T0301361

# THE NEW STOCK MARKET

# The New Stock Market

*Law, Economics, and Policy*

**Merritt B. Fox,
Lawrence R. Glosten,
and Gabriel V. Rauterberg**

COLUMBIA UNIVERSITY PRESS  New York

Columbia University Press
*Publishers Since 1893*
New York    Chichester, West Sussex
cup.columbia.edu

Copyright © 2019 Columbia University Press
All rights reserved

Library of Congress Cataloging-in-Publication Data
Names: Fox, Merritt B., author. | Glosten, Lawrence R. (Lawrence Robert),
1951– author. | Rauterberg, Gabriel V., author.
Title: The new stock market : law, economics, and policy /
Merritt B. Fox, Lawrence R. Glosten, and Gabriel V. Rauterberg.
Description: 1 Edition. | New York : Columbia University Press, [2018] |
Includes bibliographical references and index.
Identifiers: LCCN 2018021684 (print) | LCCN 2018037234 (e-book) |
ISBN 9780231543934 (e-book) | ISBN 9780231181969 (hardback)
Subjects: LCSH: Stock exchanges. | Securities. | Short selling (Securities)
Classification: LCC HG4551 (e-book) | LCC HG4551 .F69 2018 (print) |
DDC 332.64/2—dc23
LC record available at https://lccn.loc.gov/2018021684

# Contents

## PART 4: Regulation of Broker-Dealers

# Acknowledgments

We owe our gratitude to the many people who have contributed invaluably to the development of this book. This includes first and foremost The NAS-DAQ OMX Educational Foundation, our editor at Columbia University Press, Bridget Flannery-McCoy, Laura Miller, Kevin Haeberle, Menesh Patel, Anne Choike, Yuan Zou, and Polina Dovman. Academically, we owe yet more debts. Thanks to Larry Harris, whose *Trading & Exchanges*, served for so long as our touchstone for lucidly teaching about market structure, to the Fellows of the Columbia Program in the Law and Economics of Capital Markets, and to our colleagues at Columbia University and the University of Michigan.

Most of the chapters in this book reflect work previously published in article form, although all have been extensively revised and much has not been published before. Thanks to the editors of those articles and to those cited in their acknowledgments.

Merritt Fox, Lawrence Glosten & Gabriel Rauterberg, *The New Stock Market: Sense and Nonsense*, 65 Duke Law Journal 191 (2015); excerpted and revised in Meritt B. Fox, Lawrence R Glosten, & Gabriel V. Rauterberg, *High-Frequency*

*Trading and the New Stock Market Sense and Nonsense*, 29 Journal of Applied Corporate Finance 30 (2017).

Merritt Fox, Lawrence Glosten & Gabriel Rauterberg, *Informed Trading and Its Regulation*, 43 Journal of Corporation Law 817 (2018).

Merritt Fox, Lawrence Glosten & Gabriel Rauterberg, *Stock Market Manipulation and Its Regulation*, 35 Yale Journal on Regulation 67 (2018); excerpted and revised in *Global Algorithmic Capital Markets: High Frequency Trading, Dark Pools, and Regulatory Challenges*, Ch. 8 (ed. Walter Mattli: 2019).

Merritt Fox & Gabriel Rauterberg, *Stock Market Futurism*, 42 Journal of Corporation Law 793 (2017) (Symposium).

Merritt Fox & Kevin S. Haeberle, *Evaluating Stock-Trading Practices and Their Regulation*, 42 Journal of Corporation Law 887 (2017) (Symposium).

Merritt Fox, Lawrence Glosten & Paul Tetlock, *Short Selling and the News: A Preliminary Report on an Empirical Study*, 54 New York Law School Law Review 645 (2010).

# THE NEW STOCK MARKET

# Introduction

Financial trading markets can seem deeply puzzling. Central features conspicuously depart from how most markets work. This makes their study particularly interesting, but it also means there are many ways in which an unwary observer may stumble. For instance, voluntary trade is typically thought to leave both parties better off, but trade in financial markets also has a distinctively zero-sum aspect. Whereas many market transactions involve the consumption of goods that provide personal utility, transactions in financial markets involve the pursuit of claims on future cash flows and control rights.

Financial trading markets are also distinguished by their great social importance, particularly the market for corporate equities, which is the primary subject of this book. The U.S. stock market's total valuation is about $25 trillion—almost double the total assets held by the commercial banking system.[1] The stock market is the principal vehicle for the direct and indirect investment of public savings, representing roughly half of the value of the dollars saved. Its functioning is critical to the process by which changes of control in major companies take place. Famously, prices in the stock market incorporate enormous amounts of information and serve as important guides to decision making throughout the economy. For all these reasons, the stock market remains a potent national symbol of trade and commerce.

This book aims to provide an accessible yet sophisticated overview of the institutions, social functions, and economics of the secondary trading market for corporate equities. This is done with the principal ambition of understanding and improving the regulation of this market. Moreover, doing so at this particular moment presents a distinct opportunity. Driven by technology, the trading of equities occurs in a fundamentally new environment relative to just twenty years ago. As a result, the market for equities has evolved in unexpected and complex ways. The trading of any given stock is spread over dozens of different venues, rather than being largely concentrated on or within a single exchange. There are entirely new kinds of participants, such as high-frequency traders, and new institutions, such as dark pools. Our understanding of the market now also benefits from the rapidly evolving theoretical and empirical work of microstructure economics, a field dedicated to understanding the nature of trade in financial markets, which dates back only slightly more than thirty years.

Our methodology combines legal analysis and institutional description with various strands of economics—not only microstructure economics, but also financial economics more generally and the theory of the firm. What results is a functionalist explanation of how the stock market works. This approach has advantages from both a positive and normative point of view. It allows an integrated, understandable vision of the workings of the market and of the extraordinarily complex regulatory web to which it is subject, which involves federal statutory law and administrative rulemaking, state legislation, and self-regulatory rules. It also provides a basis for policy-based critiques of regulation that relate to the most basic values at stake in these markets.

In sum, we approach understanding the equity market from a distinctive perspective. Microstructure economics focuses on the differences in what market participants know. The central claim of this book is that this informational perspective significantly illuminates both the existing regulatory structure of our equity trading markets and how we can improve it. Crucially, some traders (the "informed") possess information and analyses about a company's future that provide them with a more accurate view of the value of its shares than is possessed by the rest of the market (the "uninformed"). Informed traders trade in order to make speculative profits based on their informational advantages. Uninformed traders trade for other reasons, such as seeking a place to put their savings or later selling their shares in order to finance consumption.

In choosing to focus on the institutions, economics, and regulation of one particular financial trading market—the market for equities—this book follows the lead of the financial economics literature. For a variety of reasons, including the social importance of the market for equities and the availability of data for empirical work, microstructure has overwhelmingly emphasized the equity market. At the same time, however, this book will seek to develop a theoretical framework with rich insights for other trading markets, including debt, options, commodities, and over-the-counter derivatives. Although those insights will typically be implicit, we will explicitly turn to them briefly in the conclusion.

Before turning to the contents of this book, a note on its intended audience may be helpful. This book has two audiences in mind, and thus its ambitions are sometimes in tension. On the one hand, it aims to provide newcomers to the study of trading markets—whether regulators; industry professionals; interested laypersons; or law, economics, or business students—with an accessible overview of the major issues in these markets. On the other hand, it aims to generate novel critical insights into a range of policy issues that even the seasoned scholar of these markets should find of interest. Thus, early chapters have an introductory character that the second audience may wish to skip.

Part I of this book begins by addressing the foundations necessary for understanding the equity trading market. This encompasses the institutions, mechanics, and regulatory architecture of this market; the functions it serves for society; and the economic dynamics that underlie how it operates. We begin in chapter 1 by discussing the institutions and regulation of the stock market. The central institutions of today's stock market are the trading venues themselves: the twelve stock exchanges, which account for 60 percent of trading volume; the approximately thirty active alternative trading systems; and the other forms of off-exchange trade, such as internalization, a means by which a broker-dealer transacts directly against order flow sent to it by brokers. We also introduce the federal regulatory scheme governing the structure of the stock market: principally, Regulation National Market System (NMS).

In chapter 2, we ask why equity trading markets exist, and we try to answer that question, defining the principal functions served by these markets for society. These functions include facilitating trade by investors, lowering companies' cost of capital, allocating risk, and aggregating information in prices to guide decision making in the broader economy. These functions establish the normative yardstick for assessing the performance and regulation of the equity market. This chapter also explains the emphasis in financial economics on liquidity and price accuracy as the two primary quantitative proxies for the ultimate social functions served by trading markets.

Chapter 3 explores the economics of equity trading. It presents some central results of market microstructure economics in a form accessible to nonspecialists. Its principal models formally analyze trading behavior and liquidity. They reveal that equities trading is a strategic interaction driven by differences in what traders know. The attempt by other market participants to mitigate the adverse selection arising from the trades of informed traders is the central economic dynamic of trading in the stock market.

The remainder of the book—parts II, III, and IV—generally adopts a normative approach, evaluating the practices of major participants in today's equity markets and the structures in which they interact. We canvass a range of popular and academic criticisms and consider their merits, attempting to demonstrate the usefulness of the microstructure perspective by applying it to these major issues in contemporary securities law.

Part II of the book, chapter 4, concerns the regulation of market structure. We begin with high-frequency traders (HFTs) and how they operate within today's world of multiple trading venues, each venue operating as an electronic limit order book. HFTs are a major source of liquidity in the modern stock market, posting a significant portion of the bid and offer quotes that result in trades. These quotes constitute the prices at which other traders can transact. HFTs revise their quotes at rapid speeds and high volume, employ private data feeds from exchanges, and are shrouded in secrecy. In the market, they occupy dual roles as liquidity providers and arbitrageurs. As a result of all this, they are enormously controversial. This chapter introduces the market-making role of HFTs and assesses four HFT practices that have been the subject of vigorous criticism, explaining why some of these criticisms reflect deep misunderstandings of the role of HFTs, while others appropriately target socially undesirable behaviors.

Part III of the book, consisting of chapters 5, 6, 7, and 8, addresses the regulation of traders. In chapter 5, we step back to offer a broader welfare perspective on informed trading. Trading on nonpublic or "private" information drives the stock market. Hedge funds, equity analysts, and active traders of all types, including corporate and institutional insiders, seek an informational "edge" from which to profit. Through trade, "private" information leads to more informative stock prices, which has real economic benefits. However, informed trade also leads to losses by liquidity suppliers, making trade costlier and less efficient. There is thus a fundamental trade-off in how private information affects the two principal functions served by the stock market: price accuracy and liquidity. Chapter 5 develops a general theory of the regulation of trading on private information, arguing that any given type of informed trade should be assessed based on how it affects the stock market's basic social functions. Specifically, we argue that the time horizon of private information—the latency before it would otherwise be revealed—determines both the trading strategies traders must employ and the social value of trade. To demonstrate the utility of our framework, we apply it in chapter 6 to recent controversies involving informed traders, as well as to a welter of legal rules under the Securities Exchange Act of 1934 that affect the extent of certain types of informed trade. These include the insider trading prohibitions of Section 10(b) and Rule 10b-5, the issuer mandatory disclosure regime, Section 16(b), Reg. NMS, and Reg. FD.

Chapter 7 analyzes manipulative trading. Traders may try to influence prices in ways that permit them to buy low and sell high when there has been no change in the economic fundamentals of the securities involved. Whether such manipulative trading activity is either profitable or common is highly controversial. This chapter provides a roadmap of different forms of manipulative trading, carefully separating the relevant economics of each type in order to assess its social impact. It considers the meaning of *manipulation* in terms of both market microstructure and securities law.

Chapter 8 discusses short selling. Short selling involves an arrangement by which a trader acquires shares from a third party under an obligation to return shares of the same stock to the third party at a later date. The trader sells the acquired shares immediately. If the stock's price declines by the time the shares have to be returned, the trader can acquire them for less than the proceeds received from the earlier sale and will profit accordingly. Top officials of firms subject to heavy short selling often complain that the practice is socially harmful, as do many media critics and politicians. In this largely descriptive chapter, we examine the criticisms in light of current short sale regulation and survey recent empirical evidence on the types of short selling that prevail in the market.

The last portion of this book—chapters 9, 10, 11, and 12—concerns the regulation of broker-dealers. In chapter 9, we take a tour of one of the more confusing features of trading market regulation: broker-dealer status and the duties that accompany it. Federal law currently imposes one regulatory status, that of a "broker-dealer," on any individual or institution that performs any of the following roles: 1) serving as a broker, which executes transactions on behalf of customers; 2) serving as a dealer, which facilitates order execution by trading with others as principal for its own account; and 3) operating a trading venue that is not a stock exchange.

In chapter 10, we turn to dark pools: off-exchange trading venues that promise to keep secret the existence of the orders sent to them and that can discriminate in terms of which parties they allow to trade. About 15 percent of equity transaction volume now occurs within dark pools. In chapter 10, we look at a few major criticisms of alleged practices of dark pools. For instance, some critics contend that large investment banks, which are both important providers of brokerage services and operators of most of the largest dark pools, sometimes route their brokerage customers' orders to the banks' own dark pools. They do so even when the orders will receive inferior execution there and even when the customers submitting the orders expressly direct that they be sent elsewhere.

Chapters 11 and 12 concern payments received by brokers from third parties in connection with the brokers' handling of customer orders. Chapter 11 relates to the controversial practice by most exchanges of making payments to brokers for sending the exchanges certain kinds of offers and charging brokers fees for sending other kinds: so-called "maker-taker" and "taker-maker" arrangements. Maker-taker exchanges offer rebates for limit orders that post a new offer or bid (i.e., "make liquidity") that is eventually transacted against. Marketable orders— orders that arrive on the exchange and transact immediately against a standing limit order—pay a fee because they "take liquidity." Taker-maker exchanges offer the reverse arrangement. Critics argue that these payments create incentives for brokers to direct customer orders to the venue paying the highest rebate, rather than the one that delivers best execution. Empirical evidence suggests that this may in fact be a widespread problem. In chapter 11, we assess the merits of this criticism from a legal and economic perspective and provide suggestions for regulatory reform.

In chapter 12, the focus turns to payment for order flow. When a broker-dealer receives orders from its customers, it in theory could transact against those orders directly itself, rather than directing them to an exchange or other trading venue. Doing so would be particularly attractive to a large broker-dealer with a steady stream of retail orders, which are typically uninformed and thus will have roughly the same number of buy and sell orders coming in nearly simultaneously. For technical legal reasons, the broker-dealer essentially outsources this activity, selling its customers' order flow to another broker-dealer that is instead the one being the counterparty to the buy and sell orders sent to it. This practice is known as *internalization* and payments made by the internalizing broker-dealer to the broker-dealer supplying the customer order flow is known as *payment for order flow*. Critics argue that payment for order flow is a kind of bribe that generates an agency problem, inducing a broker to sell order flow for payments (that it does not pass on to customers) rather than providing customers with best execution of their orders. In chapter 12, we likewise evaluate the merits of this criticism and provide suggestions for reform.

In the conclusion, we briefly reflect upon the informational paradigm, which possesses remarkable explanatory power in equity markets, and on the differences between equities and other major trading markets, such as the debt and derivative markets. Our general claim here is that trading markets are generally information markets, and that their economic dynamics and social functions are critically shaped by what kinds of informational asymmetries are (or are not) present. The determinants of the cost of liquidity and the role of private information will vary depending on these asymmetries. If regulation fails to carefully attend to these features, it can misfire and do more harm than good, but when it is carefully crafted, regulation can play an essential role in optimizing market structure.

Foundations | **PART 1**

# The Institutions and Regulation of Trading Markets

**ONE**

What are securities markets? They enable businesses to create and sell securities, and then allow the initial buyers of these securities ultimately to sell these securities into a market where they may thereafter be repeatedly bought and sold on an ongoing basis. A *security*, informally put, is a tradable financial instrument. A *financial instrument*, in turn, is essentially a contract that provides the contract holder with some kind of claim to the cash flows and/or control of a business. The most familiar of these securities are equity and debt. In the case of equity, the individual or institution who initially purchases the newly issued security provides the corporation with money and in return receives the promise of some bundle of control rights over the corporation and a right to its residual earnings.

Thus, by issuing equities, firms sell claims on their future cash flows in return for money from persons with savings now. This primary market for securities involves the initial transaction between a business and the first purchaser of its securities. All other transactions in that security compose the *trading market* (also known as the *secondary market*): the life of that security as it changes hands from one purchaser to another, and where the original corporation that issued the security typically has no involvement. This book is dedicated to explaining this secondary trading market for securities, particularly equities. This chapter starts with a brief overview of what the securities markets do and then focuses on five main topics: the institutions of trade; trading patterns over time; the intermediation of trade; the mechanics of trade; and the basic regulatory system.

## I. WHAT DO SECURITIES MARKETS DO?

The trading market serves related but distinct social functions. These are discussed in more detail in chapter 2, but it is worthwhile making a first introduction right at the outset. Importantly, the trading market permits individuals and institutions interested in purchasing or selling securities to do so. This is the most obvious reason for a trading market. The market brings together those interested in buying and those interested in selling. In so doing, a market makes it easier to trade.

A well-functioning secondary market also promotes a healthy primary market because investors will pay more for the securities they purchase in the primary market if they expect that they can easily sell these securities down the road. Individuals' reasons for trading will be many. They may purchase securities as a place to put savings. Later, they may sell these securities in order to generate cash with which to engage in consumption. They may buy or sell to diversify their investment portfolios across many securities in an effort to reduce risk. They may also execute strategies designed to obtain trading profits based on analyses of public or private information.

If the market is functioning well, trade occurs at prices that reflect the information available about the value of the securities being traded. Such a trading market is informationally efficient, with securities prices that reflect all relevant public information. This produces a public good for society. Individuals in the real economy can look at the prices in the trading market as informative signals: if, for example, the price of a business's stock is plummeting, this suggests that the business is performing poorly. The board of such a corporation may choose to replace current management, or cancel a project that was just announced and precipitated the fall in price.

## II. THE INSTITUTIONS OF TRADE

The idea of the stock market may still conjure images of a stock exchange trading floor in downtown Manhattan, where individuals in colored jackets furiously gesture at one another as fortunes are bought and sold. Today's trading market, however, is quite different. Before we describe the current market, though, it is important at the outset to see how much the stock market has changed in a relatively short time and to identify the forces that have led to this change.

## A. How the Stock Market Has Changed

The stock market is an institution that connects potential buyers and sellers of companies' stocks. As recently as the early 1990s, trading in the stock of each publicly traded company of any significance was still largely confined to a single venue, either NASDAQ or the New York Stock Exchange (NYSE).[1] At NASDAQ, a dealer was the purchaser of every share sold by a trader and the seller of every share bought by a trader. The dealer did so at quoted prices generated through the calculation and judgment of an individual human being. At the NYSE, where there was an actual floor, the specialist for a stock (also a human being) often played a similar dealer role, but in addition posted quotes sent in by traders willing to buy or sell at stated prices, held auctions, and helped arrange trades by brokers and traders on the floor.[2]

Today, in contrast, any given stock is potentially traded in each of almost seventy-five competing venues, including twelve exchanges and more than thirty dark pools.[3] The NASDAQ dealers and the NYSE specialists are gone. Almost all of these competing trading venues are electronic limit order books, in which a trader can post a *limit order*, which is a firm commitment (until cancelled) to buy or sell up to a specified number of shares at a quoted price.[4] A computer (the venue's matching engine) matches these posted limit orders with incoming buy and sell *marketable orders*, which are orders that have terms allowing them to execute at what is then the best available price in the market.[5]

Today, high-frequency traders (HFTs) post a significant portion of the limit orders that are matched in this fashion and result in executed trades.[6] An HFT uses high-speed communications to constantly update its information concerning transactions occurring in each stock that it regularly trades, as well as changes in the buy and sell limit orders for these stocks posted by others on every major trading venue. The HFT automatically feeds this information into a computer that uses algorithms to change the limit prices and quantities associated with the HFT's own limit orders posted on each of the various trading venues.[7] More than three-quarters of all trades in the United States are executed on one or another of these electronic limit order book venues.[8] Most of the remaining trades involve retail orders executed by off-exchange dealers in the process called internalization.[9]

## B. Forces for Change and the Role of Regulation

This transformation to the new stock market is a product of the fantastic increases in the speed of communication and calculation that have arisen from the information technology revolution. The new stock market's particular structure, though, is also due in important part to choices made by Congress and the Securities and Exchange Commission (SEC). The initial impetus for this new market structure goes back to Congress's adoption in 1975 of the National Market System (NMS) amendments to the Securities Exchange Act of 1934 (the Exchange Act).[10] Multiple, competing trading venues have the upside of the greater efficiency and higher rate of innovation that are likely to arise from competition. They have the possible downside that orders from potential traders may be fragmented among multiple venues, which makes it less likely that willing buyers and sellers can easily find each other and transact. Congress, in its adoption of the NMS amendments, foresaw that improving information technology could significantly reduce this downside by making it easier for traders to see what is going on in each of these venues.[11] The NMS amendments pushed the system to develop in this direction, a push that has been consistently supported by the SEC.[12]

This decision favoring multiple venues is unlikely to be reversed in the foreseeable future. Data concerning the speed of trading, its cost, and the apparent amount of liquidity in the system suggest that the new stock market is a substantial improvement over what came before it.[13] Today's technology, if it instead were operating within a centralized single-venue system, might of course have led to even greater improvements—a possibility that is the subject of continuing debate among academic theorists[14]—but this is entirely a matter of speculation. Moreover, as a matter of political economy, any attempt to reverse the decision for multiple venues would meet stiff resistance from those who have built businesses based on an assumption that the multiple-venue structure will continue. So, to the extent that the criticisms of the new stock market have merit, the challenge will be to design reforms within the current multivenue system.

## C. Trading Venues

One of the striking features of the modern stock market, alluded to in II.B, is the complex range of venues on which transactions occur. This section briefly describes this range of venues. An important feature to keep in mind is that the distinctions among venues are in large part an artifact of regulatory classification, rather than following strictly functional lines, a fact to which we will return in greater depth in chapter 9.

Currently, there are three principal types of trading venues: stock exchanges, alternative trading systems (ATSs), and non-ATS off-exchange trade, which is mostly internalization. The most familiar and still the most important venues for trading stocks are the national stock exchanges, of which there are currently thirteen.[15] In aggregate, around 60–65 percent of equity market trading volume typically occurs on the exchanges.[16] As defined by the Exchange Act, an *exchange* is simply any rule-based marketplace for transacting securities[17] that registers as an exchange. Registering requires the entity to act as a self-regulatory organization (SRO).[18]

The status of exchanges as SROs plays an important role in current market structure, so it is worth pausing to discuss what that status involves and the benefits and burdens that come with it. Under the self-regulatory system, exchanges act as quasi-public institutions that are delegated regulatory functions by the SEC. The exchanges are charged with partly regulating their own markets, including establishing rules of operation compliant with law and regulation, supervising the conduct of their members (i.e., the broker-dealers who trade directly on the exchange), and participating in the governance of the systems that interlink the various exchanges and other equity trading venues.[19] Important benefits also accompany SRO status, including dramatic limits on an exchange's potential civil liability to private individuals and institutions. A stock exchange is absolutely immune from liability to private plaintiffs when conducting its regulatory activities.[20]

Any transaction not occurring on an exchange occurs "off exchange," on either ATSs or non-ATSs.[21] An ATS is simply an exchange-like trading venue—a facility in which buyers and sellers of stocks can post orders and transact—that does not take on any self-regulatory functions or operate as an SRO.[22] Instead, ATSs are operated by broker-dealers.[23] ATSs can be either electronic communication networks (ECNs) or "dark pools." ECNs are open to all traders and either generally make their quotations part of the public data feeds for quotes (just like an exchange does), or are "crossing networks," whereby the venue connects buyers and sellers each willing to execute at the midpoint between the best offer and best bid available in the market. Dark pools, which are discussed in more detail in chapter 10, may restrict who can have access and do not make their quotes available. Lastly, there is non-ATS trade, which is largely "internalization,"[24] whereby a retail broker-dealer sells its customers' order flow to another broker-dealer that acts as the counterparty to the flow of buy and sell orders sent to it.[25]

## III. TRADING PATTERNS OVER TIME

How much trading activity is going on in these markets, and how has that activity trended over time? Figure 1.1 shows annual share trading volume of NYSE-listed stocks on the NYSE. This extreme "hockey stick" obscures more than it explains, however. This is because, starting in the 1970s, and escalating during the late 1990s tech bubble, many new companies were listed on the NYSE. Furthermore, as stock prices increased, many firms split their shares, transforming one old share into two or more new shares. Thus, the number of shares listed on the NYSE (the sum of all the shares eligible for trading of all the issuers listing on the NYSE) has expanded significantly over time, as illustrated in figure 1.2. As a result, the increase in trading volume does not necessarily mean a change in trader behavior.

To adjust for the number of shares listed, financial economists typically use what is termed *turnover*. This number is the per-period share volume divided by the (average) number of shares outstanding during the period, typically annually. Turnover can be thought of as merely a normalized measure of trading volume, but it can also be interpreted as measuring the average holding period of the security or securities being analyzed. An annual turnover of 1.0 indicates an average holding period of one year. An annual turnover of 3.0 indicates an average holding period of four months.

Figure 1.3 shows NYSE annual turnover (in this case it is the annual trading volume on the NYSE of its listed stocks divided by the average number of NYSE-listed shares). There are some interesting aspects to this graph. Early turnover was

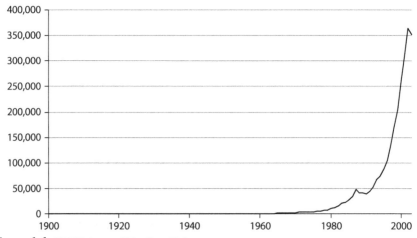

Figure 1.1 NYSE Annual Trading Volume, 1900–2003
*Source:* NYSE Factbook

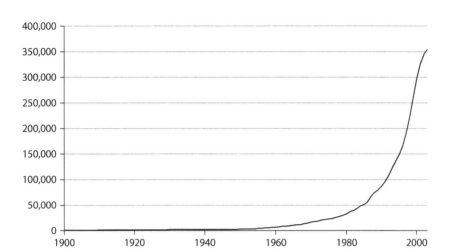

Figure 1.2 Shares listed 1900–2003, NYSE
*Source:* NYSE Factbook

remarkably high, particularly in the late 1910s and into the 1920s. We suspect that during this time the denominator (average shares outstanding) may have been quite small because founding families owned a significant number of unregistered shares. Still, each share that was eligible for trade changed hands very frequently, most often an average of once every three months. Following 1934, turnover was fairly steady and low, typically more in the range of only once every four years,

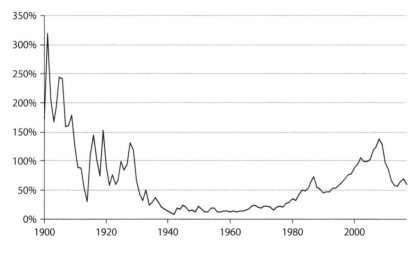

Figure 1.3 NYSE Annual Turnover (1900–2017)
*Source:* NYSE Factbooks

with another significant increase starting around 1980. Is it just a coincidence that this low-turnover period begins with the passage of the Exchange Act of 1934, with the resulting imposition of mandatory periodic issuer disclosure and a variety of new rules aimed at both broker and trader behavior? It seems plausible that there is a relationship, but it is really impossible to tell, particularly given the record after 1980. It is important to note that this was not an otherwise uninteresting timespan: it included the latter part of the Great Depression, the recovery coming with World War II and the post–World War II demobilization, and then the Korean War and the Vietnam War. The years after World War II were also a time of significant technological and social change, yet this did not appear to affect the way people handled their portfolios, at least in terms of their holding periods.

Things start changing around 1980, with relatively steady growth in turnover. This seems to represent a change in trading behavior, but it is also important to note that around this time the mix of types of firms traded was changing, with more tech stocks listing on the NYSE. The impact that the nature of the company involved has on turnover is illustrated by the much higher turnover rates over time for stocks on NASDAQ (figure 1.4), which included more high-tech and new companies.

NASDAQ turnover starts out at a bit less than 100 percent in the early 1980s (when turnover of NYSE listed stocks was at about 50 percent), and it peaks at a rather astounding 500 percent in 2000; in other words, shares were changing hands on average a little less than every two months. This high turnover then

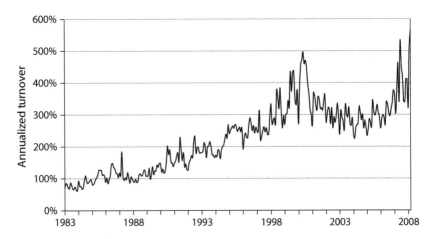

Figure 1.4 NASDAQ Turnover
*Source:* NASDAQ Trader

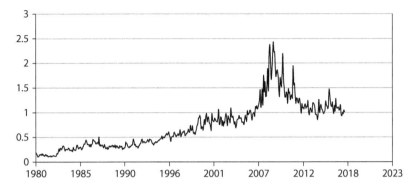

Figure 1.5 Annual Turnover, All U.S. Registered Equities

declines with the bursting of the tech bubble, but climbs back up during the late 2000s.[26] Finally, the general patterns observed in figures 1.3 and 1.4 are confirmed in figure 1.5, which shows data from CRISP and combines trading in NASDAQ- and NYSE-listed shares on all exchanges. All of these data are suggestive of the factors that may affect turnover, but we must admit that financial economists still do not understand the phenomenon very well.

## IV. INTERMEDIATION OF TRADE

Intermediation remains enormously important to the operation of trading markets. The equity market features two crucial kinds of intermediaries: brokers and liquidity providers. Both brokers and liquidity providers are regulated as "broker-dealers," a regulatory status created to regulate securities intermediaries, which is discussed in more depth in chapter 9.

## A. Brokers

A *broker* is the agent of a customer wishing to buy or sell a security. The broker represents the customer in seeking to find a counterparty for the trade the customer wishes to make; for example, by sending the order to an exchange. A sophisticated broker will design and execute entire trading strategies on behalf of institutional customers that instruct it to do so.

Brokers are necessary for a number of reasons. First, brokers must be members of the Financial Industry Regulatory Authority (FINRA), which, by regulation, is a prerequisite for direct access to trading on a stock exchange or any other trading venue. Almost no investor is a member of FINRA. Thus, everyday investors, and even the most sophisticated traders or institutions, must direct their orders to a broker, which executes it only on the customers' behalf.

Second, even if an institution were allowed to directly trade itself, it might wish to rely on a broker's superior skill in locating counterparty trading interests.

Finally, a trade on an exchange is simply an executory contract, in which one party promises to provide a certain number of shares on a certain date and the other party promises to pay a specified amount of money for those shares. The parties' respective brokers each vouch that their customers will in fact live up to their promises on the day of closing. This vouching is the product of a complex set of rules that allows each party in an anonymous market to be willing to promise to participate in an exchange of money for shares that by the time of closing might seem disadvantageous. A party does so because she has confidence that if the exchange instead turns out to be disadvantageous to the other party, the other party will still perform.

## B. Liquidity Suppliers

A liquidity provider also facilitates a trader's trading interests, but does so by trading for its own account. For instance, the liquidity provider will buy from someone who wishes to sell a stock and then subsequently sell to another trader who wishes to purchase that same stock. The service it provides is intermediation across time, rather than trade execution services. Historically, liquidity providers have gone by a variety of names, including "market makers" and "dealers." In equity markets of previous years, the institutionally designated liquidity providers on the NYSE were known as *specialists*, and on NASDAQ as *OTC dealers*. As is discussed in more detail in chapter 4, a significant portion of liquidity supply today is provided by HFTs that engage in both the frequent purchase and frequent sale of a given stock by regularly posting sell limit offers (constituting offer quotes) and buy limit orders (constituting bid quotes) on a variety of exchanges.

## V. MECHANICS OF TRADE

To understand and evaluate the stock market's function and regulation, it is necessary to first understand its mechanics.

## A. Vocabulary

Before tackling the mechanics of an electronic limit order-based market, it is worthwhile to supply more detail about some vocabulary that helps to describe both what traders are seeking to accomplish with the orders they send to trading venues and the services that trading venues offer these traders.

### 1. Quotes and depth

Suppose that at 1:59:32 PM on July 10, 2014, Maria decides she wants to buy 200 shares of Apple. She contacts her broker and discovers the best quotes for Apple: the national best bid (NBB) is $95.28 and the national best offer (NBO) is $95.29, with a depth, respectively, of 500 and 1,000 shares. In other words, according to what is reported by the national reporting system, on one or more trading venues there are one or more buyers willing to pay $95.28 per share for up to 500 shares in aggregate (but no one willing to pay more) and one or more sellers willing to provide up to 1,000 shares in aggregate for $95.29 (but no one willing to charge less).

### 2. Market orders, marketable limit orders, and marketable orders

One possibility is that Maria submits a market buy order for 200 shares: this is an unconditional order to buy at whatever is the best (lowest) price available. Because she places no limit on what she is willing to pay, the order will execute almost immediately. It will do so at $95.29 unless the NBO, as reported by the national reporting system, has changed by the time her order arrives at the trading venue to which it is ultimately sent.[27] If the NBO has changed by that time, the order would execute at the new NBO.

　　Another possibility is that Maria, knowing the current quotes, but wanting to protect herself in case the NBO moves up too much before her order can execute, places the order for 200 shares but with the caveat that she will not pay more than $95.31. In other words, Maria has submitted a buy limit order for 200 shares at $95.31.[28]

　　Given that the NBO at the time Maria sent the order, $95.29, is below—that is, at least as favorable as—Maria's $95.31 limit, we refer to her order as a *marketable buy limit order*.[29] This is because it will behave just like a market order and execute at whatever is the then-current NBO unless the NBO has changed and has moved to above $95.31 in the brief time it takes her order to arrive at the trading venue to which it is ultimately sent.[30] For this reason, we call both market orders and marketable limit orders *marketable orders*.

### 3. Nonmarketable limit orders

In contrast, a *nonmarketable buy limit* order is a buy limit order with a price limit below the NBO at the time it is sent. It is called nonmarketable because at that moment, no one in the market is willing to sell at a price this low. Similarly, a *nonmarketable sell limit order* is a sell limit order with a price limit above the NBB at the time it is sent, because at that moment no one in the market is willing to buy at a price this high.

### 4. Partially marketable limit orders

A *partially marketable buy limit order* is a buy limit order with a price limit equal to the NBO at the time it is sent, but for a quantity of shares greater than what is available in the market at that price. The portion of the order equal in size to what is available will execute at the NBO and the remainder will be sent to another exchange, if any, that also displays offers at the original NBO. If there are no such offers or they are insufficient to exhaust the purchase order, what remains will be posted as a buy limit order on the exchange to which it was sent. A *partially marketable sell limit order* is a sell limit order with a price limit equal to the NBB at the time it is sent, but for a quantity of shares greater than what is available in the market at that price. Again, the portion beyond what executes on the exchange to which it was sent will similarly be either sent to another exchange for execution or posted as a sell limit order on the exchange to which it was sent.

### 5. Where bid and offer quotes come from

The foregoing shows that equity-market trading venues provide a place for market participants to display a variety of different trading interests. In the market we have described, the best offer quote is $95.29 with a depth of 1,000 shares. This is the result of persons who had previously posted still-in-effect nonmarketable sell orders with a limit of $95.29 that aggregate to 1,000 shares (that is, sell orders with a limit price above the NBB, which in our example is $98.28).[31]

### 6. Making and taking liquidity

The persons who have posted these standing nonmarketable sell limit orders have provided Maria with the option to trade immediately at $95.29, an option she can exercise by sending in a marketable order. We say that these persons have provided liquidity or that they are makers of liquidity. Maria, who in our examples takes advantage of this ability to trade immediately by submitting either a market order or a marketable limit order, consumes liquidity. She is a taker of liquidity.

*7. The tradeoff between taking and making liquidity*

If Maria is willing to be less aggressive, she can instead attempt to acquire her Apple shares by putting in a nonmarketable limit order to buy 200 shares at $95.28. Then, if the quotes do not change by the time her order reaches the market, she will be adding 200 more shares to the already existing NBB for 500 shares at $95.28. Thus, if she follows this less aggressive strategy, she can be a maker, not a taker, of liquidity, even though, unlike an HFT, she is not in the business of liquidity supply.

If Maria follows this less aggressive strategy and a sufficient number of marketable sell orders come in before her offer expires or is cancelled, Maria's limit order will execute and she will have paid a penny less per share. If a sufficient number of such sell orders does not come in, her order will fail to execute. She then runs the risk that, if she still wants to purchase the shares, the offer quotes will have moved up, in which case she will have to pay more than the $95.29 per share she would have paid had she initially submitted a marketable order. Market orders provide speed and certainty of execution. Limit orders may obtain a better price but are less certain to execute.

*8. Order types*

In reality, Maria has a surprisingly large range of additional choices available in expressing her trading interest. One dimension is "time in force": how long a limit order will remain operational before it expires. The common default period is one day, where an order is live until it executes, is canceled, or the day ends (whichever happens first), but Maria can specify a longer or shorter time before expiration. Whatever the period before expiration, a trader can cancel her limit order at any time. She can also direct that the order be "immediate or cancel" (IOC), which means that whatever portion of the order, if any, can be filled immediately, will execute and any remainder will cancel. Alternatively, she can direct that the order have a "fill or kill" status, in which case, if the order is not filled in full, it is immediately canceled.

Another important dimension is whether the limit order is displayed in whole, in part, or not at all. The discussion so far has assumed that all standing orders are displayed. In reality, stock exchanges also allow undisplayed standing orders. The default rule is that orders, except fairly large ones, are displayed, but the customer can specify that it not be displayed instead. A nondisplayed order is posted on the limit order book at its limit price, but the quotation is not included in disseminated data feeds about the contents of the limit order book. If the nondisplayed order offers the best price, and a contra-side marketable order arrives, then the marketable order will execute against the nondisplayed limit order at its limit price, just like a displayed limit order. If, however, there is a displayed limit order at the same price as the nondisplayed order, the displayed limit order typically has priority.

*9. Timing of an order and priority of execution generally*

What if there are two displayed standing orders at the same price and a marketable order comes in that is not large enough to fully exhaust both of them? In such an event, the standing order that arrived earlier gets priority and so is executed against first.[32] If that is not sufficient to fill the marketable order, then the remainder of the marketable order is filled from the later-arriving standing limit order. The same rule would apply between two undisplayed standing orders at the same price. More generally, most stock exchanges observe price/display/time rules for prioritizing executions. That is, the standing order that offers the best price will execute, but if two standing orders are at the same price, then, as noted before, the displayed order will execute before the nondisplayed order. Also, if two displayed (or undisplayed) standing limit orders are at the same price, then the first to have arrived will enjoy priority in execution.

## B. The Mechanics of Trading on a Single Venue

To understand the dynamics of a multivenue electronic limit-order-book market and the standard approach to its depiction, it is convenient to begin the discussion by considering how trades would be depicted if we instead had just a single trading venue.[33] In Section C, we will add the complications involved with the multivenue system we have today.

*1. Depicting the initial book*

As an example, consider the initial state of an order book for a stock such as XYZ. This *book* (that is, the collection of standing limit orders) can be depicted as follows:

| Bids | | Offers | |
|------|------|------|------|
| Price | Shares | Price | Shares |
| 30.48 | 500 | 30.50 | 700 |
| 30.46 | 200 | 30.51 | 300 |
| 30.45 | 300 | 30.52 | 400 |
| 30.44 | 200 | 30.57 | 400 |

In this case, the best offer is $30.50 with 700 shares available, and the best bid is $30.48 with 500 shares available.[34] This simple description of the "top of the book" is all the information the typical retail investor receives. Notice, however, that this description does not fully describe the market. For example, this simple top-of-the-book description does not reveal that investors have bid 500 additional shares for a price within three cents of the best bid and offered 700 shares for a price within two cents of the best offer. In other words, information about the depth of the book beyond the best bid and offer is revealed only by a full order book. Notice also that even with the fuller depiction set out here, one cannot tell whether the book consists of seven offers of 100 shares each at $30.50 or one offer of 700 shares. Nor can one tell if there are any nondisplayed orders (however, for the purposes of the examples here we will assume that there are none).

### 2. Depicting a marketable buy limit order

Suppose that Anna decides she wishes to buy 400 shares of XYZ, but is not willing to pay more than $30.60 per share. Accordingly, she instructs her broker to submit a limit order to buy 400 shares with a limit price of $30.60. Because $30.60 is above the best offer of $30.50 and more than 400 shares are available at $30.50, her order is marketable and would transact immediately at a price of $30.50.

Regulation NMS requires that a report of the executed transaction—a sale of 400 shares at $30.50—be sent almost immediately to a publicly disseminated last-trade data stream that forms the national reporting system for transactions.[35] The venue is also allowed to simultaneously send the same last-trade report to persons, including co-locating HFTs, that contract with it to receive a direct feed.[36] Regulation NMS also requires that a report of the changes in the quotes—the reduction in the number of shares offered at $30.50 from 700 to 300—be sent to a publicly disseminated quote stream that forms the national reporting system for quotes[37] (and again, the venue may simultaneously send this information to persons with a direct feed).[38] The new order book, reflecting this change, would appear as follows:

| Bids | | Offers | |
|---|---|---|---|
| Price | Shares | Price | Shares |
| 30.48 | 500 | 30.50 | 300 |
| 30.46 | 200 | 30.51 | 300 |
| 30.45 | 300 | 30.52 | 400 |
| 30.44 | 200 | 30.57 | 400 |

*3. Depicting a nonmarketable buy limit order*

Suppose that another investor, Dave, prompted by this new state of the book, decides that he wishes to buy 200 shares of XYZ, but is not willing to pay more than $30.49 per share. Accordingly, he instructs his broker to submit a limit order to buy 200 shares with a limit price of $30.49. Because $30.49 is below the best offer of $30.50, his order is nonmarketable and no transaction will occur. Instead, his limit order will be posted on the bid side of the limit order book. This is because he is expressing his willingness to buy at $30.49, and so his order becomes a bid for 200 shares at this price. Because $30.49 is higher than the previous best bid, Dave's limit order becomes the new best bid, thereby reducing the spread between the best bid and the best offer by a penny (though also reducing depth at the best bid to 200 shares). The new book reflecting the posting of this new order would appear as follows:

| Bids | | Offers | |
|---|---|---|---|
| Price | Shares | Price | Shares |
| 30.49 | 200 | 30.50 | 300 |
| 30.48 | 500 | 30.51 | 300 |
| 30.46 | 200 | 30.52 | 400 |
| 30.45 | 300 | 30.57 | 400 |
| 30.44 | 200 | | |

Information about the new state of the book would be disseminated as in the previous example.

*4. Symmetry for sell orders*

We have presented the dynamics associated with buy orders: both marketable buy orders, which reduce what is available on the offer side of the book, and nonmarketable buy orders, which add to the bid side of the book. The situation is symmetric for sell orders—both marketable sell orders, which reduce what is available on the bid side of the book, and nonmarketable sell orders, which add to the offer side of the book.

## C. The Mechanics of Trading on Multiple Exchanges

With multiple exchanges, the order book dynamics are similar, but the routing of the order can be much more complicated. Part of the complication comes from Regulation NMS Rule 611, which generally requires that a marketable sell order—regardless of the trading venue to which it is originally sent—execute at a price equal to the best bid available on any exchange in the country, and a marketable buy order at the best offer.[39] To see how this works, consider the following consolidated-limit-order book, which aggregates the quotes from all the exchanges in the country. The aggregate number of shares bid or offered at any given exchange is identified by a single letter corresponding to that exchange.

| Bids | | Offers | |
|---|---|---|---|
| Price | Shares | Price | Shares |
| 30.48 | Q 300 | 30.50 | Q 500 |
|  | P 200 |  | P 100 |
|  |  |  | Z 100 |
| 30.46 | Q 200 | 30.51 | Q 500 |
|  |  |  | D 100 |
| 30.45 | Z 300 | 30.52 | Q 400 |
| 30.44 | Z 200 | 30.57 | Q 400 |

Now consider Maria wanting to purchase 1,000 shares. One way to accomplish this is for her broker to send the following market buy orders: 800 shares to Q, 100 shares to P, 100 shares to Z. Assuming the quotes are still good by the time her order arrives at these respective venues, she would pay an average price of $30.503. If speed were important and there was reason to think that the order would reach Q first, it might appear to be better to send the whole 1,000-share order to Q and pay the slightly higher average price of $30.505. Because of Rule 611,[40] however, sending the whole order to Q would not have this result. Instead, Q is required to have a system that would forward 100-share orders to each of P and Z, at which shares were also available at the NBO of $30.50. These orders would execute on these venues at this price. On Q, 500 shares would execute at $30.50 and the remaining 300 at $30.51. Again, the average price would be $30.503.

The preceding discussion, however, assumes that everyone involved is instantly aware of all newly executed transactions and all changes in quotes. It also assumes that orders can be sent and cancelled instantaneously. Things become more interesting when we drop these unrealistic assumptions. Consider first how Maria's broker became aware of the quotations and how Q knows about offers on P and Z at $30.50. Traditionally, each exchange independently provided quotation and transaction information. As discussed, however, the 1975 NMS amendments to the Exchange Act included broad provisions for consolidating information in the U.S. stock market, which reflected the congressional vision of an electronically linked market made up of competing venues trading in the stock of the same issuers.[41] Full realization of this vision, including rules leading to the construction of the national reporting system for quotes and transactions, took thirty years, culminating in the SEC's 2005 adoption of Regulation NMS.[42]

According to the NMS rules, a trading venue must participate in quote and transaction reporting plans approved by the SEC.[43] The quote plan must provide that there is a system by which the best bid and best offer quotes posted on the venue for a given issuer's stock are furnished to a processor to which all other venues also furnish quotes for this stock.[44] This processor consolidates this information with the information the processor acquires concerning the same stock from the other venues that make available quotes in the stock. From all this, the processor constructs a consolidated list depicting the best offer and best bid for the stock at each of the venues making quotes available and the corresponding sizes of these quotes. The processor must make this quote information available to the public on terms that are fair and reasonable.[45] At any point in time, the best bid and best offer on this consolidated list represent the official NBB and NBO.

A similar rule applies to data concerning the price and size of all actual transactions in a given stock occurring across all venues.[46] Again, each venue where the stock trades must enter into an SEC-approved reporting plan. The goal of this rule is to facilitate dissemination of transaction data in consolidated form as well.

## VI. THE BASIC REGULATORY SYSTEM

The regulatory system governing equity trading markets is largely a creature of statutory law adopted by Congress and administrative rulemaking by the Securities and Exchange Commission (SEC). It is astonishingly complex. We provide only the briefest overview here; further features of the regulatory scheme will be introduced throughout this book as necessary.

The backbone of the federal securities laws consists of the Securities Act of 1933 (the Securities Act) and the Securities and Exchange Act of 1934 (the Exchange Act), which, at the broadest level, are concerned with the primary market and secondary market, respectively. At the time of its initial passage, the Exchange Act was largely concerned with the national securities exchanges that then dominated the trading of stocks.

The major legislation inaugurating the modern era of market structure had to wait four decades. In 1975, Congress passed a series of amendments to the Exchange Act, known as the "NMS Amendments," because they directed the SEC to establish a "national market system" for equities. Over the next few decades, various features of the current regulatory environment were put in place piecemeal, but they are now gathered in two important sets of rules: Regulation NMS (Reg. NMS) and Regulation ATS (Reg. ATS).

Regulation NMS is the heart of the regulatory regime for the stock market. In its details, it is quite complex, but in its basic features, far simpler. Before turning to the NMS rules, however, it is worth reflecting on the basic vision of market structure embodied in the regulatory changes that preceded, and were then codified and supplemented in, Reg. NMS. This market structure involves a multivenue trading system in which the stocks of a company can trade on any trading venue (not only the exchange on which that company is listed), and in which a series of technologies and regulatory requirements interconnect all of the trading venues, such that they routinely route orders to one another and provide quote and transaction data to consolidated plans. The ultimate structure under Reg. NMS has several notable features.

First is transparency. Rules 601–603 of Reg. NMS define the requirements for what information about transactions (Rule 601) and quotes (Rule 602) must be made publicly available, and how that quote and transaction information will be consolidated and displayed (Rule 603). The information required by these rules is displayed through a transaction reporting plan that consolidates information from each exchange on its highest bid and lowest ask quotations as well as information from all venues about their last-sale prices for each stock. The reporting plan then publishes that consolidated data in near real-time.[47] The highest bid and lowest ask of all the quotes publicly reported by any venue become the national best bid and offer (NBBO) for that stock.[48]

Second is the protection of customer limit orders. Under previous iterations of equity market structure, a dealer sometimes lacked any legal obligation to display limit orders sent to it by a broker on behalf of the broker's customer. In other words, the customer may have wished to offer to sell a stock at a price superior to the one posted by a dealer in a stock, but the world would never know about. This is because the dealer, while holding the customer's order on its books in case it later found the order advantageous to trade against, would have no duty to display the order to other traders. Rule 604 required dealers to publicly display any customer limit orders that they received.[49] This is a crucial design feature. It effectively guarantees that the system's end users—the ordinary traders—could compete with its specialized intermediaries, such as the NASDAQ dealer or the NYSE specialist, in providing quotes. Perhaps more than anything else, the directive codified in Rule 604 marked the formal movement of NASDAQ from a dealer market (in which every customer purchase or sale transaction has a dealer as the counterparty and dealers provide all the quotes) to an open-limit-order book where marketable orders execute against the best available quotes that arise in a competitive market as the result of the submission of limit orders by anyone, but in practice today particularly by HFTs.

Third is disclosure. Rules 605–607 define what information broker-dealers must disclose to customers. This includes information about the quality of execution of their orders (Rule 605), of the venues to which those orders were routed (Rule 606), and about the customer's account (Rule 607).

Fourth is fair access. Rule 610 generally requires that exchanges avoid any unfairly discriminatory terms in limiting traders' access to the exchanges' facilities. This includes Rule 610(c)'s cap on the fees that exchanges can impose on a trader for accessing a quotation posted on that venue. The cap amounts to $0.003 per share in trading against a displayed quotation. One impact of this rule is to put a ceiling on the "taker" fee that can be used in connection with trading venues using the "maker-taker" fee business model in which the venue pays brokers a rebate to send the venue nonmarketable limit orders that are executed against and charges brokers an access fee for marketable orders.

Fifth is the trade-through rule, mentioned earlier and codified as Rule 611, which requires that trading centers establish and enforce procedures to prevent transactions at prices inferior to the best displayed quotes for a given stock.[50] Rule 611 applies to all trading venues.[51] When a venue receives an order to buy or sell for a stock for which its best quote is not the national best, Rule 611 in effect prompts the venue to send the order on to the (or a) venue that does have the best quote.

It should be noted that Rule 610's cap on the access fee effectively prevents a venue from undercutting the objective of the trade-through rule. Without the cap, a venue could offer a very high rebate, essentially attracting very favorably priced quotes that would be subsidized by the prospect of the rebate, and funding the rebate with a very high access fee. The trade-through rule would then dictate that a customer's marketable order, wherever it was originally sent, be directed to the venue that had used this tactic to attract these very favorably priced quotes. The effective cost of trading to the customer who had sent in the marketable order, however, would be higher than if her order had executed in a venue with a less favorably priced quote but, as well might be the case, had a lower access fee that more than made up the difference.

Rules 610 and 611 were the most controversial parts of Reg. NMS when it was adopted, and have continued to attract significant opposition. The critics reject the need for the consumer protection that the rules are intended to provide and object that these rules interfere with the workings of a competitive free market for liquidity.[52] They suggest that the market for liquidity should be allowed to work like most other markets in the economy and that a person seeking immediate execution of an order should be free to have the order executed at whatever venue she wishes, transacting at whatever is its best quote and paying whatever access fee the venue has announced that it will charge.

Sixth is Rule 612, which specifies the "tick size" or minimum price variation at which traders may post displayed limit orders. Under Rule 612, displayed orders must generally be priced in pennies or more. The phenomenon of moving to a tick size of one cent was known as "decimalization."

Some other features of Reg. NMS are worth noting, but less crucial to its overall architecture. Rules 608 and 609 address the requirements for filing national market system plans, which are the governance plans for fulfilling various requirements of Reg. NMS; and for registering securities information processors, which govern the public consolidation and display of the information required under Rules 602 and 603. Rule 600 provides definitions. Rule 613 requires the industry to develop a "consolidated audit trail" that would provide the SEC with a complete picture of quotes and transactions, including an ID for everyone entering a quote or involved in a transaction. It will be a massive project.

Regulation ATS provides a general exemption for a trading venue that meets the statutory definition of an exchange from the requirement that it register as a national stock exchange and be regulated as such. Instead, it is regulated as an alternative trading system (ATS). Under the ATS regime, venues operating under this exemption do not act as self-regulatory organizations and are free from many other exchange regulations. Regulation ATS formalized the SEC's exemption of ATSs from certain of the general regulatory requirements imposed on exchanges. As is discussed in more detail in chapter 9, these venues are instead subject to their own distinct regulatory requirements.[53] Importantly, ATSs must register as broker-dealers. Additionally, if trading volume in a given issuer's stock security on an ATS exceeds five percent of that security's total trading volume, then exchange-like requirements become imposed on this ATS: it must publicly display its best quotes for the issuer's shares and allow traders in general to transact against those quotes.

Why should we care? Why are the market for equities and the law that regulates it important, and how should we evaluate any given market practice or possible regulation? Answering these threshold questions requires an exploration of the social goals that the equities market is expected to serve and that form the justificatory basis for regulation when the market falls short.

The reason for caring is that a properly operating equities trading market generates substantial social value in four distinct ways:

- *Use of existing productive capacity.* A well-functioning equities market promotes managerial decisions that lead to the more efficient use of the economy's existing productive capacity, so as to maximize the value of the goods and services that it yields.
- *Capital allocation.* A well-functioning equities market assists in the efficient allocation of society's scarce capital, helping to steer this capital to the most promising new investment projects in our economy.
- *Allocation of resources over time.* A well-functioning equities market promotes the efficient division of currently available resources between the production of goods and services for consumption today and the generation of new productive

capacity that will allow for the greater production of goods and services for future consumption.

- *Risk allocation.* A well-functioning equities market aids in the allocation of the risks generated by the inevitably volatile cash flows of the firms traded in the market so that risk-averse investors, who hold portfolios of these firms' shares, suffer as little pain from this volatility as possible.

A critical task in evaluating any given market practice or regulation is to compare a world with and without the practice or regulation in order to see whether its presence helps or hurts the market in creating social value in these four ways. This task is greatly simplified by the fact that the equities trading market has two key characteristics—price accuracy and liquidity—that are central to this creation of social value.

- *Price accuracy* concerns the accuracy with which the market price of an issuer's shares predicts the issuer's future cash flows.
- *Liquidity* concerns the costs of transacting. Liquidity is a multidimensional concept that relates to the size of a trade, the price at which it is accomplished, and the time it takes to accomplish the trade. Generally, the larger the size of the purchase or sale and the faster one wishes to accomplish it, the less desirable the price will be. The more liquid the market is, however, the less severe these trade-offs are. For the small retail investor, the best measure of a stock's liquidity is just the "bid-ask spread": that is, the difference between the best available bid (the price at which liquidity suppliers are willing to buy such shares) and the best available offer (the price at which liquidity suppliers are willing to sell such shares).

The more accurate the market's share prices are and the greater the liquidity of the shares trading in it, the better the equity market is at generating social value in the four ways just identified.

Beyond this analysis of the impact of a practice or regulation on the equity market's capacity to generate social value, a proper evaluation requires three additional considerations:

- *Consumption of real resources.* The equities trading market consumes considerable real resources—talented personnel, equipment, communications facilities, and real estate—that would otherwise be available to produce other goods and services that people enjoy. So, in evaluating a practice or regulation, we need to know its impact on the amount of real resources society devotes to the operation of the equity trading markets and to the enforcement and compliance costs associated with its regulation, if any.

- *Innovation.* History has shown the overall system of equities trading to be very dynamic, with changes driven by innovations in technology, market participants' strategies, and regulation itself. Such innovations have often allowed the equity market to generate greater social value and/or reduce the amount of real resources that it consumes. So, in evaluating a practice or regulation, we need to know the effect of the practice or regulation under evaluation on the capacity of the system to further innovate in such favorable ways in the future.
- *Fairness.* The actual fairness of a practice is a worthy concern in and of itself. Indeed, promoting such fairness has traditionally been regarded as the core mission of securities regulation. Moreover, perceptions of the fairness of a practice, whether accurate or not, can substantially affect how well the equities trading market performs in creating social value.

This chapter summarizes the argument as to how a well-functioning equities market, through its contributions to share price accuracy and liquidity, creates social value in the four ways enumerated earlier. It also establishes a framework for taking into consideration the system's consumption of real resources, capacity for innovation, and actual and apparent fairness.

Most of this book consists of an exploration of a wide variety of market practices and current and proposed regulations. Before we get there, however, the stage is set by this chapter and by the next, chapter 3, which analyzes the underlying determinants of price accuracy and liquidity and how to determine who wins and who loses from any particular market practice. Our general approach to assessing market practices moves in two steps. First, we utilize the analysis in chapter 3 to determine the effects of a practice or regulation on price accuracy, liquidity, and on the wealth positions of various market participants. Then, based on these determinations, we employ the analysis set out in this chapter to evaluate the impact of the practice or regulation on the market's capacity to create social value, as well as its effects in terms of resource use, innovation, and fairness.

## I. EFFICIENCY IN THE USE OF EXISTING PRODUCTIVE CAPACITY AND CAPITAL ALLOCATION

A well-functioning equity trading market assists in the efficient use of the economy's existing productive capacity and the efficient allocation of its scarce capital in a number of ways. Three mechanisms are at work. First, more accurate prices play an important role in prompting managers to make decisions that maximize the value of their shares. As developed later in this chapter, the managerial decisions concerning a firm's existing productive capacity that result in the most efficient use of this capacity from the point of view of the economy as a whole turn out to be the ones that maximize share value. Furthermore, the managerial decisions concerning the choice of proposed investment projects to undertake that help most in the larger process of efficiently allocating the economy's scarce capital also turn out to be the ones that maximize share value. Second, more accurate share prices affect the terms on which firms can obtain external financing in ways that also improve the efficiency with which capital is allocated. Third, greater liquidity creates a trading environment that promotes the generation, and reflection in share price, of more fundamental value information, thereby making prices more accurate, which, in turn, leads to the benefits just noted in terms of the more efficient use of the economy's existing capacity and more efficient allocation of its scarce capital.

## A. The Role of Accurate Prices in Prompting Managers to Maximize Share Value

Firms with shares that are regularly bought and sold on organized trading venues play a very large role in our economy. In 2016 in the United States, these firms undertook investments aggregating to $1.06 trillion,[1] which represented about 45 percent of total private (i.e., nongovernmental) nonresidential investment,[2] and about 6 percent of total gross domestic product (GDP) for the year.[3] A substantial portion of these firms are "management controlled" in the sense that the holders of their shares are sufficiently dispersed that no one shareholder or organized group has a control block.[4]

The managers of such a firm, in making decisions concerning how to deploy its existing productive capacity or which proposed investment projects to implement, will be driven by the same objectives as drive most other people: desires for compensation, perquisites, respect, power, affection of those around them, and a sense of rectitude, among other things. The fundamental problem of corporate governance is how to design a structure of incentives—carrots and sticks—that channels these drives so that the decisions the managers make will be in society's best interest.[5] We argue in this chapter that, in general, these are the decisions that maximize the firm's share value. Market failures of course erode this link between share value and maximizing social utility, but we believe the argument we set out holds well enough for it to be a useful normative guide. More accurate share prices play a vital role in this story. They enable our system of corporate governance to incentivize managers to make share value–maximizing decisions in three ways: alerting investors when managers deviate from making such decisions, providing managers themselves with guidance as to what are share value–maximizing decisions, and enhancing the effectiveness of share price–based compensation.

*1. Alerting investors to behavior that does not maximize share value*

Maximizing a firm's share value means maximizing the future expected cash flows for the rest of the life of the firm (discounted to present value) paid to a holder of the share. Doing so is thus intimately related to a firm's future cash flows over time. If a share price is more accurate, it predicts these cash flows more accurately. When managers make a decision that does not maximize share value, they are making a decision that falls short of maximizing this future cash flow discounted to present value. The more accurate the firm's share price, the more likely it is that the price will pick this up and reflect the problem in part or in whole. This lower price can be a signal to the market of non-maximizing management: for example, when the firm's share price suggests a lower value of future cash flows than what is suggested by the share prices of its competitors in the same business.

This signal can prompt various reactions that may pressure the managers to change their policies—or lead to the managers' replacement. One possible reaction is through the exercise of the shareholder franchise. This would work primarily through the information that the signal provides to a firm's larger shareholders (i.e., the institutions or wealthy individuals that each hold between perhaps a fraction of 1 percent and a few percent of the issuer's outstanding shares). These shareholders have stakes large enough to overcome free-rider/collective action problems that might otherwise lead to the signal just being ignored or, even if noticed, to the unwillingness to engage in at least the minimal effort needed to coordinate their votes with other shareholders even when someone else takes the lead.[6] The growth of institutional investing means that shareholders of this kind hold in aggregate sufficiently large portions of the total shares outstanding to play a potentially critical role in voting in most publicly traded corporations that lack a controlling shareholder or group.[7] As a result, the corporate voting franchise has taken on new importance in recent years. Activist hedge funds, for example, have been able to target individual firms by acquiring a beachhead block of shares and then persuading other institutional investors to vote (or threaten to vote) with them, and in so doing, accomplish changes in managerial policy or management itself.[8]

A second possible reaction to the price signal occurs when the signal prompts a potential hostile tender offeror to investigate further and ultimately act. A third possible reaction to a signal would be action by the firm's own independent directors.

We do not need to see frequent examples of these reactions for the mechanisms described here to have a substantial influence on managerial behavior. Managers do not want to lose their jobs, and so the mere threat of replacement can lead them to avoid decisions that do not maximize share value. The more accurate a firm's share price is, the more effective are these deterrents to such decisions.

It should be noted that more accurate prices may enhance the effectiveness of the activist hedge fund and hostile tender offer threats in a second way as well: by reducing the firm-specific risk associated with the shares of the firm held by the offending managers. Greater price accuracy is likely to lead to less such risk because there will be less in the way of volatility-inducing surprises. An ordinary investor can entirely avoid suffering from firm-specific risk by having a sufficiently diversified portfolio. Activist hedge funds and hostile tender offerors, however, cannot avoid such risk because, to accumulate a large enough block of the target firm's shares to be effective, they will inevitably become less than fully diversified. The less firm-specific risk there is associated with a target firm's shares, however, the less likely it is that such risk will deter them from acting when they see signals of non-maximizing behavior. This makes the activist hedge fund and hostile takeover threats more real and hence more effective at prompting managers to make share value–maximizing decisions.

## 2. Providing guidance to managers

A firm's share price can provide useful guidance to managers as to what in fact are share value–maximizing decisions.[9] Managers ordinarily know more about what is going on within the firm than does anyone else, but they are not as expert relative to others with respect to many features of the outside environment in which the firm operates. Prices in an efficient market very usefully incorporate publicly available information concerning these features of the outside environment. Thus, market prices can incorporate better predictions of the effects of these features of the outside environment on the firm's future cash flows than the parallel predictions of the managers. The more accurate prices are, the better guidance they can give.

*3. Share price–based compensation*

Share price–based compensation is intended to help align the incentives of managers with those of shareholders and, if properly structured, to promote decisions that maximize share value. The manager is usually awarded the right to the compensation at one point in time and cannot realize a price-determined gain until some later point in time, usually measured in years. The more accurate the share price is at the time the manager realizes her share price–determined gain, the more reliable a reward mechanism it is and the more effective an incentive it is for her to make share value–maximizing decisions in the period between the award date and the realization date. If, during this period, she anticipates that the price at the time of realization, though unbiased, will not reflect with full accuracy the true consequences of the decisions she is making, she will not be as motivated to override her parochial self-interests and make share value–maximizing decisions. She knows that if she pursues share value maximization, but the price at the realization time is inaccurately low, she will not get fully rewarded for sacrificing her self-interest. Similarly, if she pursues her own parochial interests, but the price is inaccurately high at the time of realization, she will not be fully punished for neglecting to maximize share value. The more accurate prices are, the less this is a problem.

More accurate prices may be able to help the effectiveness of share price–based compensation in another way as well. The problem for managers with share price–based compensation, compared to a straight salary with the same expected value, is the undiversifiable, unsystematic risk it imposes on the manager. As noted earlier, greater price accuracy is likely to lead to less such risk because there will be less in the way of volatility-inducing surprises. Accordingly, a manager, when offered a total compensation package with a given expected value, will be willing to take a larger portion of it in share price–based form.[10]

## B. Efficient Use of Existing Productive Capacity

There are strong arguments that, in general, when managers make decisions concerning the use of a firm's existing productive capacity that maximize share value, they are making the ones that result in the most efficient use of this capacity for the economy as a whole and hence most enhance social welfare. Again, maximizing share value means maximizing the future expected cash flows for the rest of the life of the firm, discounted to present value, paid to the holder of the share. This requires a firm to use its productive capacity in each period in a way that maximizes that period's cash flow.

Assume, as a rough approximation of reality, that corporations operate in competitive markets and are properly regulated to account for their externalities. Under these circumstances, at the margin, what the corporation pays for each of its inputs used to generate this period's production equals the economic value of what it takes from society. The price of the input represents the opportunity cost to society arising from the corporation's use of the input: i.e., the value to society of the input being employed in its next best use. The price at which the corporation sells its output equals, at the margin, the economic value of what it gives back to society. Thus, in any one period, decisions that maximize the difference between the total cost of its inputs and the total revenues from selling its outputs maximize the corporation's contribution to society. Production decisions made in accordance with this principle in each period over the life of the firm are the ones that would maximize its cash flows over time discounted to present value.[11]

To be sure, reasonable readers will disagree as to how "rough" an approximate this account is, and the "what is good for the firm is good for society" reasoning admittedly sits on layers of assumptions. This book would triple in length were it to seriously defend all of these assumptions. We will simply note that this view enjoys widespread support among law and economics commentators and provides at least a rough measure of the effect of firm share value maximization on social welfare.[12]

## C. Efficient Capital Allocation

On at least a day-to-day basis, it is the top managers of a firm who decide how the funds in that firm's coffers will be deployed. These could be funds that the firm has generated internally when the revenues from the goods or services it sells exceed the costs of the inputs needed to produce those goods or services. They could also be funds raised through external financing. Persons within the firm will present various proposed investment projects to senior management. In deciding how to deploy the firm's available funds, the top managers can choose to invest in as many of these projects as they have funds for. Alternatively, they can pay out some or all of the available funds to their shareholders, who can then reinvest them elsewhere. Thus, in making these decisions, a firm's managers are participating in the larger process of determining which of the proposed investment projects in the economy ultimately receive funding.

Through the same mechanisms as discussed in section B, more accurate share prices enhance the effectiveness of the various mechanisms pressuring firm managers to make share value–maximizing decisions concerning not only how to use existing productive capacity but also which proposed investment projects to undertake. In the process, as we will see, more accurate prices play an important role in promoting capital allocation efficiency. Share prices also affect these decisions more directly; for example, through their effect on the terms on which firms can obtain external financing. These effects that more accurate prices have on the terms and availability of external financing are thus additional ways in which greater price accuracy improves the efficiency with which capital is allocated.

### 1. The Meaning of Better Capital Allocation

Before exploring the various capital-allocation benefits of share price accuracy, however, it is important to define exactly what is meant by *capital allocation efficiency*. Engage in a brief thought experiment. Imagine a nirvana world in which everyone's expectations concerning the future cash flows generated by proposed investment projects reflected all available information,[13] and expectations were uniform across all actors and were equally accurate predictions of future cash flows. The future cash flows of all of the proposed investment projects in the economy could, based on these expectations, be listed in rank order from most to least promising. Society's scarce savings would be optimally allocated—and social welfare maximized—if these savings were used to fund proposed projects, going down the list from the most promising to the next most promising and so on until the savings were exhausted.

This ultimate ideal is exactly what would happen in this imaginary world if it had freely operating markets and no transaction costs. This is because it would be mutually advantageous for people to enter into deals to make it happen. The real world, of course, involves very significant information asymmetries where different people possess different bits of information. Thus, the challenge is to design a financial system that chooses the set of projects that, in allocating scarce capital, comes as close as possible to this ultimate ideal. The discussion that follows concerns how a well-functioning secondary market for equities can play a helpful role.

### 2. Share value maximization and efficient capital allocation

A basic tenet of financial economics is that to maximize share value, a firm should avoid implementing any proposed investment project with a negative net present value (NPV), i.e., a project whose expected future net revenues discounted to present value are less than the project's cost.[14] The discount rate is determined by the price of alternative expected cash flows available for purchase in the market that have comparable amounts of undiversifiable risk.[15] The underlying idea is that, relative to the firm investing its funds in the negative NPV project, its shareholders can expect to do better if the firm distributes cash to them to reinvest in the market. As a result, the shares of the firm will be more valuable to hold if the firm avoids the project.[16]

Following this rule also makes the firm's investment decisions maximize social value. The risk-adjusted return that the shareholder can get by investing in the market is determined by the expected return on the most marginal proposed project available elsewhere in the economy. In other words, the risk-adjusted return represents the opportunity cost of the firm investing in its own project. If the firm funds its negative NPV project, the marginal project elsewhere, which has a higher risk-adjusted expected return, will not be implemented. Thus, more accurate share prices, by making more effective the forces that push managers to maximize share value, push them to avoid implementing negative NPV projects. Through this mechanism, more accurate prices not only lead to more efficient use of the firm's existing productive assets, but lead to more efficient allocation of capital as well.

It is difficult to over-emphasize the importance of having strong forces to push managers to make share value–maximizing decisions with respect to which investment projects they implement. Both theory and empirical studies suggest that left to their own devices, managers with surplus internally generated funds will often prefer to use these funds to implement negative net present value projects rather than paying them out in dividends. Because managers tend to benefit both from the process of firm growth and from running a firm of larger absolute size, managers who still have internal funds available after they have exhausted their firm's positive and zero net present value investment opportunities are likely to find it in their personal interests to implement some negative net present value projects in addition.[17] The chance that their share value–diminishing behavior will go undetected is increased by the very fact that firms with surplus internally generated funds do not engage in outside finance. As a result, their managers are not subjected to the discipline and scrutiny of the external capital market.[18] There is substantial empirical evidence, gathered in an era when the forces pushing for share value maximization were weaker, that the investment projects chosen by firms that relied predominantly on internal finance were considerably inferior to projects chosen by other firms.[19]

*3. The more direct role of share price accuracy*

More accurate secondary market share prices also improve the allocation of capital among prospective investment projects not just through their corporate governance effects, but more directly by affecting the terms of a firm's financing. These more direct effects are a feature of what we label as "institutional finance theory." Although we believe that these more direct effects are important, there is some debate about this. According to an alternative approach, what we label "classical finance theory," more accurate share prices do not have these more direct effects. These two contrasting theories are briefly discussed immediately below, with a fuller description set out in Appendix A.

Strict classical corporate finance theory suggests that share price accuracy exerts an effect on project choice *only* as a result of its impact on the quality of corporate governance. Under this theory, investment and financing decisions are separate because the determinants of whether a project has positive NPV—its expected profits and the market price of cash flows with comparable systematic risk—are unaffected by the firm's share price. Thus, when an issuer considers a proposed investment project, the terms at which outside funds can be obtained should not influence the decision as to whether to implement a project, and firms seeking to maximize share value should undertake positive NPV projects regardless of the share price.

Institutional finance theory takes a more nuanced approach to the interrelationships between financing and investment. In particular, it seeks to account for a number of features of the real world not accounted for in the classical theory, including the facts that (i) the market and legal forces pushing managers to make share value–maximizing decisions will not be fully effective at all firms at all times, and (ii) at least some firms will not generate sufficient funds internally to implement all their positive NPV projects. For instance, a firm may have a positive NPV project that it is attractive to fund through equity financing, but also face an inaccurately low share price. If the share price is low enough, the firm may fail to undertake the positive NPV project because it will have to offer so many shares to finance the project (because of these shares' current low price) that the negative effect of the dilution on the value of the existing shares more than cancels out the positive effect of adopting the positive NPV project. The institutional approach thus suggests how the accuracy of stock prices can be directly important to the viability of financing positive NPV projects and affect issuer's decisions about whether to invest in proposed projects. As described in Appendix A, share price will in fact affect a firm's willingness to undertake a proposed real investment project whatever the potential source of funding:

publicly offered equity or debt, privately placed debt or equity, bank loans, or internally generated funds.

## D. Liquidity

Greater liquidity has multiple benefits that are discussed in more detail in part II of this chapter. One benefit, however, deserves mention here. Greater liquidity reduces the transaction costs associated with speculative trading based on acquiring a variety of bits of publicly available information and analyzing them to make more accurate predictions of an issuer's cash flows. In other words, greater liquidity reduces the transaction costs associated with trading upon fundamental value information that the trader created or paid to have created.[20] Thus, greater liquidity, by lowering the costs of trading on fundamental value information not yet reflected in price, makes such trading more profitable and hence stimulates the creation of such information. The more such information is created and traded upon, the more accurate share prices are. More accurate share prices, in turn, lead to the attendant benefits in terms of more efficient capital allocation and utilization of existing productive capacity discussed earlier.

## II. ALLOCATION OF RESOURCES OVER TIME

If goods and services are to be produced for consumption in future periods, some of society's scarce resources must be used in the current period to build the needed productive capacity. Whatever resources are used to build capacity to produce in the future periods are resources not available to support current consumption. Society thus faces a trade-off between current consumption and future consumption. The secondary market for equities plays a role in determining the point on this trade-off chosen by society. As will be developed in this section, the more liquid an equity market, the closer the chosen point will be to what would be most efficient.

## A. How Secondary Market Liquidity Affects the Primary Market for Equities

During the current period, there are firms seeking to implement proposed real investment projects that, through the resulting production of goods and services in future periods, are expected to produce a future cash flow. Also during the current period, there are individuals willing to forego consumption of goods and services now so that they can consume more of these goods and services in future periods. One of the most important functions of an economy is to bring these producing firms and saving individuals together, and, in the process, allocate scarce resources so that they are used in a way that allows for the pattern of consumption over time that comes as close as possible to the one that leads to the highest level of social welfare. The more liquid the *secondary* trading market for equities, the better the *primary* market for equities works in promoting this end. This primary market simultaneously satisfies the needs of firms seeking funds for real investments (which offer shares or bonds—forms of a promise of future dollars—to implement real investment projects in return for obtaining from savers their current dollars) and the needs of savers seeking to forgo current consumption in order to enjoy future consumption (individuals who provide these current dollars in return for these promises of future dollars).

The more liquid an issuing firm's shares are expected to be, the more valuable they are to hold. For prospective purchasers of these shares in the primary market—the sellers of current dollars in return for the promise of receiving future dollars—the expectation of greater liquidity means that the purchaser will expect less cost in the future when she wishes to sell her shares in order to consume. She will also expect that her buyer will pay more for her shares because her buyer too will, for the same reasons, put a higher value on more liquid shares. Thus, when an issuer offers shares in the primary market, the more liquid investors anticipate the shares will be in the future, the higher the price at which the issuer can sell its shares (assuming all other conditions are equal). This higher primary market price translates into a lower cost of capital for the issuing firm. This is because the prospect of greater liquidity results in the issuer's expected future cash flows being discounted to present value at a lower discount rate.[21]

## B. The Effects of Illiquidity on the Choice Between Current and Future Consumption

This discussion of the benefits of share liquidity to investors and issuers lays the groundwork for seeing why a less liquid market leads to an inefficient choice as to the use of today's scarce resources in terms of the trade-off between consumption today and consumption in future periods. The less liquid shares are expected to be, the less rewarding individuals find saving to be and the less share value–maximizing firms will invest in proposed real investment projects. In welfare economics terms, just like a tax, illiquidity results in a wedge between the value of what the savers (the purchasers of future dollars) expect to receive in the future and what the entrepreneurs or issuers (the suppliers of future dollars in the form of future dividend streams) expect to give up in the future.[22] This wedge prevents certain transactions from occurring that would have occurred if the shares were expected to be more liquid. The fact that, absent this wedge, issuers and savers would have willingly entered into these transactions means the transactions prevented by illiquidity are ones that would, with greater liquidity, have made both parties better off on an expected basis. These lost transactions are projects with expected returns that are lower than the marginal project that gets funded in a world with a lower degree of illiquidity, but that nevertheless are high enough to make some individual investors feel that, absent liquidity concerns, sacrificing their current dollars for the projects' promises of future ones would be worthwhile.[23]

## III. ALLOCATION OF RISK

The future cash flows that will be produced by any given real investment project cannot be predicted with certainty. Rather, based on the best information available, one can construct a probability distribution of possible future returns, with an expected return (the probabilistically weighted average of the different possible outcomes), a variance (a measure of the potential for the realized future return to deviate on one side or the other of the expected return), and covariances with the returns on the other real investment projects in the economy (the tendency for, and extent to which, the project's realized future returns will be in the same or opposite direction as the realized return on each of the other real investment projects in the economy).

This lack of certainty concerning the future returns of the economy's real investment projects poses difficulties for investors, who are assumed typically to be risk averse. In other words, between two portfolios with the same expected return, the typical investor would choose the one for which actual realized return is likely to be closer, on one side or the other, of the expected return. The standard explanation of this preference is that most individuals gain declining marginal utility from money, which is the product of the quadratic utility function that they are typically assumed to have. With such a utility function, an investor will gain less in utility in the future, if the actual realized return is above the expected return by any given amount, than she will lose in utility if it is below the expected return by the same amount.

A very important function of the market for equities is to aid in the allocation of the risks generated by this lack of certainty as to what each investment project's actual realized returns will turn out to be. The goal is for these risks to be allocated among all the economy's investors in a way that each risk-averse investor has holdings of claims on these future cash flows (i.e., in the portfolio of shares that they hold) such that in aggregate they suffer as little risk-generated disutility as possible.[24] An individual investor seeking to maximize her economic welfare needs to achieve two ends in composing a collection of what shares to hold (taking also into account her portfolio's nonequity investments such as her human capital and any equity in her home). One end is to try to do as well as can be done in the trade-off between the overall portfolio's expected return and its overall riskiness. This can be done by taking advantage of the fact that the returns from different stocks are not perfectly correlated and so holding a collection of different stocks—*diversification*—can lead to a certain amount of cancelling-out of risk. This is because some stocks will turn out to realize returns greater than what is expected and others will turn out to realize returns less than what is expected. The second end is to have a portfolio that is as close as possible to the point in this trade-off that best satisfies the investor's particular level of risk aversion, which depends on her sensibilities with regard to risk and to her life circumstances. Portfolio theory dictates the particular collection of equity securities that best achieves these two ends.

The very existence of a reasonably liquid secondary trading market is essential for the successful working of this whole system of risk reduction through diversified shareholdings by many investors. If there were no public market for securities and ownership of each issuer was divided up among only a small number of investors, the size of the typical stake would be larger than the total invested wealth of most potential equity investors. For those investors with enough wealth to be able to hold such stakes, their fortunes would often not be large enough to hold stakes in enough different companies to gain anything like the full advantages of diversification.

A market with more than this minimum level of liquidity offers yet further advantages. Constant change in the world means that what constitutes an individual's optimal portfolio is always shifting. The more liquid the market is, by making both the purchase and sale of securities less expensive, the more the individual investor can cost-effectively fine-tune her portfolio to keep it close to the moving target of what at each moment is optimal for her.

## IV. RESOURCE USE AND INNOVATION

The equity trading market consumes substantial amounts of real resources that would otherwise be available to produce other goods and services that people enjoy. To give at least a sense of the order of magnitude of the resources involved, consider the larger financial system. It includes, in addition to the secondary market in equity, the primary market for equity, the primary and secondary markets debt, the banking system, and of course more. In aggregate, the financial system constitutes 8 percent of the country's GDP, or about $1.6 trillion in 2016.[25] Thus, it is not enough just to know what are the share price accuracy and liquidity impacts of a given practice or regulation. The practice or regulation is also likely to have an impact on the level of real resources consumed in operating the stock market and in enforcing and complying with the regulatory web within which the market functions. Even if the practice or regulation is, on a net basis, favorable for the functioning of the economy in the ways that we have surveyed in sections I through III of this chapter, it is quite possible that, at the margin, these real resource costs exceed the gains in terms of any beneficial impact the practice has on the functioning of the economy.

A good example of where the resource costs almost certainly outweigh any benefits is trading based on very recently announced information that has yet to be fully reflected in price. Such announcement information is the information contained in an announcement by an issuer or other institution with obvious implications as to the issuer's future cash flows. It retains this status as information that is not fully reflected only for the brief period between the time of the announcement and the time the information is fully reflected in price. Announcement traders profit by appreciating with lightning speed the import of an announcement (often based on machine reading) combined with technology enabling their buy or sell orders to reach trading venues very quickly.[26] The resources devoted to this practice are much greater than the benefit from the fleeting improvement in price accuracy.[27]

It is also important to recognize that the overall system is dynamic: there is always the possibility of future innovation that would allow the equity market to more effectively perform its social functions and/or reduce the real resources it consumes in doing so. Hence, we need to know the effect of the practice, and any current or proposed regulations to which that practice is or will be subject, on the capacity of the system to innovate over time. There is, for example, a lively debate as to whether it would be better to have all equity trading for a given company's stock occur on a single central limit order book (CLOB) rather than the current system in which each company's stock trades on many different venues. The multiple-venue system undoubtedly uses more resources because of all the interconnections that are necessary. By being competitive, however, the multiple-venue system is much more open to—and indeed is likely to spur—innovation.[28]

## V. REAL AND PERCEIVED FAIRNESS

So far, this chapter has exclusively addressed the effects of the trading market for equities on the efficiency with which the economy operates.[29] Much of the discussion concerning market practices, however, uses the language of fairness. Indeed, the core mission of securities regulation has traditionally been articulated in these terms. Unfortunately, allegations of unfairness are often (but not always) rather superficial. Frequently, they consist of taking a single transaction involving a trading practice, showing that the transaction benefits one party at the expense of another, and labeling the resulting transfer "larcenous," "extractive," "predatory," or simply "unfair." Serious analysis requires digging deeper. There must be a consideration of the effects of the practice as something that occurs on a repeated basis, in most cases within a competitive market. It is also necessary to take into account the reaction of the various other participants in the market to their knowledge of the practice in order to consider what the longer-run equilibrium effect of the practice will be.

This said, attention to fairness is important. The actual impact of any given practice on the fairness of the market is obviously a worthy concern in and of itself. In addition, perceptions of the fairness of a practice, whether accurate or not, can substantially affect how well the equities trading market performs its social functions. Thus, it is necessary, in the evaluation of any practice, to consider both the actual and perceived impacts on market fairness.

### A. Actual Fairness—The Larger Context

Conceptions of fairness are too many and too multifarious to address here in depth. However, fairness plays too prominent a role in public criticism of the securities markets to simply ignore. Our approach here is to take, as an exemplar, a conception of fairness that most frequently appears in commentary on securities markets. This conception criticizes a practice as unfair because each instance of its exercise leaves one or more persons worse off than they would have been had the instance of the practice not occurred. In essence, this conception argues that the practice is unfair because it results in an increase in the wealth positon of the person engaging in the practice and the decrease in the wealth position of one or more others.

In what follows, we critique this exemplar conception of fairness. Our critique builds upon a well-known line of argument first developed by Easterbrook and Fischel.[30] We recognize that our critique has its limitations and that some practices that are condemned by commentators as being unfair in this exemplar in fact raise genuine concerns that our approach does not pick up. Still, in the end, we think that as a general matter most controversial market practices can be more rigorously and perspicuously analyzed within the efficiency framework that we use throughout the rest of the book.

Our critique of the exemplar conception of fairness rests, depending on the particular practice, on one or more of the following three propositions. First, for many of the practices labelled as unfair by at least some commentators, retail investors in aggregate do not lose money from any given single exercise of the practice. Moreover each individual retail investor, and indeed each investor more generally, would typically be neither better nor worse off in terms of trading profits if the practice did not exist at all. This is because she engages in repeated transactions where she is affected by the practice and with each transaction she is as likely to benefit as to lose. Second, although the critiqued practice may increase the variance of the prices of individual stocks, each instance of someone undertaking the practice is generally independent of each other instance. Most investors engage in trades many times during their lives and are usually at least somewhat diversified. The effects of any increase in the price volatility of each individual stock as a result of the existence of the practice are likely to cancel each other out and thus impose little or no disutility. Third, trading markets are generally competitive. The assumption that these three premises are true underlies much of the normative analysis in this book. They, of course, will not always be true, and we will try to identify where the failure of one of these assumptions raises significant problems.

## B. Actual Fairness—Analysis

Take any frequently undertaken practice that is condemned as unfair under the exemplar conception of unfairness. When one market participant—call him Y—engages in the practice, some other participant—call her X—is worse off. As a general matter, X is usuallly worse off for one of two reasons. One reason involves X buying (or selling) some shares where the price would have been more favorable but for the action by Y. The other reason involves X being *induced* into purchasing (or selling) a share due to some action by Y, and, with the passage of time, the transaction turning out to be an unfortunate one for X for reasons related to Y's action. Either way, ex post, X has suffered a loss because of Y's action. The thrust of our analysis, though, is that to determine the fairness of the practice, we need to ask whether X would have been any better off in a world where the practice does not occur at all. For some practices the answer is yes. But for a broad range of practices considered in this book, the answer is no. This is because they involve one of the two situations (Situation 1 or Situation 2) described below.

*1. Situation I: Ex ante, the person whose trade was affected by the practice was as likely to have done better in terms of trading profits as to have done worse*

Consider the following three hypotheticals, which describe typical situations involving a person X whose trade was negatively affected by an instance of a given practice undertaken by another market participant Y, but where, ex ante, the negatively affected person was just as likely to have benefited from someone engaging in this practice.

First, suppose that over time, as various persons engage in a practice that Y engages in, a stock's price goes down as often as it goes up. Unfortunately for X, Y's instance of undertaking the action made the price go up, not down, and X just happened to be buying at that time. So, when some market participant engages in this practice, it is as likely to make X a gainer as a loser. She just turned out to be a loser in this instance.

Second, suppose, alternatively, that over time, as various persons engage in a practice that Y engages in, the action always moves the stock price up. Unfortunately for X, she just happened to be making a purchase at a time when someone, in our example Y, was engaging in the practice. An example, discussed in chapter 7, is where an uninformed trader purchases shares whose market price has been inflated by someone making a false positive statement. Trading profits require both a purchase and a sale, however, so X was as likely to have been a gainer at the time of sale from someone engaging in this practice as being a loser at the time of purchase. X was just unlucky that it was at the time of a purchase, not of a sale, when Y undertook this action.

Third, suppose that Y's action induced X into making a purchase that turned out to be unfortunate, but it was just as likely that an instance of the practice would have induced X into a transaction that would turn out to be favorable.

In each of these hypotheticals, whether any transaction entered into by X ultimately improves or diminishes X's wealth depends on a large number of factors as to which there is uncertainty at the time of X's decision to enter into the transaction. The possibility that the terms of any purchase or sale by X, or X's actual decision to buy or sell, has been affected by a market participant engaging in the practice undertaken by Y is just one more such risk. Probabilistically, as long as the upside of the risk associated with someone engaging in the practice is as big as the downside risk, the existence of the practice does not alter X's expected return from engaging in the transaction. X was just as likely to have enjoyed a windfall gain when she decided to transact, but in this instance happened to suffer a windfall loss instead. Moreover, if X has a diversified portfolio and/or engages in a relatively large number of share transactions over her life, the gains and losses resulting from various people engaging in the practice are likely to cancel each other out, leaving X in the same position as if she lived in a world where the practice was not occurring at all. In essence, the situation is like playing a game of chance where the dice are not loaded. If she plays on a repeated basis, she is likely to come out about even, thus there will be no significant wealth effect even viewed ex post.

In sum, with respect to the practices involved in each of these hypotheticals, it is very likely that X would not be any better off in a world where the practice does not occur at all. So in our view the wealth distribution effects of the practice are not a reason to prohibit it. Instead, the decision on how the practice should be treated under the law should be based on an efficiency analysis.

This said, we recognize that there are some salient limitations to our analysis. As Alicia Davis has shown, while it is a mathematical certainty that across all traders the expected net gain (or loss) is zero dollars, this is not true of every specific kind of trader. In a series of computer simulations Davis runs on a variety of trading strategies, a number of investor styles suffer significant gains or losses due to fraud. Further, as the number of trades increases, the probability of a trader precisely breaking even actually diminishes, eventually to zero, although the proportion of times a trader wins and loses from a practice approaches 50 percent as the number of trades increases.

Despite these limitations, we think that a direct efficiency analysis is generally a more useful lens for assessing market practices than fairness, and for two principal reasons. First, the fundamental social function of equity trading markets—the creation of wealth—is closely related to efficiency criteria. In this respect, activities associated with the stock market are quite different from many other activities. The range of activities covered by the tort system, for example, is much broader, where a plausible primary rationale for the law is expressing the equal dignity of citizens.

Second, we seek to offer a general assessment of practices based on their effects on the economy as a whole. To the extent that our regulatory recommendations differ from those of corrective justice advocates, this in part is the result of a simple difference of ambition. Corrective justice advocates emphasize losses incurred by specific traders. Under some circumstances we do not necessarily disagree that these losses may justify compensatory remedies. Our focus, however, is on the efficiency of the overall system in terms of the economic functions described above.

*2. Situation 2: Ex ante, the person whose trade was affected by the practice was not as likely to have done better in terms of trading profits as to have done worse, but the general existence of the practice leads to some kind of fully compensating change in the trader's circumstances.*

Suppose instead that in each of the preceding hypotheticals, X, as the result of someone engaging in the practice under evaluation, has less chance (if any) of making trading profits. Suppose, as well, however, that the existence of the practice leads to some kind of difference in X's circumstances that is fully compensating. If so, it is again hard to characterize the particular practice as unfair. This situation describes many of the other practices considered in the chapters that follow.

Consider just one example, discussed in more detail in chapter 5. Suppose that Y is an insider of the ABC corporation. Y sells some ABC shares on the basis of negative confidential information obtained from within ABC. X is a professional liquidity supplier and, in an anonymous market transaction, is Y's counterparty (i.e., X is the buyer purchasing Y's shares). X is likely to be a trading-profits loser when she engages in purchases at a time when someone is selling on the basis of negative confidential information.

However, as more fully explained in chapter 3, the expectation that such informed trading based on negative information will occur from time to time will lead liquidity suppliers such as X to protect themselves by quoting lower bids than they would if there were no such expectation. This allows them to pass on to the other sellers to whom they provide liquidity the costs of their unfavorable purchases from persons such as X. Because insiders can also trade on the basis of positive confidential information, liquidity suppliers also quote higher offers than if that practice did not occur. This wider bid/ask spread and reduced depth of book means that the stock will be less liquid. As we have seen in the preceding discussion, the purchase price of a less liquid stock is discounted to reflect this fact and thus purchasers in both the primary and secondary markets will not, on average, be adversely affected.

Nevertheless, this widening of the spread and resulting discounting of share prices in the secondary market has a number of indirect effects on the wealth positions of other individuals beyond X and the purchasers in the primary and secondary markets. Thus, one may also properly ask about the fairness of these more indirect wealth effects resulting from freely occurring insider trading. As we have seen earlier in this chapter, the expectation of wider spreads in the secondary market leads to lower initial public offering (IPO) share prices, which depresses the founding of new firms and hence the rents earned by potential entrepreneurs and by persons skilled at providing entrepreneurs with early financing. Wider spreads also increase the cost of transacting in shares, which means that fewer such transactions will occur, thus lowering rents to the providers of the specialized inputs required for the business of professional liquidity supply.

More specifically, in a competitive economy, suppliers of the ordinary inputs connected with the creation of start-ups and the provision of liquidity will be paid a market return comparable to what they would earn if the resources they supplied were instead deployed another way. So, the wealth positions of these persons will be unaffected by whether or not, in our example, insider trading is freely occurring. In contrast, the persons with uniquely useful abilities and skills for founding or financing start-up companies, or for the liquidity supply business, will each be paid extra in the way of rents if they pursue these respective activities rather than engaging in a different line of work. The amount extra, though, depends on the level of demand for the activity. Therefore, the lower number of IPOs and level of secondary market securities trading means that the rents going to these specialized providers of inputs will be lower with freely occurring insider trading than without it, and hence the existence of the practice of reduces their wealth positions.

It is again hard to characterize these diminished wealth positions as unfair. In a market economy, rents prompt the suppliers of specialized inputs to come forward. Under the right conditions, this is the mechanism by which these specialized resources get directed to the activity for which they are most particularly suited. As a general matter, the positive or negative effects of an equity trading market practice on the rents being paid to the suppliers of specialized inputs to any activity associated with this market would not appear to raise any greater fairness issues than do the rents paid persons with special abilities and skills across the whole market-based part of our economy. The foregoing discussion thus suggests that the prime normative question raised by practices best described by Situation 2 is, as with Situation 1 practices, whether the practice increases or decreases economic efficiency, not the fairness of its effects on the wealth positions of the various participants in the market.

Again, of course, criticisms of the market as unfair travel under many banners, and we do not mean to dismiss the concerns behind some of them. Worries about growing inequality in the United States and the role of the financial sector in exacerbating this trend are real concerns. We simply do not think that these broader social worries help us make the most accurate evaluations of the specific features of the equity market and their regulation that are the focus of this book.

## C. Perceived (Un)Fairness

Even if certain market practices are not in fact unfair, the perception that they are unfair is an important public policy concern. The stock market remains a highly effective forum in which middle-class individuals can invest their savings. If the perception that the stock market is unfair causes these individuals not to invest, or to substitute investment in less effective savings vehicles, then this could have very negative social consequences. Empirical evidence suggests that lack of trust in the stock market can be an important factor in explaining whether individuals invest in stock.[31] Far more empirical work is needed to better understand what practices investors perceive to be unfair and which might cause them to invest less or not at all.

# Appendix A

## THE MORE DIRECT ROLE OF SHARE PRICE ACCURACY: CONTRASTING CLASSICAL AND INSTITUTIONAL FINANCE THEORY

### A. Classical Finance Theory

Classical finance theory's conclusion that an issuer's share price should not affect its project choice decisions reflects the basic Miller and Modiglani tenet that investment and financing decisions should be separate.[32]

#### I. Share value maximization for real investment decisions

As we have seen, the share value–maximizing rule for *real investment* decisions is that the issuer should not undertake a proposed investment project unless the project has a positive or zero NPV. The rate used to discount expected future cash flows is determined by the market price of alternative expected cash flows available for purchase in the market that have comparable amounts of undiversifiable risk.[33] Thus, the two factors needed to make the net present value determination—this discount rate and the expected net revenues from the project—are each unaffected by the issuer's current share price.

*II. Share value maximization for external finance decisions*

The share value–maximizing rule for *finance* is that the issuer should raise external funds if and only if the funds received are greater than the discounted present value of the expected future cash flows that must be paid out in return. In the case of external equity finance, the funds received are the share price (less the transaction costs of the offering), and the future cash flows that must be paid out are expected dividends and other shareholder distributions on the newly issued shares for the rest of the issuer's life. Thus, for a manager seeking to maximize the value of her firm's currently outstanding shares, share price is important to the finance decision concerning whether to raise funds by issuing new shares, but is not important to the real investment decision as to whether to implement any particular project. Only the investment decision affects the allocation of real resources in the economy and hence its capacity to enhance social welfare through the provision of goods and services for consumption.

*III. An example of where the separation of the two decisions matters*

The importance of these rationales for separating the finance and investment decisions can be seen in the case of a firm that has inaccurately overpriced shares, but only negative NPV investment projects under consideration. Separating the finance decisions from the investment decisions suggests that the firm should sell additional shares, but should not invest the proceeds in any of the projects. The proceeds should instead be paid out to the shareholders as additional dividends.[34]

## B. Institutional Finance Theory

Notwithstanding the classical theory, there is nevertheless a significant chance that a firm's secondary market share price will affect a firm's real investment decision as to whether to undertake a proposed investment project.

*I. Firms with positive NPV projects*

Consider first the most obvious case: a firm lacking sufficient internal funds to finance a positive NPV project at a time when the secondary market price for its shares is inaccurately low. The price in the secondary trading market will largely determine the price at which the firm can publicly offer a new issue of shares, because no one is going to pay more in the public offering than they would pay in the secondary market to get a share of the same stock. Suppose that a public offering of equity would, at an accurate price, represent the least-cost method of external finance. With the secondary market price inaccurately low, however, implementing the project with funds raised in a public offering of equity may depress share value even though the project has a positive net present value. This is because with a lower share price, more shares will have to be issued to raise the needed amount of funding. The additional share dilution might depress share value more than the adoption of a positive net present value project would increase share value. If, for example, because of the agency costs of debt, other forms of finance are sufficiently more expensive than a public equity offering would have been if the share price had been accurate, then these alternative forms of external finance would also not be used. Hence, because the share price is inaccurately low, the project would not be undertaken at all even though its implementation would be socially desirable.

*II. Firms with only negative NPV projects*

Now consider a firm whose share price is instead inaccurately high and which only has a negative NPV investment project proposal. It is plausible that the forces pushing the firm's managers to engage in share value–maximizing behavior are not completely effective. In such a situation, the firm may both engage in a sale of new equity, as classical finance theory would suggest it should, and also—contrary to classical theory—implement the project. Raising the funds through a new equity sale followed immediately by a distribution of the proceeds might be awkward. Using the cash to implement the project instead, even though it does not maximize share value, would avoid this awkwardness and at the same time satisfy the managerial preference for firm growth and a larger firm size. Thus, an inaccurately high share price may lead to the implementation of negative NPV projects, which are socially undesirable.

*III. Indirect effects of inaccurate share prices*

Finally, the impact of inaccurate share prices on decisions concerning investment project implementation goes beyond their effect on a firm's use of the public equity markets. Even when the firm does have sufficient internal funds, or when a public equity offering is not the least cost method, share price may have an effect on whether the project is implemented. On the finance supply side, share price can directly affect the cost of financing a project by affecting the terms demanded by other external sources such as lenders.[35] On the demand side, an inaccurate share price can, under some circumstances, affect management's willingness to use debt to implement a new project. This is because of the prospect that the firm will subsequently want to counterbalance any new debt with new equity financing in order to maintain a perceived optimal debt/equity ratio. If share price is inaccurately low and managers are not confident that there will be a correction within the time frame that the counterbalancing equity offering would have to be effected, managers may be unwilling to take on additional debt to finance a positive net present value project. This is because of the prospect that the counterbalancing equity financing will, through dilution, be too costly to current shareholders.[36]

## IV. Additional considerations

Everything that has been said so far concerning the more direct effects of share price accuracy on capital allocation applies even if the market has no information concerning the proposed investment project that the firm is considering. Accurate share prices become even more important, however, if the market does have some such information. The more accurate the market's assessment of a project, the more likely it is that the assessment will push price in the direction that prompts the social value-maximizing decision as to whether to implement the project: pushing the price up if the project has a positive NPV and down if it has a negative NPV.

Seeing how the practices of the equity trading market's various participants affect share liquidity, share price accuracy, and wealth distribution requires a basic understanding of the market's underlying economics. Microstructure economics examines the nature of trade in securities markets and can provide a foundation for this understanding. Its principal models formally analyze trading behavior and liquidity. They reveal that trading equities involves a particular kind of strategic interaction. Traders differ in what they know. Crucially, some traders (the informed) possess information and analyses about a company's future that provide them with a more accurate view of the value of its shares than is possessed by the rest of the market (the uninformed). Informed traders trade in order to make speculative profits based on their informational advantage. Uninformed traders trade for other reasons, such as seeking a place to put their savings or later selling their shares in order to finance consumption. This chapter presents some central results of microstructure economics in a form accessible to nonspecialists.

We start by considering the different buyers and sellers in the market and their reasons for transacting. We then consider the critical role of adverse selection in the business of liquidity supply and its effect on the bid-ask spread and depth of book available to traders. Finally, we consider other costs associated with liquidity supply and their role in determining these same measures of liquidity.

## I. TRADERS AND THEIR REASONS FOR TRADING

The equity market exists in the first instance to serve traders. Traders are motivated to trade for a variety of reasons and, on this basis, can be broken down into five major categories: informed traders, uninformed traders, mistake traders, anti-mistake traders, and price-sensitive fundamental value traders. As this book progresses, we will see that the main story centers around the first two kinds of traders—informed traders and uninformed traders—and their interaction with professional liquidity suppliers. A complete picture, though, occasionally requires reference to the other three types of traders.

### A. Informed Traders

*Informed traders* are motivated to buy or sell based on private information that allows a more accurate appraisal of the stock's value[1] than the assessment of the stock's value implied by its current market price. Informed traders make money by buying when their private information suggests that a stock is underpriced and then selling what they bought when the market price comes to recognize the stock's value. They also make money by engaging in the mirror image of these transactions when their information suggests that the stock is overpriced. Distinctions among the kinds of private information that motivate informed traders are not important for a basic understanding of the mechanics behind the impact of informed trading on liquidity and prices. As will be developed in subsequent chapters, however, the extent of these impacts, and their significance in terms of social welfare, can very much depend on which kind of information is involved. The kinds of information on which an informed trader trades can be divided into four categories.[2]

### 1. Fundamental value information

A person generates fundamental value information by gathering various bits of information that are publicly available or are otherwise observable features of the world and analyzing what has been gathered in a sophisticated way that enables a superior assessment of a stock's cash flows than that implied by the current market price. Examples of fundamental value information traders are managed mutual funds, hedge funds, pension funds, and the professionally managed portfolios of very wealthy individuals and nonprofit institutions.

### 2. Announcement information

*Announcement information* is the information contained in an announcement by an issuer or other institution with obvious implications as to the issuer's future cash flows. The information retains this status only for the brief period of time between the time of the announcement and the time by which the information is fully reflected in price. Announcement traders profit by appreciating with lightning speed the import of an announcement (often based on machine reading) combined with technology enabling their buy or sell orders to reach trading venues very quickly.[3]

### 3. Information from inside an issuer

Much information held within an issuer is not yet public and thus not yet reflected in the price. Many of the cases relating to informed trading arising under the Exchange Act's Rule 10b-5 involve trades based on such information by corporate insiders or by their direct or indirect tippees. Such cases are often referred to as reflecting the "classical theory" of how an informed trader can violate Rule 10b-5.[4]

### 4. Information from inside a non-issuer source

Information relevant to prediction of an issuer's future cash flows that is not yet public or reflected in the price is also frequently held within an institution other than the issuer. This could be a potential acquirer contemplating a takeover of the issuer, or one of the acquirer's agents that is pledged to keep the takeover possibility confidential, such as its law firm or investment bank. Alternatively, it could instead be an institutional investor planning the purchase or sale of a substantial number of shares. Or it could be a brokerage, research, or media company that finds it commercially profitable to gather bits of publicly available information, analyze them in a sophisticated way, and thereafter sell and/or publicly announce its conclusions. Finally, it could be a government agency that gathers and processes information (or makes decisions) relevant to prediction of an issuer's future cash flows that the agency has not yet disclosed. Rule 10b-5 cases involving trades without permission by insiders of such institutions, or by their direct or indirect tippees, are often referred to as reflecting the "misappropriation theory" of how an informed trader can violate Rule 10b-5.[5]

## B. Uninformed Traders

*Uninformed traders* buy and sell shares without possession of information that allows a more accurate appraisal of the stock's value than the assessment implied by current market prices. Nor do they have a belief that they have such information or that prices are otherwise incorrect. One possible motivation for an uninformed trade is that purchase of the share and its later sale are a way of saving: deferring consumption from the time of the purchase to the time of the sale.[6] Thus, the purchase might be triggered by a bequest from the trader's recently deceased grandmother that is not needed for current consumption. A sale might be motivated by the need for cash to pay the college tuition bill of the trader's child. The second possible motivation for an uninformed trade is to correct for the fact that, perhaps due to changing conditions, the trader's current portfolio differs from the portfolio that would, for her, optimally balance expected return and risk.[7] As with deferred-consumption-related transactions, the triggers for these risk related portfolio adjustments are unrelated to any private information and so these transactions too will have a risk-adjusted market rate of expected return.

Index funds too are, by definition, uninformed traders. Their purchases of the shares of any given issuer are usually triggered by inflows to the fund exceeding redemptions and their sales of such shares are triggered by the opposite situation. More infrequently, index funds must trade in response to corporate decisions. To the extent that the fund holders wish dividends to be reinvested, the fund will have to buy the index components with those reinvested dividends. The index fund will also have to rebalance in the face of extensive share repurchases, selling shares of the index components that have significant repurchases. Because the triggers for all of these purchases and sales of uninformed trades are unrelated to private information about the value of the stock involved, the expected return at the time of an uninformed trader's purchase will simply be the expected return on the market as a whole adjusted to reflect the risk characteristics of the particular firm's shares.[8]

Index funds are not the only institutional sized traders who generate uninformed orders. It is quite likely that with any actively managed fund, a single informed trade will be accompanied by other uninformed trades used to fund the informed one. While the fund would like to sell shares about which it has bad news, that may not be feasible. Rather, the fund may be required to sell shares on the basis of no information. Similarly, if there are large inflows at a time when the actively managed fund has exhausted its new investment ideas, its purchases will be largely unguided by information.

Other large uninformed transactions unmotivated by information are for risk management purposes. For example, if a fund has idiosyncratic information about a single firm in an industry, it may wish to trade away from the industry risk by selling shares of other firms in the same industry about which it has no private information. It should be noted, furthermore, that these hedging trades in the other firms need to be done as quickly as the trade in the firm concerning which they have private information.

## C. Mistake Traders

*Mistake traders* believe they have information not reflected in price that permits a more accurate appraisal of an issuer's future cash flows.[9] What distinguishes them from informed traders is the fact that the information is either already reflected in price or is irrelevant. To the extent that what drives mistake traders at any given moment in time are idiosyncratic beliefs, their buy and sell trades will in aggregate tend to cancel each other out. To the extent that what drives them is a widespread fad or fashion, their trades will push a stock's price in the direction suggested by the fad or fashion. Such fad- or fashion-driven trading thus tends to drive price away from being the best estimate of an issuer's future cash flows given all publicly available information.

## D. Anti-Mistake Traders

*Anti-mistake trading* is a particular form of informed trading, discussed separately here because of the special role that it plays in the pricing process. Anti-mistake traders actively search for new information about an issuer's future cash flows and are prepared to transact in the opposite direction when they see prices move at a time when their search suggests there is no new information. Thus, when fad-driven mistake traders push price in one direction, anti-mistake traders trade in the opposite direction. Because of the synergies of engaging in fundamental value informed trading and the information search that is the basis of anti-mistake trading, the same person or entity often engages in both types of trading.

## E. Price-Sensitive Fundamental Value Traders

Each price-sensitive fundamental value trader has her own reservation price for buying and for selling a given stock that is a product of her own best estimate of the issuer's future cash flows based on her particular analysis of publicly available information, how long or short she already is in the issuer's shares, and a discount to reflect the chance that what appears to be an attractive purchase or sale price might be the result of informed trading.[10] As we will see, such traders play a role in the process by which professional liquidity suppliers manage their inventories and, with anti-mistake traders, act as an antidote to pricing distortions caused by mistake traders. Often these fundamental value traders are traders who, though not in the business of supplying liquidity like professional liquidity suppliers, have submitted nonmarketable limit orders. Thus, they are showing that they are interested in buying or selling shares of an issuer, but only if they can do so at a more favorable price than the current NBO or NBB. Because the trades of price-sensitive fundamental value traders are not motivated by either new private information (like those of informed traders), or by a search suggesting that a price change is not due to new private information (like those of anti-mistake traders), these price-sensitive traders otherwise act more like uninformed traders.

## II. PROFESSIONAL LIQUIDITY SUPPLIERS

In addition to these five types of traders, there is one more set of buyers and sellers in the market of great interest: professional suppliers of liquidity. A professional liquidity supplier engages in both the frequent purchase and frequent sale of a range of different stocks, making a business out of standing ready to buy and sell these shares up to stated amounts at quoted prices (respectively a *bid* and an *offer* or *ask*). As noted in chapter 1, the best available bid in the market is referred to as the *national best bid* (NBB) and the best available offer as the *national best offer* (NBO). Today, this professional liquidity supplier is typically a high-frequency trader (HFT). An HFT uses high-speed communications to constantly update its information concerning transactions and quotes at every trading venue, and revises its own quotes accordingly, rather than using information about the issuer itself to determine these quotes. Thus, the professional liquidity supplier is typically not "informed" in the sense that we use the term here. Indeed, because of its unique intermediary market-making role, unlike all other buyers and sellers of securities in the market, we will not refer to it as a trader.

The liquidity supplier makes money if on average it sells the shares it buys for more than the price paid. Doing so might appear easy, even in markets with a one-cent spread: buy at the bid and sell at the offer and make a half-cent per share on every transaction. Do this for a billion shares and pretty soon you are talking about real money. In fact, however, it is not so easy. Liquidity suppliers are subject to adverse selection by informed traders. Their sales to, and purchases from, informed traders occur at just the times when it is least desirable to be transacting in the direction that the liquidity supplier is transacting. The losses arising from transacting with informed traders appear to constitute the largest part of the costs of being a professional liquidity supplier and hence the largest determinant of the spreads between a liquidity supplier's bids and offers.[11]

Liquidity suppliers also require capital, which can only be obtained if the investor providing it can expect to receive a risk-adjusted market rate of return. They incur as well certain operating expenses, including paying talented personnel. Furthermore, they face risks associated with their inventories and incur costs in managing these risks. These other factors too will have an effect on the spreads between their bids and offers.

In the rest of this chapter, we consider separately the effects on the bid-ask spread from adverse selection and from these other factors. The adverse selection discussion assumes that adverse selection is the only cost facing liquidity suppliers. Indeed, this is the factor that predominantly drives the strategic interaction among the various participants and that is most affected by whatever particular regulatory mix governs the market. Hence, its isolation in the analysis is critically helpful in understanding much of the story in the chapters that follow. The subsequent discussion of the other factors then completes the picture.

## III. ADVERSE SELECTION

The persons with whom a liquidity supplier trades generally do not reveal their identities. The possibility always exists that a person (the *trader*) who places a marketable order that executes against the liquidity supplier's quote will turn out to be informed. In other words, this trader has private information that is not known to most of the market or to the liquidity supplier and hence is not yet fully reflected in price. As already noted, an informed trader of this kind will buy from the liquidity supplier when her private information suggests that the stock's value is above the liquidity provider's offer. She will sell to the liquidity supplier when her private information suggests that the stock's value is below the liquidity provider's bid. The liquidity provider will be subject to adverse selection and on average lose money when it sells at the offer to informed buyers or buys at the bid from informed sellers, and this is so whatever the informed traders' source of private information. However, as long as there are enough uninformed traders willing to incur, in order to accomplish their reasons for trading, the inevitable expected trading losses of always buying at the offer and selling at the bid, the liquidity provider can break even.[12] The spread simply has to be large enough between the bid and offer that the losses incurred by transacting with informed traders are offset by the profits accrued from transacting with uninformed investors.[13] To see how these ideas translate into a description of how liquidity suppliers set their quotes and the impact of this quote-setting on liquidity and price accuracy, we first consider a world with just informed traders, uninformed traders, and liquidity suppliers. Then we add in mistake traders, anti-mistake traders, and price-sensitive fundamental value traders.

## A. The Effect of Adverse Selection on the Setting of Quotes and Market Liquidity

There are two useful ways thinking about the calculations that liquidity suppliers need to perform to survive in a competitive market. The first, sometimes referred to as the "accounting perspective,"[14] is based on the proposition that for a liquidity supplier to survive in business, what it loses from transacting with informed traders must be offset by what it gains from transacting with uninformed traders. The second, sometimes referred to as the "information perspective,"[15] relates to how a liquidity supplier rationally should update its estimate of a stock's value depending on whether the next order that transacts against its quotes is a buy or a sell. Each of these two perspectives leads to the same bid-ask spread.[16]

### 1. The accounting perspective

At a point in time, let P be the market's assessment of the value of a share of stock given current information. If A and B are respectively the offer and bid, and the market consists entirely of traders with no private information, then the liquidity provider's expected profits are (A − P) from buyers and (P − B) from sellers. This is because a liquidity provider receives A from an uninformed buyer and gives up a share of stock worth, given current information, P. Similarly, the liquidity provider pays out B to an uninformed seller and receives a share of stock worth P.

Now suppose, however, that some traders in the market may be informed. An informed trader's private information leads to a different—on average more accurate—appraisal of the stock's value than the market assessment, P. Informed traders will buy if their appraisal of the stock value, V, exceeds A, the offer. They will sell if their estimate of value, V, is below B, the bid. The liquidity supplier knows that if a buyer is informed, its view of the value of the stock, V, will, on average, be more accurate than P, the view of others in the market. Therefore, the liquidity supplier rationally expects that if it unknowingly sells at A to a person who is informed, V is on average greater than A. It will similarly expect that if it unknowingly buys at B from a person who is informed, V on average is less than B. Hence, expected profits from transactions with informed buyers are negative, and expected profits from transactions with informed sellers are similarly negative.

The final input to the calculation is the likelihood of informed and uninformed traders. The starting point is an assumption that on average, buy and sell orders from uninformed traders will be equal in number, which seems reasonable because the trades of uninformed traders are typically motivated by concerns unique to each individual trader and not by the possession of nonpublic information or a belief that the price is too high or too low.[17] To calculate the ratio, a concrete example is useful here. Suppose that over the next short interval of time the market knows there will be an announcement. If it contains good news, the apparent value of the stock will rise from $60 to $61. If it contains bad news, the apparent value will instead fall to $59. To those without private information, it is equally likely that the news will be good as that it will be bad. Informed traders, however, know what the announcement will be. One percent of the order flow is expected to come from informed traders, who will buy if what they know is good and sell if what they know is bad. The remainder of the order flow is from uninformed traders and, as just noted, involve an approximately equal number of buy and sell orders.

If trading takes place on the basis of *positive* private information, the informed traders will submit buy orders but not sell orders. Then, the probability that a buy is from an informed trader is $(0.5 \times .01)$ (the likelihood the information is positive multiplied by the percentage of trades that will be informed), whereas the probability that it is from an uninformed trader is $(0.99 \times 0.5)$ (the percentage of traders that are uninformed multiplied by the even chance that they will be buyers rather than sellers). Setting the offer equal to A, the expected profit is $A - 61$ if the order is informed and $A - 60$ if it is uninformed. Thus, for the offer quote not to be a losing proposition, it must be at least as big as the A that solves:

$$(0.5 \times 0.01)(A - \$61) + (0.99 \times 0.5)(A - \$60) = 0$$

Solving this equation, A, the offer, must be $60.01. By the same reasoning, for the bid quote not to be a losing proposition, it should be $59.99, that is, a spread of two cents in a competitive market of liquidity suppliers. In essence, in order to expect to break even, the liquidity supplier must set its bid and ask such that the profits it expects to make from transacting with uninformed traders just equals the losses it expects to experience from trading with informed traders.

## 2. The information perspective

The second way to view the quoting problem is the following. The liquidity supplier sets its bid and offer before knowing whether the *next* order to arrive will be a buy or sell. Nonetheless, when deciding on its offer, it knows that an informed trader will submit a buy order to transact with that offer only if the trader is in possession of positive private information suggesting that the current price is too low. The liquidity supplier thus knows the arrival of a buy order will move its estimate of the stock's value upward. This is because there is some chance that the order is motivated by positive nonpublic information and no chance that it was motivated by negative information. In other words, the arrival of the buy order contains a hint about whether the information is positive or negative: a buy order increases the likelihood (in the liquidity suppliers' eyes) that the information is positive. To not regret that transaction, the liquidity supplier must, before the order arrives, set its offer quote to reflect the upward revision that will accompany the arrival of the buy order. Likewise when the supplier sets its bid: to be regret-free, the bid must reflect the anticipated downward valuation revision that would accompany the arrival of a sell order. The result is that the offer is already set at a price *conditional* on the next arriving order being a buy and the bid on it being a sell. The higher the percentage of incoming orders that the liquidity supplier expects to be informed, the greater will be these upward and downward revisions of estimated value upon the receipt of each buy order and each sell order. Thus, the spread will be greater: its offers will be more above the midpoint and its bids more below the midpoint.[18]

## 3. Impact of adverse selection on liquidity

The higher the level of informed trading expected by liquidity suppliers, the less liquid the market for the stock is. The accounting and information perspectives each show this. Consider first the accounting perspective. A liquidity supplier cannot simply set an extremely wide spread to garner large profits. Liquidity suppliers function in a competitive market. As a result, to survive, they must set their quotes aggressively enough (offers low enough and bids high enough) to attract counterparties to trade, but still earn sufficient revenue that their profits from trading with the uninformed equal or exceed their losses from trading with the informed. If the level of expected informed trading increases, liquidity suppliers must set their offers higher, and bids lower, to break even. This is true not only for each supplier's best bid and offer. This is true as well for its bids for additional shares below its best bid and offers for additional shares above its best offer. Thus, the expectation of a higher level of informed trading leads not only to wider bid-ask spreads but also to less depth of book.

Similarly, under the information perspective, each liquidity supplier sets its offer and bid to be regret-free contingent on the next order coming in being a purchase or a sale. The higher the percentage of incoming orders that a liquidity supplier expects to be informed, the greater will be its contingent-on-which-order-type-arrives upward and downward revisions of a stock's estimated value. Thus, its offers will be higher above the midpoint and its bid lower than the midpoint.[19] Again, this widening effect relates to the distance between all of a liquidity supplier's bids and offers for a given stock, not just the spread between its best bid and offer, thus meaning less depth of book.

*4. The information value of trade size*

The adverse selection model just presented is driven only by an imbalance in order flow going to liquidity suppliers and does not take into account the size of the individual marketable orders that lead to this imbalance. However, the size of an individual order—*trade size*—can also convey some information to liquidity suppliers concerning the likelihood that the order is informed and, if so, the importance of the information motivating it.[20] All else equal, a single larger order is more suggestive of informed trading than several smaller orders adding up to the same total number of shares. This fact turns out to be relevant to our analysis in chapter 4 of the impact on social welfare of the so-called electronic front-running by HFTs, as well as to our analysis in chapters 5 and 6 of the proper regulation of various types of informed trading. In Appendix A of this chapter, we provide an extension of the adverse selection model set out here that accounts for trade size.

## B. The Pattern of Transaction Prices in the Presence of Informed Trading

The information perspective highlights an important side effect of how rational liquidity suppliers set their quotes in a market with informed trading. Liquidity suppliers constantly update quotes in response to transactions. As a result, the market price eventually comes to reflect the informed trader's information. The behavior of rational liquidity providers thus reflects a kind of "invisible hand": simply as a result of their efforts to avoid losses to informed traders, liquidity providers repeatedly revise their quotes so that, with time, their quotes come to fully reflect informed traders' information.

To illustrate, consider the example in the preceding discussion concerning the accounting perspective. Assume that the informed traders have a piece of positive private information that motivates them to send in buy orders. At the same time, uninformed traders are also trading, and the number of their buy and sell orders are approximately equal because the reasons for their trades are unrelated to efforts to acrrue trading profits by finding over- or underpriced securities. So, during this period, both buy and sell orders will arrive at trading venues, but in total there will be more buys than sells because the incoming buy orders also include the orders from informed traders and the incoming sell orders do not. Accordingly, the bids and offers that liquidity suppliers set fluctuate as their estimates of value move slightly up and down with the arrival of each buy and sell order. Ultimately, though, the predominance of buy orders will cause the revised quotes to trend up, along with the midpoint between the bid and offer, until the offer gets high enough that it equals $61, the informed traders' estimate of the share's value.[21] Empirical evidence strongly supports the results from these adverse selection models: Analyses of intraday changes to quotes and the prices of executed transactions consistently show that they respond to the pattern of buy and sell orders, and that the adjustment in price described here often occurs rapidly.[22]

In sum, informed trading makes stock prices more accurate. As described in this subsection, liquidity suppliers' quotes—the prices posted on trading venues—adjust in response to private information. Because private information allows a more accurate appraisal of the stock's value than that implied by its current price, the effect of liquidity suppliers' revisions is to cause the bid and offer to move in the direction of a more accurate appraisal until they fully reflect all the private information on which the informed traders trade.

## C. Adding in the Effects of Mistake Traders, Anti-Mistake Traders, and Price-Sensitive Fundamental Value Traders

The three other kinds of traders—mistake traders, anti-mistake traders, and price-sensitive fundamental value traders—also play roles in the adverse selection story, although secondary ones relative to the roles of informed and uninformed traders.

## 1. Mistake traders

Mistake traders believe they have information that permits a more accurate appraisal of an issuer's value, but in reality that information either is already reflected in price or is irrelevant to developing a more accurate appraisal. To the extent that what drives mistake traders at any given moment of time is idiosyncratic to each trader, their buy and sell trades tend to cancel each other out. Just like uninformed trading, such idiosyncratic mistake trading creates no significant order imbalance for liquidity suppliers and thus has no significant effect on price or the bid-ask spread. To the extent, however, that a widely shared but foundationless belief drives the mistake trading, an order imbalance will result. The imbalance pushes bids and offers in the direction suggested by the fad or fashion and makes the midpoint deviate from what would otherwise be the best estimate of an issuer's future cash flows given all publicly available information.

## 2. Anti-mistake traders and price-sensitive fundamental value traders

Recall that each anti-mistake trader actively searches for new information about an issuer's future cash flows. She transacts when she infers the presence of mistake trading because prices have moved but her search shows no new information to justify this movement. Each price-sensitive fundamental value trader has her own reservation price for buying and for selling a given stock that is a product of her own best estimate of the issuer's future cash flows based on her particular analysis of publicly available information, how long or short she already is in the issuer's shares, and a discount to reflect the chance that what appears to be an attractive purchase or sale price might be the result of informed trading. A price-sensitive trader, rather than responding to new information or to a price change lacking (after search) any apparent justification, simply buys if the price drops to his reservation purchase price and sells if it rises to his reservation sale price.

To illustrate how the reactions of these two types of traders to fad-driven mistake trading work, start with a situation in which there is no informed trading and no mistake trading in an issuer's shares, so that the initial midpoint between the bid and the offer represents the best estimate of the stock's value given the available information. However, liquidity suppliers do not know that there are no informed traders. Mistake traders then acquire a widely shared but false belief that the stock's value is significantly below this initial midpoint and start selling, which creates an imbalance of sell orders arriving at the trading venues and executing against the liquidity suppliers' quotes. This pushes down the bid and the offer. The mistake traders continue this selling until the bid drops to what they (incorrectly) believe to be the stock's value. The offer drops along with the bid. The anti-mistake traders, observing this price drop and believing there is no genuinely predictive negative information to justify it, start buying at the reduced offer price. So do the price-sensitive fundamental value traders whose reservation purchase prices were below the original offer but not the new lower offer. These purchases by the anti-mistake traders and the price-sensitive fundamental value traders create an imbalance, with more buy than sell orders reaching the liquidity suppliers. This imbalance pushes the bid and the offer back up. This buying will continue until the offer reaches the initial midpoint.

*3. The interaction of mistake traders, anti-mistake traders, price-sensitive fundamental value traders, and professional liquidity suppliers*

As this story illustrates, the mistake traders, who incorrectly believe they possess negative information, suffer trading losses because they sell shares for less than they are worth. Anti-mistake traders and price-sensitive fundamental value traders enjoy trading gains because they buy shares for less than they are worth. At the end, liquidity suppliers on average just make the spread on each share purchased from the mistake traders and then sold to the anti-mistake traders and the price-sensitive fundamental value traders. This is because the midpoint between the bid and the offer is commensurably below the value of the shares both as the shares are purchased from the mistake traders and as they are sold to the anti-mistake and price-sensitive fundamental value traders, but the purchases are at the bid and the sales at the offer. Thus, the combination of fad-driven mistake trading and these other two kinds of trading does not worsen the liquidity suppliers' adverse selection problem. The mirror image of this story occurs when the mistake traders incorrectly believe they have positive information, but again the liquidity suppliers' adverse selection problem is not worsened.

## IV. OTHER FACTORS AFFECTING THE BID-ASK SPREAD

A number of other factors affect the bid-ask spread beyond adverse selection from informed traders. A liquidity supplier requires capital to cover its long and short positions, and this capital is at risk. To raise this needed capital, the supplier must offer the investor providing it the prospect of receiving a risk-adjusted expected market rate of return. The more the liquidity supplier trades in any given time period, the more such capital it needs. It also needs to maintain office space, pay fees for access to trading and quote data, and obtain sophisticated electronic equipment and software and high-speed communications lines. Also, it utilizes talented personnel who incur an opportunity cost for spending their time working for the liquidity supplier rather than doing something else (a factor explored in more detail in Appendix C to this chapter). Each of these factors adds to the marginal cost, at least in the long run, associated with each purchase and sale the liquidity supplier undertakes. Thus, in a competitive market, each of these cost factors will add to the price the supplier charges for the service of providing liquidity: the difference between the bid or ask and the midpoint.

The liquidity supplier's need for trading capital and the risks associated with its use deserve special attention here. The adverse selection model of liquidity supply set out earlier does not address how liquidity suppliers reverse the effects on their inventories from being on the other side of the order imbalance resulting from informed trade. Nor does it address the price impact when informed traders lock in their profits by reverse transactions once their private information becomes public. These issues are explored in detail in Appendix D to this chapter, but some basic intuitions are set out here.

The simplest story as to how these parts of the story could work is as follows. Assume, for purposes of illustration, that there is just one informed trader and that, based on positive nonpublic information, the informed trader purchased 10,000 shares of ABC Corporation stock per trading day over a 100-trading-day period (one million shares in aggregate). To lock in her profits so as to avoid any continued risk, the informed trader will want to reverse her purchases as soon as possible after the information on which she traded becomes public. At the moment it becomes public, the informed trader's portfolio has almost a million more shares of ABC than would a fully diversified portfolio. Similarly, the portfolios of the liquidity suppliers that sold these shares to her are in aggregate short almost a million such shares relative to where their portfolios would be if fully diversified. This means that the portfolios of the informed trader and of each of these liquidity suppliers have large amounts of extra, firm-specific, risk that could be eliminated by full diversification without any sacrifice in expected return.[23] Thus, at the moment of public revelation of the private information, the informed trader would be anxious to sell, and the liquidity suppliers in aggregate would be anxious to buy, about one million ABC shares. The transactions to accomplish this should occur at about the price per share established after this public revelation. After all, the liquidity suppliers know that there has been an abundance of buy orders leading up to an announcement of good news and hence they will expect and welcome an abundance of sell orders. To the extent that the sales by the informed trader nevertheless begin to push the bid and offer down much below this figure, anti-mistake traders, ascertaining that likely there is no private information justifying the decline in the offer, would submit a sufficient number of buy orders to maintain the price established by the public revelation.

A more complicated story would recognize that liquidity suppliers would find it undesirable to have so much capital put at so much risk for 100 trading days. They likely would seek to rebalance their portfolios regularly, rather than waiting until the informed trading stops and the private information becomes public as in the simple story offered here. Using the example again, one could imagine that after each day's 10,000-share order imbalance, liquidity suppliers would have a somewhat higher bid and higher offer than what would be called for by the pure adverse selection considerations just described. The object would be to find some price-sensitive fundamental value investors whose reservation prices were such that they would respond by sending in more sell orders and fewer buy orders than would otherwise have been the case.

When the informed trader seeks to unwind her position by selling shares after the public revelation of the information, this will again cause an order imbalance going to the liquidity suppliers. To the extent, if any, that the liquidity suppliers cannot figure out that this imbalance just represents such an unwinding, they will lower their bids and offers. In response, though, anti-mistake traders, believing there is no private information justifying the decline in the offer, would submit a sufficient number of buy orders to largely maintain the price established by the public revelation. Inventory models in microstructure economics have developed a sophisticated literature in the vein of this more complicated picture.[24]

There are two other factors that can affect the size of the bid-ask spread. One is the level of competition, explored in more detail in Appendix E to this chapter. The analysis so far has assumed that liquidity suppliers operate in a fully competitive environment, but, to the extent that the environment is instead monopolistic or oligopolistic, they can use their market power to extract a higher price in return for their services (i.e., a higher bid-ask spread). This, in fact, appears to have been the case in the days of the Nasdaq dealers and the NYSE specialist. The other factor is the minimum allowable difference in quotations, which is explored in more detail in Appendix F. Currently, the minimum is generally $0.01 (that is, no bid or ask can be quoted in an amount involving fraction of a cent), but minimum tick sizes used to be more larger than this (for example, it was traditionally $0.125 on the NYSE). A minimum tick size obviously results in a wider bid-ask spread anytime the spread as determined by all the other factors discussed previously would be smaller than the minimum tick.

## V. CONCLUSION

Combining what we have learned in this chapter with the lessons of chapter 2 yields the following key conclusions. Informed trading is the central dynamic driving our market for equity trading. Informed trading enhances share price accuracy but reduces liquidity. Price accuracy and liquidity are each social goods, and so there is a basic social trade-off.

These key conclusions powerfully shape the story that unfolds in the following chapters. As we will see, the terms of the social trade-off between price accuracy and liquidity depend a great deal on the kind of private information involved. This observation helps guide a determination of which kinds of informed trading, if any, should be subject to direct prohibition, a focus of chapters 5 and 6. It also helps guide a determination of how to regulate the structure of trading, because market structure rules can have a differential impact depending on the kind of informed trading involved. These include rules relating to HFTs, exchanges, dissemination of quote and transaction information, dark pools, and payments to brokers, the subjects of chapters 4, 9, 10, 11 and 12. Finally, an understanding of the origins of the trade-off between price accuracy and liquidity can yield new insights about two other market practices that have proved particularly elusive to commentators, manipulation and short selling, which are the topics of chapters 7 and 8.

# Appendixes

## Appendix A

### EXTENSION OF THE SIMPLE ORDER IMBALANCE MODEL TO MULTIPLE TRADE SIZES

The adverse selection model in the text of this chapter 3 is driven only by an imbalance in the order flow going to liquidity suppliers and does not take into account the size of the individual marketable orders that lead to this imbalance. It is plausible, however, that all else equal, the larger the order, the more likely that it is informed, a fact that is relevant to some of the discussions in the chapters that follow. In this appendix, we provide an extension to the simple order imbalance adverse selection model that accounts for trade size.

## A. The Basic Model

To make the exposition simple, we suppose that there are just two sizes of marketable orders: a small order of 100 shares and a large order of 300 shares. The proportion over time of small orders in the overall flow is $\pi$ and the proportion of large orders is $(1 - \pi)$. To exemplify how, in the workings of the market, order size can be a signal as to whether an order is informed, we assume that none of the small orders come from informed investors, while a fraction, $\alpha$, of the large orders come from informed investors. With regard to knowledge concerning the value of the shares, the liquidity suppliers, as in the earlier simple order imbalance example, only know that there is a 50 percent chance that it is $59 and a 50 percent chance that it is $61. The informed traders do know which it is. If it is $61, they will be buying; if it is $59, they will be selling. The liquidity suppliers know that there are traders who are informed as to which the value is. They also know that (i) all small orders come from uninformed traders; (ii) a proportion, $\alpha$, of the large orders come from informed traders, with the rest coming from uninformed traders; and (iii) the proportion of order flow over time coming from large orders is $(1 - \pi)$.

Assume that professional liquidity suppliers are the sole suppliers of the limit orders that form the limit order book and that they always submit 100 share units. This is a fairly reasonable assumption, as the modal transaction size in today's market is in fact 100 shares. An easy way to see the pricing equilibrium in the limit order book is to start with it empty. Liquidity suppliers then submit their 100 share limit orders one at a time. They pick the prices of the bids and offers that they submit based on what has happened before them in this round of quote submissions. After all the limit orders have been submitted, a marketable order arrives. After the marketable order executes, any remaining limit orders are cancelled and the game begins again. This is a reasonably realistic assumption in today's market, where each colocated HFT constantly monitors both the quotes of the others and any new transaction and where each such HFT can cancel its own quotes and submit new ones in less than a thousandth of a second.

The supplier who submits the first limit sell order knows that her 100 share offer will transact no matter what size marketable buy order arrives. If this marketable buy order is a small order, the liquidity supplier's limit order will satisfy it entirely. If this marketable order is a large order, the supplier's limit order will satisfy only 100 shares of the marketable order.

The simple order imbalance analysis in the text of chapter 3 must be modified as follows to account for this more complicated situation. The marketable buy order executing against the first supplier's offer quote can only be one of three kinds. One kind is a buy order from an *uninformed* trader submitting a *small* marketable order. Its probability is $(1.0 \times 0.5 \times \pi)$: the percentage of small-order submitters who are uninformed, multiplied by the even chance that an uninformed submitter will be a buyer rather than a seller, multiplied by the chance that the order is a small order. The second kind is a buy order from an *uninformed* trader submitting a *large* marketable order. Its probability is $(1 - \alpha) \times 0.5 \times (1 - \pi)$: the percentage of large-order submitters who are uninformed, multiplied by the even chance that the submitter will be a buyer rather than a seller, multiplied by the chance that the order is a large order. The third kind is a buy order from an *informed* trader submitting a *large* marketable order. Its probability is $[0.5 \times \alpha \times (1 - \pi)]$: the likelihood that the information is positive, multiplied by the percentage of large-order submitters who are informed, multiplied by the chance that the order is a large order. Setting the first liquidity supplier's quote equal to A, the expected profit is $A - 60$ if the marketable order is uninformed and $A - 61$ if it is informed. Consequently, the expected profit from the first liquidity supplier's 100 share offer is:

$$0.5\pi \ (A - 60) + 0.5 \ (1 - \pi) \ (1 - \alpha) \ (A - 60) + 0.5 \ (1 - \pi)\alpha \ (A - 61)$$
$$= 0.5 \ [A - 60 - (1 - \pi)\alpha]$$

Setting this expression equal to 0 (the level of profits in a competitive market for liquidity supply) and solving for A reveals that the first limit order will be priced at $60 + (1 - \pi)\alpha$. This is the level at which the first supplier needs to set her offer in order to break even. A symmetric argument will show that the break-even bid will be $60 - (1 - \pi)\alpha$.

Now consider the expectations of the liquidity suppliers submitting the second and third arrivals to the limit order book. They each observe that a first sell limit order has already been submitted. Thus they realize that their orders will transact only if the marketable order, when it arrives, is a large order. These liquidity suppliers are in essentially the same position as the liquidity supplier in the simple order imbalance model provided in the text of this chapter. Based on that model, we know that the offer will be set at $60 + \alpha$. This is because each supplier reasons that if its offer ultimately does not transact, it will be because the marketable order, when it arrives, will turn out to have been either a sell order or a small buy order. So, if its sell limit order *does* ultimately execute, the marketable order must have been a large buy order. In this case, the probability of the marketable order being informed is $\alpha$ and the probability of it being an uninformed order is $1 - \alpha$. Consequently, the expected profit from the 100-share offer by each of the second and third liquidity suppliers is:

$$0.5(1 - \alpha)(A - 60) + 0.5\alpha(A - 61) = 0.5(A - 60 - \alpha)$$

Setting this expression equal to 0 (the level of profits in a competitive market for liquidity supply) and solving for A reveals that the second and third limit orders will be priced at $60 + \alpha$. This is the level at which the second and third liquidity suppliers each need to set their offers in order to break even. A symmetric argument will show that the break-even bid will be $60 - \alpha$.

Accordingly the equilibrium in the limit order book will depend upon the parameters $\alpha$ and $\pi$. Suppose that $\alpha = 0.05$ and $\pi = 0.8$. The break-even first offer must be 60.01. The break-even second and third offers must be at least 60.05. The break-even first bid must be 59.99. The break-even second and third bids must be at least 59.95.

## B. Accounting for Shredding

Reality is somewhat more nuanced than the workings of this mathematical model. An informed trader, all else equal, would prefer to accomplish his purchase as quickly possible—that is, in a single round, using just one large marketable order. All is not equal, however, because, as the preceding model shows, using a larger order size results in trading at a less advantageous price. If the informed trader instead "shreds" his larger order into 100 share orders, each of these shreds will look like what a larger portion of the uninformed orders look like. Under the assumptions of the model in this appendix, each 100-share order, because of its small size, does not carry any signal of being informed because it is assumed to be uninformed. What happens if informed traders start shredding? Liquidity suppliers will soon notice that an order imbalance coming from small orders is correlated with a future price change and, in accordance with the adverse selection model presented in the text of this chapter, will, in their quotes, start taking account of the fact that they will be losing to informed traders from some small marketable orders as well as from some large ones. This change in quoting behavior will reduce the benefit of shredding, but there will still be some advantage as long as there was originally a benefit to shredding, namely that the proportion of large trades that are uninformed is less than the proportion of small trades that are uninformed. This is a reasonable assumption: some informed traders have information that will become public much sooner than the information possessed by other informed traders. Thus, to trade with greater speed, they will find it worthwhile to use larger, unshredded marketable orders even though it is a more expensive way to trade.

## C. Accounting for Tick Size Restrictions

One separate additional nuance should be noted, relating to the impact of a minimum tick size. *Tick size*, explored further in Appendix F, is the smallest allowable difference between quotes. It is $0.01 for most NMS stocks.

To explore the interaction of tick size with the marketable-order-size analysis presented here, go back, for simplicity of exposition, to the original model in this Appendix A, where there was no shredding. It was fortuitous that the numerical example in that discussion resulted in breakeven offers and bids that fell on even pennies. Consider now a situation in which that is not the case. For example, suppose that $\alpha$ is 0.01, rather than 0.05 as it was in the preceding numerical example. Then parallel calculations would show that the breakeven offer for the liquidity supplier submitting the first offer would be $60 + (0.01 \times 0.2) = \$60.002$. The breakeven offer for each of the subsequently submitted offers would be $60 + 0.01 = \$60.01$. With the minimum tick size of $0.01, however, all the offers will be at $60.01. This is because $60.002 is not an allowable quote and the supplier of the first offer would lose money if it quoted $60.00.

This example highlights the value of speed for a liquidity supplier in real markets. The liquidity supplier submitting the first offer has a per-share expected profit of $0.01 - 0.002 = \$0.008$, because its quote is $0.008 above its breakeven point.

# Appendix B

## EXTREME INFORMATION ASYMMETRY AND MARKET UNRAVELING

A feature of the adverse selection model in the text of this chapter is that the uninformed will trade no matter how wide the bid-ask spread. This may stretch credibility. If the upside is 61, this model suggests that an uninformed trader is as willing to buy at just under 61 as at 60 even though the downside is 59. Although the model presented in the text is able to provide in simple fashion much of the intuition for what asymmetric information does in markets, it misses out on the effect of extreme information asymmetry, which will result in the market simply closing down. We believe this happens, and it is easy to modify the model to show why.

One approach is simply to notice that uninformed traders trade for a reason, even if they have no view as to the value of a stock relative to its price (perhaps beyond some kind of faith in the efficient market hypothesis). For example, as noted in the discussion of uninformed traders at the beginning of this chapter, an uninformed investor may consider buying a share simply to find a place to put savings or selling a share simply to generate cash for consumption. Or she may consider buying or selling a share in order to help rebalance her portfolio in a way that achieves a better risk/return ratio or a ratio more appropriate for her taste in terms of the trade-off between the two. Before she acts, though, she must compare the gain from achieving one of these aims versus the cost of transacting. The cost of transacting is essentially half the spread. The greater the amount of information asymmetry, the wider the spread and hence the higher the cost of transacting. As the cost rises, each uninformed investor will find that in fewer and fewer cases will the reasons motivating a potential purchase or sale justify actually going ahead with the transaction. A potential vicious circle is established. As fewer informed traders trade, the proportion of all trading that is informed trade increases, which leads to a wider spread for the same level of information asymmetry. This wider spread in turns leads to even more informed traders deciding not to trade, and so on.

Another approach is to treat all uninformed investors as traders sensitive to movements in the absolute value of a stock's price.[25] All we need is that there be sufficient adverse selection and that uninformed traders decide, based on the quote, whether they want to trade or not. A simple way to do this is to imagine that all potential uninformed traders have private valuations that are independent of the private information creating the information asymmetry. They buy if their private valuation is above the offer and sell if their private valuation is below the bid. Suppose this private valuation is uniformly distributed among potential uninformed traders over the range of 59 to 61.

Imagine this scenario using the simple model of adverse selection presented in the text of this chapter and modifying its numerical example so that $\alpha$, the likelihood that a trade is informed, is initially equal to 0.5. Start with the prediction of this basic model that the offer should be $60.50. At this price, however, only half of the potential uninformed buyers will in fact want to buy. But this implies that the informed trades will now be $0.5/(0.5 + 0.25) = 2/3$ of the transacting order flow. Thus, the offer must be raised to 60.67. But now only one-third of the uninformed will want to buy, and the informed constitute $0.5/(0.5 + 0.083)$ of the transacting order flow. Thus, the offer must be raised to 60.86. But this again reduces the number of uninformed who wish to trade, increasing further the informed as a proportion of transacting order flow.

Calculations have become tedious, and it is not obvious where we end up. But the equilibrium can be solved as shown next.

Recall that potential informed traders learn that the future value is either 59 or 61 and they arrive at rate α. Uninformed traders, as we have just seen, each have a private valuation that is uniformly distributed among them across the range of 59 to 61. Call this random private value X, and specify that an uninformed arrival will buy if X > A, which occurs with probability 0.5(61 − A) and sell if X < B which occurs with probability 0.5(B − 59). As before, the uninformed arrive at rate (1 − α) but then choose to trade based on their private valuations. As a consequence, the expected profit on the offer side can be written, for A ≤ 61:

$$5\alpha(A - 61) + (1 - \alpha)0.5(61 - A)(A - 60)$$
$$= 0.5(61 - A)(1 - \alpha)[A - 60 - \alpha/(1 - \alpha)]$$

Recall that in a competitive liquidity supply market, the equilibrium offer will be the A that results in profits being zero, i.e., the breakeven A. The breakeven A can be obtained by setting the expression equal to 0 and solving for A. It is easy to see that one such solution is for A to equal 61. But an offer of 61 will also yield zero trade. An alternative solution is for A to equal 60 + α/(1 − α). This solution will be an offer that yields zero trade unless the resulting A is less than 61, but A cannot be less than 61 unless α is less than ½. Thus, in this numerical example, we conclude that if the rate of informed arrival is ½ or greater, the market will close down and there will be no trade.

We think that this mechanism is real. In the old days of the specialist on the NYSE, the specialist had the ability to ask the floor manager to suspend trading in a particular stock. Conversations with specialists in those days suggested that they did this reluctantly, but did so when the trading environment became dangerous. A common reason for requesting a shutdown was that a firm announcement was anticipated and that there could be informed trading ahead of that announcement.

## Appendix C

### THE EFFECT OF LIQUIDITY SUPPLIER OPPORTUNITY COST ON THE BID-ASK SPREAD

Adverse selection is not the only cost associated with liquidity supply. Among other things, liquidity requires individual effort as well. This appendix considers the contribution to the bid-ask spread of this need for individual effort.

A person who makes a career out of providing liquidity is competent to do other things instead. Hence, her compensation for providing liquidity must be at least as great as her next best opportunity. By spending the day providing liquidity, she gives up the opportunity to do something else, and therefore making liquidity involves an opportunity cost.

Three factors determine the size of this opportunity cost's contribution to a stock's bid-ask spread: the stock's total daily volume of trading,[26] the number of professionals supplying liquidity in this stock, and the opportunity cost to each professional associated with spending her day doing so. Let V equal the total stock's trading volume divided by the number of professionals providing liquidity in the stock. Let C equal each professional's opportunity cost. To isolate this opportunity cost's contribution to the spread, assume that it is the only cost associated with providing liquidity (i.e., there are no adverse selection or other costs).

Recall from the discussion in the text of this chapter that the expected gain from transacting a single share of stock is half the bid-ask spread. If S is the average spread, this means that S must be large enough to satisfy the following condition: $V \times S/2 \geq C$. Otherwise, the liquidity supply professionals will pursue some other line of work. This means that in a fully competitive market, where the supplier just breaks even, $S = 2C/V$.

This simple model can yield some important observations. First, if the total daily volume of trade for a given stock is smaller, a given level of V for each individual liquidity supplier can still be maintained by there being fewer liquidity suppliers, something that would happen naturally through the workings of market forces. If the number of suppliers is small enough, however, the market in which they operate may not be fully competitive. Relative to the model set out in this appendix, this can result in the spread being greater than the breakeven minimum indicated in the preceding formula. Moreover, if the total volume of trading in a stock is sufficiently small that the number of suppliers drops to one, then the smaller this total volume, the smaller V is, and hence the larger the breakeven minimum spread. Consistent with what we see empirically, these two considerations suggest that the spread will be wider for smaller cap stocks in which there is less trading interest than for thickly traded stocks.

The second observation concerns the impact of labor-saving technology. The more securities transactions in a given stock that a liquidity supplier can handle in a given day, the larger V will be, because each supplier can handle a bigger portion of the total volume of trade. Thus, the smaller will be 2C/V, the breakeven spread. At least as important, if a professional liquidity supplier can supply liquidity in more than one stock, her full opportunity cost for spending the day supplying liquidity is spread over multiple stocks. In essence, the C associated with each stock becomes smaller. Thus, again, the smaller $2C/V$ (the minimum breakeven spread) will be.

These two points shed light on one likely reason why spreads are smaller today than in the past. When the liquidity supplier was typically a NYSE specialist or NASDAQ dealer, quoting decisions were made by individual human beings. This put substantial limits on the number of transactions one such individual could handle in a day and the number of different stocks for which she could have quotation responsibility. For today's professional liquidity suppliers—HFTs—the number of transactions they can handle in a day is very large and the number of different stocks for which they can have quotation responsibility is substantial. An HFT firm consisting of a relatively small number of professionals is likely to be algorithmically making markets in a large number of stocks all over the world. This makes the opportunity cost contribution to the spread much less significant than it was in the past.

It is possible that this opportunity cost does play a more important role in the spreads of municipal and corporate bonds. Volume in such bonds is notoriously small and, at least so far, the level of technology devoted to the actual trading of bonds has not reached much beyond the telephone.

# Appendix D

## RISK AVERSION, FUNDING, AND INVENTORY MANAGEMENT

Much of the academic literature dealing with inventory effects is related to dealer and specialist markets.[27] However, the insights can be applied to limit order markets. The basic idea is that a liquidity supplier does not like to have too large an inventory of any stock, either positive or negative. To have such a position exposes the market maker to idiosyncratic risk, particularly when holding the position overnight. The stock may go up (good for a long position, bad for a short position) or it may go down (good for a short position, bad for a long position), so on average this possibility of share price change is not bad. What is bad is the risk. Theory predicts that in response to serving a number of buy orders and hence being short, a liquidity supplier will increase its offer, making the offer unattractive in light of other market makers' quotes and thereby reducing the expected number of future marketable buy orders. Simultaneously, the market maker will increase its bid, making this market maker's quote more attractive than other competing bids. This increases the number of marketable sell orders executing against the liquidity supplier, thereby reducing its short position. In order to prevent buying high at the increased bid and selling low at the original offer, the dealer needs to set a positive spread. The original offer must be at least as large as the increased bid needed to attract marketable sell orders. That is, in addition to there being a spread component due to asymmetric information, there should be a spread component due to risk aversion and inventory management.

There is one subtlety that must be acknowledged. Comerton-Forde, Hendershott, Jones, Moulton and Seasholes report that in 1994–2004, the NYSE specialists had long positions at the end of the day in 83 percent of the days.[28] Either they were not very good at inventory management or something else was going on. It is quite likely that during that time period, and perhaps still today, a long sale or buy was easier than a short sale: hence the positive target inventory.

With competing market makers, the inventory management just described should spread the inventory around to the other dealers. This risk sharing is the efficient thing to happen. In case that is not enough, dealer markets with competing dealers have offered a way to trade between themselves. NASDAQ created such a market, SelectNet, to effect inter-dealer trading. We see similar institutions in the interest rate swaps market.

It might be argued that the market makers can, at least imperfectly, hedge the overnight risk by using the option markets. Liquidity suppliers that are long might buy puts, for example, so that if the stock price goes down, the put position will rise in value. However, buying the puts from option market makers will leave them effectively long in the stock, leading them to sell stock to hedge their position and thus increasing the inventory position of the stock market makers. Their hedge might effectively be undone. It should also be noted that spreads in the option markets tend to be quite large. In a sample from the late 1980s to the mid-1990s, average quoted and effective spreads for a five-dollar option were, respectively, 40 cents and 25 cents.[29] These spreads are probably larger than those on the underlying stock with a much higher price. A recent review of CBOE quotes for Apple (AAPL) options priced at more than $3.00 reveals spreads of 10–15 cents, whereas the tick for AAPL options is a nickel (on options priced more than $3.00). In contrast, a recent contemporaneous bid and ask for AAPL was $173.58 and $173.59.

Scholarly articles agree on the effect of the level of inventory on the location of the spread, but disagree about the effects on the spread itself. The preceding narrative of inventory management suggests that inventory should have a relatively minor role in the spread of an individual liquidity provider itself, as opposed to the location of the spread, as both bid and offer are raised in response to a short position. Momentarily, the spread may fall as the affected market maker increases its bid while the offers of other market makers remain the same. However, as inventory is spread around, the spread should return to its original size but a new location.

In fact, there is evidence that the absolute value of an inventory position did have an effect on specialists' spreads.[30] The paper motivates the result by noting that as inventories increase in absolute value, financing requirements increase. Financing frictions may have occasionally prevented the specialist (or specialist firm) from being able to meet its obligations. In that case, the fear of larger (in absolute value) inventories is more salient than the delight at reducing them. A wider spread results. Although the study analyzed specialist data, the logic could still apply today to HFT liquidity suppliers.

Do these results from the days of specialists and dealers have relevance today? Though we do not have any hard data on HFTs' day-end inventories, anecdotal evidence suggests that HFTs prefer to end the day flat. As significant suppliers of liquidity, then, we can imagine that the desire to avoid an inventory position will affect their quoting behavior. Of course, HFTs have the ability to directly undo inventory by using marketable orders like ordinary traders (i.e., crossing the spread). However, a long position created by successive buying at a decreasing bid is not going to be profitably undone by selling at the now-depressed bid of other market participants.

## Appendix E

### THE EXTENT OF LIQUIDITY SUPPLIER COMPETITION AND THE BID-ASK SPREAD

It might be thought that the capital markets must embody the epitome of perfect competition. After all, FINRA, the SRO tasked with regulating broker/dealers, boasted 3,816 member firms with 159,641 branch offices hosting 635,367 registered representatives as of February 2017.[31] Such numbers might suggest a very competitive market as long as two conditions hold: (1) all market participants have an equal opportunity to offer liquidity to the market, and (2) all such participants have equal access to market information. The structure of the market, however, in part determines the extent to which these conditions are actually met.

With today's market structure for all more thickly traded equities, in which anyone can provide liquidity simply by sending a nonmarketable limit order to any one of twelve electronic open limit order books, the first condition—equal opportunity to offer liquidity—may appear to be met. As discussed later, this is certainly true relative to the NASDAQ dealer market of the past. It should be noted, however, that some persons—HFTs—can both send orders to, and cancel orders on, these venues faster than others because of their colocation with the venues' matching engines. Thus, they can alter their quotes more quickly than others in response to some signal. Colocation also violates the second condition—equal access to information—because each HFT learns faster than others of new transactions and changes in the available quotes, a subject to which we will return in chapter 4.

Now, for a moment, consider instead a pure dealer market, such as the NASDAQ market of the past and the over-the-counter (OTC) market for unlisted securities that still exists today. A *pure dealer market* is one in which designated dealers must be the counterparties to every single transaction. That is, if a non-dealer wishes to transact, a purchase must be from a dealer and a sale must be to a dealer. The old NASDAQ dealer market was in some sense the first electronic market, where electronic communications substituted for direct personal interaction on a trading floor. It consisted of three levels of "screens." The first level was for potential traders—i.e., the customers of brokers—and it displayed only the best bid and offer. The second level was for brokers and showed each dealer's name, and its bid and offer with quantities. The third level was only for the dealers and featured the names and quotes of the other dealers along with the ability to change quotes and send messages. The incoming orders were electronically directed to the dealer chosen by the broker. On top of the electronic portion of the market was a telephonic market in which large transactions were effected over the phone. In this case a broker representing a large order would tell the dealer the size of the order but not the side (buy or sell) of the order. The dealer would respond with a two-sided (bid and ask) quote. The broker and dealer could then negotiate, or the broker could try calling elsewhere. Notably, the bid and ask provided by the dealer could be outside of the market quote and a transaction could be effected at a bid that was lower, or an offer that was higher, than the posted best bid or offer.

In this old NASDAQ dealer market, the quotes displayed to the brokers were firm up to 1000 shares—but, significantly, any dealer could match any other dealer's better quote when an order arrived. Thus, a broker might quite reasonably send an order to a dealer whose quote was not the best with the expectation that the dealer would match the best. The dealer not quoting the best would in fact typically match in this way, for to do otherwise would leave the broker in violation of its duty to its customer to provide best execution (discussed in more depth in chapter 9). That would damage the dealer's relationship with the broker. Further, the dealers would cement their relationships with brokers by paying for order flow, just as internalizers pay for order flow today, a topic discussed in chapter 12. So, for each security, there was in essence a network in which brokers had relationships with dealers and vice versa. This resulted in a sort of "price matching" equilibrium of noncompetitive quotes in which no individual dealer had an incentive to deviate from the consensus.[32]

One might wonder where the limit orders were in this prior world. The answer is that if there were any, they were held by a dealer and executed against only when and if the dealer was ready to do so. For example, suppose a dealer's quotes are 60.25 bid, offered at 60.50 . A limit order to buy at 60.375 is then sent to the dealer. Recall that in a pure dealer market, a dealer must be the counter-party to every order. Thus, this limit order to buy would not execute until and unless the dealer's offer dropped to 60.375 or below. So, a buy limit order gets executed only after the market falls from the level it was at when the limit order was submitted, and a sell limit order only after the market rises from the level it was at when the limit order was submitted. In other words, the limit order would execute only after the market moved in a disadvantageous direction. No statistics are available, but we believe that for this reason limit orders were not often used. In any event, there is no way in which limit orders competed with NASDAQ dealers in a way that would push them to improve their quotes.

During the time of the NASDAQ dealer market, it was observed that quoted and effective spreads for NASDAQ stocks were larger than for NYSE spreads. Some asserted that this just reflected the riskier and less active nature of the NASDAQ listed stocks. There is a logic behind this explanation: riskier, less active securities require liquidity suppliers to engage in more inventory management and, as compensation, they need to charge a wider spread. The question of whether this was all that was at work, however, was put to the test by Christie and Schultz.[33] They discovered that in a sample of the 100 most liquid NASDAQ-listed stocks, 60 of them hardly ever traded on an odd eighth, and so the effective tick size for these stocks was $0.25. The authors suggested, and many agreed, that this was evidence that the price of liquidity provision—the spread—was fixed above competitive levels. This explanation appears to make sense because any dealer making a quote at an odd eighth would immediately be revealed as deviating from the rule and would be subject to punishment by the other dealers.[34] What is more, several newspapers reported the Christie and Schultz results on May 26 and 27, 1994. May 27 showed a dramatic increase in odd-eighth quotes in Amgen, Cisco Systems, and Microsoft. Apple computer traders faced many more odd-eighth quotes the following day.[35] Among the top ten NASDAQ stocks by volume, it is precisely this list of firms that had previously avoided odd eighths.

Following these studies, a number of suits were brought alleging such price fixing, as well as actions brought by the Department of Justice (DOJ) and the SEC. The dealers settled with both the DOJ and the SEC in 1996. The DOJ settlement required the dealers to stop fixing quotes, a practice to which they did not admit, but agreed to stop.[36] The SEC put into place its "order handling rules," which required each dealer to take any limit order it received that either bettered or added size to its current quote and to reflect the limit order in its book. The dealer then must allow any contra-side marketable order that subsequently arrives to execute against this limit order.[37] These two settlements appear to have been the impetus that resulted in NASDAQ morphing into the electronic limit order book that we see today.

By allowing the limit orders of other participants to compete with those of professional liquidity suppliers, the current market structure is clearly more competitive than the old NASDAQ dealer market. However, as noted above, the extent to which the 635,000-plus registered FINRA-regulated individual brokers and their customers contribute to competitive quoting is still constrained by the fact that HFTs, acting as professional liquidity suppliers, have distinct competitive advantages because each one, in response to new transactions and changes in the quotes of other participants, can cancel old orders and submit new ones faster than any other kind of participant. The implications of these advantages are explored further in chapter 4.

There are in fact, as best we can tell, only a small number of HFTs with any significant market share today. Thus, only a small number of entities enjoy the bulk of the advantages that HFTs have over all other participants in submitting nonmarketable limit orders. This structure in the HFT industry suggests that the business involves considerable economies of scale. For instance, the marginal physical cost of trading is near zero once you have the computer power. It also suggests that if the current incumbents have first-mover advantages of any kind, they may have a certain amount of market power.

It is worth noting, as an aside, that HFTs are well situated to be announcement traders as well as professional liquidity suppliers. Recall that an *announcement trader* is an informed trader whose information advantage arises from very quickly becoming aware of a public announcement as soon as it is made and acting on it before others can. Some HFTs certainly play this announcement trader role at times. Suppose that there are $N$ HFTs. Nothing in the market happens precisely simultaneously and so, for any given announcement, one of these $N$ HFTs apprehends and acts on it first. Assume, however, that each HFT apprehends and reacts to announcements generally with the same average speed. In other words, for any given announcement, there is an equal chance that any given HFT will be the first to react. Based on a model originated by Budish, Cramton, and Shim,[38] we would expect to see the following pricing equilibrium. Assume that the announcement is positive and, for simplicity, that just one of the $N$ HFTs (the quoter) has a sell limit order on any given exchange. The remaining HFTs will be "snipers." Each sniper, after apprehending the news, tries to execute against the quoter's offer before it is cancelled. Because on average they are all equally fast, each of the snipers has a $1/N$ chance of executing against the offer. The quoter, after apprehending the news, has a $1/N$ chance of cancelling its offer before any of the snipers manage to execute against it. This means the quoter will be sniped with probability $(N - 1)/N$. The quotes are set so that every HFT is indifferent between being a sniper or quoter. Based on the simple order imbalance adverse selection model in the text of Chapter 3, this in turn implies that the offer, A, for example, must satisfy the following: $.5(1 - \alpha)(A - 60) + .5\alpha(A - 61)(N - 1)/N = .5\alpha(61 - A)(1/N)$ or $A = 60 + \alpha$, exactly the same A that we derived above. Notice, though, that this offer yields a profit to the quoter of $0.5\alpha(1 - \alpha)(1/N) > 0$ on the offer side (and, by the same logic, the same on the bid side for negative announcements). No amount of competition from all the other participants— the slow broker/dealers and their customers—can alter this.

## Appendix F

### THE EFFECT OF TICK SIZE ON THE BID-ASK QUOTE

The *tick* is the smallest difference between allowable quotes. In the United States, it is set to be $0.01 by Rule 612 of Regulation NMS for most NMS stocks. For most of the history of the market, the tick was $0.125 (1/8 of a dollar) and then was briefly $0.0625 (1/16). In 1997, it dropped to the current tick of a penny. It is pretty clear from the data that at least part of the observable spread is due to the tick, because so many stocks typically have spreads of exactly one penny. Most stocks priced between $10 and $40 trade, most of the time, on a spread equal to $0.01. This suggests that were these stocks allowed to trade on fractions of a penny, spreads could be smaller than a penny.

When stocks started trading on pennies, many market professionals bemoaned the smaller number of shares bid and offered at the NBB and NBO. In other words, a marketable order of a size that previously could be fully executed at the NBB or NBO now requires going into the book a penny at a time. The important point, though, is that the cost of trading for the part that does execute at the NBB or NBO will in fact be lower in any case where the larger tick of the earlier era would have had any effect on price.

It is also important to note that the tick as a percent of stock price (the *relative tick*) is within the control of the firm. Should a firm think that a penny is too small a tick, by simply engaging in a stock split (making one share become two, for example) the firm can decrease its price per share so that the relative tick doubles.[39] In fact, there is scant evidence that firms believe that a penny tick is too small. There was not a riot of stock splitting when the tick went to a penny. Also, despite the fact that the market is up more than 100 percent since early 2010, reducing by half the relative tick represented by a penny absolute tick, the past few years have set records for the lowest number of stock splits. There were just seven splits among S&P 500 stocks in 2016.

## Appendix G

### MEASURING THE SPREAD AND THE COST OF TRADING

The theory outlined in this chapter, including the appendices, suggests that just knowing the quoted spread at a given moment will not tell a potential liquidity supplier how profitable it is going to be to provide liquidity at that time. If the entire spread is due to adverse selection, then the spread can be quite wide but submitting nonmarketable limit orders reflecting this spread will not be better than a break even proposition. Similarly, our discussion of order types in the first chapter suggests that just knowing the quoted spread at a given moment will not tell a marketable order user how much it is going to cost to trade. This is because existence of hidden limit orders may make it less costly since there may be hidden liquidity inside the NBBO.

There are several notions of average spread that appear in the academic literature and that are referred to in regulatory and legal discourse: (1) time-weighted average quoted spread, (2) trade-weighted average quoted spread, (3) effective spread and (4) realized spread. To calculate the *time weighted average spread* for a given period of time, observe the spread for a given stock every second (or every 10th second or every minute) and take the average. To calculate *the trade-weighted average spread* for a given period, observe the quoted spread at the time of each transaction and average. We would expect the first to be greater than the second if there is variation in the quoted spread. This is because if at some point the spread is unusually high, then a marketable order user is likely to be free to wait until the spread narrows to send in an order.

The *effective spread* for a transaction is represented by the formula: (Transaction price – Spread Midpoint) × Q, where Q is +1 if the marketable order is a buy and –1 if the marketable order is a sell. The average over a number of executions yields the *average effective spread*. As already noted, this should be less than the trade-weighted average spread if there is hidden liquidity. Finally, the *realized spread* for a period of time is the average over transactions occurring during that period of (Transaction Price – Spread Midpoint 5 minutes later) × Q, again where Q is +1 if the marketable order is a buy and –1 if the marketable order is a sell. By using the delayed midpoint, this measure accounts for the effect of orders on future price in the way contemplated by the adverse selection model in this chapter. Thus, if adverse selection is the only determinant of the spread, the realized spread will be zero. If there is no adverse selection, then the realized spread will equal the effective spread. In the data, it is not uncommon for realized spreads to be negative, meaning that during that period of time the spread does not fully compensate for adverse selection.

Trading Market Practices | **PART 2**

As discussed in chapter 1, today, any given stock potentially trades on each of a large number of competing venues. Almost all of these competing trading venues are electronic limit order books, where a trader can post as a limit order its firm commitment, until cancelled, to buy or sell up to a specified number of shares at a quoted price. A computer (the venue's matching engine) matches these posted limit orders with incoming buy and sell marketable orders, which are orders from traders willing to trade at what is presently the best available price in the market. High-frequency traders (HFTs) post a significant number of the limit orders that are matched in this fashion and result in executed trades.[1] An HFT uses high-speed communications to constantly update its information concerning transactions occurring in each stock that it regularly trades, as well as changes in the buy and sell limit orders posted by others on every major trading venue. This information is automatically fed into a computer that uses algorithms to change the limit prices and quantities associated with the HFT's own limit orders posted on each of the various trading venues. One study of the speed with which HFTs do this has clocked the duration between when an HFT's limit order is executed at an exchange and when the HFT is able to adjust its orders in response as taking around 30 to 60 microseconds—that is,

30 to 60 millionths of a second.[2] More than three-quarters of all trades in the United States are executed on one or another of such electronic limit order book venues.[3]

At the heart of HFT operations is colocation. Colocation involves the HFT having a computer located right next to an exchange's matching engine. This arrangement allows the HFT to find out about transactions occurring on the exchange, and about changes in quoted prices, sooner than regular traders, many of which are not similarly colocated. It also allows the HFT to very quickly cancel old limit orders posted on the exchange and submit new ones. The HFT's colocation facility at each exchange is connected to its colocation facility at every other exchange by specialized high-speed communications equipment, which permits extremely rapid communication among the HFT's colocation facilities at the different exchanges, most of which have their matching engines in northern New Jersey.

Because of the speed at which HFTs can acquire and act on market information, they have become enormously controversial. This chapter assesses the three HFT practices subject to the most frequent criticism: "electronic front-running," slow market arbitrage, and exploitation of midpoint limit orders posted in dark pools. This chapter also assesses criticisms that HFTs are contributing seriously to market volatility. Some of the criticisms of HFTs reflect misunderstandings of the role HFTs play as major suppliers of liquidity in today's market. Others, however, appropriately target socially undesirable behaviors.

After the assessment of these three practices and the role of HFTs in volatility, we will make some tentative policy suggestions.

## I. ELECTRONIC FRONT-RUNNING

So-called *electronic front-running* involves a situation in which an HFT, before others in the market, learns of a transaction that has occurred at one exchange and infers from this that similar orders may still be in transit heading toward other exchanges. The HFT races ahead of these still-in-transit orders to the other exchanges and, before they arrive at their destinations, changes its quotes on these other exchanges.

This practice has come in for harsh criticism. For example, Charlie Munger, vice chairman of Berkshire Hathaway, has objected that high-frequency trading is "legalized front-running[,] . . . and it should never have been able to reach the size that it did."[4] Similarly, while he was New York Attorney General, Eric Schneiderman complained that "[w]hen blinding speed is coupled with early access to data, it gives small groups of traders the power to manipulate market movements in their own favor before anyone else knows what's happening."[5] Michael Lewis's *Flash Boys* makes what he terms electronic front-running its principal focus.[6] Shortly after its publication, a prominent class action suit was filed against all of the nation's exchanges that, in support of its claim of fraud, included allegations that the exchanges cooperated with HFTs in facilitating this practice.[7]

Substantively, all of these criticisms focus on the fact that when an HFT engages in an act of "electronic front-running," the HFT can be expected to be better off and some other trader worse off. It should be noted at the outset, however, that the HFT practice labeled as "electronic front-running" is distinctly different from the kind of behavior that has traditionally been termed "front-running." Traditional front-running, which is clearly illegal, relates to a situation involving a customer giving her broker an order to handle. Then the broker, which has a legal duty to its customer not to use knowledge of its customer's order to its own advantage, breaches this duty by engaging in a trade on its own behalf that executes ahead of the customer's order.[8] In contrast, when an HFT engages in the practice Lewis labels "electronic front-running," it has no preexisting relationship with the trader placing the order that the HFT detects, and thus there is no relationship between the two that could give rise to a duty on the part of the HFT akin to what a broker owes its customer. The matter of whether there should be rules to prevent HFTs from engaging in this practice is of course an appropriate issue for policy analysis, which we undertake here. It is important to note, however, that the practice involves no breach of duty or of mutually agreed-upon terms between contracting parties, nor does it involve any obvious breach by HFTs of the federal antifraud laws. Further, the use of "front-running" seems inapt because the HTF is not even accused of taking a position in anticipation of another trader's order; it simply adjusts its quotes. As a result, we refer to what many other commentators refer to as "electronic front-running" as *anticipatory order cancelation*, a term which, while infelicitous, more accurately describes what HFTs do and avoids prejudging the practice's welfare effects.

## A. An Example

We will examine the practice of anticipatory order cancelation through use of an example. For simplicity of exposition, just one HFT, Lightning, and two exchanges, BATS Y and the NYSE, are involved in this example. Lightning has colocation facilities at the respective locations of the BATS Y and NYSE matching engines. These colocation facilities are connected with each other by high-speed communications equipment.

An actively managed institutional investor, Smartmoney, decides that Agilent's future cash flows are going to be greater than its current share price suggests. The NBO is $48.00, with 10,000 shares being offered at this price on BATS Y and 35,000 shares at this price on NYSE. Smartmoney decides to buy a substantial block of Agilent stock and sends a 10,000-share market buy order to BATS Y and a 35,000-share market buy order to NYSE.[9] The 35,000 shares offered at $48.00 on NYSE are all from sell limit orders posted by Lightning.

The order sent to BATS Y arrives at its destination first and executes. Lightning's colocation facility there learns of the transaction very quickly. An algorithm infers from this information that an informed trader might be looking to buy a large number of Agilent shares and thus may have sent buy orders to other exchanges as well. Because of Lightning's ultra-high-speed connection, it has the near instantaneous ability to send a message from its BATS Y colocation facility to its colocation facility at NYSE, which in turn can extremely rapidly cancel Lightning's 35,000-share $48.00 sell limit order posted on NYSE. All this can happen so fast that the cancellation occurs before the arrival at NYSE of Smartmoney's market buy order. If Lightning does cancel in this fashion, it has engaged in anticipatory order cancelation.

The fact that Lightning has the technical capacity to cancel its sell limit order on NYSE does not necessarily imply that it will. Why, then, might it wish to? One possibility is that given its inference that a large market buy order is likely to arrive at NYSE soon, Lightning wishes to submit, in place of its cancelled order, a new sell limit order for the same number of shares at a higher price: say at $48.02. If Lightning does so and Smartmoney's buy order executes against this new higher quote, Lightning will be better off, and Smartmoney worse off, by $.02 per share (i.e., $700).

Note though, that the HFT will be able to improve its position in this way only if there is room in the NYSE limit order book so that the $48.02 offer price is still more attractive to potential buyers than any other offers with respect to Agilent already posted on NYSE. Suppose, for example, that prior to Lightning's cancellation, the next best offer on the NYSE was 15,000 shares at $48.01 and the best offer after that was 20,000 shares at $48.02. The price and time priority rules would mean that Smartmoney's buy order would execute against these other two standing offers, not against any new $42.02 offer by Lightning.

This cautionary note, though, hides a more critical point: Lightning may wish to cancel its $48.00 sell limit order even if in fact there is no room in the book to improve its position by selling to Smartmoney at a higher price. Recall that to survive in a competitive market, a liquidity supplier such as Lightning must set its quotes aggressively enough to attract business, but not so aggressively that the money it makes by buying from, and selling to, uninformed traders is less than what it loses by engaging in such transactions with informed traders. $48.00 was what Lightning calculated at the time it posted its sell limit order to be the optimal price for an offer of 35,000 shares, based on what it knew then about the likelihood of the existence of positive private information. Now, however, Lightning knows something more: a large buy order has transacted on BATS Y. This will cause Lightning to revise its assessment of the value of a security upward, to be higher than the market previously thought. The upward revision is very possibly great enough that $48.00 is no longer the optimal price at which to offer to sell shares. In that case, Lightning will be better off cancelling its $48.00 limit offer on NYSE.

## B. Wealth Transfer Considerations: A First Cut

To see the distributive effects of anticipatory order cancelation, we need to consider how the world would differ if the practice were eliminated. To preview, our central conclusion is quite intuitive: traders seeking to transact rapidly and in large volume lose as a result of the availability of anticipatory order cancelation, while all other traders benefit from its existence. Understanding the efficiency consequences of anticipatory order cancelation, however, requires a considering precisely which kinds of traders win and lose as a result of the practice. As a first cut, we will begin our discussion of the practice's wealth and efficiency effects, with only three kinds of market participants: HFTs, informed traders who trade on the basis of fundamental value information, and ordinary retail uninformed traders.[10] Later, we will take a more granular look at how different kinds of informed and uninformed traders are affected by anticipatory order cancelation.

### 1. Anticipatory order cancelation narrows spreads

As the analysis of the example makes clear, the practice of anticipatory order cancelation by HFTs allows them to better detect and respond to the possibility that informed market orders are headed for their limit orders and to alter their standing limit orders accordingly. If HFTs did not have these abilities, they would know that a larger percentage of the trades that will execute against their limit orders will come from informed traders. A primary cost of being a liquidity supplier—the losses incurred from dealing with informed traders—would therefore go up. Accordingly, the HFTs would increase their initially posted spreads to compensate.

Going back to our example, if Lightning were not able to electronically front-run, it might have initially posted its sell limit order for 35,000 shares at $48.01 instead of $48.00. For the same reasons, it would also have posted a lower bid. Thus, with anticipatory order cancelation being allowed, its bid would have been $47.96, whereas without the practice its bid might instead have been $47.95.

## 2. Anticipatory order cancelation helps uninformed investors and hurts informed investors

If anticipatory order cancelation were eliminated, uninformed traders and informed traders will each suffer from the resulting larger spreads—the higher offers and lower bids—because for both it will be more expensive to trade. For uninformed traders, that is the end of the story. Informed traders, however, would get a more-than-compensating benefit.

To see why, the starting point again is the fact that the elimination of anticipatory order cancelation would make it more difficult for HFTs to detect indications of possibly informed trades, and so more informed trades would execute against their quotes. Trading is a zero-sum game. Thus, if HFTs did not increase their spreads in response to the end of the practice, the gains enjoyed by informed investors would just equal the increased losses suffered by HFTs. In fact, however, the elimination of anticipatory order cancelation, as just noted, will lead HFTs to increase their spreads and to do so by an amount just sufficient to cover what these increased losses to informed traders would otherwise be.[11] The increased spreads will be borne by all traders, informed and uninformed alike, because the HFTs cannot condition their exchange-posted limit orders on the identity of the person who sends the market orders against which their limit orders execute.[12] This means that informed traders come out ahead: the gains they would have enjoyed without the increase in spreads are not fully dissipated by the extra they must pay with the widened spread that in fact occurs. This is because the rest of what HFTs need to break even comes from uninformed traders, who must pay the increased spread too.

In sum, without anticipatory order cancelation, HFTs would find it harder to detect indications of possible trading on private information and as a result would increase their spreads. Informed traders would get all of the gains from being better able to hide the informed nature of their trades. But they would pay, through the increased spreads, only part of the added costs incurred by HFTs as a result of entering into more losing transactions. The rest of these added costs would be borne by uninformed investors, who receive no such benefit. So, the practice of anticipatory order cancelation benefits uninformed investors and harms informed ones.

### 3. The ultimate incidence of anticipatory order cancelation

Anticipatory order cancelation has been regularly attacked as harming "ordinary investors."[13] This first-cut analysis, however, suggests that this attack is unmerited. To start, consider retail investors, the paradigmatic ordinary investors. Retail investors generally lack any significant private information and hence are properly assumed to be uninformed. Uninformed investors, as we have just seen, are helped, not hurt, by anticipatory order cancelation, because without it the bid-ask spreads that they confront would be wider.

What about ordinary people who invest in actively managed mutual or pension funds? These entities do fundamental value research and thus have the potential of being informed investors. The preceding analysis suggests that anticipatory order cancelation hurts informed investors. It is true that, at least under the assumptions in this part of the discussion in which fundamental value traders are the only informed traders and index funds are not taken into account, these actively managed funds can be expected to enjoy gains from the elimination of anticipatory order cancelation.

These gains, however, might well not be passed on to the ordinary people who invest in the managed funds. The investment industry and those who work in it each appear to operate in fairly competitive markets. To the extent that these markets are in fact competitive, much of whatever above-market returns are generated by these institutions' informed trading will be captured in the form of higher fees or salaries for the professionals who make the actual investment decisions.[14] In other words, any gains in these entities' trading returns that might result from the elimination of anticipatory order cancelation are likely to go primarily to increase these fees and salaries, not to the ordinary persons on whose behalf the professionals trade. Thus, even the ordinary investors whose investments are in actively managed funds may not be hurt by anticipatory order cancelation.

The beneficiaries of anticipatory order cancelation, according to the critics of the practice, are the exchanges and the HFTs themselves.[15] Here the critics are closer to the mark. An exchange charges HFTs fees for permitting colocation: namely, the right to place the HFT's server very near the exchange's matching engine. If anticipatory order cancelation were eliminated tomorrow, HFT colocation facilities would be worth less to the HFTs and they might consequently not be willing to pay as much in fees. This might reduce the rents collected by the exchanges.[16] Any such reduction in rents certainly would hurt the exchanges, at least in the short run.[17]

Similarly, the lower volume of HFT business that would result from the elimination of anticipatory order cancelation would reduce the profits of firms now in the HFT business and thus lower the value of their existing assets. In the longer run future, though, investments in the industry can be expected to earn a competitive return, with or without the practice. Persons with abilities and skills that are uniquely valuable to the business of HFTs would, however, suffer both a short- and longer-term diminution in the rents accrued on the basis of these abilities and skills and so would experience a reduction in wealth positions from an elimination of anticipatory order cancelation.

In sum, at least on the basis of this first-cut analysis, the differences in wealth distribution between a world with and without anticipatory order cancelation do not seem to raise serious fairness issues. In particular, the claim that anticipatory order cancelation hurts the ordinary investor seems unmerited.

It is also worth noting the important role technology can play in determining how many traders can be subject to the practice of anticipatory order cancelation. The significance of anticipatory order adjustment vanishes insofar as other market participants can find a technological solution to it. For instance, if software becomes widely available that enables traders to time the arrival of orders such that HFTs are no longer capable of adjusting quotes at one venue, based on executions at another before those traders' orders arrive, then attempts at anticipatory order cancelation will not be effective. Indeed, if this technology is in sufficiently widespread use, anticipatory order adjustment may have become a creature of the past. Developments in smart routers suggest that many traders may have adopted precisely such a solution.

## C. Efficiency Considerations: A First Cut

To see the efficiency effects of anticipatory order cancelation, we again need to consider how the world would differ if the practice were eliminated. At least under the assumption that fundamental value information is the only basis of informed trade, elimination of the practice would increase share price accuracy, which enhances efficiency. In addition, it would reduce the resources going into HFT activities, which, under all circumstances, also enhances efficiency.

At the same time, it would reduce the efficiency with which risk and resources over time are allocated.

*1. Improved share price accuracy*

We have just seen that informed traders would be net gainers from the elimination of anticipatory order cancelation. Their cost of trading would go up from the increase in spreads, but this would be more than compensated for by the more advantageous trades they can make with HFTs because of the HFTs' reduced ability to detect indications of possible informed trading.

Because these informed traders buy when their superior estimate of share value suggests that a stock is underpriced and sell when it indicates that a stock is overpriced, their activities make share prices more accurate. The elimination of anticipatory order cancelation would make it more profitable for these traders to engage in their activity, and so they would do more of it. As a result, prices will be more accurate. As discussed in chapter 2, more accurate prices benefit the economy by helping to allocate the economy's scarce capital to the most promising potential real investment projects and by improving the utilization of the economy's existing productive capacity through optimizing the signals provided to management about investment decisions and the signals given to boards and shareholders about the quality of management decisions.[18]

*2. Reduced resources going to HFT activities*

The second positive effect from eliminating anticipatory order cancelation relates to the productive resources that are currently being devoted to undertaking the practice, including the skills and abilities of highly sophisticated technical personnel, advanced computers, and fiber-optic networks. With the elimination of anticipatory order cancelation, this infrastructure and human capital would no longer be needed to support the practice and would be freed up to increase other productive activities in the economy.

Although high-frequency traders are notoriously secretive, HFT Virtu Financial, Inc. (Virtu) does make certain public disclosures as a publicly traded company.[19] In 2016 alone, Virtu spent approximately $71 million on communication and data processing and $85 million on employee compensation and payroll taxes.[20] Because Virtu has only 148 employees, this means it pays an average salary of about $574,000.[21] It is interesting to note that by 2016 year end, Virtu Financial had net trading income of just over $645 million, down from \$757 million in 2015.[22] Virtu is just one of several large HFTs, and there are many smaller ones as well.

*3. Allocation of resources over time and allocation of risk*

The elimination of anticipatory order cancelation, by widening spreads, would make the market for equities less liquid. This has an unambiguously negative effect on the efficient allocation of resources over time. As we saw in chapter 2, the prospect that an issuer's shares will have less liquidity in the secondary trading market increases the issuer's cost of capital. Just like a tax, illiquidity results in a "wedge" between the value of what the savers (the purchasers of future dollars) expect to receive in the future and what the entrepreneurs or issuers (the suppliers of future dollars in the form of future dividend streams) expect to give up in the future. This blocks transactions that both parties would otherwise have found advantageous had the market for the stock been expected to be more liquid, and hence diminishes economic welfare.

Less liquidity would similarly have an unambiguously negative effect on the efficient allocation of risk. The greater transaction costs deter each investor from adjusting her portfolio as finely when circumstances alter what would be optimal in terms of diversification and suitability to her risk preferences.

Permitting anticipatory order cancelation thus seems to pose a difficult trade-off between the basic functions of a trading market: doing so decreases price accuracy, but increases liquidity.

## D. Wealth Transfer and Efficiency Considerations: Taking Other Kinds of Informed Traders and Uninformed Traders into Account

The preceding discussion relied on two stylized characterizations of the market, both of which we must further complicate. First, as mentioned, there are several distinct types of informed traders, and anticipatory order cancelation may affect them differently with complex welfare consequences. Second, there are uninformed traders who may wish to make large trades rapidly, whereas we have previously assumed that only informed traders would have reason to do so.

Taking these various kinds of private information into account does not change our previous conclusions that the elimination of anticipatory order cancelation would have negative effects on ordinary uninformed traders, as well as on the efficiency with which risk is allocated and resources are allocated over time. Nor does it alter the fact that the elimination of anticipatory order cancelation would save the real resources that it consumes, which could be used instead to improve economic welfare by increasing the production of other useful goods or services. It also may not change the conclusion that its elimination would be helpful to informed traders as a group. However, as discussed in the rest of this section, taking account of these additional kinds of private information may well reverse the first-cut conclusion that anticipatory order cancelation reduces share price accuracy. Indeed, for us, this additional consideration leads us to the conclusion that regulatory changes specifically aimed at eliminating anticipatory order cancelation would be ill-advised.

In contrast, as discussed in subsections D.1 – D.4, eliminating anticipatory order cancelation, depending on the facts, could be helpful rather than harmful to some uninformed traders, which also adds a caveat to some of the conclusions reached in the first-cut analysis.

*1. Why anticipatory order cancelation may give a competitive advantage to fundamental value informed trading versus other kinds of informed trading*

The different kinds of informed traders are in one sense in competition with each other. This competition arises because the more of any one kind of informed trading that occurs, the more it increases the bid-ask spread and hence the more it raises the costs of trading for the other three kinds. Thus, the higher the levels of the other kinds of informed trading, the more they crowd out fundamental value informed trading. Appreciating this fact is the key starting point for understanding why inclusion of the other kinds of informed trading in the analysis may reverse our first-cut conclusion that anticipatory order cancelation reduces share price accuracy.

Suppose—as we argue in the next paragraph—that anticipatory order cancelation is much more helpful at enabling liquidity suppliers to respond to trading based on announcement information than to trading based on fundamental value information. Suppose as well that trading on the basis of announcement information constitutes a significant portion of informed trading generally. In that case, most of the increased trading gains from elimination of the practice would be enjoyed by announcement traders. If anticipatory order cancelation were eliminated, HFTs would need to increase spreads sufficiently to cover their corresponding increased trading losses, most of which would be due to announcement traders. With the elimination of anticipatory order cancelation, fundamental value information traders would thus have to pay as much extra per trade from the increased spread as traders on the other kinds of private information. They would, however, get only a small portion of the additional trading gains permitted by elimination of anticipatory order cancelation (i.e., the increased percentage of their marketable orders able to execute against standing limit orders posted by HFTs). Thus, it is quite possible that fundamental value informed traders actually benefit from anticipatory order cancelation and that only traders on announcement information would benefit from its elimination. If so, anticipatory order cancelation improves share price accuracy in a socially beneficial way.

A key factor in this story is the premise that fundamental value informed trading is in fact relatively less susceptible to detection by anticipatory order cancelation compared with the other three kinds of informed trading. Announcement information traders are clearly particularly susceptible because they need to do all of their trading in a very short period of time. They therefore need to engage in larger transactions. Larger transactions are easier for HFTs to detect and react to.[23] Persons trading on the basis of the two kinds of inside information are also likely to need to do their trading in a relatively concentrated period of time because they will tend to wait to trade until shortly before they expect the information to become public. Doing so reduces the period during which they are exposed to firm-specific risk before locking in their profits, a point discussed in more detail in chapter 5.

A fundamental value trader, in contrast, is often able to execute her planned purchases or sales on a more relaxed schedule. This is because she developed the information herself or paid someone to do so. Thus, her own trading aside, the information is less likely to be reflected in price anytime soon. As a consequence, she can break the total amount she wishes to transact into small packets that look more like the trades of uninformed traders and submit these packets over time. This difference in trading patterns suggests that the elimination of anticipatory order cancelation would indeed result in fundamental value informed traders enjoying less of a gain from an increase in the percentage of their trades executing against uncancelled HFT limit orders relative to the other three kinds of informed traders. Thus, it is very possible that fundamental value traders would be hurt by elimination of the practice: enjoying less in the way of trading gains vis-à-vis HFTs than they lose by having to pay an increased bid-ask spread.

*2. Giving a competitive advantage to fundamental value informed trading can improve share price accuracy*

As explored in more significant detail in chapters 5 and 6, society has a stake in the competition among informed traders. Every kind of informed trading accelerates when prices come to reflect the existing accumulation of information in the world. However, two other factors are also important in the social welfare contribution of an informed trade's improvement in price accuracy: how much the informed trade advances the time at which the information on which it is based becomes reflected in price, and the extent to which the prospect of profits from trades based on new information stimulates the production of new information.[24]

Persons trading on the basis of announcement information advance its reflection in price only by a moment because the information is already public. Persons trading on the basis of most issuer and other-entity inside information do not speed up its reflection in price by much more because, as just discussed, typically they do not trade until a short period before the information is to be announced. Moreover, with each of these other three types of private information, the prospect of trading profits usually does not stimulate the production of new information. The traders utilizing the information generally neither worked to develop the information themselves, nor paid someone else to work to develop it.

Whether or not the trades based on these other three kinds of private information are legal depends on the circumstances, a matter addressed in chapter 6. Legality aside, however, it is hard to justify the gains that the announcement trader enjoys as representing a socially useful incentive. These gains come at the expense of other traders through the decrease in liquidity, and, in particular, the decrease in liquidity resulting from announcement trading discourages the activities of fundamental value informed traders.

*3. Considering the impact of large uninformed investors trading rapidly and in size*

Our earlier analysis basically took informed traders—particularly, announcement informed traders—to be the traders who seek to trade simultaneously at multiple venues, and who are thus directly affected by the availability or unavailability of anticipatory order cancelation. Some uninformed traders, however, may also seek to trade this way. For instance, certain index funds may have reasons to trade rapidly in large size. An ETF may attempt to rapidly re-balance its holdings during trading hours, rather than at the close. Or, as discussed in chapter 1, a large institution with liquidity or hedging needs may try to sell a position rapidly while trying to minimize impact on price. The question then is how our conclusions change if we add in such large, uninformed investors that transact rapidly and in large volume? Such traders are by definition uninformed: their purchases and sales are not prompted by any kind of private information. What differentiates these investors from other uninformed investors' trading behavior is the size and pattern of their trades. In this regard, at such times, these entities trade more like the announcement informed traders described above. For simplicity, we will refer to these simply as "large, uninformed funds" in the following discussion, but what is meant is any investor who lacks private information, but who is interested in executing at multiple exchanges simultaneously and doing so in significant volume.

Adding large, uninformed funds to the mix does not change any of the preceding discussion concerning the effect of anticipatory order cancelation on price accuracy. The presence of large, uninformed funds simply makes large trades a noisier proxy of whether informed trading is going on. It is still more probable that a large trade is informed than a small one. Thus, being able to adjust orders still helps protect HFTs against informed trading—just not as effectively. Nothing in this discussion concerning the effects of anticipatory order cancelation on price accuracy (in both the first-cut and second-cut analyses) depends on it being a more versus a less powerful protection, as long as it is some kind of protection.

Adding large, uninformed funds to the mix may change some of the preceding discussion concerning the wealth transfer effects of anticipatory order cancelation, which is important because many of the persons whose money is invested in these funds may count as ordinary investors. For the same reasons, it may also change some of the preceding conclusions with regard to the effect of anticipatory order cancelation on the efficiency with which the market allocates risk and resources over time. Whether taking account of large, uninformed funds should in fact change these conclusions is an empirical question for which there is no clear answer at the moment.

The starting point is to note that if we were to assume that the size and pattern of large, uninformed funds' orders and of each of the four kinds of informed traders were all identical, then there would be no doubt that eliminating the practice would decrease the cost of trading for all of them, including large, uninformed funds. Under this assumption, all of them would pay the same cost for needing to use a particular size and pattern of trading—a size and pattern that suggests an increased probability of being an informed trader. This cost is less when the HFTs cannot, in the face of such orders, engage in the order adjustment that is the core of anticipatory order cancelation. This conclusion (based on the assumption of identical order sizes and patterns) that eliminating anticipatory order cancelation would decrease large, uninformed funds' cost of trading suggests that the wealth impact of anticipatory order cancelation on ordinary people is ambiguous. This is because such ordinary people participate in the market both as ordinary retail investors, whose cost of trading is lowered by the practice; and as investors in large, uninformed funds, whose cost of trading is, given the assumption concerning identical order size and pattern, increased by the practice. This ambiguity extends as well to the effect of anticipatory order cancelation on the market's efficiency in risk allocation and resources-over-time allocation. The practice aids market efficiency (by lowering the cost of trading) to the extent that investors buy and sell shares for these reasons as individuals. It has the opposite effect (by increasing the cost of trading) to the extent that they buy and sell shares for such reasons indirectly through the use of large, uninformed funds.

The assumption that the size and pattern of large, uninformed fund orders and of orders of each of the four kinds of informed traders are all identical is not true, however. Because of this, it is possible that anticipatory order cancelation in fact lowers the cost of trading for all uninformed traders, both ordinary investors and large, uninformed funds. We have already seen how the fact that fundamental value informed traders typically do not have the same urgency to trade as do the other kinds of informed traders may turn around conclusions about the impact of the practice on the cost of trading for fundamental value informed traders. If the size and pattern of large, uninformed orders more resemble those of fundamental value informed traders than they do those of the other three kinds of informed traders, it is possible that the practice also lowers, not increases, the large, uninformed fund cost of trading as well. The argument in essence would be that on the one hand, large, uninformed funds would enjoy the lower spreads that result from anticipatory order cancelation. On the other hand, they do not pay a big price that arises from the anticipatory order cancelation that brings these lower spreads because the size and pattern of their orders make them less likely to be identified as informed. As a result, they are unlikely to be hurt anticipatory order cancelation. Rather, it is the announcement and inside information traders that pay much of this price, and it is their paying the price that in significant part results in anticipatory order cancelation lowering the spread.

## 4. Conclusion

To reach a definitive answer to the question of whether anticipatory order cancelation decreases or increases social welfare through its effect on price accuracy, we would need to know more than we currently do. Existing empirical research is not very enlightening concerning several important factors: the proportion of informed trades based on each of the four of kinds of private information, the average value to the real economy of the acceleration of information into price with regard to each, and the exact sensitivity of the trading patterns associated with each of the four kinds of informed trades to detection by anticipatory order cancelation. The same can be said as to whether anticipatory order cancelation increases or decreases the cost of large, uninformed funds' trading.

Still, the analysis here leads us tentatively toward the conclusion that anticipatory order cancelation in fact increases, not decreases, social welfare in terms of its effect on price accuracy. We cannot know for certain if it increases or decreases the cost of large, uninformed fund trading. If it decreases the cost of large, uninformed fund trading and we are correct about its impact on price accuracy, then the practice unambiguously enhances all three ways in which the stock market can contribute to economic efficiency: share price accuracy, allocation of resources over time, and allocation of risk. In this case as well, the practice also unambiguously results in no negative wealth transfers in terms of ordinary investors. Even if the practice adds to the cost of large, uninformed fund trading, these conclusions may still hold because individuals buy and sell shares both directly as ordinary investors and indirectly through large, uninformed funds. At a minimum, any argument that anticipatory order cancelation damages efficiency in any of these three ways or leads to some kind of unfairness to ordinary investors is unproven. This suggests that efforts to change policy by restricting the practice would be ill-advised at this time.

The problem in answering these questions, of course, is that both the identity of traders and the substance of their trading style are anonymous. Nonetheless, one noisy proxy for those who trade rapidly in large size has been studied empirically. The *intermarket sweep order* (ISO) is a complex order type utilized by traders who are seeking to trade in very large size as close to instantaneously as possible. They thus submit an order type—the ISO—that enables them to drill through a given venue's book of orders until a given limit price is reached. The kind of trader who uses an ISO can often find anticipatory order cancelation to pose a problem. The limited empirical research on who uses ISOs suggests that they are disproportionately deployed by the informed.[25] Insofar as these findings are general, it strengthens the case that anticipatory order cancelation is in fact desirable because it reduces the cost of liquidity and because the price accuracy effects of more announcement trading are negligible or negative.

It should also be noted that to the extent that introducing large, uninformed funds into the analysis muddies our earlier conclusions, it also lessens the stakes of whether to allow anticipatory order cancelation or not. To the extent that large, uninformed funds suffer increased trading costs because HFTs mistake their orders for those of informed investors, the fact that they make these mistakes renders anticipatory order cancelation less effective as protection against informed trading. In using it, HFTs run the risk that by cancelling their limit orders, they will miss out on a transaction with an expected profit (i.e., a transaction with an index fund, which by definition is uninformed). With the stakes lowered, there is less of a case for regulatory change in the face of ambiguity.

## II. SLOW MARKET ARBITRAGE

Slow market arbitrage can occur under the following scenario. An HFT has posted a quote representing the NBO or NBB on one exchange. Subsequently someone else posts an even better quote on a second exchange. The HFT learns of the new, better quote before it is reported by the national system. If, in the short time before the national report updates, a marketable order arrives at the first exchange, the order will transact against the HFT's now stale quote.[26] The HFT, using its speed, can then make a riskless profit by turning around and transacting against the better quote on the second exchange.

Slow market arbitrage was a target of criticism in *Flash Boys*,[27] which in turn reflected growing discontent among commentators in the years preceding its publication.[28] The practice has also formed a basis for litigation. For example, in the City of Providence's class action against all the exchanges for their cooperation with HFTs, the complaint alleged that HFTs engaged in slow market arbitrage and claimed that the practice "generate[d] billions of dollars more a year in illicit profits than front-running."[29]

### A. An Example

To understand the practice in more detail, let us return to our HFT, Lightning. Suppose that Lightning has a sell limit order for 1,000 shares of IBM at $161.15 posted on NYSE. This quote represents the NBO at the moment. Mr. Lowprice then posts a new 1,000-share sell limit order for IBM on EDGE for $161.13.

The national reporting system is a bit slow, and so a very short period of time elapses before it reports Lowprice's new, better offer. Lightning's colocation facility at EDGE very quickly learns of the new $161.13 offer, however, and an algorithm sends an ultra-fast message to Lightning's colocation facility at NYSE informing it of the new offer. During the reporting gap, though, Lightning keeps its $161.15 offer posted. Next, Ms. Stumble sends a marketable buy order to NYSE for 1,000 IBM shares. Lightning's $161.15 offer remains the official NBO, and so Stumble's order transacts against it. Lightning's colocation facility at NYSE then sends an ultra-fast message to the one at EDGE instructing it to submit a 1,000-share marketable buy order there. This buy order transacts against Lowprice's $161.13 offer. Thus, within the short period before the new $161.13 quote otherwise would have been known more broadly, Lightning has been able to sell 1,000 IBM shares at $161.15 and purchase them at $161.13, creating for it a $20 profit.

It is worth noting that the first step in this story—Lowprice's posting of the $161.13 offer on EDGE—does not guarantee that Lightning can make this profit. It may be that no marketable buy order arrives at NYSE during the reporting gap. Also, even if one does, by the time Lightning is able to submit its marketable buy order at EDGE, some other person may already have submitted a marketable buy order to EDGE that picks off the $161.13 offer. This becomes particularly likely if, as is the case in the real world, there are a number of HFTs besides Lightning with colocation facilities at EDGE and at the other exchanges. Depending on the nature of their own respective offers posted on various exchanges, one or more of these other HFTs may be competing with Lightning to pick off the one $161.13 offer. This latter point indicates the inappropriateness of the use of the term "arbitrage."

## B. Wealth Transfer Effects

Who is helped and who is hurt in the example in subsection A, and what are the larger distributive consequences with slow market arbitrage as an ongoing practice?

*1. The trader whose order executes against the stale quote is not a loser*

In the example, the first thing to note is that Ms. Stumble, the person who, during the reporting gap, submits the marketable order that transacts against Lightning's stale $161.15 offer, is not harmed by Lightning's slow market arbitrage activities. Stumble would have suffered the same fate if Lightning had not engaged in slow market arbitrage, because that course of action would also have left the $161.15 offer posted on NYSE and so Stumble's buy order would still have transacted against it.

*2. The arbitraging HFT is the gainer and ordinary traders, both informed and uninformed, are the losers*

Still, someone must be worse off: Lightning is better off than if it had not engaged in the slow market arbitrage, and trading is a zero-sum game. To see who this worse-off person might be, consider first why Lightning is better off. Lightning is in the business of buying and selling shares, not of holding onto long or short positions for any significant period of time. Thus, it will wish to reverse quickly each transaction into which it enters. Here, it sold shares when Stumble's order transacted against Lightning's $161.15 offer on NYSE. To reverse this transaction, Lightning needed to buy shares. By engaging in slow market arbitrage, it did so by seizing the best offer in the market—Lowprice's $161.13 offer on EDGE—before some others in the market even knew the offer was available. If Lightning had not detected this new offer ahead of others and seized it, Lightning's reversal of the situation would occur through its posting a bid that a marketable order transacts against. We know from chapter 3 that the sale of the shares at $161.15 and their repurchase as a result of this posting of a new bid would each, on an expected basis, have been a break-even transaction. By successfully engaging in slow market arbitrage, Lightning instead made a certain $0.02 profit per share sold and purchased.

To figure out who is hurt from Lightning engaging in slow market arbitrage—i.e., detecting the $161.13 offer and seizing it—consider who would have been better off if Lightning had posted a new buy limit order instead of seizing Lowprice's $161.13 offer. The person or persons helped would come from one of two groups of potential liquidity takers. One group is potential sellers who submit marketable sell orders: the posted bid that Lightning would need filled would improve the terms for the marginal seller. The other group is potential buyers who submit marketable buy orders: the opportunity by members of this group to seize Lowprice's $161.13 offer that Lightning seized instead. This offer was better than anything else available in the market at the time and thus, if it had been available, would improve terms for the marginal buyer.

The results from this example can be generalized. The persons who are hurt by HFTs engaging in slow market arbitrage on an ongoing basis are regular traders, both informed ones and uninformed ones.[30] In contrast to anticipatory order cancelation, where the practice decreases the effective cost of trading for uninformed traders but increases it for informed traders, slow market arbitrage increases the effective cost of trading for both groups.

## C. Efficiency Considerations

In most situations, arbitrage activities, at least if they do not consume any real resources, have positive economic welfare effects. The actions of arbitrageurs tend to equilibrate prices in two markets, each of which has its own group of potential participants. As a result, presumptively welfare enhancing transactions occur that otherwise would not have been entered into. The arbitrageurs do this by buying in the low price market, thereby putting upward pressure on the price there, and selling the same item in the high price market, thereby putting downward pressure on the price there. As a result, there is a group of potential sellers in the initially low price market who would not find it worthwhile to sell at the initial lower price, but who do find it worthwhile to sell at the higher equilibrating price. There is a group of potential buyers in the initially high price market that are in the exact mirror-image situation. The transactions entered into by these two groups of people, which would not occur but for arbitrage, are presumptively welfare enhancing because they are entered into voluntarily by both parties to each of the transactions.

Slow market arbitrage, however, has little in common with ordinary arbitrage, and thus does not enjoy this presumption of welfare enhancement. Unlike the ordinary arbitrage situation, the HFT engaging in slow market arbitrage is not moving prices in two markets, each with its own distinct separate group of traders, whereby the link by the arbitrageur improves the welfare of each group. As the slow market arbitrage example shows, the added third party, the liquidity supplier, is the only gainer from the activity, in contrast to the ordinary arbitrage situation. Regular traders, both informed and uninformed, are in fact losers because their cost of trading goes up.

This increase in the cost of trading for both informed and uninformed traders has an unambiguously negative impact on social welfare. Consider first the effect of the increased effective cost of trading for fundamental value informed traders. Slow market arbitrage, by raising their effective cost of trading, makes it less rewarding to seek out bits of publicly available information and to analyze their implications in a sophisticated way. This reduces share price accuracy, which, as we have seen, would in turn have negative effects on the allocation of capital for new real investment projects and the efficient utilization of existing productive capacity. The increased effective cost of trading on uninformed traders now has the familiar negative effects on the efficient allocation of resources over time and on the efficient allocation of risk.

Slow market arbitrage consumes real resources, which is another efficiency consideration, but perhaps ultimately not a very important one. If it were the only HFT practice dependent on colocation facilities and ultra-fast connections, it would use substantial amounts of real resources that could otherwise be usefully employed, increasing the production of other goods and services. If HFTs continue the practice of anticipatory order cancelation, however, the marginal cost in real resources of engaging in slow market arbitrage as well is probably fairly low.

## III. HFT EXPLOITATION OF MIDPOINT ORDERS

A trader will often submit to a dark pool a "midpoint" buy or sell limit order, the terms of which are that it will execute against the next marketable order with the opposite interest to arrive at the pool and will do so at a price equal to the midpoint between the best publicly reported bid and offer at the time of execution. Midpoint orders appear to have the advantage of allowing a buyer to buy at well below the best offer and sell well above the best bid. It has been noted for a number of years, however, that traders who post such orders are vulnerable to the activities of HFTs.[31] Midpoint order exploitation again involves an HFT detecting an improvement in the best available bid or offer on one of the exchanges before the new quote is more generally known. The HFT puts in an order to transact against the new improved quote, and then sends an order reversing the transaction to a dark pool that contains midpoint limit orders with the opposite interest that transact at a price equal to the midpoint between the now-stale best publicly reported bid and offer.

### A. An Example

Let us again bring back our HFT, Lightning. Suppose that the NBO and NBB for IBM are $161.15 and $161.11, respectively, and each are for 1,000 shares and are posted on NYSE by HFTs other than Lightning. Then the $161.15 offer is cancelled and a new 1,000-share offer is submitted at $161.12. Lightning, through its colocation facilities at NYSE, learns of these changes in advance of their being publicly reported. During the reporting gap, the official NBO remains $161.15.

Lightning knows that midpoint orders for IBM are often posted on Opaque, a well-known dark pool, and Lightning programs its algorithms accordingly. Because Opaque does not disclose what is in its limit order book, Lightning cannot know, however, whether at this moment any such orders are posted on Opaque, and, if there are, whether they are buy orders or sell orders. Still, there is the potential for making money.

Using an ultra-fast connection between the colocation facility at NYSE and Opaque, a sell midpoint order for 1,000 shares is sent to Opaque with the condition attached that it be canceled if it does not transact immediately (a so-called *IOC order*). This way, if there were one or more midpoint buy orders posted at Opaque for IBM, they will execute against Lightning's order at $161.13, halfway between the now-stale, but still official, NBB of $161.11 and NBO of $161.15. If there are no such midpoint buy orders posted at Opaque, nothing is lost.

Assume that there are one or more such midpoint buy orders aggregating to at least 1,000 shares and so Lightning's sell order of 1,000 shares transacts at $161.13. Lightning's colocation facility at NYSE is informed of this fact through Lightning's ultra-fast connection with Opaque. A marketable buy order for 1,000 shares is sent almost instantaneously to NYSE, which transacts against the new $161.12 offer. Thus, within the short period before the new $161.12 offer on NYSE is publicly reported, Lightning has been able to execute against this offer, purchase 1,000 IBM shares at $161.12, and sell them at $161.13, for a $10 profit.

## B. Wealth Transfer and Efficiency Considerations

The regular practice of HFT exploitation of dark pool midpoint orders clearly provides rents to HFTs: they are able to make profitable trades that they would otherwise not be able to make. There is no pro-social incentive effect from this activity, because it is unrelated to the positive social function that we have attributed to HFTs: providing liquidity in a world with both uninformed and informed traders. Because trading is a zero-sum game, if the HFTs gain, certain regular traders must lose. Because of the practice, the expected cost of trading using midpoint orders in a dark pool goes up. This would hurt those who are deterred from using dark pool midpoint orders because of this higher cost of trading, as well as those who still do use them but have to incur these higher costs.

The efficiency effects of the practice closely resemble the efficiency effects of the abuses by investment banks and dark pool operators that are the subject of chapter 10. Suffice it to say here, dark pools are a place for uninformed traders to lower their cost of trading by finding other uninformed traders with which to trade. Midpoint exploitation undermines their ability to do this, at least to some extent. The practice increases the effective cost of trading for those uninformed traders who use dark pools. This hurts both those who use dark pools despite the higher effective cost of trading and those who would have used them but for this higher cost. For the same reasons as discussed with respect to the earlier practices, this will reduce the efficiency of both the allocation of resources over time and the allocation of risk in the economy. At the same time, as will be discussed more fully in chapters 9 and 10, to the extent that the practice steers more uninformed traders to trade in the exchanges, it leads to a narrowing of spreads on the exchanges, thereby reducing the cost of fundamental value informed trading and thus improving share price accuracy.

## IV. HIGH-FREQUENCY TRADING AND VOLATILITY

Although much of the controversy about high-frequency traders has focused on their trading strategies, a different, but also important, strain of criticism has alleged a causal connection between HFT activity and greater volatility in equity markets.[32] One criticism is that HFTs have made the markets more volatile from moment to moment on an ongoing basis, month in and month out. A second criticism is that HFTs exacerbate volatility in a very extreme manner on an occasional basis when there has been some kind of disruption in the market, such as the infamous "Flash Crash" of May 6, 2010.

### A. HFTs and the Ongoing Level of Volatility

There is a widespread perception that HFT trading aggravates volatility as a general matter. Michael Lewis, for example, asserts in *Flash Boys* that the intra-day price volatility of the stock market was 40 percent greater between 2010 and 2013 than it was between 2004 and 2006, and associates this change with the enactment of Reg. NMS and the rise of HFTs.[33] A harder look at the data does not bear out this perception. In particular, Lewis's use of a comparison between the 2004–2006 period and the 2010–1013 period seems particularly mistaken. One big problem is that the years 2004–2006 are a poor comparison sample because they had uncharacteristically low volatility, below any other two-year period from 1998 to 2012.[34] Another big problem is that the years 2010–2013 are also uncharacteristic, as they followed the most severe financial crisis since the Great Depression and would be expected to show high volatility due to the increased uncertainty associated with the fundamental values of securities.[35]

A better comparison sample would be 2012 to the present, which shows market volatility that is generally lower than the 1990s and early 2000s, despite the greatly increased role of HFTs in the latter period. As one prominent article has noted, current "[i]ntra-day volatility is below the levels of the pre-electronic 1990s."[36] As best one can tell so far, there is no serious empirical evidence showing that the rise of HFTs has led to ongoing increased volatility. Rather, HFTs happen to have arisen to prominence during a period of greater volatility, which was due to extraneous causes, not to the HFTs themselves. There is also no general theoretical reason for expecting greater volatility due to HFT activity. Instead, the majority of academic evidence on the subject suggests that, if anything, HFTs reduce volatility.[37]

## B. The Flash Crash

The second criticism—that HFTs exacerbate volatility in a very extreme manner when some kind of major disruption occurs in the market—is more interesting. The classic case of such a disruption is the infamous May 6, 2010, "Flash Crash." The Flash Crash occurred within a window of less than 30 minutes. Over this short period, the Dow Jones Industrial Average (DJIA)—a benchmark of general market performance—dropped about 1,000 points, losing 9 percent of its value, and then recovered almost its entire loss.[38] In this incident, the DJIA suffered the greatest one-hour decline in its history[39] and several individual stocks displayed astonishing volatility. Accenture, for instance, fell from trading at $39.98 at 2:46 to $0.01 at 2:49, only to return to $39.51 by 2:50.[40] Apple, in contrast, at one moment traded for almost $100,000 per share.[41]

The Flash Crash was widely taken to "highlight[] the risks of electronic trading," as NYSE's then head of operations suggested.[42] In the years since, blame has been persistently attributed to HFTs, and commentators have suggested that HFTs generally increase the severity of market crashes.[43] However, the report eventually issued by federal regulators explained the Flash Crash as the result of a large sell order that triggered a flight of liquidity from the market. This flight involved HFTs, but only in the sense that many HFTs (which, as we saw in chapter 3, play a critical role in the supply of liquidity) temporarily left the market altogether in response to the large sell order. Without them, the market was being supplied with substantially less liquidity.[44]

The crucial question is: Why would a large market sell order trigger a flight by HFTs, when the business of HFTs is to make money by providing liquidity to persons submitting marketable orders? The answer to this question returns us to the overarching theme of this book: that comprehension and intelligent regulation of the modern stock market is impossible without a thorough appreciation for the role of adverse selection in shaping the provision of liquidity.[45] A large, aggressive sell (or buy) order suggests to liquidity providers that the order submitter may have important private information. As we saw in chapter 3, HFTs know that if this apparent private information in fact turns out to exist, they will lose money from trading at the quotes that they set before learning of this order. Their usual reaction to such an order is to widen their spreads. If the order is such that the threat of being adversely selected becomes extreme, the HFTs know that, to protect themselves, the spread would have to be widened a great deal. They may be unsure, however, as to how much widening is enough. Under these circumstances, many or all liquidity providers may find it safer just to temporarily exit the market altogether. As a result, the only available quotes will come not from professional liquidity suppliers, but from limit orders at very extreme prices posted by individuals on the chance that they can make money from some fluke event. As a result, market orders will execute at prices far from any plausible estimate of a security's fundamental value.[46]

This exit by HFTs and its predictable consequences is, in essence, what happened on a large scale during the Flash Crash.[47] The crash was triggered by a very large sell order that, given its size and aggressiveness, was perceived by the HFTs as having a high probability of being motivated by significantly negative private information.[48] HFTs removed their quotes to minimize their risk of suffering major trading losses, and liquidated any long positions they had accumulated, particularly exacerbating pressures on the price decline side.[49] Because HFTs provide a large share of liquidity, in their absence, soon the only quotes left were ones lying far from the true price of a security.[50]

## C. Wealth Transfer and Efficiency Considerations

Assessing the wealth transfers resulting from major gyrations such as in the Flash Crash is equivalent to asking who wins and who loses when HFTs stop providing liquidity. HFTs cannot make money if they do not trade. They were just unheroic, not the predators that they were portrayed to be by their Flash Crash critics.

What about traders during such gyrations? To the extent that the trades were not broken by the exchanges, the losers are persons who put in market sell orders for stocks that temporarily went way down and market buy orders for stocks that temporarily went way up. The winners were the persons who posted previously way-out-of-the-money limit orders against which these market orders transacted.

We do not think that either wealth transfer or efficiency concerns call for major changes in response to events such as the Flash Crash. We hold this position despite the fact that some commentators believe that such events, which appear bound to occur from time to time, are more frequent with an HFT-dominated system for providing liquidity than in the pre-HFT past. That belief appears to be based on the facts that the specialist was supposed to "lean against the wind" to provide liquidity in the old NYSE system, and that in the old NASDAQ dealer system, human beings, who could stop for a moment and take stock of things, made the trading decisions.

Although some commentators believe that the old system was less prone to major market gyrations, we are not confident they are correct. However, more central to our position that occasional brief moments of liquidity collapse such as the Flash Crash do not signal a need for major reforms is the fact that such gyrations are not fundamentally important in terms of our touchstones for efficiency. Very brief sharp deviations of share prices from fundamental values do not seriously undermine the role of share prices in aiding the efficiency with which capital is allocated to new real investment projects and with which existing productive capacity is utilized. It is accuracy *most of the time* that matters.

The trader seeking immediate execution who places an order when no gyration appears to be occurring, but who seeks to guard against one occurring immediately thereafter, has a simple way of protecting herself. Instead of using a market order, she should use a limit order with a limit price that would appear to make it marketable. In other words, the limit should be enough over the apparent latest available best offer in the market, or enough below the latest available best bid, that the order would be sure to execute in any ordinary market, but not so far above or below as to be out of the range of a plausible assessment of the stock's fundamental value. Traders who might otherwise have wanted to trade during a brief period when such a gyration has already begun can protect themselves by simply staying out of the market during the brief period of time before the gyration has runs its course. They can follow this advice without seriously undermining the efficient allocation of resources over time or the efficient allocation of risk, neither of which requires investors to seek instantaneous execution.

The bottom line here is that we do not think it would be worthwhile to return to the old NYSE specialist and NASDAQ dealer system just to avoid the occasional individual stock or even market-wide price gyration, even if it were practical to require such return. The modern stock market's overall performance in terms of liquidity provision and operational costs is far better than that of the market of the past, which matters more for the ultimate social goals promoted by a well-functioning equity market than avoidance of the occasional price gyration.

## V. POLICY CONCLUSIONS

Potential regulatory responses prompted by the preceding survey of HFT controversies fall into two groups. Each of the proposals in the first group goes to curbing the informational advantages enjoyed by HFTs. These proposals are aimed at preventing anticipatory order cancelation, slow market arbitrage, and exploitation of dark pool midpoint orders, all of which depend on these informational advantages. The second group of proposals arises from concerns about the relationship between HFTs and market volatility and involves adaptations to the entire market's reliance on this form of liquidity supply.

## A. HFT SPEED IN OBTAINING MARKET INFORMATION

Because anticipatory order cancelation, slow market arbitrage, and exploitation of dark pool midpoint orders all involve HFTs acquiring market information ahead of at least some others, once we have assessed the social desirability or undesirability of each of these practices, any possible reform will have to take account of its effect on all three. In this section we expand upon our assessments of each of these practices and then discuss possible reforms.

### 1. Would it be desirable to eliminate anticipatory order cancelation?

Persons transacting in stocks have always played a cat-and-mouse game whereby each tries to figure out what the others are up to. One function of regulation is to step in and prohibit particular informational advantages when such intervention can lead to improved social outcomes. The question is whether the informational advantages that HFTs deploy in anticipatory order cancelation call for such an intervention.

The first step to answering this question requires a policy analysis that compares a world with and without anticipatory order cancelation. As we have seen, the unfairness case against anticipatory order cancelation is at best unproven, and in fact anticipatory order cancelation may well have no unfairness associated with it. We also tentatively conclude that the practice enhances efficiency. In any event, the best arguments that can be made for eliminating anticipatory order cancelation are, at least based on what we know today, insufficiently strong by themselves to justify a regulatory intervention that reduces the informational advantages currently enjoyed by HFTs.

#### A. ACTUAL UNFAIRNESS

The rhetoric of the critics of anticipatory order cancelation focuses primarily on what they see as the unfairness of the resulting wealth transfers. Deeper analysis, however, shows that a compelling case for elimination of the practice cannot be made on this basis of unfairness. As we have demonstrated earlier, the practice actually appears to benefit ordinary people to the extent that they invest directly in the market as retail customers because it lowers spreads and thus their costs of trading. It is unclear whether anticipatory order cancelation is helpful or harmful to ordinary people to the extent that they instead have channeled savings to mutual funds or pension funds that invest all or a portion of their funds in equities on an index basis and execute their purchase and sale transactions on exchanges.[51] To the extent that ordinary people invest through actively managed mutual and pension funds—which, by definition, seek to be informed traders—the net benefit, if there is one, that would arise from elimination of the practice is, as discussed earlier, likely to be substantially captured by the persons running the funds in the form of the higher fees and salaries that they would be able to command.

## B. EFFICIENCY

A stronger case can be made for the elimination of anticipatory order cancelation on efficiency grounds. As at least based on our first-cut efficiency analysis of anticipatory order cancelation, elimination of the practice would involve an unavoidable efficiency trade-off. The increase in price accuracy resulting from elimination of the practice would lead to efficiency gains in the form of better capital allocation and utilization of the economy's existing productive capacity. However, the reduction in liquidity resulting from the elimination would lead to efficiency losses in the form of less efficient allocation of resources over time and allocation of risk. A priori, there is no obvious reason for choosing the point in this trade-off associated with elimination of the practice over the point associated with continuation of the practice. Also, our more nuanced analysis, which takes into account the presence of announcement information traders and inside information traders, suggests that it is quite possible that eliminating anticipatory order cancelation would in fact reduce, rather than improve, price accuracy, so that there is no trade-off and the practice is unambiguously efficiency-enhancing in terms of its price accuracy effects.

## C. RESOURCES CONSUMED

What is clear from an efficiency analysis is that the HFT informational advantages that make anticipatory order cancelation possible have real costs. If HFTs were not able to pursue these advantages, the very substantial human and material resources that pursuing them requires would be freed up to be used elsewhere in the economy in some more clearly productive way.

## D. APPEARANCE OF UNFAIRNESS

Although our previous analysis suggests that anticipatory order cancelation does not actually result in unfairness, HFT practices of this sort are clearly viewed by a substantial portion of the public as being unfair. Much of this perception is of course due to the very criticism of HFT practices that this chapter seeks to subject to more serious analysis. Normally, the better response to misunderstanding is education, not a change in what people are allowed to do where the activity does not in fact pose a problem. Still, if, unlike us, one were persuaded that an efficiency analysis leans toward the conclusion that the practice is on balance socially undesirable, the existence of an unfounded but persistent sense of unfairness can, as discussed in chapter 2, add to the desirability of prohibition of that practice.

*2. Adding slow market arbitrage and dark pool midpoint order exploitation to the analysis*

There are, presumably, large synergies in terms of the use of real productive resources between anticipatory order cancelation, slow market arbitrage, and dark pool midpoint order exploitation. Thus, resource use is not an independent consideration with regard to these other two speed-based HFT practices. Still, in contrast to anticipatory order cancelation, these two practices each seem unquestionably undesirable.

There is no fairness argument that slow market arbitrage helps any ordinary investors: it hurts all regular traders, uninformed and informed alike, by increasing their effective cost of trading. Because of this, its economic welfare effects are unambiguously negative as well. The increased effective cost of trading for informed traders means that it is less rewarding to seek out bits of publicly available information and to analyze their implications in a sophisticated way. As a consequence, share price accuracy, with its beneficial effects on the real economy, is reduced. The increased effective cost of trading on uninformed traders has negative effects on the efficient allocation of resources over time and on the efficient allocation of risk.

Dark pool midpoint order exploitation hurts uninformed investors and in so doing again has negative effects on the efficient allocation of resources over time and on the efficient allocation of risk. It arguably helps share price efficiency by deterring uninformed traders from using dark pools so that they use exchanges as well, where they cause spreads to decrease, reducing the effective cost of trading for fundamental value informed traders.[52] Nevertheless, if it is in fact good social policy to push uninformed traders into the market to subsidize such informed trading, there are more direct ways of doing it than allowing HFTs to profit in this particular fashion.

### 3. The desirability of curbing HFT informational advantages: An evaluation

How should we come out on the question of a regulatory intervention aimed at reducing HFT informational advantages when we consider both anticipatory order cancelation, which we tentatively view as efficiency enhancing, with slow market arbitrage and midpoint order exploitation, which we view as clearly negative activities, and add in the substantial resources that HFTs consume in undertaking these three practices? A great deal depends on how prevalent the latter two practices in fact are. There is some empirical evidence to suggest that they are a sideshow relative to anticipatory order cancelation.[53] When we combine all these conclusions, tentative as they may be, with the fact that greater share price accuracy can yield significant gains in terms of the efficient functioning of the real economy, then the real resources that go into pursuing the informational advantages on which anticipatory order cancelation rest appear more than worth the costs. In sum, at the moment, we would not favor a regulatory intervention aimed at reducing HFT informational advantages.

### 4. Measures to curb HFT informational advantages if deemed desirable

Nevertheless, future empirical studies might well shed a different light on our evaluation that anticipatory order cancelation enhances efficiency in the real economy, or might show that slow market arbitrage and midpoint order exploitation are more prevalent than we currently think. Moreover, we recognize that even based on what is known now, reasonable minds can differ on the question of whether trying to curb HFT informational advantages would be desirable. Hence, it is worth asking how any such regulatory intervention should be designed and whether it can be accomplished at reasonable cost.

The recent controversy surrounding HFTs—and anticipatory order cancelation in particular—has resulted in at least three different proposals for addressing HFTs' activity, each of which offers a range of potential benefits and costs. The first two proposals address HFT conduct by taking aim at high-frequency changes in quotes.[54] One provides financial disincentives for high-volume quoting, such as NASDAQ's former surcharge on each order above a 100:1 order-to-trade ratio (the number of posted quotes to ones that are actually executed against).[55] These fees may simply force HFTs to internalize their quoting's otherwise unpriced consumption of bandwidth. Things get more complicated, however, if the fees are higher than what is necessary to tax this externality and are aimed at reducing practices such as anticipatory order cancelation. In their efforts to fight adverse selection and manage their inventories, HFTs revise their quotes for many reasons other than to engage in anticipatory order cancelation. If in fact HFTs are often revising quotes at a high enough rate to exceed the 100:1 order-to-trade ratio, then fees on quotes in numbers exceeding this limit would create disincentives for all quote revisions, not just the ones associated with anticipatory order cancelation. Thus, these fees can be expected to widen spreads and reduce depth because, beyond anticipatory order cancelation, the fees make it harder for market makers to control adverse selection and inventory risks.[56] This is not a concern if these fees are voluntarily imposed by an exchange in active competition with other exchanges. Traders are its customers and they can decide whether they like the trade-offs implied by the ultimate results. But it would be a concern to us if the fees were mandated on all exchanges by regulation as a way to stop the three controversial practices.

The other proposal aiming at reducing the three controversial practices by reducing quote revisions would impose a minimum time-in-force for quotes, prohibiting them from being canceled, within, for example, 100 milliseconds of submission.[57] Again, HFTs cancel orders faster than 100 milliseconds for reasons other than anticipatory order cancelation and the other two controversial practices. The costs of such a plan in terms of liquidity provision could be substantial. Such a plan sets a floor on the length of the option offered by liquidity providers to liquidity takers, increasing their chance of being adversely selected. Again, the result will be a widening of spreads.[58]

The third proposal aimed at limiting the three controversial practices is the much-discussed idea to alter the current market trading structure itself.[59] Stock exchanges currently conduct continuous two-sided (i.e., buy and sell) auctions for each security. Budish et al.'s proposal is to replace this with frequent batch auctions, say, every 100 milliseconds.[60] Batch auctions would consist of uniform-price, sealed-bid auctions conducted at discrete time intervals. Budish and his co-authors' motivation for their proposal is a concern about the real resources consumed by HFTs. They argue that HFTs seek speed because current equity market structure permits frequent technical arbitrage opportunities based on who is first to exploit symmetrically available public information, creating a socially wasteful "arms race" to exploit these opportunities. Frequent batch auctions would eliminate the value of minute speed advantages. Although Budish et al.'s proposal may have significant merit in this regard, much would depend on implementation. To eliminate anticipatory order cancelation and the other two practices, every exchange would have to have its auction (nearly) simultaneously. Furthermore, these auctions would have to be synchronized with auctions in derivatives markets. If auctions were sufficiently frequent and at different times at each venue, then inter-venue HFT exploitation of tiny speed differences based on informational advantages (and the associated use of real resources) might persist.

If curbing these HFT information-speed advantages were deemed to be desirable, we think there is a simpler approach, both in terms of implementation and in terms of achieving the needed legal changes. None of these three practices would be possible if private data feeds did not effectively make market quote and transaction data available to some market participants before others. Thus, one potential regulatory response in furtherance of curbing HFT informational advantages is to require that private dissemination of quote and trade information be delayed until the exclusive processor under the Reg. NMS scheme, referred to as the SIP, has publicly disseminated information from all the exchanges. In fact, mechanically, it would likely be necessary to delay the arrival of exchanges' entire proprietary data feeds until the public feed arrived, because changes in depth-of-book information would allow HFTs to backward-engineer most, if not all, changes to core data.

Rule 603(a)(2) of Reg. NMS prohibits exchanges from "unreasonably discriminatory" distribution of market data.[61] In its adopting release for Reg. NMS, the SEC outlined its interpretation of that provision, which is that privately "distributed data could not be made available on a more timely basis [to private clients] than core data is made available to a Network processor [the SIP]. . . . Rule 603(a) prohibits an SRO or broker-dealer from transmitting data to a vendor or user any sooner than it transmits the data to a Network processor."[62] *Core data* is composed of last-trade reports and each exchange's current highest bids and lowest offers for each security, from which the exchange's NBB and NBO are ascertained.[63]

The SEC's interpretation of the "unreasonably discriminatory" distribution language of Rule 603(a)(2) appears to say that it is permissible for core data information to reach an HFT more rapidly than the public recipients of the SIP as long as the signal sending the data to the HFT does not precede the signal sent to the SIP. Certainly the exchanges and the HFTs, in agreeing to their colocation arrangements, have assumed this interpretation to be correct. The SEC's choice of enforcement actions constitutes an implicit confirmation of this interpretation as well. On the one hand, no actions have been brought against colocation arrangements where the signal was sent simultaneously to the colocated HFTs and to the SIP. Indeed, the SEC, in a 2010 Concept Release, acknowledged the existence of exchanges' widely known practice of submitting data simultaneously to the SIP and private feeds and the fact that, as a result, private feeds will reach subscribers far faster than the SIP distributes its data.[64] On the other hand, in a 2012 proceeding, the SEC did find that NYSE had been sending market data, including best bids and offers, to private subscribers *before* it sent that data to the SIP, and fined NYSE $5 million.[65]

Certainly the language of Rule 603(a)(2) could plausibly be interpreted in a different fashion. Sending the signal simultaneously to an HFT and to the SIP arguably is "unreasonably discriminatory" distribution of core data to the end users because, given colocation and other technological differences, it is predictable that some traders will consistently receive it faster than others. This interpretation of Rule 603(a)(2)'s language already has its advocates. The market research firm Nanex has repeatedly insisted that the exchanges are in standing violation of Reg. NMS for this reason.[66]

In terms of its legal basis, this interpretation of "unreasonably discriminatory" may seem unusually demanding, but it is no stranger to securities law. Rather, the revisionist interpretation of Rule 603(a)(2) is more consistent with the SEC's usual approach to regulating the dissemination of information in securities markets than the current one. Most importantly, in the SEC and courts' approach to regulating insider trading, information has been held to be no longer nonpublic when it reaches end users, rather than when a public announcement is made.[67] The adopting release for Regulation Fair Disclosure uses a similar definition of information as nonpublic "if [the information] has not been disseminated in a manner making it available to investors generally."[68] Thus, to make information public in the SEC's eyes, "it must be disseminated in a manner calculated to reach the securities market place . . . and public investors must be afforded a reasonable waiting period to react to the information."[69]

The SEC's ability to alter its interpretation of Rule 603(a)(2) may be the path of least legislative or regulatory resistance to ending HFT advantages that are based on knowing quote changes and transaction data before others. However, one may feel that too much has already been invested in reliance on the SEC's apparent original interpretation for a prohibition to be imposed without the normal procedures of an administrative agency rule change. If so, then the ordinary process of rule change, including notice and comment, can be followed and the rule amended.

## B. HFTs and Volatility

Overall, we concluded earlier in this chapter that there is no evidence of a relationship between HFT activities and a general increase in market volatility. We concluded as well that the connection between HFTs and episodic volatility is not due to predatory behavior on their parts, but rather to their rational with-drawal from the market at certain moments of stress.

There are, nonetheless, a number of existing proposals seeking to address the alleged link between HFT activity and volatility. These proposals fall into two groups: one group seeks to ameliorate trading volatility generally and would incidentally affect HFTs; the second group seeks to target a specific link between HFTs and volatility.

As to the first group, soon after the Flash Crash, the SEC phased in sin-gle-stock circuit breakers, which impose a 5-minute halt in the trading of an individual stock if its price moves by more than 10 percent within 5 minutes.[70] This trading pause is designed to give liquidity providers breathing room to consider whether or not order imbalances actually reflect private information. Similarly, the SEC also approved a "limit up-limit down" plan that pauses trading in a stock if transactions move more than a certain amount, often 5 percent, away from the security's average price over the past five minutes.[71] These are moderate proposals, which should have salutary effects in moderating future crashes.

The second set of proposals tackles the important question of whether mar-ket makers, however they be defined, should have stronger affirmative liquid-ity-providing obligations than they currently do. Exchanges already impose a range of affirmative obligations on institutionally identified market makers at their venues. For instance, the NYSE has "designated market makers," who have specific obligations to help maintain an orderly and continuous trading market in particular stocks.[72] Some commentators want to go further down this road and to impose on HFTs legal responsibilities resembling those imposed on the institutionally designated market makers of yesteryear, such as the specialists of the pre-2005 NYSE.[73]

There is an obvious attraction to proposals that might moderate the flight of liquidity provision from the market during periods of extreme volatility. How-ever, the historical evidence suggests that strong paper obligations have proved insufficient in the past to motivate market makers to continue supplying liquidity during periods of extreme volatility.[74] Commentators have also noted problems with strengthening such affirmative obligations, emphasizing that any system that requires liquidity providers to take heavy losses during periods of extreme adverse selection must compensate them for doing so at other times. At least two associated problems result: first, determining the value of that compensation is extremely difficult; and second, during times of crisis these designated liquidity providers will be the prime targets of informed traders.[75] Thus, we are skeptical about such proposals, especially given our conclusion that the consequences of episodic volatility in terms of wealth transfer and efficiency are not substantial.

Regulation of Traders | **PART 3**

Informed trading—trading on information not yet reflected in a stock's price—drives much of the stock market.[1] Such information, as we have seen, involves a more accurate appraisal of a stock's value than what its current price implies. The trader may have obtained this information from astute analysis of varied bits of publicly available information or observations of the world; from newly disclosed public information not yet incorporated into a stock's price; or from confidential information possessed by the issuer of the stock or another entity, such as a potential acquirer.

No issue in securities law has garnered more attention from law and economics scholars and the larger public alike than insider trading, where a trader transacts based on nonpublic information obtained from inside an issuer or another entity.[2] The legal literature has thought far less about how the other forms of informed trading are affected by current law and how the law should ideally regulate them. The ambition of this chapter is to advance thinking on both fronts. We argue here that these two types of insider trading are better regulated as part of the more general phenomenon of informed trading, and that securities regulation could better promote social welfare if it was designed with an awareness of both what all types of informed trading have in common and how they differ.[3]

As we have shown in chapters 2 and 3, informed trading generally leads to more accurate share prices, which in turn increase the efficiency with which the economy produces goods and services. Informed trading also reduces market liquidity, which makes trading costlier and leads to a variety of inefficiencies in the economy. There is thus a fundamental trade-off in how informed trading affects the two principal social functions served by equity markets: providing accurate prices and facilitating liquidity. This chapter takes this basic trade-off and goes back to first principles (using the tools developed in the preceding chapters) to try to identify which forms of informed trade are in fact socially desirable, which are socially undesirable, and how to best regulate the market as a result.[4] A key observation is that the time horizon of the information on which an informed trade is based—the latency before it would otherwise be reflected in price—crucially determines both the strategies of those trading on it and the social value of such trading.[5] Disaggregating traders and trading strategies in this way provides powerful new insights into how we can use regulation to deter socially undesirable forms of informed trading and promote socially desirable ones.

Informed trading in the United States is currently affected by a complex, and far from coherent, jumble of legal rules. Relevant federal provisions include rules coming out of the convoluted case law interpreting § 10(b) of the Securities Exchange Act of 1934 (the Exchange Act)[6] and Rule 10b-5 promulgated thereunder (neither of which explicitly refers to trading on nonpublic information), Exchange Act § 16(b) (requiring insiders to return to the issuer profits made from short-swing trading),[7] the Exchange Act's mandatory disclosure regime (requiring the filing of Forms 10K, 10Q, and 8K), Regulation Fair Disclosure (Reg. FD) (requiring immediate public disclosure of material information given privately to analysts or particular traders),[8] and Regulation National Market System (Reg. NMS) (setting forth the basic rules of equity market structure). Certain provisions of state law and stock exchange regulations are relevant as well.[9]

As will be discussed in more detail in chapter 6, under this range of provisions, some informed trades are prohibited or deterred, while others are allowed or even encouraged. Our analysis has both good news and bad news with regard to this current regulatory structure. The regulation of trading based on inside information, despite its tortured doctrinal basis in Rule 10b-5, has more policy coherence than many commentators appreciate. For example, under the "misappropriation theory," a trade based on nonpublic information possessed by an entity *other than the issuer* is legal if the entity has given the trader permission, but is, in general, illegal if permission has not been granted. This distinction is criticized on both the "left" and the "right" because the counterparty to the trade has the same regrets whether permission was granted or not.[10] Our analysis suggests that the real injury is reduced liquidity, which is the same in either case. The legal distinction still makes sense, however, because trades without permission undermine the incentives to acquire information that makes share prices more accurate, whereas trades with permission enhance these incentives. In contrast, New York's former Attorney General, Eric Schneiderman, utilized New York's Martin Act to launch a heated, but we believe misguided, public campaign against institutions that release market-moving information early to a subset of traders, attacking what he called "Insider Trading 2.0."[11]

Also, under current law, a tippee's trade based on a tip from an insider *within an issuer* is prohibited only if the tipper received a "personal benefit."[12] This result has been similarly criticized because the counterparty to the tippee's trade is equally injured whether or not the tipper enjoyed a personal benefit.[13] What constituted a personal benefit was at the center of the dispute in *United States v. Salman*,[14] a tippee case recently decided by the Supreme Court. Again, our analysis suggests that the real social injury from the tippee's trade is not the injury to the counterparty, but reduced liquidity. That too is the same whether the tipper received a personal benefit or not. Still, there may be reasons to refrain from imposing liability on a direct tippee when the tipper received no personal benefit because of the social value of engagement between issuer representatives and equity analysts. Admittedly, if trades based on information gleaned from analyst interviews are outside the reach of Rule 10b-5, then some interviews will reveal *material* nonpublic information that will be traded upon. This, viewed in isolation, is as unfortunate as a trade based on the same information by an issuer insider and thus would seem to call for imposition of Rule 10b-5 liability. But imposing liability is likely to chill the occurrence of analyst interviews. Avoiding chilling such interviews has a benefit: they allow analysts to gather and analyze pieces of *immaterial* nonpublic information that they can use to develop, and trade on, a superior analysis of the value of the issuer's shares. The net social gain from the second kind of trades is arguably greater than the net social loss from the first.

On the other hand, we find that announcement trading—trading based on information relevant to a stock's value made public so recently that it is not yet fully reflected in the price—though perfectly legal today, reduces liquidity without any redeeming social benefit from its effect on price accuracy. This is because the information would be reflected in price very quickly even without such trading. Moreover, significant resources are devoted to such trading. Although it is probably impractical to try to make such trades illegal, they can be deterred through appropriate rules governing the structure of trading markets.

This chapter uses the evaluative framework and analysis of the economics of trading markets from chapters 2 and 3 to assess each of the four types of informed trade—fundamental value, announcement, issuer insider, and non-issuer insider—to determine whether, and under what circumstances, it is socially desirable or undesirable. Fundamental value informed trading is found to be socially desirable. Announcement trading is found to be undesirable. Trading on the basis of information from inside an issuer is found to be generally undesirable, but with exceptions; for example, trading on the basis of an evaluation of the company based on a variety of small bits of nonpublic information as opposed to being based on a major piece of information about to be announced. The desirability of trading based on information from inside a non-issuer institution depends on whether the institution agrees to its use. When it does, allowing such trading adds to the incentives for the institution to generate valuable information and hence is socially desirable. When the institution does not agree, the opposite is the case.

Chapter 6 goes on to explore this pattern of regulatory impacts to see how close what is prohibited or discouraged comes to what the analysis in this chapter suggests are the socially undesirable informed trades and how close what is encouraged comes to what it suggests are the socially desirable ones. Four types of legal rules are considered: rules that outright prohibit certain kinds of informed trades; rules that require, under certain circumstances, the return of profits from the informed trader to the issuer of the shares; mandatory disclosure rules; and rules governing the structure of the markets for secondary trading.

## I. FUNDAMENTAL VALUE INFORMED TRADING

Fundamental value information arises from a person gathering bits of publicly available information and observations of the world and analyzing what the person has gathered or observed in a sophisticated way that allows a superior assessment of these cash flows than what is implied by current market pricing. Hedge funds and actively managed mutual funds, pension funds, and endowments of non-profits are examples of informed traders using such information.

In determining the social value of such trading, we start with an analysis of its wealth impacts, from both an ex post and an ex ante perspective. The ex post perspective relates to who is better off, and who is worse off, after a single such informed trade. The ex ante perspective relates to the effect on the expected wealth positions of the different market participants when such trading occurs as an ongoing practice within a competitive environment. These analyses allow us to make determinations about the fairness of the practice and the incentives that it creates. We consider as well the extent and duration of price accuracy improvement associated with the practice relative to its negative impact on liquidity, and the resources its practitioners consume that would otherwise be available for other socially useful purposes.

Our ultimate conclusion is that fundamental value informed trading is fair and enhances the efficiency of the U.S. economy. Thus, it is socially desirable. This conclusion is not really very controversial: few have suggested that those who, through their own hard work and use of publicly available sources, come up with superior assessments of an issuer's share value should be prohibited from trading on this information to their profit.[15] The way we come to this conclusion, however, sharpens the analysis considerably and provides a roadmap for analyzing the other, more controversial forms of informed trading.

## A. Wealth Effects: The Ex Post Perspective

Understanding the wealth transfer implications of fundamental value informed trading is most easily understood by starting with an example. Suppose X does substantial research, gathering various bits of publicly available information about the potential sales of automobiles operating on pure ethanol obtained from switchgrass and about the economic practicality of this process. ABC is known to be the auto firm furthest along in developing an engine that can burn this fuel. X concludes that the switchgrass process is more practical, and consumer interest greater, than is generally believed. ABC's NBB is $59.95 and NBO is $60.05 and X's research suggests the stock is worth $70.00. X starts using a large number of small market buy orders, averaging in aggregate 10,000 shares per day. For expository simplicity, assume that during X's buying period, X is the only informed trader of any kind, there is no mistake or anti-mistake trading, and there is no publicly released information relevant to the value of ABC's shares. So, if X had not been buying, the NBB and NBO would have remained at about their initial levels.

X continues his buying until, given the continued imbalance of buy orders over sell orders received by liquidity suppliers, the NBB has risen to $69.90 and the NBO to $70.00. By this point, X has been buying for 100 trading days and has acquired 1,000,000 ABC shares at an average price of $65.05. X then gives his research to a prominent business journalist, who checks it out and publishes an article in a widely read business magazine based on X's research, at which point ABC's NBB inches up to $69.95 and its NBO to $70.05.[16] Who gained and who lost in this story?

## 1. Informed traders

X, the informed trader, appears to have a trading gain of slightly less than $5 million, the difference between the average purchase price and what he can sell them for after the announcement. Because trading is a zero-sum game, the gains and losses of all the other players in the market must aggregate to a loss of the same amount.

## 2. Liquidity suppliers

The liquidity suppliers would, over the 100-trading-day period, have received and executed against their quotes, 1,000,000 more buy orders than sell orders. This is because X would have submitted 1,000,000 buy orders and no sell orders. As we saw in chapter 3, the uninformed traders, because they trade for reasons unrelated to making trading profits, would in aggregate have submitted an approximately equal number of buy and sell orders. Thus, the liquidity suppliers would be short by 1,000,000 shares at the time the business journalist publishes the story.

The liquidity supplier makes on average $0.05 (half the spread) for each purchase from, and for each sale to, an uninformed trader, but that would have happened even if X had not traded. So, as a result of X's purchases, the liquidity traders sold, for an average of $65.55, 1,000,000 shares that are now implicitly valued by the market at $70.00; that is, the liquidity traders' short positions translate into a loss equal to the same approximate $5 million gain enjoyed by X.[17]

## 3. Uninformed traders

Because the uninformed buy and sell orders each day are essentially equal in number, the gradual increase in the bid and offer during the period of X's trading will be a wash for uninformed traders as a group. Compared to if X had not placed his orders, however, sellers are better off and buyers are worse off, with the gains for sellers just equaling the losses of buyers.

## B. Wealth and Resource Allocation Effects: The Ex Ante Perspective

The ex ante perspective compares, in long-run competitive equilibrium, a world where the practice of fundamental value informed trading occurs freely versus one where it does not and considers the differences in terms of the wealth positions of the market's various participants and in terms of the allocation of resources. It assumes, not unrealistically, that all the participants have unbiased (though not necessarily highly accurate) expectations concerning the prevalence of informed trading by fundamental value informed traders.

### 1. Fundamental value informed traders

Fundamental value informed trading will generate positive trading profits on an expected basis, as illustrated in the example above, even though the existence of the practice widens the spreads that its practitioners incur. The business of such trading requires skilled and unskilled labor and physical, organizational, and financial assets.[18]

In a competitive economy, suppliers of the ordinary inputs will be paid a market return comparable to what they would earn if the resources they supplied were deployed instead in another way. Thus, the practice of fundamental value informed trading has no effect on their wealth positions. The persons with uniquely useful abilities and skills for fundamental value trading will be paid greater rents than they would be paid if they had to work in a different business. Thus, the wealth positions of these persons are greater in the world where the practice occurs freely than where it is prohibited.

### 2. Liquidity suppliers

As discussed in chapter 3, liquidity suppliers will incur expected trading losses when they transact with informed traders. At the same time, liquidity suppliers gain in their transactions with uninformed traders, making on average half the spread with each purchase or sale. To survive in a competitive market, a liquidity supplier must set its bids and offers so that these losses and gains balance out, plus cover the returns paid to its personnel, a market return on the capital needed for real estate and equipment and for engaging in the trading itself, and compensation for the undiversified nature of the portfolio that the business will be holding much of the time. With spreads wider than this, the liquidity supplier will not attract orders. With spreads narrower than this, at least some of the liquidity supplier's inputs will be receiving less than a market return and thus the supplier will not be able to survive in the longer run.

Despite liquidity suppliers being able to pass on to traders their losses due to the free occurrence of fundamental value informed trading (through wider spreads), the practice does have a negative effect on the wealth positions of certain persons associated with the liquidity supply business. Higher prices for buying shares and lower prices for selling them increase the cost of trading. When trading costs more, less of it occurs. This means that fewer resources are needed for the business of liquidity supply to operate, thereby reducing the rents paid to inputs uniquely well suited to such a business.[19]

### 3. Anti-mistake traders

Anti-mistake traders buy at the offer and sell at the bid. To the extent that fundamental value informed trading widens the spread, it increases the anti-mistake traders' costs of doing business, making their business less profitable, decreasing the resources drawn into it, and reducing the rents paid to its specialized inputs. These points are softened, though, by the fact that there are synergies for a person or entity to engage in the fundamental value informed trade business and the anti-mistake trading business at the same time.

### 4. Uninformed traders: actual costs and their ultimate incidence

Because an uninformed trader trading on an exchange buys at the offer and sells at the bid, she pays the spread between the two in the full cycle of the purchase and sale of a share. Freely occurring fundamental value trading makes this spread larger and so this cost of trading will be greater for her.[20] As discussed in chapter 2, calculating the ultimate incidence of this larger cost on the wealth positions of the various market participants is complicated, however. When an issuer's entrepreneurs and early investors engage in an initial public offering, the shares they offer will be discounted to reflect the anticipated spread paid with each subsequent purchase and sale in the secondary market.[21] So, the wider spread from freely occurring fundamental value informed trading reduces what the entrepreneurs and early investors receive selling shares when they take their firms public. This discount continues at the same level for as long as the firm appears to have a long-run future.

### 5. Uninformed traders: illusory losses and gains

A number of other uninformed trader losses and gains appear to be associated with fundamental value informed trading, but, upon closer analysis, prove to be illusory. An uninformed seller may sometimes regret a sale that occurs at a time when, unknown to her, an informed trader is making purchases. But, because the uninformed trader's motivations for trading are not prompted by either new information or price change, she would have sold anyway even if the informed trader had not traded. Thus, the regret is not properly related to the informed trader's purchases.

Indeed, as the previous example illustrates, the informed trader's purchases, by pushing up the bids and offers quoted by liquidity suppliers, mean that the uninformed seller will receive more for her shares than if the informed trader had not been purchasing. From an ex ante point of view, however, this gain is also illusory: the uninformed trader was just as likely to be a buyer as a seller when the price has been pushed up in this way and so the practice on an ongoing basis is as likely to hurt her as help her. A parallel set of illusions would accompany an uninformed trader's purchase when an informed trader is selling based on negative information.

## C. Fairness Analysis

Overall, it is hard to argue that fundamental value informed trading creates unfairness. Liquidity suppliers will suffer trading losses, as illustrated in the ex post example. The ex ante analysis, however, shows these losses simply to be a cost of doing business that is passed onto traders through wider spreads. The ex post example shows that uninformed traders trading in the same direction as the informed trader are worse off. For example, when an informed trader is buying, he pushes prices up, thereby increasing what uninformed buyers have to pay. But the informed trading makes uninformed traders trading in the opposite direction (in this example, the sellers) better off by an equal amount. Therefore, the practice is as likely to help as hurt an uninformed trader as she enters into any given transaction. Given this, a loss in any one transaction is likely to be canceled out by a gain in some other transaction, particularly if the investor ameliorates this risk, along with the myriad other risks of equity investing, by holding a diversified portfolio.

Freely occurring fundamental value informed trading does widen the spread that uninformed traders have to pay. However, this widened spread, as we have seen, neither helps nor hurts the uninformed traders on average because share prices are commensurately discounted to reflect this widened spread.[22] The cost of this widened spread thus ultimately falls on entrepreneurs and early investors that face a higher cost of capital because of this discount. These same entrepreneurs and early investors benefit, however, from the practice's resulting improved price accuracy, which, as we will discuss, lowers the cost of capital.

The ex ante analysis shows that freely allowing fundamental value trading draws resources into this business, thereby improving the wealth positions of the suppliers of its specialized inputs. It also diminishes resources drawn into the liquidity supply and anti-mistake trading businesses, thereby decreasing the wealth positions of their specialized input suppliers. As noted in chapter 2, however, in a market economy, the offer of rents, which prompt the suppliers of specialized inputs to come forward, is the mechanism by which these resources get directed to the activity for which they are most particularly suited. Thus, the practice's positive or negative effects on the rents being paid in these three businesses do not appear to raise any greater fairness issues than do the rents paid persons with special abilities and skills across the whole market-based part of our economy.[23]

## D. Efficiency Considerations

The foregoing discussion suggests that the more serious normative question raised by fundamental value informed trading is whether the practice increases or decreases economic efficiency, not whether those who suffer losses as a result of such a trade have experienced unfairness. Indeed, because the analysis of the wealth impacts of the other three types of informed trading will follow lines similar to the analysis here, we will conclude with them too that efficiency, not fairness, should be the prime normative concern.

Freely occurring fundamental value trading positively affects economic welfare by increasing share price accuracy. It negatively affects economic welfare by reducing liquidity and by consuming resources that would otherwise be available for the production of other goods and services of value to society. These effects and how they likely net out are discussed in the following subsections.

### 1. Positive effects on price accuracy

Trading by any type of informed trader moves prices in the direction of what they would be if the trader's information was fully reflected in price. As a consequence, all kinds of informed trading make prices more accurate. The distinguishing feature of fundamental value informed trading is that, unlike the other three kinds of informed trading, the information on which it is based did not exist before it was generated as the result of the trader's own actions. This distinguishing feature has two important implications. These implications, in turn, suggest that, relative to other types of informed trading, fundamental value trading's effect on price accuracy has a much larger positive impact on the functioning of the real economy and its capacity to provide society with goods and services.

A. TRADING PROFITS CREATE INCENTIVES TO PRODUCE NEW INFORMATION

With fundamental value informed trading, the prospect of trading profits creates an incentive to increase the stock of information in the world relevant to
predicting an issuer's long-term future cash flows. This is not the case with the
other three kinds of informed trading, each of which involves simply taking
already existing information and trading on it.[24]

B. PRICE ACCURACY IS IMPROVED OVER A LONGER SPAN OF TIME

Price accuracy relates to the accuracy with which the market price of an issuer's
shares predicts the events that determine an issuer's future cash flows. Compared to the information that is the basis of other types of informed trading, the
information motivating fundamental value informed trading is likelier to relate
to the probability of an event in the medium- or long-term future.

To illustrate, consider the previous example. X does substantial research,
gathering various bits of publicly available information about the potential sales
for automobiles operating on pure ethanol obtained from switchgrass and on the
practicality of the process. Using smart analysis, he concludes that they are better
than generally believed. He therefore purchases shares of ABC, the auto company known to be furthest along in developing an engine that can burn this fuel.

Now consider the timing relating to the types of nonpublic information that
are more typically the basis of the three *other* types of informed trading. One
such type of information relates to an event that has already occurred and had
an effect on the cash position of the issuer available to shareholders. An example would be knowledge of an embezzlement that leaves the corporate treasury
$100 million short of what is publicly believed to be the case. Another such type
of information relates to an event that has already occurred and that will have
a definite effect on future cash flows. An example would be knowledge of a yet-
to-be-announced FDA approval of a new patented drug for which there should
be large demand. Yet another relates to an event that is very likely to occur in
the near future and, if it does, will have a definite effect on future cash flows, but
where the facts suggesting this high likelihood are not yet public—for example,
facts suggesting a high likelihood of such FDA approval very soon.

C. CONSEQUENCES FOR THE EXTENT OF POSITIVE IMPACT ON ECONOMIC WELFARE

Keep in mind these two implications associated with fundamental value informed
trading—its incentive effects and its capacity to improve price accuracy for a
long period of time—and consider how the world would differ with and without
this kind of informed trading. Then compare this difference with how the world

would differ with and without each of the other three kinds of informed trading. For each of the four types of informed trading, if that particular type was effectively banned, then a stock price would still become, at some later point, as accurate a predictor of the issuer's cash flows as the price would have been *earlier* had that type of informed trading been allowed. The question is how much earlier this price accuracy improvement would have occurred if this type of informed trading had been allowed.[25] If fundamental value informed trading were allowed, this price accuracy improvement would often have come considerably earlier. For most informed trades of the other three types, the price accuracy improvement would have come only slightly earlier because the information would have been publicly announced and fully reflected in price very soon anyway. In essence, freely occurring fundamental value informed trading tends to make share prices consistently more accurate: information with predictive value is created and the resulting improvement in the accuracy with which the price predicts the cash flow involved occurs considerably earlier than otherwise relative to when the cash flow is realized.[26]

This assessment suggests that the positive effects on price accuracy from fundamental value informed trading result in a greater contribution to social welfare than the contribution from the free occurrence of the other three kinds. To see why, recall from chapter 2 that more accurate prices benefit the economy by helping to allocate the economy's scarce capital to the most promising potential real investment projects and by improving the utilization of the economy's existing productive capacity through optimizing the signals provided to management about investment decisions and the signals given to boards and shareholders about the quality of management decisions. Informed trades based on information that will be fully reflected in price anyway very soon after the trade occurs do little to help share prices perform this kind of guiding work in the real economy. Conversely, informed trades that are based on information that would not otherwise have been created and that improve price accuracy well in advance of the cash flows they are predicting do help prices perform this guiding kind of work. Put another way, *efficient allocation of capital and good corporate governance depend much more on how much information is reflected in price, not on slight improvements in the timing of price accuracy improvements.* What is important about informative prices is that they impound information into prices at time intervals relevant to the important decisions being made by actors in the real economy. Important capital raising, takeover, and investment decisions tend to be made over the course of many months. They are thus unlikely to be affected by an improvement in price accuracy for the short period between an informed trade and the information on which it was based being disclosed in a company's regular course of business.[27]

*2. Comparison of benefits with costs*

The social gains from freely occurring fundamental value informed trading must be compared with the social losses therefrom, which are straightforward. Freely occurring fundamental value informed trading increases illiquidity, which reduces social welfare because of the resulting misallocation of resources over time and of risk. Such trading also draws resources into the business of fundamental value informed trading that could be used elsewhere in the economy to produce useful goods and services.[28]

In our view, the improvements in the real economy induced by fundamental value informed trading's increased price accuracy—better capital allocation and better utilization of the economy's existing productive capacity—outweigh the social losses associated with such trading. In essence, the decision to allow fundamental value informed trading is a decision to encourage the production of the information on which it is based by the higher spread paid by uninformed traders and ultimately borne by entrepreneurs and by persons investing in firms prior to their becoming publicly traded.[29] Although our conclusion involves some speculation, fundamental value information would probably be under-produced from a social welfare point of view absent this subsidy. Empirical evidence suggests that informed trading contributes significantly to the information impounded in share prices.[30] There is also ample empirical evidence to suggest that accurate price signals do in fact have efficiency-enhancing effects on managerial decisions, both in terms of new investment decisions and the utilization of existing productive capacity. Theory suggests that the many imperfections in the market for the development of knowledge mean that the information reflected in share prices would be underprovided if fundamental value informed trading were prohibited: in essence such knowledge has the qualities of a public good.[31]

## II. ANNOUNCEMENT INFORMATION

*Announcement information* is information contained in an announcement by an issuer or other institution with direct implications for the issuer's future cash flows.[32] This information remains announcement information only for the brief period of time between when the announcement is made and when the information becomes fully reflected in price. Success in announcement trading is based on a capacity to act with great speed.[33] For instance, this could involve a capacity to rapidly machine-read a public announcement and determine whether it has positive or negative implications for the issuer involved, combined with rapidly sending buy or sell orders to the relevant trading venues, all before a human could possibly blink.

## A. Wealth Transfers and Fairness

The ex post and ex ante wealth transfer implications of announcement informed trading are essentially identical to those of fundamental value informed trading: just substituting "announcement trading" wherever "fundamental value informed trading" appears in the discussion above. Accordingly, freely occurring announcement trading results in more resources than otherwise being drawn into this business and hence increases the rents paid to the suppliers of its specialized inputs. Because liquidity suppliers protect themselves against such trading with wider spreads, it increases the cost of trading and hence lessens demand for their services and reduces the rents paid to the suppliers of their specialized inputs. The wider spreads also make all trading, including all informed trading, more expensive. In essence, this is a crowding-out effect, which reduces the rents paid to the suppliers of their respective specialized inputs. As was discussed earlier, such effects on the rents paid to the suppliers of specialized inputs needed by the various market participants do not raise serious fairness issues.

Uninformed traders are on average neither advantaged nor disadvantaged by announcement trading. Again, because uninformed traders' decisions are not motivated by either information or price, they are as likely buyers as sellers if they happen to trade during the brief moment before the announcement is fully reflected in price and thus are as likely to be benefited as harmed by the price impact of an announcement trade. Announcement trading will widen the bid-ask spread but, as discussed in chapter 2, share prices are discounted to reflect the extent to which it does so. The cost of this increased spread again ultimately falls on entrepreneurs and early investors, who face a higher cost of capital because of this discount.

In sum, the conclusion is the same as with fundamental value informed trading: rather than fairness, the more important normative question concerning announcement trading concerns its efficiency effects.

## B. Efficiency Considerations

In our view, announcement trading is socially undesirable. Its capacity to augment the speed with which market prices reflect already existing new information is of socially insignificant benefit. The ways in which price accuracy improves the efficiency of the real economy do not require anything like this speed. Moreover, announcement trading's negative social effects are substantial. Announcement trading has all the same negative efficiency effects from its adverse impact on liquidity as does any other type of informed trading. Particularly important, it consumes scarce resources—talented people and sophisticated equipment—that could be usefully employed elsewhere to provide goods and services of value to society. Also, its crowding-out effect reduces the level of fundamental value informed trading, which we have concluded is a socially desirable activity.

## III. INSIDE INFORMATION: THE ISSUER AS SOURCE

*Issuer inside information* is information not yet publicly available that is obtained from within a stock's issuer and that is relevant to predicting the future cash flows paid to its shareholders. Few topics have divided law and economics scholarship as deeply as informed trading by issuer insiders. There is vociferous disagreement not only concerning the justification for prohibiting such insider trading, but also about whether a prohibition should exist at all.

For the first thirty years after the beginnings of federal securities regulation, there was a widely shared perception on behalf of commentators that such insider trading was unfair because it gave corporate insiders unique opportunities to capture the wealth generated by corporations—a view still frequently expressed in judicial opinions and by some prominent commentators.[34] A sea change was triggered by Henry Manne's 1966 publication of *Insider Trading and the Stock Market*.[35] Manne insisted that not only is such insider trading perfectly fair, but that it is actually socially beneficial because it enhances efficiency, and thus should be legal. Trading by issuer insiders enhances efficiency, in his view, because it results in the speedier incorporation of information into stock prices and because it serves as an effective form of incentive compensation for corporate managers.[36]

In this section, we examine both the fairness and efficiency implications of issuer insider informed trading. We will conclude that it is indeed not unfair, although public perceptions to the contrary may still provide some justification for its prohibition. But we will also conclude, contrary to Manne, that it makes the economy less, not more, efficient, although this argument weakens and may, in fact, reverse itself in the case of trades based on some forms of immaterial inside information—the accumulation of many small bits of nonpublic information that are not likely to be reflected in price for some time.

Significant parts of the analysis that follows here is synthetic—surveying and briefly summarizing aspects of the vast scholarly literature addressing insider trading. We cannot hope to even touch on all the insightful work in this area. Still, we believe we put the subject in a fresh light. And, in particular, what follows enables us to sharpen our own analysis of the tipper and tippee trading issues that only last year occupied the Supreme Court (discussed in chapter 6) and will likely preoccupy lower courts for years to come.

## A. Wealth Transfers: Their Incentive and Fairness Effects

Understanding the wealth transfer implications of trading based on issuer inside information is again most easily understood by starting with an example and seeing the ex post effect of the trade, and then considering, from an ex ante perspective, what the impact of the practice is as a generally known ongoing phenomenon. Much of this analysis parallels our analysis of fundamental value informed trading and announcement trading and need not be repeated here, but there are enough differences that it is worthwhile starting with a new example for the ex post analysis.

### 1. Ex post perspective

Suppose Y obtains from within EDF Inc. information, not known publicly or otherwise reflected in price, that EDF is developing a new low-pollution engine that is likely to pass the last few tests being held over the next two weeks. If, as expected within EDF, the engine does pass the tests, EDF will be able to enter into some very profitable contracts that will significantly improve the future cash flow paid out to holders of EDF shares compared to what is currently expected. Y uses a large number of orders, averaging in aggregate 100,000 per trading day, to purchase 1,000,000 EDF shares over the ten trading days in the two-week period. Prior to Y's purchases, EDF's NBB was $59.95 and its NBO was $60.05. For expository simplicity, assume that during this period Y is the only informed trader of any kind and there is no publicly released information relevant to the value of EDF's shares. Thus, if Y had not made these purchases, the NBB and NBO would have remained at or close to these levels throughout the two-week period. Instead, at the end of two weeks, EDF's NBB is $62.95 and its NBO is $63.05, with Y having paid an average of $61.55 for each of his shares. The engine passes the tests, and at the end of the two-week period, EDF announces the development, at which time the price jumps such that the NBB is $79.95 and the NBO is $80.05.

From the point of view of trading gains and losses, the analysis of who is helped and who is hurt as a result of Y's purchases during these two weeks is identical to the example of X's trading in ABC shares used in the ex post analysis of fundamental value informed trading, except that it is concentrated over two weeks instead of stretched over five months. The same is true of the analysis as to why the NBB and NBO each increased as a result of the informed purchases. Y appears to have a trading gain in the neighborhood of $18.5 million. Because trading is a zero-sum game, the gains and losses of all the other players in the market must aggregate to a loss of the same amount.[37] The liquidity suppliers would receive, and have executed against their quotes, 1,000,000 more buy orders than sell orders and thus would be short by 1,000,000 shares at the time the announcement of the engine development is made. As a result of Y's purchases, the liquidity suppliers sold, for an average of $61.55, 1,000,000 shares that are now valued by the market at $80.00; in other words, the liquidity traders' short positions translate into a loss equal to the same approximate $18.5-million gain enjoyed by Y.[38] For the uninformed traders as a group, the increase accompanying Y's purchases of $3.00 over time in the bid and offer is a wash, with sellers as a group being better off than if Y had not placed its orders, and buyers being equally worse off.

## 2. Ex ante perspective

Now consider the ex ante wealth effects of freely occurring issuer insider trading in longer-run competitive equilibrium, assuming again, not unrealistically, that all the players have unbiased (though not necessarily accurate) expectations concerning the prevalence of issuer insider informed trading.

### A. ISSUER INSIDERS

In a world with freely occurring issuer insider trading, an insider, as a result of her employment, gains the opportunity to obtain, and trade on, pieces of non-public information. In a competitive market for managerial talent, the expected value of this perquisite will reduce commensurately the aggregate value of the other components of her compensation package relative to a world without issuer insider trading. In either world, in equilibrium, the insider will receive a compensation package with the same total expected value and the shareholders will ultimately pay for this package. Thus, once again, the real normative question concerning the desirability of this type of informed trading relates to the efficiency of this kind of compensation, not to its fairness.

Having said this, it should be noted that the managerial labor market appears to be very sticky.[39] Therefore, a regulatory change that would allow an increase in the level of such trading would, for some period of time, enrich managers who have access to nonpublic issuer information. A regulatory change that would decrease the level of such trading would have the opposite effect.

## B. LIQUIDITY SUPPLIERS AND ANTI-MISTAKE TRADERS

The analysis for liquidity suppliers directly parallels the analysis for them with regard to fundamental value informed trading and announcement trading: freely occurring issuer insider informed trading will lead them to quote a wider bid-ask spread than if the practice were prohibited. Cross-country empirical studies suggest that difference in liquidity would be substantial. One study examined the 103 countries with stock markets in 2002 and found that laws against insider trading existed in 87 of them, with 38 of those countries having made at least one prosecution under their laws.[40] There was a significant reduction in firms' cost of capital, presumably reflecting greater share liquidity when a country first enforced an enacted prohibition against insider trading.[41] Freely occurring issuer insider trading, by widening the spread and hence increasing the cost of trading, would reduce the amount of liquidity supply demanded. Fewer resources being drawn into the liquidity supply business would reduce the rents paid to the suppliers of its specialized inputs.

## C. UNINFORMED TRADERS

The more significant conclusion, but one that flows from the identical analysis in the cases of fundamental value informed trading and announcement trading, is that uninformed traders are on average neither directly advantaged nor disadvantaged by the free occurrence of issuer insider informed trading. This again is because share prices are discounted to reflect the extent to which such trading increases the bid-ask spread, with the cost of this increased spread ultimately falling on entrepreneurs and early investors who face a higher cost of capital at the time of public offering because of this discount.

It is worth noting again, given the much more heated debate concerning this kind of informed trading, the illusory nature of some other losses and gains that some might say are experienced by uninformed traders. The typical uninformed seller in our example would likely regret her sale because, but for her sale of shares at some point during the two weeks of Y's purchases at an average price of $61.45 shares,[42] she would have been holding stock that could instead be sold for $79.95. Y's purchase, however, did not cause her to miss out on this jump in price, because she would have sold whether Y had traded or not.[43] So, her regret is not properly related to Y's purchases. Indeed, the average uninformed seller's price of $61.45 is $1.50 higher than it would have been but for

Y's purchases. From an ex ante point of view, however, this average $1.50 gain is as illusory as the regret, because the uninformed trader is just as likely to be a buyer as a seller when the price has been pushed up in this way.

D. FUNDAMENTAL VALUE INFORMED AND ANTI-MISTAKE TRADERS

Freely occurring issuer insider trading's widened bid-ask spread will increase the cost of business for fundamental value informed traders and thus will reduce the level of such trading, in essence crowding it out,[44] and thus reduce the resources going into this business and the rents paid to the suppliers of its specialized inputs.[45] The negative effect on the amount of information reflected in share prices can be serious: cross-country studies demonstrate a significant positive relationship between the effectiveness of a country's prohibition on issuer insider trading and a measure of the amount of information reflected in the share prices of its issuers.[46]

## B. Efficiency Effects: Claimed Social Benefits

The claimed positive efficiency effects of freely occurring issuer insider trading relate to price accuracy and its desirability as a form of managerial compensation.

### 1. Price accuracy effects

Trading by informed issuer insiders, like all informed trading, moves price in the direction the information's content implies. Thus, in this narrow sense, such trading makes prices more accurate. There is a serious question, however, as to whether it actually accelerates the reflection of already existing information in price. Even if it does, it generally advances the moment by which information gets reflected in price by very little, which renders the social gain, if any, insignificant.

A. DELAYING VERSUS ACCELERATING ISSUER DISCLOSURE

Freely occurring issuer insider trading may, in many cases, actually delay, not accelerate, the moment when existing information gets reflected in share prices.[47] Insiders would have an incentive to cause the issuer to delay disclosure of the information on which they are trading in order to maximize the profitability of their trades by slowly buying large amounts of stock.[48] Although these trades will move price in the right direction, typically only with public disclosure will the information be fully reflected in price.[49]

There is a response to this argument: insider trading might actually create incentives for faster public disclosure because once insiders' trading ceased, they want the information disclosed immediately and fully reflected in price. The insider can then close her position and take her full profits as quickly as possible,[50] thereby ending the risks associated with her concentrated position in the issuer's stock.

## B. UNIMPORTANCE OF ANY DELAY OR ACCELERATION

Ultimately, this debate is not very fruitful. The question of delay versus advance is an empirical one, and rigorous work on the issue is largely lacking. More fundamentally, the kind of insider trading that a prohibition can effectively catch, and that in the absence of prohibition would be most tempting, will probably be a trade shortly before an anticipated corporate announcement. Thus, the period over which price would be improved, whether accelerated or delayed, is going to be very brief in any case. As discussed above, when informed trading improves price accuracy for only a brief period of time, the acceleration will not have any important effects on enhancing the efficiency of the real economy.[51]

To explore this argument, we assembled a small dataset by coding SEC enforcement releases concerning insider trading. We studied two issues: First, what is the time lag between when the insider traders acquire their position and when the information on which they trade would have otherwise become public? Second, what is the informational content on which they typically trade? Based on results from 2016, covering insider trading on 90 separate events, we find that the time lag between the insider's initiating transaction and public disclosure of the event on which the insider traded ranges from one day to 101 days, with three days being the modal time lag between the unlawful transaction and public disclosure. The average lag is 25 days, and the median lag is 19 days. Interestingly, in the vast majority of enforcement actions, the information on which the insider trades concerns an impending acquisition. The few other pieces of nonpublic information involve asset acquisitions, earnings announcements, and licensing announcements. In other words, those insiders that the SEC actually prosecutes for illegal trading overwhelmingly trade on forms of information that they do not need incentives to carefully analyze and probe, and which would have become public soon in any event.

### 2. Managerial compensation

A second efficiency argument for issuer insider trading, again pioneered by Henry Manne, is that insider informed trading can serve as a particularly effective compensation arrangement to induce managers in large bureaucratic corporations to act more entrepreneurially.[52] If managers can freely profit from trading based on their knowledge of an issuer's future performance, they have additional incentives to achieve accomplishments that, when announced, will constitute the kind of good news that drives up the issuer's share price. However, this argument too is open to significant rebuttals.

## A. DISTORTED INCENTIVES TO CHOOSE RISK OVER EXPECTED RETURN

The managerial incentives provided by insider trading may in fact be neutral. Selling after undertaking undisclosed actions that will drive firm performance down is just as profitable as buying after undisclosed actions that will drive it up. Even if these bets against the firm could be fully deterred by rules such as Exchange Act § 16(c)'s prohibition on short selling by issuer officers and directors, this rebuttal is suggestive of another point: insider trading can incentivize managers to make the riskier decision—because of its bigger upside, even where the less risky choice would have a higher expected return and thus would be the better one for shareholders and for the efficiency of the economy as a whole.[53]

## B. INEFFICIENT ALLOCATION OF RISK

Allowing insider trading is an inherently risky form of compensation and as such allocates risk between managers and shareholders inefficiently.[54] An issuer is a wealth-generating entity whose residual returns, after paying for labor and other inputs, are shared between managers and shareholders. The returns on this wealth-generating entity are inherently volatile, with much of this volatility coming from firm-specific risk. The typical managerial compensation arrangement divides these volatile residuals up between managers and shareholders. At one extreme would be a straight fixed salary with no insider trading allowed. At the other extreme would be no salary but permission to engage in insider trading to the extent that the expected value of this right equals that of the straight salary. On an expected basis, each of these two compensation arrangements is equally costly to shareholders. In the first, the volatility in future residuals is fully borne by the shareholders. In the second, the shareholders bear only a portion of this volatility, with the rest being borne by the managers.

Shareholders are the more efficient bearers of this risk.[55] This is because they can diversify their portfolio of stock holdings and completely eliminate the firm-specific portion of the risk. Managers, in contrast, are already inherently undiversified, because they have developed substantial firm-specific human capital.[56] The firm-specific portion of the residual volatility that they take on with the insider trading arrangement, which also cannot be diversified away, just adds to the problem and will cause them disutility. Thus, managers will be willing to agree to a package with lower expected compensation if it does not include a risky insider trading right. Shareholders, because of their capacity to diversify, suffer no disutility from bearing this package's extra risk. Thus, a package without an insider trading component, if it can be effectively enforced, would be the one that both managers and shareholders would choose.

### C. POORLY FOCUSED REWARD FOR PERFORMANCE AND DISTORTED INTERNAL COMMUNICATIONS

The idea of insider trading profits as an effective compensation tool also suffers from being unrealistic because there is generally a low correlation between who is responsible for the accomplishments that, when announced, will constitute good news and who might be able to profit from trading in anticipation of the announcement. So, for instance, the head of a division responsible for a major development is likely to represent only one of many corporate insiders who will be aware of this news prior to its public disclosure and able to profit by trading on it. The result is a poorly focused incentive scheme where the person most responsible for corporate improvements will internalize only a small fraction of insider trading profits.

An insider trading enthusiast might try to rebut this concern by saying that it underestimates the extent to which management acts as a team and that positive accomplishments are the result of team, not individual, effort. True as this rebuttal may be, it only points to a potentially even more serious problem: the opportunity to inside-trade might result in corporate insiders working less effectively as a team. For instance, those acquiring information first may, rather than sending it immediately to others, hold back until they can maximize their own trading profits without the competition of these others.[57]

### 3. Efficiency considerations: social losses

Freely occurring issuer insider informed trading has substantial negative social effects. It has the same adverse impact on liquidity as does any other type of informed trading. As discussed, less liquidity reduces social welfare because of the resulting misallocation of resources over time and misallocation of risk.[58] It also significantly reduces the level of fundamental value informed trading, which we have concluded is a socially desirable activity.

Issuer insider informed trading has an additional social cost not present with fundamental value informed trading and announcement informed trading. Although we find that issuer insider informed trading is not unfair, much of the public feels that it is. This perception of unfairness is demoralizing: it harms people to think that a major social institution is corrupt. It also discourages direct and indirect ownership of equities by persons who, absent this perception, would find equities to be an investment vehicle that suits some of their needs, thereby blocking what would otherwise be welfare-improving transactions. Normally, the better response to public misunderstanding is education. This perception of unfairness may be very hard to eradicate, however, and a generally effective prohibition on insider trading is another way of dealing with the perception's unfortunate effects.

## C. Overall Policy Conclusions

The foregoing discussion strongly suggests that freely occurring informed trading by issuer insiders would be socially undesirable. Though the practice does not, as many believe, work a wealth-redistributing unfairness, it does generally lead to inefficiency. Both the share-price-accuracy and compensation-efficiency social benefit arguments for allowing such trading are unpersuasive. Also, as just recounted, its costly effects on liquidity clearly have a number of negative effects on efficiency, as does the widespread perception that it is unfair.

Four further questions must be addressed, however. First, is it necessary that informed trading by the insiders of all issuers be banned, or would this be better decided on an issuer-by-issuer basis? Second, does all trading based on inside information need to be banned, or just trades based on material information? Third, what are the social consequences of trades based on tippees of issuer insiders? Finally, do the conclusions concerning the social undesirability of trading by issuer insiders apply as well to issuers themselves?

### 1. Should issuers be able to consent to insider trading?

Nothing in this analysis so far suggests that it matters whether or not the issuer consents to the trading by its insiders. If the preceding analysis is correct with regard to every issuer, the claimed efficiency benefits are just as unpersuasive, and the negative efficiency effects are just as substantial, with or without the issuer's consent. We cannot be sure, however, that the preceding analysis is indeed correct as to every single issuer in the market. Thus, an argument can be made that each issuer should be able to adopt a policy allowing its insiders to trade, as long as the policy is publicly announced.[59]

The argument in favor of allowing each issuer to choose whether to ban its insiders from trading goes as follows. Suppose our conclusion that insider trading diminishes efficiency *is* in fact correct with respect to a given issuer. The market will price the issuer's stock lower if it nevertheless allows its insiders to trade. Because the entrepreneurs and original investors want as high a share price as possible when they take the issuer public, they would have strong incentives to impose a binding permanent prohibition on insider trading in its shares.[60] If, instead, the analysis is *incorrect* with respect to a given issuer, allowing insider trading would result in a higher share price at the time that the issuer goes public. In this event, the entrepreneurs and original investors would allow insider trading because they could get a higher price for their shares by doing so. In essence, the reaction of the market would force the persons taking the issuer public to absorb the loss if trading by its insiders is inefficient and to enjoy the gain if it is efficient. Thus, the market would guide these persons to the most efficient choice.

There is some force to this argument, but we are ultimately skeptical. One reason for skepticism is that there are probably substantial economies of scale in an effective enforcement mechanism against issuer insider informed trading.[61] So, if there are good reasons to believe that it is inefficient for most issuers, the restriction should apply to all.[62] Another reason relates to all companies that are already publicly traded. Even if allowing issuer insider informed trading would be inefficient at such a firm, its managers typically own only a small portion of the stock. They would likely have much more to gain from being able to inside-trade than they would lose from the decline in the value of their stock. If the managers have either the power to decide the question or a heavy influence on a shareholder vote on the question, firms will consent to allowing such trading even when it is socially undesirable for them to do so.

### 2. Insider trading on small bits of nonpublic information

As discussed, the reasons for finding issuer insider informed trading to be socially undesirable are strongest for a trade executed shortly before an anticipated corporate announcement. This is the kind of insider trading that a prohibition can most effectively catch and that, in the absence of prohibition, would be most tempting. It is also the kind with the poorest ratio of social benefits to social costs.

Consider, in contrast, a purchase by a corporate insider who concludes, based on a myriad of individually small pieces of nonpublic information about which she is inevitably aware, that the issuer's shares are worth more than the current market price. Her purchase will move the price in the direction of reflecting these many small pieces of information and thus make the price more accurate. Most of these pieces of information will probably never be disclosed, either voluntarily or pursuant to mandatory disclosure. This is because there are so many of them, each of which is individually of little importance. In addition, blanket disclosure of all these bits of information would often be unnecessarily harmful to the issuer's ability to compete. Absent insider trading based on this information, it will not be reflected in price until much later when the good or bad results that they predict materialize. Thus, allowing such trading is likely to improve price accuracy in ways that are meaningfully beneficial for the real economy.

The complaint that allowing this type of insider trading would incentivize managers to take risky decisions at the expense of expected return is also inapplicable to this kind of insider trading. In making purchases based on such information, managers would need to face both the upside and downside risks since they would need to make their purchases well before the results of their decisions were in.

There is considerable evidence that this kind of insider trading occurs and is profitable. Officers and directors are required under Exchange Act § 16(a) to report all purchases and sales. Presumably most officers and directors comply except for trades that violate Rule 10b-5. Officers and directors appear to make above-market returns on their reported purchases and sales of their own firms' shares that they report in their § 16(a) filings.[63]

### 3. Trading by tippees

A trade by a tippee of an issuer insider is no different in its negative effect on liquidity than a trade by the insider herself. Moreover, if the insider receives a benefit in return, or the satisfaction of making a gift to someone, allowing such tippee trading has just the same managerial incentive effects, good and bad, as allowing trades by the insider herself: the insider just gets the benefit or satisfaction instead of getting the profit from the trade. We have concluded that on balance these managerial incentive effects are negative. Things are even worse, though, if the tip is not a gift and no benefit is received by the insider. In that case the trade does not even serve as an alternative form of compensation that can reduce the size of other components of the compensation package. In sum, absent some additional considerations relevant to a particular case, informed trades by tippees are at least as socially undesirable as trades by insiders.

*4. Trading by an issuer possessing material information or by persons to whom it gives the information*

Trading by an issuer possessing material nonpublic information is socially undesirable. It has the same positive price accuracy effects and negative liquidity effects as trading by an issuer insider. This is a trade-off that we concluded involves a net social loss. There are no obvious other efficiency benefits when it is the issuer that is trading instead, and so the same conclusion should apply to this type of trading as well. In contrast, trading by an issuer that is not in possession of material nonpublic information but is, as would inevitably be the case, in possession of many bits of immaterial nonpublic information, is very similar to trading by insiders on the basis of immaterial nonpublic information and for the same reasons is probably socially desirable to allow.

We also concluded that trades by direct or indirect tippees of issuer insiders are socially undesirable. Again, the analysis behind this conclusion applies as well to trades made by outsiders authoritatively given such information by the issuer, whether directly or indirectly.

## IV. INSIDE INFORMATION: A NON-ISSUER SOURCE

Trades can also be based on confidential information relevant to predicting an issuer's future cash flows that is obtained from within an institution other than the issuer. This institution could be, for example, a potential acquirer of the issuer (or the potential acquirer's investment bank or law firm), a hedge fund or other institutional investor, or a financial research company. The analysis of the social desirability of such trades largely tracks the analysis of the desirability of trading based on information generated within the issuer, in particular the wealth transfer and fairness parts of the analysis. Ultimately, however, we will reach a somewhat different conclusion regarding this situation. We found trades based on material information generated within the issuer to be socially undesirable no matter who executes them. In contrast, we find many kinds of trades based on information generated within a non-issuer institution to be socially desirable. This difference in conclusions relates to how sensitive the generation of each of the two types of information is to the prospect of profits from trading on it. Specifically, most material information from within an issuer is the synergistic byproduct of the operations of the underlying business and thus will be generated whether or not the issuer or its insiders are allowed to trade on it—and it will be reflected in price soon in any event. Much of the information material to an issuer from within a non-issuer institution, however, would not be generated unless the institution, or others approved by it, are allowed to trade on the information.

## A. Socially Desirable Trades

Recall the definition of *fundamental value informed trading*: trading based on information generated by a person who gathers various bits of information that are publicly available or observable and analyzes them in a sophisticated way that enables a superior assessment of an issuer's cash flows to that implied by the current stock price. When an institution other than the issuer develops confidential material information about the issuer that enables such a superior assessment, it is very likely to be fundamental value information—indeed, sufficiently likely that it seems appropriate for our purposes here to classify all such information developed by a non-issuer institution as fundamental value information. Thus, in accordance with our earlier analysis, a trade by a non-issuer institution based on confidential material information that it has developed is socially desirable. It reduces liquidity with the consequent negative effects on efficiency in the same way that an issuer insider trade does. However, this efficiency loss is more than counterbalanced by the efficiency gains arising from the incentives that are created to do the hard work of generating price-accuracy-enhancing information and to get it reflected in price.[64]

Using the same logic, where the institution allows someone else, whether an insider or outside person, to trade on such information, this trade is socially beneficial as well. The institution can be expected to try to maximize the returns it can garner from generating such information by authoritatively deciding to whom (if anyone) to communicate the information and specifying the terms of its use, including whether it can be traded upon by the recipient; whether it can be recommunicated one or more times; and, if it can be recommunicated, the terms that each recommunicating person must impose on the recipient. The institution presumably authorizes such use only when it calculates that its benefits from doing so equal or exceed any resulting loss in its own trading profits.

This logic also applies as we contemplate the information being handed down through a chain of recipients. The more money the institution's direct recipient can make from trading on it or communicating it to yet others, the more consideration the direct recipient will be willing to provide the institution originally generating the information. If the direct recipient is permitted by the institution's terms to communicate the information to others, the direct recipient will go through the same calculations in determining its terms, and so on down the chain if further communications are allowed by the originating institution and each prior recipient. Thus, if there are one or more levels of authorized indirect recipients, there will be a whole network of agreements and duties specifying who is allowed to trade and under what conditions.[65] It is socially desirable to allow all the trades that are permitted pursuant to this network.

## B. Socially Undesirable Trades

Any trading not approved by this network of agreements and duties is socially undesirable. Such unapproved trading reduces liquidity, with the consequent negative efficiency effects, to the same extent as would trading by the outside institution itself or by trades approved by this network. But unlike trading by the institution or approved by this network, *unauthorized* trading creates no compensating, efficiency-enhancing incentives to gather and analyze price-accuracy-improving information.[66] Rather, the unapproved trade has the opposite effect, reducing the profitability of the institution's efforts to gather information and analyze it in a superior way. If the institution itself is planning to trade, the unapproved trades that precede the institution's trades makes the price of these trades less advantageous. There is also a reduction in profits from developing the information if the institution instead seeks to gain from selling the information to someone else who will trade on it or from simply publicly announcing the information. The information is less valuable to the purchaser if an unapproved person has already begun to move price in the indicated direction by trading on it first.

In sum, where the institution is allowed to provide confidential information to others to trade on or otherwise utilize, its incentives for generating such information are at least as great or greater than if it were the only one that could trade on the information. This depends, however, on the system of informed trading prohibitions that prevent trades outside of what is authorized by the resulting network of agreements and duties. The more effectively the prohibitions do this, the greater are the incentives of outside institutions to engage in the socially desirable practice of generating information that enhances share price accuracy.

## V. CONCLUSION

This chapter provides a general framework for analyzing the social desirability of different types of informed trading. Decades of debate surrounding insider trading have made both academics and the public widely familiar with one type of informed trading: information obtained from within a stock's issuer or other institution, generally known as insider trading. The universe of informed trading, however, is much larger.

Informed trading makes share prices more accurate, which enhances efficiency in the real economy. However, informed trading also, through the trading losses imposed on liquidity suppliers, makes markets less liquid, which is costly in efficiency terms. There is thus a fundamental trade-off in how informed trading affects the two principal social functions served by the stock market: accurate pricing and provision of liquidity.

We analyzed all of the distinct types of informed trading, and argued that doing so illuminates how the different types of private information nonetheless vary markedly in their social value. The trade-off between the social benefits from price accuracy and the social costs of decreased liquidity depends importantly on the time horizon for when the improvement in price accuracy would otherwise occur without the informed trade. Some types of informed trading, such as announcement trading, impose a social cost, through negative effects on liquidity, while creating no social benefit. Other forms of private information, such as fundamental value information, also impose a cost on liquidity, but create important positive social benefits in terms of the incentives they create for producing price-accuracy-improving information that then gets reflected in price. Trading based on various forms of confidential information from inside issuers and from inside other institutions can now be placed in a broader context, revealing that while some types are clearly undesirable, others may in fact be useful.

# Appendix A

## INSTANCES WHEN TRADING BY ISSUER INSIDERS ON MATERIAL NONPUBLIC INFORMATION WOULD LEAD TO GREATER EFFICIENCY IN THE REAL ECONOMY

A more nuanced analysis of trading by issuer insiders on nonpublic material information from within the issuer would recognize that there may be instances in which the resulting improvement in price accuracy can make a meaningful contribution to the efficiency of the real economy. This is illustrated by the following example. We ultimately still conclude, however, that on average such trading is socially disadvantageous and for this reason should be illegal.

The example works as follows. A firm starts with a value of $100 (the value of the expected future cash flows from its current assets discounted to present value) and has 100 shares outstanding. The value of these expected cash flows is fully understood by the market and so the firm's shares are priced at $1.00 ($100/100). The firm then develops two possible real investment project ideas. These are mutually exclusive projects, so only one of them will be implemented. Each project would require $300 to implement, which can only be raised by a public offering of new equity.

Project 1 would generate an additional expected future cash flow to the firm, discounted to present value, of $350. Thus, if implemented, the firm would have an expected value of $450 ($100 + $350), making the net present value (NPV) associated with implementing the project $50. Project 2 would generate an additional expected future cash flow to the firm, discounted to present value, of $400. Thus, if implemented, the firm would have an expected value of $500 ($100 + $400), making the NPV of the this latter project $100.

The prospects of Project 1 can be easily and credibly described to the market. The prospects of Project 2 will be more difficult to describe and any effort to do so will not be fully credible and will be met with a "talk is cheap" reaction. As a result, at the time of the equity offering that would be needed to fund Project 2, it will not be seen to add any more to the present value of future cash flows than its $300 cost. That is, the market will incorrectly see the NPV of Project 2 to be only $0, even though, based on the best information available that is held only by the firm, the project's NPV is really $100.

If the firm announces that it is pursuing Project 1, the market would instantly recognize that doing so will result in a firm with a total expected future cash flow discounted to present value of $450 ($100 + $350). The share price will rise to $1.50 because the market will know that the firm can raise the needed $300 to cover the project's costs by offering 200 shares, thereby increasing the total number outstanding to 300. In other words, it will foresee a firm with an expected value of $450 and with 300 shares outstanding. Accordingly, it will price shares at $450/300 = $1.50.

If the firm announces that it is pursuing Project 2, the market would at that moment believe that doing so will result in a firm with an expected future cash flow discounted to present value of $400 ($100 + $300). The share price will stay at $1.00 because the market will know, given this belief, that the firm can only raise the needed $300 to cover the project's costs by offering 300 shares, thereby increasing the number outstanding to 400. In other words, it will foresee a firm with an expected value of $400 with 400 shares outstanding. Accordingly, it will price shares at $400/400 = $1.00. However, the firm, based on its superior information, expects that, after the project has been implemented, its initial results will convince the market of the cash flow that can actually be expected to be generated by the project, at which point the price would rise to $1.25 ($500/400).

Under these circumstances, the firm would choose Project 1. This is the one that would make its current shareholders better off, even after allowing for the fact that the market would eventually have appreciated the greater expected cash flow promised by Project 2 and assuming that all current shareholders would continue to hold their shares at least until that point. This choice of Project 1 is socially unfortunate because, from a real-economy point of view, a more valuable use of society's scarce resources—represented by the $300 cost—would be Project 2, which transforms these resources into something worth $400 rather than $350.

If insider trading were allowed and a decision to implement Project 2 would result in enough such trading to stimulate price to rise to at least $1.29, the firm would instead in fact choose Project 2. This is because with a public offering of shares at $1.29 or more, the $50 greater addition to the value of the firm from choosing Project 2 has a greater positive effect on the ultimate share price than the negative effect from the dilution that occurs from offering shares at less than they are really worth. This can be seen by considering the following expression: $500/(100 + 300/p) > 1.50$. Solving this for $p$ shows that any $p$ greater than $1.286 will make the firm ultimately have a share price above $1.50 once the results of the implemented project convince the market of the project's actual expected cash flow.

This possibility—that trading by issuer insiders based on nonpublic material information from within the firm could in certain instances lead to firms making welfare-increasing investment decisions—does not, however, persuade us that such trading should be legal. Out of all the situations where insiders have valuable information to trade on, the circumstances when it would have this result appear to be fairly rare, as the assumptions behind the example suggest. Thus, we still think that on average the practice is socially disadvantageous, and for this reason should be illegal. This is because in most instances of the practice, as described in the text of this chapter, the social benefit from its positive effect on price accuracy is trivial but the social loss from its negative effect on liquidity is substantial. Also, from an administrative point of view, it would be difficult to define the boundaries of an exception to a general prohibition. A general exception for insiders of any firm soon to engage in an equity offering would create a carte blanche for trades that are really based on any kind of material inside information. It might also lead to a defense for trades solely for the manipulative purpose of raising the offering price.

# The Regulation of Informed Trading **SIX**

As noted in the introduction to chapter 5, the level of informed trading of various types is affected in the United States and elsewhere by an amalgam of legal rules. These rules directly prohibit some types of informed trades and indirectly discourage or encourage others. In this chapter, we explore this pattern of regulatory impacts to see how close what is prohibited or discouraged comes to what our preceding analysis suggests are the socially undesirable informed trades and how close what is encouraged comes to what we argue are the socially desirable ones. Four types of legal rules are considered: rules that outright prohibit certain kinds of informed trades; rules that require, under certain circumstances, the return of profits from the informed trader to the issuer of the shares; mandatory disclosure rules; and rules governing the structure of the markets for secondary trading.

## I. RULES PROHIBITING CERTAIN INFORMED TRADES

The most prominent U.S. prohibition of certain informed trades emerged out of the courts' and SEC's interpretation of Exchange Act § 10(b) and Rule 10b-5 promulgated thereunder.[1] After an exploration of the history and current reach of these prohibitions, we will consider, in subsequent sections, the use of New York's Martin Act to stop certain informed trades and two comprehensive statutory schemes for regulating informed trading: the EU's Market Abuse Directive and the proposed U.S. Insider Trading Prohibition Act.

## A. Section 10(b) and Rule 10b-5: History of Development of the Current Law

The Exchange Act is the primary statute in the United States regulating the secondary trading of securities. No provision of the Exchange Act, including § 10(b), explicitly prohibits any kind of informed trading as such. Section 10(b) simply prohibits certain "manipulative or deceptive device[s] or contrivance[s] in contravention of" rules and regulations prescribed by the SEC "as necessary or appropriate in the public interest or for the protection of investors."[2] The SEC promulgated Rule 10b-5 in 1943 pursuant to § 10(b), but that rule too contains no explicit prohibition of any type of informed trading. The closest it comes to doing so is to prohibit, "in connection with the purchase or sale of any security," employing "any device, scheme, or artifice to defraud" or engaging "in any act, practice, or course of business which operates or would operate as a fraud or deceit upon any person."[3] A brief history of the evolving interpretation of these phrases in the statute and the rule can help explain Rule 10b-5's current, rather jury-rigged, set of prohibitions on certain types of informed trading.

### 1. The early history of the development of the doctrine

It was thirty years after the passage of the Exchange Act and more than twenty years after the promulgation of Rule 10b-5 before either the SEC or a court rendered the first opinion holding that § 10(b) could be violated by some kind of informed trading on a secondary trading venue. This opinion, by the SEC in *Cady, Roberts & Co.*,[4] related to the appropriateness of a Rule 10b-5-based disciplinary action against a broker who received nonpublic information from a company's director that the company was about to announce a dividend cut. The broker, ahead of the announcement, quickly sold the company's shares for various accounts over which he had discretion.[5] The source of the information— the director—was apparently under a reasonable, but mistaken, belief that the news was already public and phoned the broker to find out the market reaction. Not reaching the broker, he left a message that effectively communicated the cut.[6] The Commission ruled that a person who has a special relationship with a company and is privy to its internal affairs, violates Rule 10b-5 if she trades in its stock without disclosing any material nonpublic information in her possession.[7] The broker was a partner in a brokerage firm for which the dividend-cutting company's director was a registered representative, and this connection with the company was enough to find the needed relationship.[8]

Four years later, the Second Circuit, in dicta in *SEC v. Texas Gulf Sulphur Co.*,[9] citing *Cady Roberts*, dispensed with the need for a relationship with the issuer, an interpretation that greatly expanded the range of persons whose informed trades would violate Rule 10b-5. The court stated "*anyone* in possession of material inside information must either disclose it to the investing public or . . . must abstain from trading in or recommending the securities concerned while such inside information remains undisclosed."[10]

### 2. Chiarella and its aftermath

The Second Circuit's very broad dicta in *Texas Gulf Sulphur* was rejected twelve years later by the Supreme Court in *Chiarella v. United States*, which held that "a duty to disclose under § 10(b) does not arise from the mere possession of nonpublic market information."[11] The defendant, Chiarella, learned of several yet-to-be-announced hostile tender offers from his work at a financial printing firm preparing the offering documents. Chiarella's employment contract pledged him to keep confidential, and not to trade on, what he learned at work. He nevertheless purchased shares of each target and resold them for a predictably higher price after the offer's announcement. The district court found Chiarella guilty of a criminal violation of Rule 10b-5 and sentenced him to a year in prison, which the Second Circuit upheld. Chiarella then appealed to the Supreme Court.

At the Supreme Court level, each of the Supreme Court Justices in the *Chiarella* case appears to have believed that more than mere possession of material nonpublic information was necessary for a trader to violate Rule 10b-5. A majority, based on the narrow holding that mere possession was not enough, voted to reverse the Second Circuit's affirmation of the convictions. The nine Justices splintered, however, on how much more than mere possession was needed and whether evidence of whatever more the particular Justice Chiarella believed was needed was presented to the jury in this case.

#### A. THE CLASSICAL THEORY OF INSIDER TRADING

Justice Powell was joined by three other Justices in his opinion setting out the "classical theory" of insider trading. Under this theory, there needs to be "a relationship of trust and confidence between the parties to a transaction."[12]

Powell stated that Chiarella had no such relationship with the sellers of the target companies' securities and that "[h]e was, in fact, a complete stranger, who dealt with the sellers only through impersonal market transactions."[13]

## B. THE MISAPPROPRIATION AND STRUCTURAL ACCESS THEORIES

Justice Burger's dissent set out the "misappropriation theory" of insider trading. Under this theory, trading by someone not in such a relationship with his counterparty nevertheless violates Rule 10b-5 if he trades on material nonpublic information that he has "misappropriated."[14] Applying this theory, Burger believed Chiarella violated Rule 10b-5 because the breach of his confidentiality agreement with his employer meant his trades were based on misappropriated information.[15] Two other Justices, Stevens and Brennan, expressed a willingness to entertain the misappropriation theory, but joined the part of Justice Powell's opinion reversing the conviction based on the narrow holding that mere possession while trading was not enough for a violation. They did so because they did not believe the misappropriation theory had been presented to the jury.[16]

Justice Blackmun, joined by Justice Marshall, set out in a separate dissent yet a third theory of insider trading, "structural access." Under this theory, trading on material nonpublic information by someone who was neither in a relationship of trust and confidence with the other party, nor was trading on the information in violation of a duty owed to some third party, would nevertheless violate Rule 10b-5 if she obtained the information as the result of a "structural informational advantage."[17]

A clear majority in *Chiarella* believed that not only was mere possession insufficient, mere structural access was insufficient as well. The status of the misappropriation theory, however, was unclear. This uncertainty was finally resolved by the Court seventeen years later in the *O'Hagan* case.[18] The defendant, O'Hagan, was a lawyer who learned of the confidential plans of his firm's client to engage in a hostile tender offer and purchased the proposed target's shares. O'Hagan was convicted in a trial based on the misappropriation theory. The majority opinion, written by Justice Ginsburg, affirmed the conviction, holding that a Rule 10b-5 violation "may be predicated on the misappropriation theory"[19] and found that trading on nonpublic material information violates Rule 10b-5 where the trade was "in breach of a duty [of loyalty and confidentiality] owed to the source of the information."[20]

## C. TIPPER AND TIPPEE LIABILITY FOR INFORMATION COMING FROM WITHIN THE ISSUER

The tipper/tippee situation arises when there is trading by a person (the recipient) who learns material nonpublic information, directly or indirectly, from a person (the source) who, if she traded on it herself, would, as an insider to the issuer, violate Rule 10b-5. Consider first where the source is an insider of the *issuer*, the recipient has no connection with the issuer, and the insider source willingly, but without the issuer's permission, provides the information to the recipient. The insider source would violate Rule 10b-5 if she herself traded in the stock because she would be regarded as being in a relationship of trust and confidence with the issuer's shareholders.[21] But it is the recipient, not the source, who is trading. The recipient has no special relationship of trust and confidence with either the persons with whom he deals or with the source. So, at first blush, neither the tip by the source, nor the trade by the recipient, would appear to violate Rule 10b-5 under either the classical theory or the misappropriation theory.

Justice Powell, in dictum in his *Chiarella* opinion, found an inventive way around this problem. He suggested that the insider source, who is deemed to be in such a relationship with the issuer's shareholders, breaches her duty to these shareholders by providing the information to someone likely to trade on it, and the recipient, by trading on it, becomes a "participant after the fact" in the source's breach.[22] This theory became the basis of a holding three years later in *Dirks v. SEC*, where Justice Powell, writing for the majority, held that "a tippee assumes a fiduciary duty to the shareholders of a corporation not to trade on material nonpublic information only when the insider has breached his fiduciary duty to the shareholders by disclosing his information to the tippee and the tippee knows or should know that there has been a breach."[23]

In *Dirks*, however, Powell added another wrinkle that went beyond his dictum in *Chiarella*. He concluded that a breach of duty to the shareholders requires that the tipper "personally . . . benefit, directly or indirectly, from [her] disclosure,"[24] not just that the transfer of information was in violation of the issuer's determination that it be kept confidential. Thus, for the source to violate Rule 10b-5, she must have this personal benefit, and for the direct recipient to violate the Rule, he must be aware of this benefit. The personal benefit requirement is also met, however, when the information is a gift to a relative or friend.[25] Justice Powell apparently added the personal benefit requirement to avoid chilling analyst interviews, which he regarded as socially beneficial.[26] Without it, the source and the recipient in such an interview could each violate Rule 10b-5 when they mistakenly thought that the information was not material or was already public.[27]

Now consider trades by more remote tippees: those who receive the information directly or indirectly from the direct recipient. They can violate Rule 10b-5 in either of two ways. One is where the trader is aware of the breach by the original source, including the source's personal benefit. Such a trader is as much a participant after the fact in the breach by the original source of his duty to the issuer's shareholders as would be a direct recipient who trades.[28] The other way is when the trader has a relationship with the person providing him the information that imposes on the trader a duty of confidentiality. The trade, as a breach of the recipient's duty to this provider, is a Rule 10b-5 violation based on the misappropriation theory, a violation that does not depend on his knowledge concerning the original breach by the insider.[29]

In *Salman v. United States*, the Supreme Court elaborated upon the gift branch of the personal benefit test in ways particularly relevant to remote tippees.[30] The tipper and the direct tippee in this case were brothers who each pled guilty to a Rule 10b-5 violation. There was evidence that they had a close relationship. The defendant, Salman, was the tipper's brother-in-law and, as part of a close extended family, received the information from the direct tippee and traded upon it. Thus, he was obviously aware of the relationship between the tipper and direct tippee. He also knew the tipper was the origin of the information on which he traded. Salman argued that he had not violated Rule 10b-5, however, because there was no evidence that the tipper received anything of a pecuniary or similarly valuable nature in exchange for the information, evidence that Salman said was required by some of the language in the recent Second Circuit decision in *U.S. v. Newman*,[31] which had been decided shortly before. Salman was found guilty at trial and his conviction was upheld by the Ninth Circuit. The Supreme Court granted certiorari on the question of whether the *Dirks* personal benefit test "require[s] proof of 'an exchange that is objective, consequential, and represents at least a potential gain of a pecuniary or similarly valuable nature,' as the Second Circuit held in [*Newman*] ..., or is it enough that the insider and the tippee shared a close family relationship," as the Ninth Circuit held in this case.[32]

In its unanimous opinion, the Court cleared up some confusing language in *Newman* that appeared to eliminate altogether the gift branch of the *Dirks* personal benefit test.[33] Equally important, it addressed the question of what kind of evidence is sufficient for a jury to infer that the source received a personal benefit in the form of making a gift. It concluded that evidence of the existence of a close family or friendship relationship—all that Salman appeared to know—was by itself sufficient.[34]

D. TIPPER AND TIPPEE LIABILITY FOR INFORMATION COMING FROM WITHIN AN INSTITUTION OTHER THAN THE ISSUER

Now consider information that comes from within an institution *other than the issuer*. As a first hypothetical, suppose that the source owes a duty to this institution to keep the information confidential and not trade on it; the recipient has no relationship with either the institution or the source; and the source willingly, but without authority, provides the information to the recipient, who trades on it. The source in this hypothetical has violated Rule 10b-5: the breach of the confidentiality duty is a misappropriation that is in connection with the purchase or sale of a security because the tip was provided to someone likely to trade on it.[35] If the recipient is aware of the breach by the source, he too violates Rule 10b-5 as a participant after the fact in the source's breach.[36]

As a second hypothetical, suppose again that the source owes a duty to the institution to keep the information confidential and not to trade on it, and may, or may not, be authorized to provide it to the recipient. The recipient, who trades on it, has no relationship with the institution but does have a duty of confidentiality to the source. The trade breaches this duty and is thus a straightforward Rule 10b-5 violation under the misappropriation theory. It does not matter whether or not the communication was unauthorized and, if it was, that the recipient was aware of this fact.

More remote tippees who trade on the information or tip themselves may, depending on the particular circumstances, violate Rule 10b-5 based on various possible combinations and permutations of the participant after the fact and misappropriation theories as they might be applied to the persons in the chain in a way similar to these two hypotheticals.

One issue remains unresolved with regard to cases where the misappropriator is not a trader, but a tipper. Significant disagreement exists among the circuit courts concerning whether the tipping misappropriator must receive a "personal benefit" for there to be a Rule 10b-5 violation, as is required under *Dirks* for tippers from within the issuer.[37] The Second Circuit historically did not require that a tipping misappropriator receive a personal benefit to violate Rule 10b-5 and, despite recent dicta going the other way, still arguably has no direct holding that a personal benefit is required.[38] The First Circuit has, in its own words, "dodged the question."[39] The Eleventh Circuit has held that a personal benefit *is* required in misappropriation cases, and that may be the trend in more recent cases.[40] As discussed below in our evaluation of Rule 10b-5's informed trading prohibitions, we believe that imposing this added test is doctrinally unnecessary and leaves a large number of socially undesirable trades beyond the prohibitions of Rule 10b-5.[41]

### E. INFORMED TRADING BY AN ISSUER

The prevailing view in the lower courts is that issuers themselves are prohibited under Rule 10b-5 from trading in their shares based on their own nonpublic material information. The leading case is *Shaw v. Digital Equipment Corp.*,[42] where the court said that "Courts, including this one, have treated a corporation trading in its own securities as an 'insider' for purposes of the 'disclose or abstain' rule."[43] As discussed in chapter 5, such a prohibition is good policy. The Supreme Court, however, has never addressed this question and the prohibition is difficult to justify in terms of the Court's doctrinal foundations in this area. It certainly could not be justified under the misappropriation theory and it does not fit easily under the classical theory either. It is a stretch under corporate law to say that the corporation itself, as opposed to its insiders, owes fiduciary-like duties to its shareholders.[44]

## B. Section 10(b) and Rule 10b-5: Evaluation

How does the reach of Rule 10b-5's prohibitions on informed trading compare with what the analysis in chapter 5 suggests are the socially undesirable informed trades?

### 1. Fundamental value informed trading

We have concluded that fundamental value informed trading is socially desirable. Consistent with this recommendation, fundamental value informed trading is not prohibited by Rule 10b-5. It is not a violation under the classical theory because there is no relationship of trust and confidence between a fundamental value informed trader and the person with whom she transacts. It is also not a violation under the misappropriation theory: the fundamental value informed trader develops the information herself based on collecting bits of publicly available information and so there is no breach of a duty of confidentiality to the information's source as required under that theory.[45]

### 2. Announcement information

We concluded that announcement informed trading is socially undesirable. Announcement trading is not prohibited by Rule 10b-5 because it involves trading on information that is, as a literal matter, publicly available. A new law imposing an outright ban on announcement trading is probably impractical: it would be difficult to define in legal terms what the reach of the prohibition should be in a way that would actually diminish the practice without at the same time chilling socially desirable trading. However, it can be reduced, as discussed later, by rules relating to the structure of market trading and to the timing of issuer announcements.

## 3. Inside information: the issuer as source

We concluded that trades based on material nonpublic information from within an issuer are, as a general matter, socially undesirable. This conclusion includes trades by the issuer itself and by issuer insiders and by their direct and indirect tippees. Consent from the issuer is irrelevant. As reviewed earlier, existing interpretations of Rule 10b-5 clearly prohibit such trades by the issuer and its insiders.[46] The status of direct and indirect tippees is more complex.

As we have seen, under *Dirks*, the Supreme Court finds some, but not all, selective disclosures of material nonpublic information from inside an issuer to be Rule 10b-5 violations, and the same with respect to some, but not all, trades by outsiders based on these disclosures. For the tip by the insider to be a violation, it must be a breach of duty to the issuer's shareholders. This requires a violation of the insider's duty to the corporation to keep the information confidential and, in addition, that the insider receive a personal benefit. The trade of the outsider recipient is a violation only if it makes her a "participant after the fact" in the insider's breach.[47] This requires that she be aware of both the duty of confidentiality violation and the insider's personal benefit.[48]

The personal benefit test is an additional wrinkle added by Justice Powell in the *Dirks* case, apparently out of a fear of chilling analyst interviews. Our analysis in chapter 5 makes us sympathetic to the concern that imposing liability on either the insider tipper, or the outsider tippee, when the insider receives no personal benefit for passing on material information, is likely to chill analyst interviews. The starting point for understanding this concern is to note that an analyst interview can give rise to either of two bases for profitable trading. One basis is where the interview reveals a large number of individually *immaterial* pieces of nonpublic information that the analyst can use to develop a superior analysis of a stock's value. For trades motivated by this basis, the social gain from the resulting price-accuracy improvements is likely to be greater than the social loss from the decline in liquidity. This conclusion holds whether the number of such immaterial bits is small or large. It rests on reasoning identical to the reasoning behind our conclusions in chapter 5 that there is a net social gain associated with fundamental value informed trading (which involves doing the same kind of analysis, but with publicly available or observable immaterial pieces of information).[49]

The second basis for an interview generating a trade is the revelation of a piece of *material* nonpublic information. A trade on this basis would have exactly the same impact on price accuracy and liquidity as a trade by an insider based on the same information, a trade which we have concluded involves a net social loss and should be prohibited. Determining whether or not to punish this second type of interview-generated trades—the socially undesirable ones based on material information—depends, however, on the effect of such punishment on the level of the first type of interview-generated trades—the socially desirable ones based on an analysis of immaterial information. We believe that if analyst interviews are unfettered by fear of liability (absent a personal benefit to the issuer spokesperson), there will be many more of them and that there will be a substantial increase in the first type of trades and only a modest increase in the second type of trades. This is because the protection arising from a lack of personal benefit only extends to unauthorized disclosures[50] and so they likely only occur by accident.[51] Thus, we think that with unfettered interviews, the net social gains from trades motivated by the first basis will be greater than the net social losses from trades motivated by the second basis. This said, using a personal benefit test of some kind is best paired with a provision, such as Regulation FD (discussed later in this chapter), that in essence prohibits a firm from the intentional selective disclosure of material information when it is likely to be traded upon and requires immediate public disclosure of such information if the firm discovers an inadvertent selective disclosure of such information.

The current law's imposition of the personal benefit test in tipper/tippee cases is one way of engaging in the doctrinal gymnastics of converting, as best one can, an anti-fraud rule into a policy-based regulation of informed trading capable of protecting analyst interviews. If the only choices were to retain or to eliminate the rule, we would choose to retain it for this reason. As discussed later, however, we believe that the test too often provides defenses for indirect tippees trading on such information: trades that are just as socially undesirable as ones by an insider based on the same information. We advocate an approach that presents much less of this problem, while still not chilling analyst interviews and while continuing to respect the doctrinal foundations laid down by Supreme Court in *Chiarella*.

### 4. Inside information: a non-issuer source

Now consider material nonpublic information relevant to predicting the future cash flows paid to the holders of an issuer's shares that comes from within an institution other than the issuer. The starting point is that, unlike trading by an issuer based on its own nonpublic material information, trading by a non-issuer institution based on non-public material fundamental value information that it developed or acquired is both socially desirable and perfectly legal. We, however, concluded in chapter 5 that trading by anyone else who, directly or indirectly, acquires this information is socially undesirable, but, unlike trading based on information from within the issuer, only when the source—the non-issuer institution—has failed to give permission. The reach of Rule 10b-5's prohibitions on trades based on such information generally includes the trades we believe are socially undesirable and leaves untouched the socially desirable ones. Again, the one problematic area relates to tippers and tippees, especially indirect tippees.

## A. TRADING AND TIPPING BY INSIDERS OF AN INSTITUTION OTHER THAN THE ISSUER AND TRADING BY THE DIRECT OUTSIDE RECIPIENTS OF THE TIP.

Under the misappropriation theory, approved by the Supreme Court's majority opinion in *O'Hagan*, trading on nonpublic material information originating from an institution other than the issuer violates Rule 10b-5 when the trade involves a breach of a duty of confidentiality.[52] Thus, when an insider of the institution, with its permission, trades or provides the information to others, there is no violation because there is no breach of a confidentiality duty. Similarly, when an agent of the institution in an authorized way provides such information to an outside recipient who trades on it or passes it on to others to trade on, there is no Rule 10b-5 violation because there is no breach by the insider with respect to which the recipient could be a participant after the fact. The exception to this would be a situation in which the outside recipient agreed to keep the information confidential or is otherwise in a relationship with the institution that imposes a duty of confidentiality—circumstances that would impose liability without reliance on the participant-after-the-fact theory.

## B. PROVIDING COHERENCE TO THE MISAPPROPRIATION THEORY

Although we approve of the results in the Supreme Court's decision in *O'Hagan* affirming the misappropriation theory, the majority opinion justified the decision in part by saying that the prohibited trades are harmful to others in the market.[53] This justification is incoherent because trades based on the same information that are approved by the non-issuer institution are equally harmful to others in the market. Yet, these trades do not violate Rule 10b-5 under the misappropriation theory, a point made forcefully by Justice Thomas in dissent.[54] The analysis here provides an alternative, more coherent justification for the distinction between the transactions prohibited by the theory and those not prohibited. Each of these two kinds of trades, by decreasing liquidity, causes the same amount of harm to other market participants. The transactions prohibited by the theory discourage production of and trading upon fundamental value information, whereas the transactions permitted by the theory encourage these socially valuable activities.

## C. TIPPERS AND TIPPEES OF INFORMATION FROM WITHIN A NON-ISSUER ENTITY

Now consider information originating from an institution other than the issuer that, without the institution's authority, is selectively disclosed by one of its insiders or by a person owing the institution a duty of confidentiality. Assume also that trading upon the information is predictable and that the direct or indirect recipient who trades on it owes no duty of confidentiality to the institution or to any person in the chain through which it reached him.

As analyzed in chapter 5, the prospect of such trades reduces the incentives of outside institutions to produce such socially useful information. Such trades are thus socially undesirable. An optimal rule would prohibit any such trade when the trader knows, or should know, that the information was confidential, came originally from within the institution, and was selectively disclosed by an insider without the institution's authority. This optimal rule should not pose a challenge to the Supreme Court's Rule 10b-5 doctrinal foundations. The insider's original disclosure of the information without authority violates Rule 10b-5 under the misappropriation theory because it involves a breach of a confidentiality duty to the institution in connection with a predictable purchase or sale of a security. The trade makes the trader a participant after the fact to this breach.

As noted earlier, however, there is disagreement among the circuits: some courts have sought to add the personal benefit test—a test that was originally developed for issuer insider tippers—as an additional requirement. We think that inserting the personal benefit test into the misappropriation theory is seriously misguided as a matter of both policy and doctrine.[55] The central factual issue under the misappropriation theory is whether the insider of the non-issuer institution breached a duty of confidentiality to it by tipping or trading. When he has, it means that the institution has not waived this duty, although it could have done so. This institution thus finds the insider's conduct disadvantageous whether or not the insider benefited personally, so allowing trading when there is no personal benefit is just as harmful to incentives to do fundamental value research as when there is a personal benefit. The Supreme Court added the personal benefit requirement in *Dirks* for a policy reason that is inapplicable to non-issuer-information cases: namely, the fear that socially valuable analyst interviews will otherwise be chilled, rather than a more general concern with the flow of information in markets. Insiders of companies considering hostile takeovers, financial printers, law firms, or investment banking firms do not give socially valuable interviews to market analysts about the future prospects of companies about which they have knowledge, and the engagement of issuer representatives with other participants in the market ecosystem has a far more general role than engagement between non-issuers and the market. Likewise, there is no social role to spouses sharing confidences with their mates. Adding the personal benefit test in these kinds of cases leaves many socially undesirable trades beyond the reach of Rule 10b-5's prohibitions for no good reason.

## C. The Way Forward Under Rule 10b-5

Overall, the current reach of Rule 10b-5 conforms reasonably closely to what is recommended in chapter 5. Fundamental value informed trading, which we find socially desirable, is permitted. Announcement trading, which we find undesirable, is also permitted, but we do not believe that an outright prohibition is the best way of dealing with announcement trading. Rule 10b-5's current reach prohibits trading by *issuer* insiders based on *material* nonpublic information from within the issuer. This is consistent with our findings that such trades are on average socially undesirable and that it is not administratively practical to distinguish the desirable from the undesirable trades based on the nature of the information, the timing of the trade, or the issuer's particular circumstances. The current reach of Rule 10b-5 permits trades by *issuer* insiders based on *im*material nonpublic information from inside the issuer: trades which we find on average to be socially desirable. We also find to be socially undesirable *unauthorized* trading in an issuer's shares by an insider of an *entity other than the issuer* based on *material* nonpublic information from within that entity. This trading too is prohibited under Rule 10b-5's current reach.

The one problematic area with respect to the regulation of trading based on both types of inside information is the current law's application of Rule 10b-5 to tippers and tippees. In terms of its direct impact on liquidity and price accuracy, a trade by a tippee, whether direct or indirect, is just as socially desirable or undesirable as if the trade were instead undertaken by the insider herself. Ideally then, as a policy matter, there should be a blanket prohibition on all tippee trades (and the tipping that led to them) where the trade would have been prohibited if instead the inside tipper herself had been the trader.[56] The one exception would be a trade by an analyst (or the entity that employs him) who receives material nonpublic information in an interview with an insider when granting the overall interview is within the insider's authority but not the disclosure of the particular piece of nonpublic information. Although such a trade is just as socially undesirable as if the insider had made it, we concluded in chapter 5 that it should be shielded from punishment in order to avoid chilling analyst interviews.

Rule 10b-5's prohibitions on tippee trading, based on existing court interpretations, fall short of this ideal. As for trading by outsiders based on information originating from within the issuer, the personal benefit rule protects from punishment far more such trades than should be protected to avoid the chilling of analyst interviews. As for trading by outsiders based on information originating from within an entity other than the issuer, courts have been increasingly applying the personal benefit rule in determining whether there has been a Rule 10b-5 violation. Doing so is not justified for policy reasons because punishing such trades would in no way chill analyst interviews.

These existing interpretations of Rule 10b-5 are not written in stone, however. They are the product of a common law process that will continue to evolve. The challenge going forward is to shape the future evolution of the law in a direction that comes as close as possible to the ideal set out in this section, while also paying due deference to the doctrinal roots of the process.

### 1. Problems with the existing law concerning trading by outsiders based on information originating from within the issuer of the traded shares

We have seen that under existing case law, a person outside of an issuer who trades shares on the basis of material nonpublic information originating from within the issuer and who owes no independent duty of confidentiality to his information source cannot be found in violation of Rule 10b-5 unless the government or other plaintiff can show that the trader knew both that (i) the insider source, in communicating the information to someone outside the issuer, breached her duty to the issuer to keep the information confidential, and (ii) the insider source received a personal benefit from doing so.[57]

This requirement to show personal benefit will usually not pose a significant obstacle for the government or other plaintiff to establish a Rule 10b-5 violation in cases where there is in fact such a personal benefit and it takes the form of a *gift*. However, it poses a more significant obstacle where the benefit instead takes the form of a *quid pro quo*, especially in cases against indirect tippees.

#### A. PERSONAL BENEFIT IN THE FORM OF A GIFT

The government or a private plaintiff should usually not face great difficulty in showing that an insider tipper enjoyed a personal benefit by making a gift when this is in fact the case.

Where the insider tipper did in fact enjoy a personal benefit but it was in the form of making a gift to the direct tippee, the government or other plaintiff will usually not have much difficulty making the required showing of this fact. This is true whether the defendant is the direct tippee or an indirect tippee.

Consider first a case against a direct tippee. In *Salman*, the Supreme Court decided that evidence of the existence of a close family or friendship relationship is, by itself, sufficient for a jury to infer that the insider tipper was making a gift of a kind that satisfies the personal benefit test.[58] Because people do not tend to do random acts of kindness, most gift cases presumably involve such a relationship. Where such a relationship exists and the case is against the initial tippee, the tippee would obviously be aware of the relationship because he would be a party to it. Therefore, under *Salman*, simply showing the existence of the relationship should be sufficient to show the outsider recipient's knowledge of the gift and hence the insider's personal benefit.

Things should not be a great deal more difficult for the government or other plaintiff when the action is instead against an indirect tippee, and the insider tipper and the initial tippee have a close family or friendship relationship. Any indirect tippee who knows enough to have good reason to believe that the original source of the information was an insider and that the information is reliable would be unlikely to have come to these conclusions without also knowing about the existence of the relationship between the insider and the initial tippee.[59] Again, evidence that the indirect tippee knew of this relationship is sufficient under *Salman* to show the indirect tippee's knowledge that the insider's tip was a gift and hence the insider enjoyed a personal benefit.

## B. PERSONAL BENEFIT IN THE FORM OF A QUID PRO QUO

Now consider the situation in which the insider tipper enjoyed a personal benefit, but it was in the form of a quid pro quo—such as the sharing of profits with his initial recipient or the prospect of reciprocal tips. The government or other plaintiff will often have much more trouble making the required showing of a personal benefit. If the defendant is the direct tippee, she would clearly be aware of the benefit that she conferred upon the insider, but evidence establishing that she gave such a benefit is often hard for the government or other plaintiff to obtain. The problem is compounded in the case of an indirect tippee. Not only does the government or other plaintiff need to find sufficient evidence that the direct tippee provided the tipper with a quid pro quo, it must also show that the indirect tippee had actual knowledge of this fact. This will not be possible in many cases. It is again true that the tip is unlikely to impel the indirect tippee to trade unless he has good reason to believe that the original source of the information is an insider and that the information is reliable. The indirect tippee, however, can easily acquire sufficient facts to come to these conclusions without acquiring any facts specifying that the insider received a quid pro quo from the initial tippee (even though he might well speculate that this is the case).

## 2. An alternative approach to outsiders trading on information originating from within the issuer

To solve the problems described in the preceding subsection, we propose an alternative approach that involves a reversal of the evidentiary burden concerning personal benefit. Relative to the current court interpretations of Rule 10b-5, this alternative will likely subject to punishment many more trades by direct and indirect tippees based on material nonpublic information coming from within the issuer and hence deter far more such trades from occurring. Yet it should be no less protective of analyst interviews than is current law. This alternate approach is also equally consistent with the doctrinal foundations laid out in *Chiarella* concerning the application of Rule 10b-5 to informed trading as are current court interpretations.

### A. THE SUBSTANCE OF THE ALTERNATIVE APPROACH: THE INSIDER TIPPER AND THE DIRECT TIPPEE

Under the alternative approach, the insider source would be found to violate Rule 10b-5 if she disclosed to an outsider nonpublic material information likely to be traded upon *unless* the insider provides persuasive evidence that the reason she did so was *not* for a *Dirks*-type personal benefit. Similarly, if the direct tippee knows, or has good reason to believe, that the information came from an insider source and trades on the information (or tips it to someone else likely to trade on it), he would be found to have violated Rule 10b-5 unless he provides the same kind of persuasive evidence that the insider tipper had a reason other than personal benefit for disclosing.

When an issuer insider makes a selective disclosure to an outsider of material nonpublic information that she can expect will be traded upon, there must be some reason motivating the disclosure. Four possible reasons largely exhaust the possibilities. Three relate to disclosure of information when the issuer deemed it should be kept confidential with respect to anyone who might trade on it: (1) an expectation of a quid pro quo, (2) an intention to benefit the outsider initial recipient, and (3) any other motivation for the disclosure of the information. A fourth possible reason relates to disclosure of information when the issuer deemed that it be kept confidentially generally, but that it be selectively disclosed to a person likely to trade on it, and when the insider conveying the information to the outsider was simply the issuer's authorized agent for doing so.[60] The rationale for our proposed alternative approach will become clear as we consider how this approach would work in connection with disclosures made for each of these four reasons.

**I. Trades based on tips made for personal benefit reasons**   Suppose that the tipper's disclosure was in fact motivated by one of the first two reasons: the expectation of a quid pro quo or the tipper's intention to benefit the tippee. If all the facts were known to the parties at the time of the tip, and to the court later on, the insider tipper and the initial tippee would clearly be found to have violated Rule 10b-5.[61] As we have seen, the problem under existing law is that it is often very difficult for the government or other plaintiff to find affirmative evidence that the insider tipper enjoyed a personal benefit, at least where that benefit takes the quid pro quo form. Under the proposed alternative approach, however, it will be much easier for the government or other plaintiff to successfully prosecute a Rule 10b-5 case against the tipper and direct tippee. This is because the tipper and direct tippee would each have great difficulty affirmatively producing convincing evidence that the reason for the initial source's disclosure was *not* for one of these first two reasons when in fact it was. Thus, under the alternative approach proposed here, personal benefit considerations would be much less likely to obstruct punishment of persons involved in a transaction that was in fact motivated by one of the first two reasons. This is a transaction that would be found to violate Rule 10b-5 under current law if all the facts were known and that our analysis in chapter 5 suggests is on average socially undesirable.

**II. Trades based on the unauthorized selective disclosure of information for reasons other than personal benefit**   Now consider the situation in which the disclosure was motivated by the third type of reason: any reason for making an *un*authorized selective disclosure of material nonpublic information other than for personal benefit. The most common example would be where the recipient is an analyst and the disclosure occurs during an interview—facts easy for both the insider source and the direct recipient to establish. Absent anything to the contrary, this evidence would be sufficient to establish the absence of personal benefit. Thus, in this situation, the alternative approach would protect both the insider tipper and direct tippee from being found to have violated Rule 10b-5, the same result as under current law. In other words, our proposed alternative approach would be just as effective at protecting analyst interviews—the concern that prompted the personal benefit test—while making it much easier to prosecute cases involving trades for either of the first two reasons—ones which would be found to have violated Rule 10b-5 if all the facts were known.[62]

**III. Trades based on authorized selective disclosure**   Finally, consider trades motivated by the fourth reason: an issuer-authorized selective disclosure of material nonpublic information to someone likely to trade on the information. The individual insider making the disclosure could very well be making the disclosure without personal benefit. If so, and if the disclosure occurs within the context of an analyst interview, both the insider tipper and the direct tippee will again almost certainly be in possession of, and able to introduce, persuasive evidence to this effect, and therefore the presumption of personal benefit can easily be rebutted. However, recall, as noted earlier in this chapter, that existing case law and commentary suggest that Rule 10b-5 is violated when an issuer trades in its own shares based on material nonpublic information that it possesses. They also suggest a violation when the issuer tips this information to an outsider likely to trade on it, who in turn can be liable as a participant after the fact in the issuer's violation. Thus, the issuer and the tippee trader would be found to violate Rule 10b-5 if all the facts were known, as would the individual tipper in his actions as the agent of the issuer. The proof problem here for the government or other plaintiff does not, even today, relate to personal benefit. It relates to demonstrating that the tip was authorized and, for the action against the direct tippee, that the tippee was aware of this fact.

## B. THE SUBSTANCE OF THE ALTERNATIVE APPROACH: THE INDIRECT TIPPEE

What about an indirect tippee? When disclosure by the insider tippee is made for one of the first two reasons, the indirect tippee is in very much the same position as the direct tippee: she will have great difficulty affirmatively producing convincing evidence that the reason for the initial source's disclosure was *not* for one of these first two reasons when in fact it was.

When the disclosure is made for the third reason, the indirect tippee is in a different position than the direct tippee. Unlike the direct tippee, she might well not be able to provide evidence that the disclosure was for the third reason when in fact it was. Thus, under the proposed alternative approach, the indirect tippee of such a disclosure might well be found to violate Rule 10b-5. This result, however, is good from a policy point of view. The indirect tippee's trade is just as socially undesirable as if the insider tipper had traded on the information himself. In addition, unlike punishing the insider tipper or direct tippee when the disclosure is made for the third reason, punishing the indirect tippee for trading on the same disclosure will not chill analyst interviews, because the indirect tippee is not a party to such an interview. This result also does not create any serious doctrinal problems. Given the available evidence, it would be assumed under the proposed alternative approach that the initial tipper either enjoyed a personal benefit, or was authorized to make the selective disclosure to someone likely to trade on it and hence was participating in the issuer's illegal tipping. Whichever it is, the insider tipper would be assumed to have violated Rule 10b-5 and the indirect tippee would be assumed to know of the violation. This would allow the indirect tippee to be considered a participant after the fact to a Rule 10b-5-type breach by the insider source. Effectively, the alternative approach says to the indirect tippee: you are on notice that there is a significant chance that the disclosure was made for one of the first two reasons and you should not trade unless you inquire and acquire sufficient evidence that is was not. [63]

When the disclosure is made for the fourth reason, again the indirect tippee might not be able to provide evidence suggesting no personal benefit even when in fact there was not any. Thus, under the proposed alternative approach, this indirect tippee might well be found to violate Rule 10b-5 even though the government or other plaintiff offered no evidence that the tip was authorized and that the indirect tippee knew of this. Again, however, it is not unfortunate that the indirect tippee be found to have violated Rule 10b-5. The indirect tippee's trade is socially undesirable and there is no reason to protect him from punishment in order to avoid chilling analyst interviews. It would be evidently illegal if all the facts were actually known. Again, he should not trade unless he inquires and acquires sufficient evidence that the reason for the disclosure was not the first, second or fourth reasons.

## C. IMPLEMENTATION

As discussed earlier, a tippee trade does not fit easily under the classical theory first articulated by Justice Powell in his opinion in *Chiarella*. The problem is that the tippee does not have the relationship of trust and confidence with the counterparty to his trade required by this theory. Recall, however, that in the same opinion, Justice Powell, in dicta, suggested a solution to this problem by saying that the tippee could be considered a "participant after the fact" to the tipper's breach of fiduciary duty.[64] Powell's *Chiarella* opinion makes no mention of the insider needing to have enjoyed a personal benefit for there to be a breach of his fiduciary duty when he makes an unauthorized selective disclosure of material nonpublic information to someone likely to trade on it. Nor does it make mention of the tippee needing to be aware of such a benefit. The authorities cited by Powell also make no mention of requiring that the tipper enjoy a personal benefit or that the tippee be aware of the benefit. Powell's policy concern in *Chiarella* is with the unfairness of the ex-post loss suffered by others trading on unfavorable terms because the insider breached his duty to keep the information confidential. This loss is just as present whether the insider enjoyed a personal benefit or not. The idea of imposing a personal benefit test does not appear in the law until three years later in Powell's opinion in *Dirks*. There, after expressing concern that analyst interviews could be chilled unless both the insider representative of the issuer and the analyst were protected from liability, Powell holds that the insider must enjoy a personal benefit for there to be a violation.

Against this background, how could the law evolve to implement the alternative approach's reversal of the evidentiary burden? The more modest way would be for the courts to establish a rebuttable presumption that an insider who is making a disclosure of confidential information to someone likely to trade on it is receiving a personal benefit. Again, the two-step rationale for such a presumption is straightforward. First, a significant portion of such disclosures involve a personal benefit. Second, it is generally easier for the insider source and original outside recipient to come up with evidence that the insider disclosed for a non-personal-benefit reason (when this is the case) than it is for the government or a private plaintiff to come up with evidence that the reason for the disclosure was a personal benefit (when that is the case).

Implementing our proposed alternative approach by creating a presumption has the advantage of being just an evidentiary rule based on its own internal logic. Thus, it does not involve a direct challenge to the Supreme Court's earlier holding in *Dirks*. This route to implementation has the important disadvantage, however, that the law governing criminal procedure generally disfavors use of a presumption in criminal cases. Indeed, we might find a presumption in the criminal insider trading context troubling on multiple grounds—especially if the presumption was crafted by courts—because of fair notice and due process concerns.[65]

The more ambitious route to implementation is for Congress to directly revise the holding in *Dirks* in accordance with the alternative approach proposed here. Revising the *Dirks* holding in this way is supported by sound reasoning. The revision is as plausible an outgrowth of the foundational *Chiarella* decision as is any approach dictated by the holding in *Dirks*. It would be as effective as the *Dirks* holding in avoiding the chilling of analyst interviews, which was the reason for adding the personal benefit test in the first place. It also has the advantage of making it less difficult to establish a Rule 10b-5 violation in both civil and criminal cases against direct and indirect tippees.[66]

*3. Trading by outsiders on the basis of nonpublic information originating within non-issuer entities*

As discussed earlier, there is currently legal uncertainty as to whether the personal benefit test applies only to cases based on the classical theory of insider trading, where it was originally developed, or whether it extends as well to cases based on the misappropriation theory. The key distinction between the two theories is that the classical theory deals only with cases involving information coming from inside the issuer whose shares are being traded, whereas the misappropriation theory was developed to deal with cases involving information coming from within an institution other than the issuer. As also discussed earlier, there are both strong policy and strong doctrinal reasons to conclude that the test should *not* extend to cases based on the misappropriation theory. Here the way forward is simple. The Supreme Court, or some developing consensus among the lower courts, simply needs to make clear that the personal benefit test should be confined to cases based on the classical theory.

## D. Use of the Martin Act Regulation to Stop Informed Trading

Many states also have anti-fraud securities laws, but they have not historically been a potent source of prohibitions on informed trading. Former New York Attorney General Eric Schneiderman's use of the state's Martin Act is an exception.[67] As detailed in this section, Schneiderman shut down Thomson Reuters' practice of privately providing to select traders the latest results of the Michigan Consumer Sentiment Survey moments in advance of announcing the results publicly.[68] Schneiderman condemned the practice as "insider trading 2.0."[69] Under the same banner, he persuaded BlackRock, the largest asset manager worldwide, to stop surveying the opinions of financial analysts before the analysts published their reports.[70] This extension of the range of prohibitions on informed trading to cover these practices is ill-advised in our view.

### 1. Practices not prohibited by Rule 10b-5

The practice of a non-issuer institution privately providing select traders with information in advance of its public announcement is clearly not prohibited by Rule 10b-5 because it does not fit under either the classical theory or the misappropriation theory. Neither the information-generating institution nor the select traders have a relationship of trust and confidence with the counterparties to the select traders' trades, and a subsequent public announcement does not change this. Therefore, failure by the select traders to provide the information to these counterparties breaches no duty to them, as required under the classical theory. The institution voluntarily gives the information to the select persons to trade upon. Thus, the recipients do not, by trading, deceptively breach a duty of confidentiality to the source of their information, as required under the alternative misappropriation theory.

### 2. The successful Martin Act campaign against "Insider Trading 2.0"

Notwithstanding the legality under Rule 10b-5 of Thomson Reuters tipping select traders in advance of its public announcement of the Consumer Sentiment Survey, Schneiderman, through use of the Martin Act's investigatory powers, was able to stop the practice without even filing a complaint.[71] The Attorney General terminated his investigation of Thomson Reuters (and later BlackRock) when each agreed not to engage in this practice in the future.

### 3. Evaluation

The Thomson Reuters affair involved an ill-advised use of the Attorney General's investigatory power under the Martin Act. As set out in this subsection, a simple extension of our analysis in chapter 5 concerning recipients of confidential information from within a non-issuer entity shows that the practice of a non-issuer institution privately providing select traders with information in advance of its public announcement is unlikely to be socially undesirable. Indeed, it appears that allowing such informed trading is socially positive, though probably just modestly. Thus, the absence of a federal prohibition on this practice gets it right, and thus it was bad public policy to use the investigatory powers under New York's Martin Act to stop "insider trading 2.0."

#### A. POSSIBLE USES BY OUTSIDERS OF THE INFORMATION THEY GENERATE ABOUT ISSUERS

Consider a non-issuer institution that has generated information of value for assessing an issuer's stock (or has purchased such information, directly or indirectly, from a person that has generated it). The starting point for the analysis is to note that this institution can use this information in three possible ways: (1) trade on the information, (2) provide it privately to certain other traders subject to whatever terms and conditions the institution wishes to impose, or (3) announce the information publicly. As discussed in chapter 5, we view it as socially desirable to allow such an institution to use the information in the first or second way or in a combination of the two. This is based on our conclusion that the social gains from the resulting additional incentives for non-issuer institutions to generate information that enhances price accuracy outweigh the social losses in terms of real resources needed to generate the information and the negative impact on liquidity. Thus, for example, it is socially undesirable to prevent Thomson Reuters from providing the Michigan Survey results to select traders ahead of its public announcement.

### B. USING GENERATED INFORMATION TO MAKE A PUBLIC ANNOUNCEMENT

If this earlier reasoning concerning the first and second uses of the information is correct, the third use—publicly announcing the information—must also be socially desirable. A non-issuer institution that contemplates this third use presumably incurs the expense of generating or obtaining the information because it expects to be compensated by the goodwill or enhanced reputation that results from a public announcement of the information. Thus, allowing public announcement of this information provides a desirable additional incentive. As with allowing the institution to trade on the information itself or to sell it privately to others to trade upon, there is also a liquidity-decreasing downside to allowing its public announcement, in this case from the trading of announcement traders. This negative impact on liquidity, however, is certainly no greater than if the institution had instead just traded on the information, a practice which we have concluded on balance should be allowable.

### C. COMBINING PROVIDING THE INFORMATION TO SELECT TRADERS PRIVATELY WITH SUBSEQUENTLY ANNOUNCING IT PUBLICLY

Finally, if, as we conclude here, each of these three uses of a piece of information should be allowable on its own, there is nothing in the logic justifying each of these uses to suggest that the uses suddenly become toxic when two or more are combined. This includes the combination of providing the information privately to select persons to trade and announcing it publicly thereafter.

## E. The Broad-Scale Legislative Approach to Informed Trading Prohibitions

A broad-scale legislative approach is an alternative to the scheme of informed trading prohibitions developed in a common-law fashion through court interpretations of Rule 10b-5. Two such legislative approaches are considered here: the EU Market Abuse Directive[72] and the proposed Insider Trading Prohibition Act[73] that was introduced in the 114th Congress. Each corrects for some of the shortcomings of the prevailing U.S. Rule 10b-5 scheme, but neither includes within its reach the full set of informed trades that optimally should be prohibited. Moreover, the Market Abuse Directive calls for prohibiting some informed trades that optimally should be allowed. Ultimately, we conclude that it would be better for the United States to continue to use the current Rule 10b-5 regime and adopt only narrowly crafted legislation to fill in some of its holes.

## 1. EU Market Abuse Directive

The EU Market Abuse Directive directs member countries to prohibit a wide range of persons[74] from trading on the basis of, or tipping, "inside information," which is defined as information relating to an issuer that is "of a precise nature which has not been made public . . . and which, if it were made public, would be likely to have a significant effect on" the price of the issuer's securities.[75] Thus, this approach does not depend on the existence of any relationship of trust and confidence or duty of confidentiality and does not differentiate between information coming from within the issuer and from within a non-issuer institution. On the surface, the Directive looks like it calls for a "parity of information" approach that goes beyond even Justice Blackmun's structural access theory in his dissent in *Chiarella*. A closer look, however, reveals that the Directive in fact excepts from its prohibitions a variety of kinds of informed trading.

### A. FUNDAMENTAL VALUE, ANNOUNCEMENT, AND ISSUER INSIDER INFORMED TRADING

The Directive's prohibitory language (quoted in the preceding subsection) appears to reach so broadly that it would prohibit all fundamental value informed trading based on information of significance. A "whereas" clause, however, clarifies that "research and estimates developed from publicly available data should not be regarded as inside information."[76] Like Rule 10b-5, the Directive appears to permit announcement trading because "inside information" includes only information "not made public."[77] Also like Rule 10b-5, it prohibits issuer insiders from trading on material nonpublic information from inside the issuer,[78] but permits them to trade on immaterial information from this source.[79] Thus, in these regards, the Directive, like Rule 10b-5, prohibits a number of kinds of informed trading that chapter 5 of this book suggests should be prohibited and allows a number of kinds that it suggests should be allowed.

### B. TIPPERS AND TIPPEES WITH REGARD TO INFORMATION FROM WITHIN THE ISSUER

The treatment of tippers and tippees is less perfect. First, consider tippers and tippees of information coming from within the issuer. The Directive, judged by the recommendations of chapter 5, is in some ways superior, and in other ways inferior, to Rule 10b-5 as currently interpreted. For there to be a violation, the Directive does not require that an issuer insider receive a personal benefit for making the tip of nonpublic material information. Instead, it has a general prohibition against "disclosing inside information to any other person," but excepts disclosures made "in the normal course of the exercise of [the disclosing person's] employment, profession or duties."[80] The exception works as well as the personal benefit test (or our proposed alternative) in immunizing *issuer representatives* participating in analyst interviews, thus avoiding chilling their participation. However, contrary to the recommendations in chapter 5 and to Rule 10b-5, *analysts* who trade on material information received in such interviews, or who privately recommend that their employer or others trade on the information, would be in violation,[81] thus chilling analysts' willingness to engage in such interviews. Thus, the way that this general prohibition and exception operate in combination does not appear to work as well as Rule 10b-5 in avoiding chilling analyst interviews, because the scheme does not seem to recognize that such interviews are two-sided.

The Directive has a catchall provision, Article 4, which applies to any person beyond those with respect to whom there are specified prohibitions relating to informed trading and tipping. Article 4 prohibits trading or tipping if such a person "possesses inside information while that person knows, or ought to have known, that it is inside information."[82] It is therefore much easier to make the case that such person has committed a violation than under Rule 10b-5, which currently requires a showing that the person knew of the original tipper's personal benefit. Thus, the Directive's provisions more effectively deter a range of trades based on information from inside an issuer that our analysis finds socially undesirable: trades by direct tippees outside the analyst interview situation and by indirect tippees generally.

## C. TRADES BASED ON INFORMATION ORIGINATING FROM WITHIN AN ENTITY OTHER THAN THE ISSUER

Trades based on nonpublic material information initially selectively disclosed by an insider of a non-issuer institution are treated differently under the Directive depending on the nature of the information. Consider first the situation in which the information is purely the result of an analysis. Informed trading based on this information, whether the trader receives it directly or indirectly, appears to be allowed because it is not considered "inside information." This is so even in situations where the trader has good reason to believe that the institution did not authorize disclosure of the information, or where the trader has some kind of duty of confidentiality to her source. Chapter 5 suggests that these trades are socially undesirable and the discussion earlier in this chapter shows that they would violate Rule 10b-5.[83]

Next, consider the situation in which the analysis leads to a plan to engage in a purchase (for example, a takeover bid) or to sell enough of the issuer's stock to likely have a significant effect on price. Suppose the institution discloses the plan to a select group of traders. Knowledge of the planned transaction would fit the definition of inside information even though the analysis that prompted the planned transaction would not. The Directive's catchall Article 4 would appear to prohibit all trades by outsiders based on knowledge of the planned transaction as long as the trader has good reason to believe that the information is material and nonpublic.[84] These are trades that our analysis in chapter 5 suggests should be allowed and that our discussion earlier this chapter shows would not violate Rule 10b-5.

D. SUMMARY

In sum, the reach of the EU's Market Abuse Directive's informed trading prohibitions is somewhat different from the reach of Rule 10b-5's prohibitions. Each system prohibits some tips and trades that our analysis suggests should be prohibited and that the other system fails to prohibit. The Directive also prohibits some trades that our analysis suggests should be allowed and that are not prohibited under Rule 10b-5. Overall, the Directive is not hobbled by the personal benefit rule test or a requirement to show knowledge by the trader of a prior breach of some duty in many situations where it would be socially desirable to punish a trade, but it is less attuned to the need to allow certain trades where the resulting profits create incentives to generate information that improves price accuracy.

## 2. Insider Trading Prohibition Act

A bipartisan group of Congress members, aided by our colleague Professor John C. Coffee, introduced in the last Congress a proposed statute,[85] the Insider Trading Prohibition Act (the Trading Act),[86] that would provide a comprehensive scheme to regulate informed trading. The Trading Act prohibits trades in an issuer's securities if the trader is in possession of material nonpublic information and the trader "knows, or recklessly disregards, that such information has been obtained wrongfully, or that such [trade] would constitute a wrongful use of such information."[87] It also prohibits the communication of such information if the communication is wrongful or the communicator has good reason to believe the information was obtained wrongfully and the recipient (or a direct or indirect tippee of the recipient) predictably trades on it.[88] A trade or communication would be a wrongful use of such information if it is obtained by such illegal acts as theft or constitutes misappropriation of the information.[89] Knowledge that information has been wrongfully obtained requires only that the trader or communicator be "aware, or recklessly disregard . . . that such information was wrongfully obtained or communicated."[90]

### A. FUNDAMENTAL VALUE, ANNOUNCEMENT, AND ISSUER INSIDER INFORMED TRADING

The Trading Act would allow fundamental value informed trading because such information is not wrongfully obtained, nor is it contrary to any other law or obligation. The Trading Act also would allow announcement trading because such trading is based on public information. It would prohibit issuer insiders from trading on material nonpublic information from inside the issuer because, as a breach of the relationship of trust that issuer insiders have with the issuer's shareholders, doing so is wrongful. The Trading Act would permit trading by issuer insiders on the basis of immaterial information from inside the issuer because the Trading Act only relates to material information. Thus, in all these regards, the Trading Act, like Rule 10b-5, prohibits all the kinds of informed trading that we suggest should be prohibited and allows all the kinds that we suggest should be allowed.

## B. TIPPERS AND TIPPEES WITH REGARD TO INFORMATION FROM WITHIN THE ISSUER

With regard to tippers and tippees of information from within the issuer, the Trading Act, judged by our recommendations in chapter 5, is superior to Rule 10b-5, though still not optimal in its reach. Consider analyst interviews. The Trading Act, although it does not explicitly include a personal benefit test, would appear to avoid chilling analyst interviews. If an issuer representative authorized to conduct an analyst interview accidentally provides material inside information, he has not communicated the information wrongfully, which is what would be required for a violation. Because the information was not wrongfully communicated to the analyst, she also would not violate the Trading Act by trading on it or by communicating it, directly or indirectly, to someone who predictably trades on it. For the same reasons, neither of the Trading Act's twin prohibitions—wrongful communication and use of wrongfully obtained information—is triggered if the information received by the analyst is then passed to others (beyond the analyst's principal) who trade on it or communicate it to yet others who predictably trade on it.

The immunization of the issuer representative and the analyst is consistent with our policy conclusions. The immunization of the indirect recipients is not consistent with our policy recommendations: the indirect recipient's trades result in the same damage to liquidity as trades by insiders and immunizing them is not necessary to avoid chilling analyst interviews. They would be immunized in a Rule 10b-5 regime also, however, and so the Trading Act is not a step backward in this regard. It is still inferior to our proposed alternative, however.

Relative to the current Rule 10b-5 regime, which is based on case law, the major advantage of the Trading Act with respect to information from within an issuer relates to direct and indirect tippees outside of the analyst interview context. The Trading Act prohibits trades and tipping by persons possessing material nonpublic information "if such person knows, or recklessly disregards, that such information has been obtained wrongfully."[91] Unlike the Rule 10b-5 regime, the

Trading Act explicitly does not require the person "to know the specific means by which the information was obtained or communicated, or whether any personal benefit was paid or promised."[92] This eliminates major obstacles under the current Rule 10b-5 regime to imposing sanctions on tippees, especially indirect ones. Again, however, it does not go as far as would an optimal regime, which would prohibit any trade or tip if the indirect tippee has good reason to know that the nonpublic material information came from within the issuer.

## C. TRADES BASED ON INFORMATION ORIGINATING FROM WITHIN A NON-ISSUER INSTITUTION

Consider now the reach of the Trading Act's prohibitions with respect to trades based on nonpublic material information generated by a non-issuer institution and traded on by an insider of that institution or by an outsider. We concluded earlier that such trades are socially desirable if approved by the institution and, in the case of a trade by any indirect outside recipient of the information, by the intermediary recipient or recipients. The basis of approval comes from what can grow to be a whole network of agreements and duties specifying who is allowed to trade and under what conditions. We concluded that any trading not approved by this network of agreements and duties is socially undesirable.

The Trading Act helps in two ways to prevent trades outside of what is permitted by this network of agreements. First, it prohibits anyone from trading on the information, or communicating it to others who predictably trade on it, when such trading or tipping is wrongful. The Trading Act is thus violated by an insider, or any outside recipient, direct or indirect, who trades or tips contrary to his agreement with his source or some other legal duty.[93] This prohibition, therefore, reinforces the already existing legal sanctions for the recipient's breach of contract with his source or breach of some other duty.

Second, the Trading Act prohibits trades or tips based on information that the user has good reason to believe was wrongfully obtained or communicated.[94] These are persons not themselves bound by any agreement or other obligation not to trade or tip. Instead, they receive the information as the result of a breach by someone who is so bound. This prohibition acts as a backstop to help prevent trades that would otherwise occur as a result of the breach by the person who was so bound.

In these regards, the reach of the Trading Act's prohibitions are identical with the reach of what we believe, doctrinally and policy-wise, is the better view of the reach of Rule 10b-5 based on the misappropriation theory, the view that does not insert the personal benefit test. The Trading Act contains an explicit provision that no showing of knowledge of personal benefit is required to establish a case based on the use of information wrongfully obtained or communicated.

An optimal regime would go further, however, and prohibit any trade based on material nonpublic information relating to an issuer generated by an outside institution when the trader (i) has good reason to believe that the information originated with that institution, and (ii) does not have a good reason to believe that the trade is in accordance with what is called for by the network agreements and duties associated with the authorized dispersion of the information and approval to trade on it. Given the value of material nonpublic information, it is predictable that the institution that generated it and each subsequent legitimate recipient would lay down terms for its use such that, if the terms were respected, the information would not be available to be freely picked up and traded upon. Thus, if someone has such nonpublic information that she has reason to believe came from the institution and does not know the route by which the information got to her and whether the information got to her legitimately, the likelihood is that a trade based on it is not in accordance what is called for by the network of agreements and is thus socially undesirable.

## 3. An alternative approach

As the preceding discussion shows, judged against what would be optimal, the reach of the EU Market Abuse Directive's prohibitions on informed trading is in some ways an improvement upon the reach of the current U.S. Rule 10b-5 regime and in some ways is less satisfactory. The proposed Insider Trading Regulation Act is an unambiguous improvement, but still falls short of the optimal set of prohibitions.

One way for the United States to have an optimal regime is to adopt a broad-scale statute that goes a step further than the proposed Insider Trading Regulation Act by including within its prohibitions the socially harmful trades (specified earlier) that the Trading Act does not reach. However, a preferable and more conservative approach would be to recognize that the current Rule 10b-5 regulation already gets most things right and provides a rich set of precedents. For an extended period of time, these precedents will generally provide more predictable outcomes than will a whole new statutory scheme with all the interpretative issues of first impression that its wording will inevitably raise. All that is really necessary to convert the current Rule 10b-5 regime into one that imposes the optimal range of informed trading prohibitions is a narrowly crafted statute that appropriately clarifies the ambiguities in the current case law and provides the desirable extensions in the range of prohibitions.

As we have seen, all of the shortcomings of the Rule 10b-5 regime relate to tipping and trading by direct and indirect tippees. With regard to material nonpublic information from within an issuer, the statute should provide that the personal benefit test applies only to an issuer insider and his direct recipient, not to indirect tippees, and should reverse the evidentiary burden so that it simply provides a defendant with an affirmative defense if he can produce persuasive evidence that the reason that the insider source disclosed was a reason other than personal benefit. Other than the trades and communications that are covered by this reverse-burden personal benefit rule, the statute should prohibit any trade (and any tip that predictably results in a trade) where the trader or tipper is in possession of material nonpublic information and has good reason to believe that it came from within the issuer. The statute should also clarify that the personal benefit rule does not apply to trades or tips based on material nonpublic information generated by an institution other than the issuer.

Finally, as discussed earlier, the object of regulating tips and trades based on such information is to maximize the incentives for such institutions to generate such information, given its attendant socially useful enhancement of share price accuracy. To accomplish this, the statute should prohibit any tip or trade based on such information where the trader has good reason to believe that it originated within that institution and does not have a good reason to believe that (i) the institution generating the information authorized its initial disclosure; (ii) each subsequent recommunication, if any, was authorized by the institution whose agent is recommunicating it (where the recipient in fact was an institution rather than an individual); (iii) each subsequent recommunication, if any, was made in accordance with the terms imposed by the originating institution and by each preceding recommunicating entity; (iv) each subsequent recommunication, if any, was not prohibited by any other obligation arising from the communicator's status; and (v) the trade itself is in accordance with the terms imposed by the originating institution and by each preceding recommunicating institution and is not prohibited by any other obligation of the tipper or trader arising out of its status.

## II. MANDATORY AFFIRMATIVE DISCLOSURE

The United States, through multiple trigger mechanisms, imposes its Exchange Act periodic disclosure regime on most of the country's publicly traded issuers.[95] This regime requires the issuer, on a regular basis, to answer in a public filing a large number of questions concerning its business and finances. The most detailed filing is the annual 10-K filing, with some of its questions requiring updates each quarter in a 10-Q filing. Specified important events, such as entering into important agreements, changes in control, senior officer changes, and material asset acquisitions and sales, trigger an 8-K filing obligation within four business days of the event. The U.S. periodic disclosure regime also includes Regulation FD, which is intended to be an antidote to some corporations' practice of selectively disclosing material information to certain outsiders who are expected to trade on it. Each European country has its own somewhat different mandatory disclosure system, but these systems are all shaped by an EU directive mandating that they all have a requirement that the issuer disclose all new nonpublic material information as soon as possible.

## A. The Relationship of Mandatory Affirmative Disclosure to Informed Trading

One purpose of affirmative disclosure requirements is to directly make share prices more accurate. The efficient market hypothesis tells us that once information is publicly disclosed, it is fully reflected in price very quickly.[96] Affirmative disclosure requirements, however, have a second important function as well: reducing or eliminating informed trading based on the information and the harm to liquidity that accompanies such trading. The less information from within an issuer is nonpublic, the less insiders and their tippees can engage in their socially undesirable informed trade.

The benefits of mandatory disclosure go beyond this, however. The increased liquidity in an issuer's stock resulting from less informed trading means that fundamental value informed traders face lower trading costs and hence will increase their level of activity. In other words, there will be less crowding-out of this socially valuable fundamental value informed trading. Admittedly, because securities filings are pubic announcements, more mandatory disclosure could lead to more announcement trading, which is also socially undesirable. But this damage to liquidity could be largely avoided if the SEC's release of the content of a filing was postponed until after the end of regular trading hours and if firms were similarly constrained in their own announcements, absent a pressing need such as a developing flood of trading by insiders and their tippees.[97]

Mandatory disclosure can favorably affect the level of fundamental value informed trading in another way as well. When an issuer discloses more about itself, fundamental value informed traders may find it more worthwhile to gather and analyze additional information. This is because the information that is received may constitute a valuable input to the process of further discovery. Thus, for example, it may be more worthwhile for an investor to gather and analyze information (not yet gathered and analyzed by others) concerning the market for the product of an issuer that has disclosed basic financial information about itself than to gather and analyze information concerning the market for the product of a firm that has not engaged in such disclosure.[98]

## B. Regulation FD

Regulation Fair Disclosure (Reg. FD),[99] adopted in August 2000, is intended to stop the practice of "selective disclosure," whereby an issuer withholds material information from the general public but furnishes it selectively to certain outsiders such as analysts, institutional investors, or shareholders likely to trade on the information.[100] Reg. FD provides that when the disclosure of material information to such outsiders is intentional, the issuer must simultaneously make the information available to the general public, and when it is unintentional, the issuer must make the information publicly available promptly thereafter.[101]

On the whole, the effects of Reg. FD are consistent with what our analysis in chapter 5 recommends. This analysis suggests that it would be undesirable for issuers to buy or sell their securities while in possession of material nonpublic information and that tipping by an issuer would therefore also be undesirable. The Reg. FD ban on intentional selective disclosure therefore makes sense. So does the requirement of prompt public disclosure after an unintentional selective disclosure of material information, especially when combined with the reverse-burden personal benefit rule for Rule 10b-5 actions recommend earlier in this chapter. On the one hand, we want to avoid chilling analyst interviews, which is the rationale for a personal benefit rule of any scope. On the other hand, avoiding such chilling is the sole purpose of the personal benefit test. If, by accident, material information is released in an analyst interview, it is undesirable that it become the basis of informed trading. Reg. FD does the best that can be done to minimize this informed trading without chilling analyst interviews (and related discussion among financial professionals).

There has been considerable controversy in the empirical literature as to whether Reg. FD improves price accuracy and whether it lowers the cost of capital.[102] A number of possible stories can be told in these regards.[103] The imposition of Reg. FD might have decreased price accuracy because, before FD, an issuer, by providing tidbits of selectively disclosed material information, may have been able to attract a following by analysts who would otherwise not find it worthwhile to follow that issuer.[104] Alternatively, Reg. FD might have increased price accuracy because it ended a corrupt game by which an issuer gave such tidbits in return for overly positive analyst reports.[105] Reg. FD's reduction in the amount of informed trading would definitely be expected improve liquidity and have a favorable effect on the cost of capital, although the empirical literature on whether it in fact has led to a liquidity improvement is mixed.[106] If Reg. FD increased price accuracy as well, then it would be an unambiguous improvement from a social welfare perspective, but there is no clear empirical answer to this.

The basic problem is that although the passage of Reg. FD indeed generated a fairly large literature on its effects, it is hard to imagine a worse time for the study of such an event. Reg. FD went into effect in October of 2000. That was in the midst of the bursting tech bubble, which started in early 2000 and ended eighteen or so months later. Furthermore, stocks started trading on pennies, rather than sixteenths, in early 2001. In fact, there was only one quarter of price data following Reg. FD in which stock prices continued to trade on sixteenths. Other events that affected the informational environment included the Enron failure in 2001, which along with other scandals, led to the enactment of Sarbanes-Oxley. This law had a significant effect on how auditing was done and regulated. Finally, there was the Global Settlement in 2003 in which the ten largest financial firms doing equity analysis paid fines totaling $1.435 billion and agreed to separate their banking and analysis groups.

One consensus seems to have been reached in the literature: Reg. FD on balance may not in many respects have affected the informational environment of larger firms. Specifically, earnings surprises were no bigger or smaller after the issuance of Reg. FD. It appears that while analysts found it more difficult to make predictions without the private information they had received in the past, at least some firms responded by providing more voluntary disclosures. Reg. FD may have made things worse for smaller firms, particularly in the technology sector, but that could be just the effects of the bubble showing up in the properties of transaction prices.[107]

Regardless of which story concerning Reg. FD's effect on price accuracy is correct, there is a better solution that would both reduce the amount of informed trading and allow issuers to attract analyst followings that enhance share price accuracy: keep Reg. FD but allow issuers to openly pay analysts to follow them in the same way that they pay accountants to certify their accounts. This arrangement would encourage the development of an analyst business in which a reputation for objectivity is an asset, because such a reputation makes the analysts' reports more valuable to investors. Once this reputation is established, the analyst would not want to jeopardize it by giving a falsely optimistic report in return for getting or retaining one more firm's business. The arrangement would be strengthened if permitting the payment to the analyst was conditioned on the arrangement involving a long-term contract spanning at least a few years. This way, a bad report could not lead to an issuer immediately dropping the analyst in retaliation.

## C. European Continuous Disclosure Regime

The EU Market Abuse Directive subjects issuers to a continuous disclosure regime concerning inside information.[108] This regime requires an issuer to disclose as quickly as possible inside information directly involving that issuer.[109] This approach has virtues and defects. If an issuer suspects that insiders or their tippees are trading based on the internal information, then it is certainly desirable for an issuer to publicly disclose that information. However, if there is no reason to suspect insider trading, the issuer may have a good business reason to keep the information secret, which would benefit the shareholders by allowing the issuer to generate a larger expected cash flow. In terms of the real-economy efficiency benefits from greater price accuracy, little is gained from a slightly earlier disclosure of this information. Even if the issuer can be exempted when it has a good business reason for withholding disclosure, placing the burden on the issuer to show that such a reason exists may lead, on average, to earlier disclosure than is desirable. Issuers may disclose despite the harm to their businesses just out of a desire to avoid the cost and risks of a fight with regulators.

## III. RETURN OF INSIDER PROFITS

Section 16(b) of the Securities Exchange Act is the only provision in the Act that deals expressly with the issue of insider trading.[110] Section 16(b) requires insiders to disgorge to their firm any profit they gain from "any purchase and sale, or any sale and purchase, of any equity security" of the company within a six-month period.

Critics have argued that § 16(b) is ineffective because all the insider has to do is wait six months to engage in the reverse transaction that realizes her profit. The analysis in chapter 5, however, suggests that the provision can be quite useful. It substantially reduces insiders' incentives to trade based on any form of material nonpublic inside information, other than information that should have a considerably longer-term impact. This is because regardless of what information motivates the insider to engage in an initial transaction, whether purchasing or selling, the insider will have to wait six months before transacting again. During those six months, a large number of market-moving events are likely to affect a company's stock price. Accordingly, § 16(b) makes trading based on inside information less attractive by mandating that insiders can only rebalance their portfolios after a considerable amount of time, thereby leaving them in a riskier position during the interim because of the reduced portfolio diversification due to the inside trade.[111] The kind of information that will remain rational to trade on will be information likely to have a price impact only over a very long period of time, which is precisely the kind of information we suggest is most likely to actually be socially valuable, rather than harmful, for insiders to trade on.[112]

## IV. MARKET STRUCTURE RULES

Rules governing the structure of the stock market can also be tailored to help promote socially desirable trading and reduce socially undesirable trading. This is especially so with announcement trading, which we find socially undesirable, but which, because it involves information that is already public, is not prohibited by Rule 10b-5 and would be difficult to cost-effectively regulate by outright prohibition.

We briefly consider two potential market structure responses here: one involving stock exchange announcement rules and the other involving regulation of the electronic connections among stock exchanges and with liquidity suppliers.

### A. Stock Exchange Announcement Rules

The New York Stock Exchange *Listed Company Manual* requires firms to quickly release material new information. Section 202.05 ("Timely Disclosure of Material News Developments") provides that listed companies should "release quickly to the public any news or information which might reasonably be expected to materially affect the market for its securities."[113] Section 202.06 ("Procedure for Public Release of Information; Trading Halts") similarly requires that "substantive items of unusual or non-recurrent nature," such as dividend announcements, mergers, acquisitions, tender offers, stock splits, or major management changes, "should be handled on an immediate release basis."[114]

A rule that that a listed issuer should disclose important news as soon as is practical makes sense in terms of our analysis when an issuer has reason to suspect that important, yet-to-be-announced news has already become the basis of insider trading. Otherwise, however, it would be better that the issuer be required to wait until after regular trading has stopped for the day. To announce during the trading day is to invite announcement trading. Thus, it would be beneficial to revisit this NYSE rule and its NASDAQ equivalent. The revised rule should require that, except when there are strong reasons to believe insider trading is already occurring, such announcements be made only outside regular trading hours. Under such a scheme, the announcement will essentially be known to market makers and market participants alike when active trading resumes, and thus the announcement will not involve any spread-widening information asymmetry during regular trading hours.

## B. Market Connection Regulation

As discussed in chapter 4, high-frequency traders (HFTs)—the suppliers of significant liquidity in modern markets—utilize a number of technologies. Stocks of any significance trade on each of a number of different trading venues, the listing exchange (in almost all cases either NYSE or NASDAQ) being just one. Each venue is essentially just a matching engine: an electronic system that matches standing limit orders that constitute the bids and offers with incoming marketable orders. An HFT typically has computers colocated right next to each venue's matching engine. Each of an HFT's colocated computers is connected to each other one by high-speed fiber-optic cable, which allows is to constantly update information concerning transactions occurring in every stock in which the HFT regularly trades, as well as changes in the bids and offers posted by others on each trading venue. This information is automatically fed into a computer that uses algorithms to change the HFT's own bids and offers posted at each venue.

Through this setup, an HFT can learn of a transaction at one venue and change its quotes at every other venue with lightning speed. So, for instance, an algorithm can learn of a very large transaction at one venue, suggesting that large orders may also be heading to the other venues that would transact against the HFT's bids or offers at these venues. The HFT can potentially make these changes before these large orders arrive at the other venues.

As we have noted, critics have labeled this practice of changing quotes "electronic front running" (what we refer to as "anticipatory order cancellation") and have suggested various ways of stopping it, most of which involve curbing the informational advantages the HFTs enjoy from using these high-speed connections.[115] As we argued earlier, this may be too narrow a view. Because the persons sending these large orders are informed traders, the availability of anticipatory order cancellation allows HFTs to better protect themselves by being able to change their quotes when such transactions suggest that informed trading is going on. This means that HFTs face lower costs from dealing with informed traders and, because they are in a competitive business, results in their narrowing their spreads.

Anticipatory order cancellation, as we suggested in chapter 4, probably has quite different effects on different types of informed trading. Trading in large amounts in rapid time is expensive to do as a general matter because it involves running through the book transacting against less and less favorable quotes. Thus, a trader is unlikely to do it unless the information motivating a trade is going to become fully public very soon. The ultimate example of such a trader is an announcement trader: a person who trades in the brief time after the announcement before the price has fully adjusted. The next best example is an insider who knows of a corporate announcement to be made very soon. When the information one possesses has a longer-term horizon before becoming public—fundamental information—there is no reason to trade in massive size rapidly. Thus, anticipatory order cancellation stands to make announcement trading, which is socially undesirable, less profitable, and may do the same for some issuer insider trading as well. It should have much less direct effect on fundamental value trading. Indeed, by discouraging announcement traders and perhaps some insider traders and hence lowering spreads, anticipatory order cancellation is likely to help fundamental value information traders, which is a socially desirable activity. As discussed previously, in chapter 4, all of this cautions against a precipitous adoption of reforms aimed at ending anticipatory order cancellation.

## V. CONCLUSION

This chapter explored the range of different regulations that in one way or another touch upon informed trading. The object was to see how close what is prohibited or discouraged comes to what the analysis in chapter 5 suggests are the socially undesirable types of informed trades and how close what is encouraged comes to what the analysis suggests are the socially desirable ones. In chapter 5, we concluded that (a) fundamental value informed trading is socially desirable; (b) announcement trading is socially undesirable; (c) trading based on nonpublic information from within an issuer is undesirable whether or not the issuer consents, but only if the information is material; and (d) trading based on material nonpublic information from inside an entity other than the issuer is socially undesirable if the trading is not allowed by this entity (or, in the case of a trade by an indirect tippee, by any authorized intervening recipient of the tip). The more effective the legal regime is at prohibiting or discouraging the undesirable kinds of informed trade, the more it encourages socially desirable informed trading. This is because of the tendency of different kinds of informed trading to crowd each other out.

In the United States, the primary outright prohibitions of informed trades arise out of court and SEC-based interpretations of Rule 10b-5. The reach of Rule 10b-5's prohibitions largely conform to the informed trades that we believe should be subject to prohibition. The primary shortfalls arise in connection with tippers and tippees. With regard to tipping cases based on nonpublic information from inside the issuer, the insertion of the personal benefit test, while usefully protecting analyst interviews from being chilled, makes more difficult many other cases in which enforcement would be socially valuable. We have recommended reversing the evidentiary burden with regard to existence of a personal benefit. This is a way of easing what is currently a major obstacle to enforcement while at the same time continuing to protect analyst interviews.

The reach of Rule 10b-5's prohibitions properly does not include announcement trading, which is better discouraged in other ways. Nor does it include trades by issuer insiders based on nonmaterial nonpublic information or fundamental value information trading, both of which we believe to be socially beneficial.

Exchange Act § 16(b) requires issuer officers, directors, and greater-than-10-percent shareholders to return to the issuer profits from purchases and sales, or sales and purchases, of the issuer's shares made within six months of each other. As we show, § 16(b) is more helpful than many critics suggest. This is in part because § 16(b) significantly adds to the risk associated with insider trading by forcing the trader to be less diversified for a considerable period of time. Also, it is particularly effective at discouraging the most socially undesirable issuer insider informed trades: ones that just briefly accelerate an improvement in price accuracy.

Mandatory disclosure discourages issuer insider trading because when more information from within the firm becomes public, there is less private information for insiders and their tippees to trade upon.

The trading gains available to fast-acting announcement traders can be eliminated to the extent that it is practical to steer corporate announcements to nontrading hours. For announcements that continue to be made during trading hours, continuing to permit HFTs to "electronic front-run" is also a way of combating announcement trading, because anticipatory order cancellation is particularly effective at helping protect HFTs from the adverse selection associated with this particular type of informed trading.

Manipulation has been stock trading's most confusing concept for lawyers and economists alike. More than eighty years after federal law first addressed stock market manipulation, the federal courts remain fractured by disagreement and confusion concerning manipulation law's most foundational issues.[1] There remains, for example, a sharp split among the federal circuits concerning the central question in manipulation law: Whether trading activity alone can ever be considered illegal manipulation under federal law? Academics have been similarly confused: economists and legal scholars cannot agree on whether manipulation is even possible in principle, let alone on how to properly address it in practice.[2]

This confusion is particularly striking because preventing manipulation was a primary motivation for enacting the U.S. securities laws. In the midst of the Great Depression, manipulation struck Congress and varied commentators as a principal cause of the 1929 stock market crash and the ensuing economic collapse.[3] As a result, the Securities Exchange Act of 1934 (the Exchange Act) expressly prohibits manipulation in §§ 9 and 10(b).[4] The continued confusion is also striking because if one uses the rough proxy of SEC enforcement, the problem of manipulation is of a similar scale to insider trading. In its statistics for the past five years, the SEC reported bringing a combined 237 civil and administrative enforcement actions for insider trading and 229 for market manipulation.[5] Yet, while there is a vast legal and economic literature addressing insider trading, efforts to analyze manipulation have been far more limited.

The difficulties for manipulation law begin with the statutory provisions themselves. The Exchange Act gives remarkably little guidance as to the conduct they cover. Section 9(a)(2) prohibits effecting "a series of transactions" in a security (i) that "creat[e] actual or apparent active trading" or affect its price, (ii) "for the purpose of inducing the purchase or sale of such security by others."[6] The first half of the proscription targets conduct that will be involved in virtually *any* trading strategy: buying or selling a security inherently involves the creation of an actual trade and frequently affects its price. The bite of the prohibition is thus left to the vague clause relating to purpose. Similarly, § 10(b) baldly prohibits the use, in violation of an SEC rule, of "any manipulative or deceptive device" in connection with the purchase or sale of a security.[7] The statute, however, fails to define "manipulative" and the only SEC attempt to do so in rulemaking simply refers back to § 9.[8]

Surprisingly little progress has been made in defining these statutory terms since the passage of the Exchange Act. As a result, manipulation may be the most controversial concept in securities law. Many commentators believe that it is simply not a sufficiently meaningful concept to justify a ban on any kind of trading.[9] Other jurists, legal scholars, and economists believe manipulation is a useful concept, but have struggled to define the term and identify its harms, typically using an overly broad or circular definition, constrained in some cases by "I know it when I see it" bromides.[10]

The result is a legal framework that lacks precision, cogency, and consistency of application. The associated confusion as to what constitutes illegal manipulation produces unpredictable and disparate outcomes for cases with similar facts. Disparate outcomes and unpredictability raise issues of fairness. More fundamentally, a confused standard with a poorly articulated normative basis produces enforcement that is both under- and over-inclusive in comparison to whatever is the ideal baseline. The law thus does a bad job both of discouraging socially harmful transactions and enabling socially beneficial ones. The importance of improving securities law in these regards is highlighted by the dollar magnitudes involved in recent cases in closely related areas of financial regulation. The economist Adam Clark-Joseph recently detailed how a subset of high-frequency traders in commodities markets makes a significant fraction of their profits from arguably manipulative activities. The last decade has also seen a number of large alleged manipulations involving financial benchmarks, resulting in multibillion-dollar fines or settlements, some of the largest ever paid by financial institutions.[11]

This chapter seeks a way out of the morass. First, we start with some simple constraints on a theory of what should constitute an illegal manipulation. Specifically, for a trading strategy to be considered such a manipulation, four essential questions must be answered in the affirmative: First, is the strategy, purely as a conceptual matter, distinguishable from other, clearly acceptable trading strategies, and does the strategy cause social harm? Second, does the strategy plausibly fit under the broad dictionary meaning of the term *manipulation*? Third, are there circumstances under which the strategy can yield positive expected profits, and do they occur frequently enough to cause concern? Fourth, are there practical procedures for implementing a ban on the strategy whereby the social gains from its reduction or elimination exceed the social costs of doing so, including deterring socially valuable transactions that might be erroneously identified as examples of the practice?[12]

In essence, this four-question approach begins with some minimal rules of statutory interpretation to define the outer borders of what is plausibly within the reach of the prohibitions of manipulation in §§ 9 and 10(b). Our approach then focuses on three types of market manipulation that, under one name or another, have been the subject of commentary both in the case law and by legal and economics scholars.[13] What has largely been missing in the treatments of each of these practices, however, is a perspicuous identification of exactly who is harmed and who is helped if the practice is left unregulated and how this would change if the practice instead were legally prohibited. Our framework allows a comparison of the two worlds in terms of economic efficiency and the fairness of the various market participants' resulting wealth positions. We then use that analysis to derive an approach that can enable regulators to deter genuinely socially undesirable activity without unnecessarily deterring similar appearing, but socially useful, trades. Indeed, whereas objections to manipulation are often framed in terms of its unfairness, we argue that manipulation is undesirable on straightforward efficiency grounds.

Our framework draws its normative and analytical building blocks from chapter 2, and its analysis of the main social functions of trading and chapter 3's discussion of how the secondary equity market typically functions. With these foundations in hand, we show in this chapter that open market manipulation will typically harm both of the stock market's central social functions, which are providing liquidity and price accuracy. Although most commentary focuses on the impact of manipulation on price accuracy, the harm to liquidity can be more important. Whether there is also harm to price accuracy turns on when, if ever, the manipulation is corrected by an event (say, a corporate disclosure) that causes a stock's price to revert to its accurate level after a successful manipulation has distorted it. Surprisingly, our analysis reveals that the core harm of a manipulation will actually depend on the speed and nature of such price "correction." If the correction to a manipulation occurs rapidly, then the social harm of manipulation arising from its effects on price accuracy will typically be trivial. The manipulation's focal harm will be to liquidity.[14] If, in contrast, a manipulation's effects on price are only corrected slowly—or are never corrected—then the harm due to its effects on price accuracy may be more significant. We discuss conceptually the various possibilities for how correction may occur (or fail to).

This chapter proceeds as follows. Part I provides an overview of three types of manipulation trading strategies, which we term naked open market manipulation, open market manipulation with an external interest, and misstatement manipulation. Parts II, III, and IV consider, respectively, these three basic forms of manipulation in depth. Part V deploys what has come before it to illuminate and assess the existing statutory framework and case law relating to these three types of manipulation.

## I. OVERVIEW

## A. Types of Manipulation

We ultimately identify three types of trading strategies that generate affirmative answers to our four foundational questions. Each, in our view, should be banned as a type of illegal manipulation, but in each case the ban requires appropriately designed enforcement procedures relating to burdens of going forward and persuasion as well as to appropriate evidentiary presumptions. These three trading strategies are not necessarily exhaustive of the types of trading strategies that should be banned under the Exchange Act as manipulative, but the list represents a reasonable distillation of the types of manipulation cases that have come up so far under the Exchange Act regarding which we think a ban is justified.

### 1. Naked Open Market Manipulation

*Naked open market manipulation* involves the purchase of a number of shares,[15] with an upward push on prices, and then their resale under circumstances in which the corresponding downward push on prices is less severe, thereby resulting in the average sale price exceeding the average purchase price.[16] This strategy will yield positive expected profits when, at the time of the purchase, the trader has good reason to believe that the likelihood of such an asymmetric price reaction is sufficiently great that the transaction will yield gains from trading that are greater than the costs involved.[17]

As will be developed later in this chapter, we believe that this reasonably predicted asymmetric-price-reaction condition for positive expected profits is met under certain circumstances, but that those circumstances arise relatively infrequently. As a result, we ultimately conclude that such a trader should be subject to legal sanctions, but only when it can be proven that she had, at the time of her purchase, good reason to believe that this asymmetric-price-reaction condition was met. Imposing sanctions without requiring such proof is likely to deter socially useful purchases followed by sales that look very much the same to an external observer. The most important example of this is fundamental value informed trading, in which a trader buys a stock based on an analysis enabling a more accurate appraisal of its value than is reflected in the then-current price, and resells when the market price catches up with her appraisal.

### 2. Open Market Manipulation with an External Interest

*Open market manipulation with an external interest* involves a trader that has some kind of economic interest in the price of a security *independent* of the price at which she can buy and sell it in the open market. An example is an executive with a compensation scheme that is tied to her company's stock price at a particular moment in time. Shortly in advance of this moment, the trader purchases a number of shares and the resulting upward push on prices leads to a gain based on the external interest. Once this moment has passed, she would likely resell the shares that she previously purchased because pushing the price up is the only reason she added these shares to her portfolio in the first place and her purpose has now been accomplished.[18] To yield an expected gain, this second manipulation strategy does not require that the likelihood of an asymmetric price reaction be sufficiently great that it makes up for the costs of the trading involved. It only requires that the expected gain derived from the external interest be greater than the costs of trading, a condition that would easily be satisfied for an external interest of any real size.

We ultimately conclude that legal sanctions should be imposed when it is proven that a trader with such an external interest makes a purchase just in advance of the moment at which the security's price determines the gain that arises from the trader's external interest. Doing so is very unlikely to deter any socially useful transactions because it would be highly coincidental that a trader would wish to engage in a purchase at just that moment for any purpose other than obtaining the external gain.

### 3. Misstatement Manipulation

*Misstatement manipulation* involves a trader who makes a materially false negative statement concerning an issuer that pushes down the issuer's share price, purchases a certain number of shares in the market, waits until the truth comes out, and then resells the shares. We ultimately conclude that legal sanctions should be imposed on this trader as well. The conclusion may not seem very controversial, but the primary reason for reaching it—that the prospect of such trading will decrease market liquidity rather than that the transaction is unfair to other traders in the market—involves new insights.

## B. The Role of Purpose

As noted in the introduction to this chapter, in actions based on § 9(a)(2), a great deal turns on the "purpose" of the transactions involved. Similarly, the concept of a "manipulative . . . device" under § 10(b) implies some kind of scienter. Trying to determine whether a given set of trades was undertaken for an illegitimate purpose raises interesting questions. A person's purpose for trading is inherently subjective. Therefore, the questions of what is an improper purpose, and what is satisfactory evidence of such a purpose, are, as a practical matter, inseparable. This is why we address them together in our recommended four-question test. We believe that identifying situations in which there are affirmative answers to our four basic questions is the best approach to determining both what constitutes an improper purpose and what is satisfactory evidence that a particular instance of trading activity had such a purpose.

This idea is worth a bit more explication. Conceptually, finding the answer to the first of these questions—what is an improper purpose—really may not be too difficult. In essence, we start by trying to imagine every possible kind of purpose for engaging in trading activities (unaccompanied by a misstatement) other than solely to move price. Most of these are either socially useful or are already outlawed by other aspects of securities law. Chapters 2 through 6 provide a good survey of the many possible purposes for trading other than just to move price.[19]

As chapter 3 makes clear, all exchange-based trades, whether or not for one of these purposes, may result in an expected price change. If all or a portion of a person's trading activity is not due to one of these purposes and yet is expected to be profitable, the expected profits must be coming from the expectation of the price movement alone. The resulting price change, just as with a wash or matched sale, is socially undesirable viewed by itself, and the trade otherwise has no socially redeeming features. This approach to the concept of what is socially undesirable manipulative trading is very close to that adopted by Lawrence Harris.[20] It is also close to a concept recognized by Fischel and Ross, even though they do not think it can be operationalized.[21] Thus, the second question—what constitutes satisfactory evidence that the motivation of at least some portion of a person's trading activity is simply to move the price—is the key one.

## C. The Extent and Nature of Manipulation

The fact is that we know relatively little about the extent of manipulation in the equity markets. Of course, we can count the number of manipulation actions by the SEC, and a couple of papers have done so. Aggarwal and Wu[22] combed the SEC's litigation releases for those announcing the filing of a complaint from 1990 to 2001, identifying 142 cases. Most of those cases involved small illiquid securities and almost half of the sample traded on over-the-counter (OTC) venues. Prosecuted manipulation cases involving the established exchanges are relatively rare. An interesting feature of these cases is that 48 percent had an insider defendant, 32 percent had a large (more than 5 percent) shareholder defendant, and 64 percent had a broker defendant.[23] The Aggarwal and Wu paper also shows that any one manipulation can put together pure trade-related strategies with the propagation of rumor, false news, and broker encouragement, thus combining, for example, a naked open market manipulation with a misstatement manipulation.

Comerton-Forde and Putniņš[24] examined a specific manipulative strategy, manipulation of the closing price, which is presumably a type of manipulation with an external interest. Between 1999 and 2005, there were eight complaints involving 31 securities and 184 specific stock/day manipulations. The search was limited to stocks traded on NYSE, AMEX, TSE, and TSE-V (New York Stock Exchange, American Stock Exchange, Toronto Stock Exchange, and Vancouver Stock Exchange). Using a sophisticated statistical technique that separately models the probability of manipulation and the conditional probability of prosecution given manipulation, the paper projected—perhaps speculatively—that on average an astonishing 1 percent of transactions involve a manipulation. These manipulations are not uniformly distributed over time and across firms. Manipulations are more likely at month end and quarter end. They are also more likely to occur in entities that have higher mutual fund ownership.

This latter result harkens to the indirect evidence of closing price manipulation in Carhart et al.[25] The paper reports that net asset value (NAV) returns of nonindex equity mutual funds are abnormally high on quarter-end days, beating the S&P 500 return by 50 to 200 basis points. Significantly, the funds underperform on the day after the quarter-ending day, as, it is argued, prices revert to their unmanipulated level. These two papers are clearly looking at what we term open market manipulation with an external interest.

We also have evidence of naked open market manipulation. Hillion and Vermaelen[26] describe the experience of 467 so-called floating-priced convertible bonds issued by 261 firms during 1994 to 1998. These convertibles are structured so that it does not matter to the holder of the bond what the future stock price is because the conversion price is the future stock price. For example, suppose the face value of the bond is 100. If the issuer's future stock price at conversion turns out to be $10, the holder of the bond will get 100/10 = 10 shares upon conversion, each worth $10, for a total value of $100. If the future price turns out to be $5, the bond is convertible into 100/5 = 20 shares each worth $5 for a total value of $100.[27] If the bondholders engage in aggressive short selling of the issuer's shares in advance of conversion, they can generate significant expected profits for holders of such bonds. This is because short sales gradually push the share price down, with the shorting bondholders receiving the average of the prices at which the short sales were executed. So, this average price received for the shares that were sold short would be greater than the price received for the last share sold in this fashion. Upon completion of the short sales, the manipulator immediately converts his bonds, allowing him to convert at a rate based on the price of the last share sold. He can then use the shares obtained from the bond conversion to unwind his short position.[28]

While this might look like a market manipulation with an external interest, it is easier to understand as naked market manipulation. The short position is taken with significant negative impact on the stock price. The short position is undone using the shares received from conversion. Thus, the manipulator's reverse transaction has no price impact at all—the ultimate asymmetric price reaction. Hillion and Vermaelen shows that after an issuer sold such convertible bonds, on average its stock price fell 34 percent during the ensuing year. In 85 percent of the cases, returns over the year following announcement of the convertible issuance were negative. The authors conclude that this is evidence of aggressive short selling on the part of the convertible investor, driving down the price.

Though there may be other explanations for short selling by holders of floating-priced convertible bonds, the SEC considered it to be a manipulation in a complaint filed against two brothers who were holders of such bonds issued by Sedona Corp., as well as against various brokers and dealers that it alleged had facilitated the sales.[29] Notably, the contract pursuant to which the brothers purchased the bonds from Sedona included a clause prohibiting them from shorting. According to the complaint, the brothers ignored this clause and shorted Sedona shares prior to converting their bonds. Moreover, they attempted to disguise their actions by failing to mark these sales as "short," a violation of SEC rules. Furthermore, the SEC obtained recordings of the brothers calling on their agents to "clobber" Sedona. The older brother was convicted and fled the country. The younger brother and broker-dealers settled with the SEC in December 2012.[30]

Adam Clark-Joseph provides fascinating indirect evidence of manipulative behavior in the eMini S&P 500 futures contract that appears to involve instances of naked open market manipulation.[31] Clark-Joseph offers the following facts: There are, in the Commodity Futures Trading Commission (CFTC) data, eight high-frequency traders (HFTs) who regularly lose money on a series of small marketable orders. These same traders also make considerable money at times from a sequence of large marketable orders.

Clark-Joseph argues that the small marketable orders are exploratory, designed to determine whether the order book is "fragile" on one side or the other. A *fragile order book* on a given side is one where the quantity of shares available at prices at or near the best quote is relatively small and does not refill immediately as marketable orders execute against the visible quotes that do exist. In such a situation, a large marketable order executing against these quotes will move price significantly. If the exploratory trades reveal that the book is fragile on the offer side, then the HFT will be able to move the price up with large, aggressive buy orders. If the HFT also forecasts that there will be a large number of marketable buy orders coming in (something that is often predictable), then it will be able to quickly unload the shares that it just purchased without a similarly strong downward pressure on price. The algorithm is thus: (1) determine if there are likely to be sizable marketable buy orders or sell orders in the very near future; (2) if sizeable buy orders are anticipated, submit small marketable buy orders to detect fragility on the offer side of the order book; (3) if the order book is robust on the offer side, do nothing; (4) if the order book is fragile on the offer side, buy aggressively with additional marketable buy orders; (5) then reverse the position by selling to the anticipated sizable marketable buy orders; (6) if instead sizable marketable sell orders are anticipated, do the mirror image of steps (2)–(5). In this story, putting the position on has large price impact when the book on that side is fragile; taking off the position is expected to have a small price impact because it involves transacting with the anticipated sizable marketable orders.

Finally, in the Appendix we describe an open manipulation case that was first brought forward in November 2016 and remains, at this writing, unsettled and unlitigated. The alleged manipulation involved two brokerage accounts. One sent orders to an exchange, while the other sent orders to internalizers (recall that internalizers are over the counter market makers usually set up to execute retail order flow). According to the complaint, orders sent to the exchanges had large impact, while orders sent to the internalizer had very small impact. Shorting the stock on an exchange reduced the price, allowing for a large buy from the internalizer at an attractive price. This would be followed by buy orders on the exchange and then subsequent large sell orders internalized at inflated prices. The profits made were significant.

## II. NAKED OPEN MARKET MANIPULATION

Naked open market manipulation involves the purchase of a number of shares, with the resulting upward push on prices as discussed in chapter 3, and then their resale under circumstances where the corresponding downward push on prices is less severe, thereby resulting in the average sale price exceeding the average purchase price.[32] The manipulator is not an informed trader in terms of knowing anything special about the issuer's future cash flows. Rather, his profits come purely from the trading profits yielded by this asymmetric price response.

The analysis in this section suggests that naked open market manipulation is a trading strategy that affirmatively answers each of the four foundational questions posed at the beginning. It is socially harmful in a way that makes it distinguishable as a conceptual matter from other trading strategies. It also fits under a broad dictionary meaning of the word *manipulation*.[33] There are circumstances under which the strategy can yield positive expected profits. Finally, there are situations in which it will be provable that a trader has reason to know of the existence of these circumstances, meaning that if legal sanctions are only imposed when such a situation can be proven to have existed, not many socially valuable transactions—ones not driven by this strategy—will be deterred.

### A. Wealth Transfers: Efficiency

Understanding of the wealth transfer implications of naked open market manipulation is most easily gained by starting with an example and seeing the ex-post effect of the trade. Then we can consider, from an ex-ante perspective, what the impact of the practice is as a generally known ongoing phenomenon occurring over the longer run within a competitive environment. From this analysis, we can make conclusions about the efficiency implications of the practice in terms of both liquidity and share price accuracy.

## 1. Ex-post perspective

Mani is a skilled manipulator who wishes to manipulate the price of NetSuite's stock by taking advantage of his rational assessment that it is probable that there will be an asymmetric price reaction to his purchases versus his later sales. For simplicity, assume that during the period of Mani's purchases and subsequent sales, although liquidity suppliers are unsure of whether any new private information has emerged or has been developed relevant to NetSuite, in fact none has. So, Mani's trading is the exclusive cause of first the trending upward, and then the trending downward, in NetSuite prices.

### A. THE ACTUAL MANIPULATION

Mani uses a large number of market orders, averaging 5,000 shares per hour, to purchase 10,000 NetSuite shares over two hours. Prior to Mani's purchases, the national best bid (NBB) for NetSuite was $10.00 and the national best offer (NBO) was $10.10. Under our assumptions of no new information, uninformed investors are the only other persons submitting orders. Their order flow arriving at trading venues during this period involves, as one would expect from the analysis in chapter 3, an essentially even number of buys and sells, because neither new information nor price changes motivate their trades. Thus, Mani's buy orders will leave liquidity suppliers facing an excess of 5,000 shares bought from them over shares sold to them each hour. Because the liquidity suppliers fear that the excess might be due to informed trading based on positive information, each 5,000 shares of excess buy orders push their bids and offers up, assume by $0.50. Therefore, at the end of two hours, NetSuite's NBB is $11.00 and its NBO $11.10. Had Mani not traded, NetSuite's NBB and NBO would have remained roughly at $10.00 and $10.10.

Mani now turns around and begins to sell his inventory of 10,000 NetSuite shares, this time selling 5,000 shares per hour for two hours. This means that liquidity suppliers now face an order imbalance of 5,000 more shares sold to them than bought from them each hour. Mani's rationally based expectation that the price response will be asymmetric proves correct: each 5,000 shares of excess sell orders push the bids and offers down by only $0.25. Thus, at the end of his two hours of selling, the NBB and NBO are, respectively, $10.50 and $10.60.

Buying at the offer as the NBO rises, Mani accumulates 10,000 NetSuite shares for an average price of $10.55. Selling at the bid as the NBB falls, Mani sells these 10,000 shares at an average price of $10.75. Mani thus achieves a profit of 10,000 × $0.20 = $2,000.

The distributive question is: Who has benefited from these trades and who has been harmed? Because secondary market trading in pursuit of profits is a zero-sum game,[34] gains and losses by different market participants are mirror images of each other and must sum to zero. In the example, Mani makes profits of $2,000. The liquidity suppliers, who sold him his shares for an average of $10.55 and repurchased them for an average of $10.75, have suffered a corresponding loss of $2,000.[35] In aggregate, uninformed traders experience the change in stock price as a wash, with sellers being better off than if Mani had not traded and buyers being reciprocally worse off.

## B. THE PRICE CORRECTION AFTER THE MANIPULATION

This is not the end of the story, however, even though the liquidity suppliers are back in balance, having purchased from Mani as many shares as they originally sold to him. When Mani finishes his sequence of trades, the NBB and NBO are, respectively, $10.50 and $10.60, not down to $10.00 and $10.10, the prices that would have prevailed absent the manipulation. To be successful, the open market manipulator must cause the stock price to deviate from what represented the market consensus of its value. The dynamics of when, if ever, the stock price's distortion is "corrected," with the impact of the manipulation being eliminated, are crucially important to the welfare effects of manipulation. We see four plausible possibilities: three different ways in which the price can be corrected and then the stark possibility that correction never occurs.

The first two possibilities involve the price going back down to $10.00/$10.10, both of which involve further losses to the liquidity suppliers. One way in which this could happen is for NetSuite to credibly announce that there is no undisclosed information within its possession that could explain the rise to $11.00/11.10 followed by the only partial return to $10.50/$10.60. It would then be clear to the market that there was no reason the price should not be back at $10.00/$10.10. Announcement traders would be briefly able to profit at the expense of liquidity suppliers as the price quickly adjusted down to $10.00/$10.10.

Absent such an announcement, a second way that the price could adjust back to its original level is through the action of anti-mistake traders. This may take considerably longer and involve considerably larger additional losses to the liquidity suppliers. The searches of the anti-mistake traders to see whether there was new information justifying the price changes took too much time for them

REGULATION OF TRADERS | 212

to have had the confidence to engage in trades that would have counteracted the price increases caused by Mani's purchases or that would have accentuated the price decreases caused by Mani's sales. Eventually, however, an increasing number of anti-mistake traders will become convinced that there is no new information that can justify the $10.50/$10.60 price level and will start to sell. As they do, they are, as noted earlier, engaging in a special kind of informed trading (in the sense that they have good reason to believe that there is no such price-justifying information when others do not know this). Just like sales by a regular informed trader in possession of negative information, the sales of the anti-mistake traders create an order imbalance that causes liquidity suppliers to acquire shares at a price above what the anti-mistake trader correctly believes is their value and so leads to additional liquidity supplier losses. Furthermore, just like sales by a regular informed trader in possession of negative information, the continuing order imbalance will prompt the liquidity suppliers to gradually lower their bids and offers until they reach the neighborhood of $10.00/$10.10, at which point the trades of the anti-mistake traders will stop.[36] Anti-mistake trading cannot be assured to occur with every naked open market manipulation, however, because the potential anti-mistake traders may not be sufficiently confident that there is no new information to justify the elevated price after the manipulation is completed.

A third way in which price can return to its proper level is simply the materialization, at some later date, of what, immediately prior to the manipulation, were the future cash flows being predicted by the premanipulation price. For example, if the share price immediately prior to the manipulation suggested that expected future cash flows would remain steady in perpetuity at a given level, but the elevated price after the manipulation suggested an increase in expected future cash flows above this level, the price would return to its original, pre-manipulation level (barring any other news) once subsequent earnings reports showed that in fact cash flows had not increased. Obviously, this final process could take considerable time, leaving prices inaccurate for a significant period.

## 2. Ex-ante perspective

Now assume, not unrealistically, that all the players have unbiased (though not necessarily accurate) expectations concerning the prevalence of successful naked open market manipulation, and that all the players operate within a competitive environment. We want to compare what the longer-run equilibrium would look like in a world where such a trading strategy is occurring freely with the equilibrium in a world where it is somehow blocked. The objective is to see how the availability of the practice affects the wealth positions of the various participants and what the implications of these effects are, through the incentives they create, on efficiency.

## A. MANIPULATORS

Naked open market manipulation will generate positive trading profits on an expected basis to the extent that its practitioners can accurately predict when asymmetric price responses will occur. The resources necessary to conduct a business in such trading are a combination of ordinary and specialized inputs. The ordinary inputs are physical, organizational, and financial assets that could be deployed equally usefully elsewhere in the economy. The specialized inputs are the efforts of key persons who possess abilities and skills uniquely useful for predicting such situations and acting on them. All of these inputs will be drawn into this business up to the point where, at the margin, the expected profits from successfully predicting and acting on such situations equal the costs of paying for the inputs. This activity occurs in an openly competitive environment and so the suppliers of the ordinary inputs will be paid a market return comparable to what they would earn if the resources they supplied were deployed instead another way. Thus, whether naked open market manipulation occurs freely or not has no effect on the wealth positions of the suppliers of these inputs. The persons with uniquely useful abilities and skills will be paid greater rents than they would be paid if, because naked open market manipulation was somehow blocked, they had to work in a different business. Thus, their wealth positions will be enhanced if such manipulation is allowed to occur freely.

## B. LIQUIDITY SUPPLIERS

As we have seen from the ex-post example, liquidity suppliers will lose in their transactions with a successful naked open market manipulator because the reversing purchases from the manipulators are on average at higher prices than the initial sales to them. The liquidity suppliers lose a second time in their transactions with the announcement or anti-mistake traders that bring the price back to the level it would have been without the manipulation.[37]

From the ex-ante perspective, however, all these losses are passed on by the liquidity suppliers to the other traders in the market. This is because, as discussed in chapter 3, liquidity suppliers gain in their transactions with uninformed traders, making half the spread with each sale to the uninformed trader and half from each purchase from an uninformed trader. To survive in a competitive market, a liquidity supplier must set its bids and offers so that these losses and gains balance out (plus, if we add some real-world flavor to the description, cover the returns paid to its personnel, a market return on the capital needed for real estate and equipment and for engaging in the trading itself, and compensation for the undiversified nature of the portfolio that the business will be holding most of the time). If its spreads are wider than this, it will not attract orders because it will be undercut by other liquidity suppliers. If they are narrower than this, at least some of its inputs will be receiving less than a market return and thus the business will not be able to survive in the longer run.

Notwithstanding the fact that liquidity traders pass on these losses, the existence of naked open market manipulations will still have a negative effect on the wealth positions of certain persons associated with the liquidity supply business, but only indirectly. As we have seen, the way that ex-post trading losses are passed on is through a wider spread between the bid and offer. This wider spread increases the cost of trading, and so traders trade less. Less trading means less use of both their ordinary and specialized inputs. Suppliers of the ordinary inputs will earn the same ordinary market return whatever the level of liquidity supply activity. However, persons with abilities and skills uniquely useful for liquidity supply will be paid less in rents and so their wealth positions would be negatively affected by successful manipulation of this type.

## C. UNINFORMED TRADERS

The expected cost to uninformed traders from naked open market manipulation is the need, in the cycle over time of a purchase and sale, to pay the increase in spread due to the occurrence of this kind of manipulation: the uninformed trader will purchase at the offer but only be able to sell at the bid. Calculating the ultimate incidence of this cost on uninformed traders is a bit complicated, however. As discussed in chapter 2, when an issuer's entrepreneurs and initial investors engage in an initial public offering, the shares they are offering will be discounted to reflect the prospect that the spread must be paid with each subsequent sale and purchase in the secondary market, as well as the prospect that any future equity offerings by the issuer over time will be similarly discounted. Thus, the entrepreneurs and early investors receive less than if there were no impact on the spread from this kind of manipulation. This discount continues at the same level for as long as the firm appears to have a long-run future. For uninformed investors who buy and sell less frequently than average, this discount makes the purchase a bargain and so they are gainers from naked open market manipulation. Those who buy and sell more frequently than average are hurt by repeatedly paying the spread more than they are helped by the discount, and so they are losers from the practice.

Informed traders of each kind pay the same increased spread due to the presence of naked open market manipulation as do uninformed traders. This increase in their cost of doing business has a depressing effect on the level of each of the kinds of informed activity. This decreases the level of resources going into each of these activities, with a negative wealth impact on the suppliers of the specialized inputs. The level of fundamental value informed trading will be most sensitive to this increase in cost. This is because fundamental value informed traders create, at a cost to them, the information on which they trade. A wider spread means their trading will be less profitable and so they have less incentive to create information. In contrast, the level of issuer insider and non-issuer insider informed trading and trading based on the tips of such insiders depends mostly on the opportunities that the insiders encounter in their employment.

The decrease in the level of fundamental value informed trading is unfortunate because, as we concluded in chapter 5, the social gain from its contribution to long-run price accuracy exceeds the social costs of the activity. Thus, the social disadvantage from a lower level of fundamental value informed trading is likely to dominate the advantage from the likely smaller decrease in the other, socially undesirable, forms of informed trading.

E. ANTI-MISTAKE TRADERS

The prospect of naked open market manipulation will draw resources into the business of anti-mistake trading, which increases the level of resources going into this activity, with a positive wealth impact on the suppliers of the specialized inputs.

## 3. Fairness considerations

Based on the preceding survey, we can see that freely occurring naked open market manipulation will not affect the wealth position of uninformed traders from an ex-ante point of view because they are as likely to benefit as to be hurt when the price at which they buy or sell is influenced by such a manipulation. It may add to the riskiness of their trading, but this is a risk that can typically be eliminated by holding a diversified portfolio. They will face an increase in the bid-ask spread, but on average this will be compensated by the lower cost of buying shares that earn a given expected return.

The wider bid-ask spread will result in fewer resources being drawn into the businesses of liquidity supply and fundamental value informed trading, thereby decreasing the wealth positions of their specialized input suppliers. The prospect of profits will draw resources into the business of manipulation and the business of anti-mistake trading, thereby increasing the wealth positions of their respective specialized input providers. As discussed in chapter 2, prospective flow of rents is not an entitlement, however. In a market economy, the offer of rents to prompt the suppliers of specialized inputs to come forward is simply the mechanism by which these resources get directed to the activity for which they are most particularly suited. Again, the effects on the rents being paid in the case of the four businesses being considered here do not raise any greater fairness issues than do the rents paid persons with special abilities and skills across the whole market-based part of our economy. As with informed trading, the bottom line is that the more serious normative question concerning naked open market manipulation is whether its effect on the allocation of resources enhances or decreases efficiency.

## 4. Efficiency considerations

From an efficiency point of view, naked open market manipulation has unambiguously negative effects. It consumes resources that could be usefully employed elsewhere in the economy and has a negative impact on both price accuracy and liquidity. It has no redeeming virtues to counteract these negatives.

### A. PRICE ACCURACY

As our discussion of the workings of the market shows, in the absence of manipulation, market prices have the remarkable quality of reflecting a large amount of information relevant to predicting an issuer's future cash flows. Naked open market manipulation moves price away from where it otherwise would be, at least temporarily (and sometimes for longer) reducing price accuracy. In essence, it acts as a kind of informational pollutant, making stock prices noisier signals of actual value. Interestingly, however, although most commentators and jurists focus on the price distortion effects of the practice, reduced price accuracy may be the less important of naked open market manipulation's negative social consequences. Recall from chapter 2 that the ways in which accurate prices benefit the economy include helping to allocate the economy's scarce capital to the most promising potential real investment projects and by improving the utilization of the economy's existing productive capacity through optimizing the signals provided to management about investment decisions and the signals given to boards and shareholders about the quality of management decisions. Very short-run distortions in price of the kind that will typically occur with naked open market manipulation will not seriously undermine the role that share prices play in guiding the real economy in these ways.

However, if neither of the first two corrective forces discussed earlier comes into play, then the price can remain significantly inaccurate for a substantial period of time. In this event, the manipulation would result both in inefficiencies arising from longer-term price inaccuracies and in the negative efficiency related to liquidity, wasted resources and diminished market confidence that we discuss in the following subsections.

## B. LIQUIDITY

The prospect of freely occurring naked open market manipulation has an ongoing negative impact on the liquidity of an issuer's shares because liquidity suppliers will defend themselves against the possibility of losing to such manipulators, and losing again in the price correction process, by widening their bid-ask spreads and decreasing their depth of book. As we have seen, less liquidity reduces social welfare because of the resulting misallocation of resources over time and misallocation of risk. By raising the costs of fundamental value informed trading and thereby lessening the incentives to search out and trade on new information, less liquidity also reduces longer-run share price accuracy.

## C. WASTED PRODUCTIVE RESOURCES

The business of engaging in naked open market manipulation uses real resources in a way that creates no social benefit, and the prospect of it occurring pulls additional resources into the anti-mistake trading business. Although anti-mistake traders perform the socially useful function of correcting prices from their distorted level at the end of a manipulation, these efforts would not be needed in the first place absent the manipulation. Without the manipulation, the resources consumed by these two activities would be available for use elsewhere in the economy, positively contributing to the production of goods and services.

## D. MARKET CONFIDENCE

There is one additional, more nebulous efficiency consideration: market confidence. Even if naked open market manipulation does not in fact decrease the wealth position of ordinary investors and the additional risk created by it can be diversified away, public awareness that it occurs may hurt everyday investors' "confidence" in the stock market. Such manipulations may strike the public as unfair and improper in some way that is harmful to them. As a result, to the detriment of both them and others, they may participate in the stock market to a lesser degree.[38] Typically, the best response to public misunderstanding is to resolve it through education, but, as discussed in chapter 2, when a perception is especially difficult to eradicate and it is causing damage, then that perception may provide an independent policy ground for prohibiting the relevant conduct.

## B. Are There Expected Profits?

The previous example of Mani suggests that there can be expected profits associated with naked open market manipulation. This is in sharp contrast to the conclusions of Daniel Fischel and David Ross's seminal article, in which they conclude that manipulation should not be legally prohibited.[39] One of their two principal reasons for reaching this conclusion is that open market manipulation cannot have expected profits associated with it. Thus, it need not be made illegal because it is self-deterring. We believe this is incorrect because, as developed here, there are situations in which an asymmetric price response can reasonably be expected.

### 1. The Fischel and Ross arguments as to why profitable manipulation is impossible

Fischel and Ross make two arguments as to why profitable manipulation is not possible.[40] First, they say, most securities markets, and especially the stock of large public firms, are highly elastic and liquid.[41] Because of this, they reason, purchases, for example, will typically have no effect on price, because holders of the security will simply sell it to the purchaser and substitute into a different security with a similar cash-flow profile. This argument, though, ignores basic lessons from microstructure economics. As we saw in chapter 3, to a liquidity supplier in an anonymous market, all trade is potentially informed trade and thus trade in fact will generally move price, at least to some extent.

Fischel's and Ross's second line of argument at least recognizes the possibility that a trade could be interpreted as indicating that someone has information not yet reflected in price. Here, they say that bids and offers may move up if a trader putting in purchase orders is perceived to be informed by the market, in which case quoting behavior will adjust to reflect the information thought to be motivating a transaction. The trader, however, will, according to them, also be thought to be informed as she sells, thereby on average driving bid and ask back down to where they were.[42] Moreover, the would-be manipulator will buy at the offer on the way up and sell at the bid on the way down. So, on average, she will actually suffer a net loss. Given this, in the long run would-be manipulators will certainly lose, and so Fischel and Ross conclude that market manipulation is self-deterring.[43] Anyone foolish enough to try manipulation will eventually learn her lesson and stop trying.

The problem with this second argument is that it fails to recognize the possibility of an asymmetric price response.[44] Empirically, we observe that the price response to new orders relating to any stock can in fact vary over time.

*2. Can an asymmetric price response ever be anticipated?*

The mere fact that the price response to new orders varies over time does not by itself prove that naked open market manipulation can generate expected profits. It is also necessary that circumstances arise under which an asymmetric response has some degree of predictability. Note that in the example set out earlier involving Mani, we posit that he rationally assesses that it is probable that his purchases will push the price up by more than his subsequent sales will push them down, but we do not discuss his basis for this expectation.

Thus, a key question is: Are there in fact circumstances under which, more likely than not, there will be an asymmetric price response in a particular direction? The answer is that there are, and in the rest of this section we give examples of a few such circumstances.

A. A PERIOD OF UNUSUAL UNCERTAINTY

One such circumstance is when it is predictable that there would be more fear of informed trading before a certain moment in time than after that moment. An example is when an issuer was expected to announce its earnings on a certain date and there was uncertainty as to what would be announced, with the possibility that it might be either above or below some mean expectation. In the run-up to the announcement, a liquidity supplier would find an order imbalance in either direction to have heightened significance because of the greater-than-usual likelihood that an issuer insider, or her tippee, was trading. Thus, if during this period of extra uncertainty, the manipulator put in orders creating such an imbalance, it would prompt a greater-than-usual adjustment in the supplier's bid and offer. Once the announcement is made, the fear of issuer insider trading diminishes and the liquidity suppliers' bid and ask adjustments in response to order imbalances diminish along with it. Thus, the manipulator can reverse her transactions with less impact on price and end up with a profit.

We should note, however, that while this kind of circumstance may arise quite often, it may not prompt very much manipulation. A manipulator trying to take advantage of such a circumstance will put herself in an unusually risky situation. The very reasons that make the liquidity supplier so sensitive to order imbalances mean that there is a heightened chance that informed trading is in fact going on. If it is, there is a 50/50 chance that the informed trader or traders are trading in the opposite direction from the manipulator, who is uninformed and hence has no idea of any informed trading occurring in the opposite direction. In such a case, the manipulator would need to transact in a very large number of shares for the price to move significantly, because her orders would just be canceling out the imbalance created by the informed trader or traders. At the end, the manipulator would be stuck with a huge inventory of shares at the time of the announcement, which, as predicted by the informed traders, moves the price in the opposite direction from what the manipulator wants.

## B. SHOPPING FOR STOPS

Another circumstance, sometimes referred to as "shopping for stops," arises when there are an unusually large number of stop-loss orders existing at the moment. On the offer side, a *stop-loss order* is an order to buy if the price goes above a certain level. It would typically be placed by someone who is in a short sale position. He does so in order to place some kind of ceiling on his potential losses if the share price goes above a certain point. If there is an usually large number of stop-loss orders on the offer side, the manipulator's purchases on the way up will have a supercharged effect on price because, as his orders drive the price up, the stop-loss orders are tripped, thereby triggering more buying orders. When the manipulator turns around to sell, the prices in the market, as they go down, will on average be well above the bid-side stop-loss orders (typically put in by someone in a long position seeking a ceiling on her losses). Thus, prices do not decline as fast in reaction to the manipulator's sales because none of the bid stop-loss orders are tripped. The tricky part of this game, though, is that stop-loss orders that are posted with exchanges are not revealed. Also, they may just be resting with a broker who is directed to submit them if the price reaches a certain level, or simply be built into the algorithm that a trader is using to determine and execute his purchases and sales. Still, with aggressive trading to test the state of the market, a manipulator might be able to detect a situation with an unusually large number of stop-loss orders, though it could be expensive to do so.

## C. BOOK FRAGILITY

A third possibility is that the manipulator detects that there is less depth of book than usual (a *fragile book*) on one or both sides of the market. Recall that a fragile book on the offer side, for example, would have standing visible offers for fewer shares than usual at prices above, but still close to, the NBO, and the book would not refill quickly once marketable orders executed against these quotes. A fragile book on the bid side is just the mirror image of this with the NBB as the baseline. If the fragility is on just one side, the manipulator's orders in that direction will run through the limit orders in the book, quickly moving the price. But, when he reverses and starts submitting the opposite orders, there will be more limit orders on this side of the book, which will absorb his orders and soften their price impact. The trick again is to determine what the state of the book is given that many orders are not displayed. Again, however, this can be tested by putting in smaller orders and seeing if the visible book refills immediately or not. As discussed earlier, there is empirical evidence suggesting that just such exploratory trading occurs often in the commodity futures market and is followed by naked open market manipulative trading.[45]

D. DIFFERENT TRADING VENUES

A final possibility relates to the existence of different types of trading venues. Chapter 1 explains the concept of internalization: retail brokerage houses commonly receive payment for order flow from over-the-counter dealers with the promise that the order will execute at prices better than the NBBO. What is important to note, here, is that the internalizers are willing to pay for this order flow because they expect to execute against largely uninformed orders. These executions will be reported via the TRF, a different vehicle for reporting than used by the exchanges. Market participants see the executions reported on the TRF and reasonably infer that these executions are likely to have been generated by uninformed orders. At the same time, because a significant number of retail orders are executed by internalizers, the likelihood that executions on the exchanges are effected by informed orders is increased. Thus, we would expect to see a greater price impact from an execution reported by the exchanges than those reported by the internalizers. This plausibly differing price impact creates an incentive for a manipulative strategy. For example, sell on an exchange, then buy from an internalizer, then buy on an exchange, and sell to an internalizer. The first internalizer sell has greater impact lowering price than the subsequent exchange buy increases price. And the exchange buy has greater price impact than the subsequent internalizer sell. The Appendix provides more detail from the SEC complaint concerning an actual implementation of this strategy.

## C. The Appropriateness of Legal Sanctions

The other principal reason that Fischel and Ross oppose the legal prohibition of manipulation is that no observable conduct separates manipulative trading from trading for other purposes. Determining the purpose of a transaction is highly speculative. Thus, they argue, making open market manipulation illegal will deter many worthwhile transactions as well. This is because persons contemplating these worthwhile transactions will fear that their transactions will be mistaken for manipulative ones. Here, we agree with Fischel's and Ross's concern, but take issue with their assumption that there is never observable conduct to distinguish manipulative transactions from socially useful ones.

Consider the four circumstances we have just discussed in which it may be possible for a manipulator to assess that an asymmetric price response is more probable than not. In the case of the first circumstance—unusual uncertainty that will be resolved soon—there is indeed no observable conduct that would separate the manipulator from an investor who simply buys based on hard work analyzing the future of the issuer, and then sells when his best guess turns out to be correct and the issuer's price increases. Thus, although, at least as a conceptual matter, there may be times in such a situation when naked open market speculation will have positive expected profits, we see no way of intelligently imposing legal sanctions, except where there is direct evidence, such as an email, as to the trader's purpose.

In contrast, in two other circumstances—shopping for stops and book fragility—a manipulative trader, to enjoy expected profits, would need to engage in observable market conduct: a testing of the market to see what the stop-loss or book fragility situation is. We thus advocate a rule that imposes legal sanctions for a series of purchases followed by a series of sales (or vice versa) that yield a profit when the first set of transactions was preceded by this kind of testing of the market that reveals a fragile book or an unusually high number of stop orders.[46] This kind of conduct would strongly suggest that the trader was entering into these transactions at least in part to profit from the socially negative practice of naked open market manipulation, and that quite possibly this was the only motivation. In other words, there is a low risk that the rule would deter transactions solely motivated entirely by some other socially worthwhile purpose. There is nothing wrong with deterring transactions that are motivated both by a desire to profit from such manipulation and by some other socially worthwhile purpose. This is because something affirmative and observable—the testing of the market—was necessary for the socially negative manipulation motive to be included. So, imposing legal sanctions should deter undertaking the affirmative conduct, which is the vehicle for acting on the manipulative motive, but should not deter transactions that further a socially worthwhile purpose.

The fourth example—using different venues to put on and take off one's position—may be problematic, at least in the longer run. As the analysis in the

Appendix shows, the losers in this manipulation are the internalizers. Indeed, the complaint claims that the respondent made frequent brokerage house changes to try and hide his behavior from the internalizers. The internalizers are sophisticated market participants and, now that they are aware of the potential of this strategy, may be able to develop better techniques for detecting and avoiding such orders.

## III. OPEN MARKET MANIPULATION WITH AN EXTERNAL INTEREST

*Open market manipulation with an external interest* involves a trader who has some kind of interest in the price of a security independent of the price at which she can buy and sell it in the open market. Shortly in advance of the moment when the price will determine the value of this independent interest, the trader purchases a number of shares, and the resulting upward push on prices leads to a gain based on the increase in the value of the external interest. Once this moment has passed, the trader resells the shares that she previously purchased to push the price up.[47] To yield an expected gain, this strategy does not require that the likelihood of an asymmetric price reaction be sufficiently great to make up for the costs of the trading involved. It only requires that the expected gain derived from the inflated price pushing up the value of the external interest be greater than the costs of trading. This is a condition that would be easily satisfied for an external interest of any real size.

The following analysis suggests that open market manipulation with an external interest is also a trading strategy that produces an affirmative answer to each of the four foundational questions posed at the beginning of this paper, and hence is an appropriate target of a ban under the Exchange Act. Again, it is socially harmful in a distinguishable way that would fit under the broad dictionary meaning of the word *manipulation;* there are circumstances under which the strategy can yield positive expected profits; and there is a legal rule available to deter it that will not deter many socially valuable transactions at the same time.

### A. The Example of *United States v. Mulheren*

Open market manipulation with an external interest is well illustrated by the famous case of *United States v. Mulheren.*[48] The history of this case is as follows: Carl Icahn and Ivan Boesky had accumulated a substantial minority ownership position in Gulf & Western Industries, Inc. (G&W), and approached Martin Davis, the chairman of G&W, about Boesky's interest in taking control of G&W or securing board seats on the company.[49] Davis was adamantly opposed to both of Boesky's proposals. Boesky then called Davis and offered to sell back his block of shares to G&W at $45, which was higher than its current trading price on the NYSE. Davis replied that G&W would buy back Boesky's block, but only at whatever price the company traded at on the NYSE at the time of the purchase. Soon thereafter, Boesky contacted John Mulheren. Their conversation was the centerpiece of the prosecution's case. According to Boesky's testimony, Boesky told Mulheren that he liked G&W's stock, which was then trading at $44.75, and that "I would not pay more than 45 for it and it would be great if it traded at 45," to which Mulheren replied, "I understand."

At 11:00 AM on the morning after Boesky's conversation with Davis, Mulheren's trading firm submitted orders to buy 75,000 G&W shares. So far that morning, G&W had only traded 32,000 shares total, still at $44.75. By the time Mulheren's orders had transacted, however, the price of G&W stock had risen to $45 per share. Within ten minutes of those transactions, Boesky and Icahn then called Davis to take him up on his offer to buy their G&W shares at the market price. As a result, they were able to sell to G&W their combined 6,715,700 G&W shares at $45 per share, generating $1,678,925 (6,715,700 × $0.25) more in proceeds than if the sale to G&W had occurred at $44.75. G&W closed at the price of $43.63 that day, leading to a loss for Mulheren of $64,406.

## B. Wealth Transfers: The Efficiency Effects of Their Incentives

We will discuss the tortured legal history of the *Mulheren* case later in this chapter. In any event, the case provides an excellent illustration of open market manipulation with an external interest if we assume, as the jury did, that Mulheren's purchases were made as a favor to Boesky: to increase the price of G&W stock so that Boesky could gain more out of his arrangement with Davis. The case shows that a manipulative scheme can be enormously profitable if there is a separate deal referring to or dependent on the stock's price, even if direct trading of that security on the exchange system turns out to be unprofitable. So, although Mulheren may have lost $64,406, Boesky and Icahn profited by almost $1.7 million as a result of the price rise that accompanied Mulheren's purchases. The alleged schemers stood to profit not from Mulheren's trades themselves, but from the off-market side deal between Boesky and Davis, which referred to a market price.

Other than the impact on the immediate parties, this kind of open market manipulation has little in the way of wealth consequences. Because there is no predictable price response asymmetry, professional liquidity suppliers suffer no expected losses from such a manipulation. In fact, it gives them extra business, just as additional uninformed trade does. Thus, the prospect that such manipulation will occur from time to time will not lead to liquidity suppliers widening their spreads and making stock trading less liquid. Uninformed and informed traders who happen to be trading in the same direction as the manipulator during the period that the price is distorted will be hurt, but those trading in the opposite direction will be helped by the same amount. As a result, ex ante the practice has no effects on the wealth positions of either uninformed or informed traders.

What about the efficiency effects of freely occurring open market manipulation with an external interest? As we have just seen, it will not affect liquidity because liquidity suppliers do not need to widen their bid-ask spreads to protect against the possibility that they are trading with such a manipulator. It will lead to a temporary distortion in price, but, just like the temporary distortions caused by the typical naked open market manipulation, these distortions will not seriously undermine the role that share prices play in guiding the real economy.

The real concern raised by this kind of manipulation is its effect on the cost of contracting. At least in principle, the government could take a caveat emptor approach toward financial arrangements that refer to manipulable market prices. Sophisticated parties could be relied upon either to eschew such terms or to require counterparties to avoid manipulative behavior and to then carefully monitor whether they comply. Suppose two parties enter an arrangement referring to a market price, but the contract fails to prohibit price-changing trading. One might maintain that the party that loses as a result of price-changing trading by the counterparty simply entered into a freely negotiated, but not very intelligently considered, contract and that he should be held to it. One could reach a similar conclusion in the situation in which the contract did contain such a prohibition but the trading occurred anyway and the negatively affected party failed to monitor the trading of the other party. In other words, the negatively affected party has no one to blame but himself because he could have negotiated a better arrangement. In the *Mulheren* example, for instance, rather than simply pegging his arrangement to the NYSE price at a given moment, Martin Davis could have pegged his deal with Boesky to the volume-weighted average price for the stock over the course of an entire day, making it effectively impossible to manipulate profitably. It certainly makes contracting more expensive if parties must also monitor for manipulation, but that only clarifies that the real efficiency question here concerns the relative competence of private parties and the government in determining and enforcing contract terms and monitoring their compliance.

It is fairly obvious that the parties to almost all contracts making reference to stock prices would want a prohibition on manipulation, at least if each thought about the matter and there was reason to expect a high level of compliance. This is because allowing manipulation undermines the very purpose of the reference to a firm's share price. Moreover, a number of factors counsel that the government may be a more efficient party to rely upon for this monitoring task than private parties. First, simply avoiding the use of market price terms will not be easy. Hundreds of trillions of dollars in financial contracts make use of market prices as referents for the simple reason that they provide enormously important information about pertinent economic realities.[50] Second, the government is likely to enjoy significant economies of scale in monitoring for misconduct and prosecuting wrongdoers.

One might argue that it is inappropriate to use the securities laws to enhance simple contracting. Something very similar, however, is being done in cases involving trading by an insider of a non-issuer entity (for example, an insider of an acquirer in a potential hostile tender offer). As we saw in chapter 5, when such an insider trades on the basis of the confidential material information that he has learned in his job, he violates Rule 10b-5 under the misappropriation theory. However, this insider is being punished not for a breach of duty to the person with whom the securities transaction is being conducted, but for a breach of duty to the insider's source of information. In other words, the securities laws are being used to reinforce a more general legal obligation—not to use information gained from a principal for personal profit—simply because a securities transaction happens to be the means of making this profit.

## C. The Appropriateness of Imposing Legal Sanctions

Assuming that one is comfortable with using the securities laws to protect contracting that depends on securities prices, the argument for imposing legal sanctions on open market manipulators with an external interest is strong. As the *Mulheren* example (or just one's imagination) shows, there are definitely circumstances under which the practice can generate large positive expected profits.[51] If the practice were freely occurring, it would be socially costly because its free occurrence makes contracting more costly and contracting is socially valuable.

In our view, legal sanctions should be imposed where it is proved that a trader with such an external interest makes a purchase just in advance of the moment at which the security's price determines the gain that arises from the trader's external interest. Doing so is very unlikely to deter any socially useful transactions because it would be highly coincidental that a trader would want to engage in a purchase at just that moment for any purpose other than obtaining the external gain.

## IV. MISSTATEMENT MANIPULATION

*Misstatement manipulation* involves a trader who makes a material false negative statement concerning an issuer that pushes down the issuer's price, purchases a certain number of shares in the market, waits until the truth comes out, and then resells the shares.[52] Even though the misstatement manipulator may have no connection with the issuer, he may be able to affect the price of its shares. The statement could be the trigger for a false rumor that spreads through the market, or it might be a public statement from a source that investors regard as trustworthy and knowledgeable concerning some aspect of the issuer's future. Our analysis suggests that misstatement manipulation is also a trading strategy that gives rise to an affirmative answer to each of the four foundational questions posed at the beginning of this chapter, and hence is an appropriate target of a ban under the Exchange Act. Again, it is socially harmful in a distinguishable way that would fit under the broad dictionary meaning of the word *manipulation*, there are circumstances under which the strategy can yield positive expected profits, and there is a legal rule available to deter it that will not deter many socially valuable transactions at the same time.

### A. Misstatement Manipulation as a Kind of Informed Trading

Misstatement manipulation is actually a special kind of informed trading. Just like a corporate insider trading on confidential information that he obtained from his employer, the misstatement manipulator makes his purchases on the basis of something that he knows and the market does not: the falsity of the price-depressing misstatement for which he is responsible.

As we demonstrated in chapter 5, ordinary informed trading, on the one hand, moves share price on average in the direction of greater accuracy, and, on the other hand, reduces liquidity. Thus, it is necessary to net out the trade-off between the positive social impact from improved share price accuracy and the negative social impact from decreased liquidity. We concluded that trading on the basis of fundamental value information is socially desirable, whereas trading on the basis of announcement information, issuer inside information, and/or non-issuer inside information (unless permitted by the non-issuer institution that generated the information) is socially undesirable. Our efforts at netting out that led to these conclusions are just reasoned judgments, however. Misstatement manipulation is different. It is true that the act of trading itself moves price in the direction of greater accuracy because the purchases push the price up somewhat from its depressed level. However, the larger strategy of which this trading is part includes the misstatement that created the inaccuracy in the first place. Thus, the overall strategy of misstatement manipulation unambiguously damages social welfare both by making prices less accurate and by reducing liquidity. An arsonist does not become a hero by putting out the fire that he started in the first place.

## B. Wealth Transfers: The Efficiency Implications of the Incentives Created

The ex-post and ex-ante wealth transfer analyses are essentially the same as those for informed trading discussed in chapter 5, with the misstatement manipulator substituted for the informed trader.[53] The manipulator makes money because he buys the securities for less than they are worth and sells them back for what they are worth (minus the bid-ask spread per share). The liquidity suppliers lose the same amount of money because they sell shares to the manipulator at a price below their value and buy them back from the manipulator at a price equal to what they are worth (again, these losses are reduced by the same bid-ask spread per share). Anti-mistake traders and price-sensitive fundamental value information traders may similarly lose to the extent they may sell at a price below share value. Uninformed traders who sell during the period that the price is depressed receive too little (though this is somewhat ameliorated for those who sell after the manipulator's purchases), but the uninformed traders who buy during this period acquire an equal number of shares and pay commensurately too little.

Ex ante, the liquidity suppliers will increase their spreads to compensate for the prospect of losing money to misstatement manipulators, so the only wealth effects are diminished rents to specialized inputs that occur because a wider spread means less business for liquidity suppliers. Uninformed investors are unaffected ex ante by the prospect of the practice because they are as likely to be winners as losers from it. Although they will have to pay the additional spread, share prices will be discounted at the time of their original issue and in ongoing secondary trading to reflect this additional spread.

From an efficiency point of view, misstatement manipulation both makes prices less accurate and decreases liquidity. Again, the decrease in liquidity may be the more serious socially negative effect. Particularly in the case of a misstatement that is the start of a false rumor, the truth may come out quickly. So, as with the other two forms of manipulation, the price distortions from misstatement manipulation will not seriously undermine the role that share prices play in guiding the real economy.

## C. The Appropriateness of Legal Sanctions

We find appropriate a rule that imposes legal sanctions when a trader (i) knowingly makes a materially false or misleading statement under circumstances in which a reasonable person would expect it likely to have an effect on price, and (ii) then makes a securities transaction in the direction that would yield positive expected profits given the misstatement's effect, followed by later transaction(s) in the opposite direction. This kind of conduct strongly suggests that the trader was entering into these transactions at least in part to profit from the socially negative practice of misstatement manipulation. As with our proposed rules for the other two kinds of manipulation, there is little risk that the rule would deter transactions motivated entirely by some other socially worthwhile purpose. Again, there is nothing wrong with deterring transactions that are motivated both by a desire to profit from such manipulation and by some socially worthwhile purpose as well. This is because something observable and affirmative—the false or misleading statement—is necessary for the socially negative manipulation motive to be included. So, again, imposing legal sanctions should deter people from undertaking the affirmative conduct that is the vehicle for the socially negative motive, not transactions to the extent that they are based on the socially worthwhile motive.

## V. THE LAW OF SECURITIES MANIPULATION

Mirroring the confusion among popular and scholarly commentators, the federal district and circuit courts of appeal are riven by a series of splits regarding some of the most foundational questions about manipulation: What is open market manipulation? Is any form of open market manipulation unlawful under Rule 10b-5, the workhorse of securities enforcement? What is the relationship between a fraud claim and a manipulation claim involving a misrepresentation under Rule 10b-5, and are they subject to different pleading requirements? After reviewing the relevant array of precedents relating to each of these questions, we will offer our view as to how these issues should be resolved.

The principal tools for attacking all three types of equity market manipulation discussed in this chapter are §§ 9(a) and 10(b) of the Securities and Exchange Act.

## A. Open Market Manipulation

The courts have not made a formal distinction between naked open market manipulation and open market manipulation with an external interest, and so we discuss the law relating to these two together. Two provisions of the 1934 Act are relevant here: §§ 9(a) and 10(b).

### 1. Section 9(a)

Section 9(a)(1) prohibits individuals from engaging in two specific forms of manipulation—"wash sales" and "matched sales"—whose anti-social aspects are relatively uncontroversial.[54] These sales involve, respectively, a trader who trades with himself and a trader who trades with a prearranged counterparty.[55] These trades result in no effective change in beneficial ownership and so serve no socially useful purpose as trades. They are socially harmful, however, in terms of the transaction reporting that they generate. Other traders do not know that the reported transactions involve wash or matched sales. They assume that the reported prices reflect the valuations of persons who are engaged in genuine purchases and sales of the stock and they react accordingly, to their disadvantage. Moreover, at least briefly, the share price is made less accurate. For reasonably thickly traded stocks, the efficient market hypothesis assures that prices fully reflect all publicly available information. This assumes that the reported prices are the result of trades genuinely involving value calculations on the part of all buyers and sellers (other than the uninformed, who have no influence on price). Wash or matched sales cause the price to deviate from this efficient price and hence make it a less accurate appraisal of an issuer's future cash flows.[56]

Section 9(a)(2) relates to a wider range of activity. It prohibits effecting "a series of transactions" in a security (i) that "creat[e] actual or apparent active trading" or affect its price, (ii) "for the purpose of inducing the purchase or sale of such security by others."[57] As discussed in Section I, for this prohibition to have practical meaning, its bite must come from defining what constitutes an illegitimate purpose. The case law reviewed here shows how difficult this has been for the courts to do and the help that can come from the approach we develop, which involves identifying those situations that satisfy our four basic questions. Recall that in the end, this simply boils down to the issue of what constitutes satisfactory evidence that the motivation behind at least some portion of a person's trading activity is simply to move the price.

The case law on manipulation is littered with references to § 9(a)(2),[58] yet there has been a consistent failure to substantively analyze, precisely identify, or even define the improper purpose required by the provision or to discuss what evidence would satisfactorily prove it. Rather, the cases typically reiterate the language of the statute[59] or provide such question-begging statements as the Seventh Circuit's: "[t]he essence of the offense is creating 'a false impression of supply or demand,' for example through wash sales, where parties fictitiously trade the same shares back and forth at higher and higher prices to fool the market into thinking that there is a lot of buying interest in the stock."[60]

Nonetheless, a few cases have offered helpful nuggets. For instance, *In re the Federal Corp.*[61] involved the purchase of shares in the secondary trading market in order to drive up the price at which a new primary offering could be made. This manipulation with an external interest was successfully prosecuted under § 9(a)(2) pursuant to an action brought by the SEC's Enforcement Division and ultimately adjudicated by the SEC. Noting that manipulative purpose must almost always be proved circumstantially, the SEC determined that "where a person is taking the legal steps necessary to make a substantial offering of a given stock . . . and he then artificially stimulates the demand by taking all the stock offered in that market at a given price," thus "raising the market by more than 14 percent and making it likely that his proposed offering will net him substantially more than it would on the basis of the untampered market price," a manipulative purpose would be found.[62] In fact, the SEC articulated quite explicitly a special case of our more general principle that an external interest creates an evidentiary presumption, noting that "it appears to us that a *prima facie* case exists when it is shown that a person who has a substantial direct pecuniary interest in the success of a proposed offering takes active steps to effect a rise in the market for outstanding securities of the same issuer."[63]

Other decisions finding a violation of § 9(a)(2) have also involved external interest manipulation cases, and at least demonstrated courts' willingness to approve prosecution of this species of manipulation under the banner of § 9(a)(2). *Securities & Exchange Commission v. Resch-Cassin & Co.*[64] involved the underwriter of a stock offering who made promises that stock that was being offered for $10 per share would be trading in the aftermarket at $20 or better. To persuade investors to purchase the unsold portion of the offering, the underwriters promised that by a certain date it would be trading at or above $20.[65] The underwriters then made sufficient purchases in the secondary market to drive the price up to this level by the specified date. As the court concluded that the defendants "had an obvious incentive to artificially influence the market price of the security in order to facilitate its distribution or increase its profitability. Here the defendants used the manipulated after-market to sell the . . . stock to the public."[66] The court provided an analysis of § 9(a)(2), noting that the defendants "engaged in a series of transactions . . . which created actual and apparent trading in, and raised the price of, that stock for the purpose of inducing its purchase by others."[67] The manipulative outcome of this conduct "was to artificially stimulate the so-called market price of the stock while making it appear to be the product of the independent forces of supply and demand when, in reality, it was completely a creature of defendants' subterfuge."[68]

Another case involving an open market manipulation with an external interest under § 9(a)(2) is *Crane Co. v. Westinghouse Air Brake Co.*[69] The case involved two companies, Crane and American Standard, each seeking to take over Air Brake. Crane was seeking to do so by a tender offer at $50 per share. American Standard's effort involved a merger agreement, proxy support for which was being sought by Standard from Air Brake's shareholders. The day that the Crane tender offer was scheduled to expire, Air Brake's stock opened at $45.25. Standard purchased 170,200 shares during the day and the price quickly rose to $50. Standard's average purchase price for the shares was $49.08. Prior to the opening, Standard had agreed in a private transaction to sell 100,000 Air Brake shares for $44.50, more than $4.50 less than the average price of its purchases that day. This strongly suggested to the court that Standard's purchases were not for the purpose of increasing the number of Air Brake shares in its portfolio, but rather to push the price of Air Brake up in order to make the Crane tender offer look unattractive and discourage Air Brake shareholders from tendering to Crane.[70] By doing so, Standard cleared the way for its merger with Air Brake to succeed. The court rejected Standard's claim that the purchases can "be explained solely by an alleged 'purpose' to acquire voting control" [71] of Air Brake and concluded that "a finding of manipulative purpose is prime facie established."[72]

Notwithstanding these few cases, the overall historical record shows that § 9(a)(2) has played only a minimal role in the development of manipulation jurisprudence in securities law, despite the obvious relevance of its language. The principal reason is that for most of its history, until 2010, § 9(a)(2) was only applicable to alleged manipulations involving *exchange* traded securities.

This made it inapplicable to most open market manipulations for two reasons. First, stocks that trade on exchanges tend to be traded in larger volume and be more liquid, whereas open market manipulation is much more likely to move price significantly with more thinly traded over-the-counter stocks. So, for most of § 9(a)(2)'s history, the lower-float, lower-volume securities most likely to be the victims of a market manipulation were outside its reach.[73] Second, NASDAQ—a principal trading venue for stocks—did not even become an exchange until 2006.[74]

## 2. Section 10(b)

Because of this history, the jurisprudence concerning open market manipulations has centered predominantly on the circumstances, if any, under which such manipulations violate § 10(b) of the 1934 Act. Section 10(b) prohibits any person from using in a securities transaction "any manipulative or deceptive device" in contravention of an SEC rule promulgated thereunder.[75] Rule 10b-5 is such a rule. It defines more specifically prohibited forms of conduct, rendering it unlawful to engage in various enumerated practices.[76] Although adopted without fanfare, Rule 10b-5 has become the foundation for prosecution of financial misconduct by the SEC as well for suits by private litigants.[77] There is a certain awkwardness, however, when behavior is challenged as manipulation under this rule. Despite the broad language of § 10(b) itself, Rule 10b-5 reads much more as a provision focused on fraud than on manipulation, a term that the language of the rule does not even include.

Supreme Court precedent that narrowly interpreted § 10(b) in cases far removed from open market manipulation unfortunately set the stage for lower court confusion regarding what open market manipulation is and whether it is unlawful under Rule 10b-5. In a series of decisions issued during the 1970s and 1980s, the Supreme Court repeatedly emphasized the role of deceit and misrepresentation in a § 10(b) claim, almost transforming § 10(b) into a statute that only caught fraud and fraud-like claims within its ambit.[78] This culminated in statements by the Court such as, "Section 10(b) is aptly described as a catchall provision, but what it catches must be fraud."[79] In the aftermath of this development, the lower federal courts were uncertain as to whether it was even possible that any open market trading behavior (whether naked or involving an external interest) could by itself constitute illegal manipulation.

The lingering effect of these Supreme Court precedents is a sharp circuit split regarding whether open market manipulation, without an additional act that is unlawful by itself, is ever prohibited under § 10(b). Both sides in this split agree on the black letter statement of the general elements of a private damages manipulation claim under Rule 10b-5: "(1) manipulative acts; (2) damages (3) caused by reliance on an assumption of an efficient market free of manipulation; (4) scienter; (5) in connection with the purchase or sale of securities; (6) furthered by the defendant's use of the mails or any facility of a national securities exchange."[80] The key question is what constitutes a "manipulative act." On one side is a series of court opinions that have been read to assert that actual trading behavior *on its own* cannot constitute a manipulation; some additional unlawful act is necessary as well. In essence, this would mean that open market manipulation per se is not illegal under Rule 10b-5. Other circuits have come to the opposite conclusion, at least under certain circumstances.

The Third Circuit is one that can be read as being in the first group. In *GFL Advantage Fund, Ltd. v. Colkitt*,[81] it stated that "[r]egardless of whether market manipulation is achieved through deceptive trading activities or deceptive statements as to the issuing corporation's value, it is clear that the essential element of the claim is that *inaccurate* information is being injected into the marketplace."[82] The facts of the case make clear that trading for the sole purpose of moving a securities price was not enough, in the court's view, to be considered an injection of inaccurate information into the marketplace. Hence, in its view, such trading by itself would not be an illegal manipulation under Rule 10b-5. What was being plausibly alleged in this case was open market manipulation with an external interest. The defendant was alleged to have depressed the price of the issuer's stock in order to profit from a prior arrangement in which the plaintiff agreed that the defendant could convert debt into equity at a discounted version of the average market price.[83] According to the Third Circuit, because the trading behavior was itself lawful, it could not be considered as creating inaccurate information and therefore was not deceptive trading behavior.[84]

The Second Circuit's current view is especially hard to discern. In 1991, in *United States v. Mulheren*,[85] the Second Circuit overturned the defendant's jury conviction regarding manipulative activity in an opinion expressing highly skeptical dicta on the question. Although the specific ground for the reversal was a determination that there was insufficient evidence that Mulheren was acting on Boesky's behalf, the Second Circuit also stated that "although we have misgivings about the government's view of the law, we will assume, without deciding on this appeal, that an investor may lawfully be convicted under Rule 10b-5 where the purpose of his transaction is solely to affect the price of a security."[86] It noted as well that "[n]one of the traditional badges of manipulation are present in this case. Mulheren conspicuously purchased the shares for Jamie's account in the open market."[87]

By 2000, a district court could note, however, that "[t]he law of the Second Circuit on so-called open-market manipulation—where the alleged manipulator has made otherwise legitimate trades, yet with the subjective intent to affect the stock price thereby—is not yet fully settled."[88] More importantly, in 2015, the Second Circuit, in *Fezzani v. Bear, Stearns & Co.*, clarified its view to the extent of saying in dictum that manipulation under § 10(b) does *not* require "reliance by a victim on direct oral or written communications by a defendant."[89] A manipulation can stem from "'market activity' intended to mislead investors by sending 'a false pricing signal to the market,' upon which victims of the manipulation rely."[90] The *Fezzani* decision built on the Second Circuit's discussion in *ATSI Communications, Inc. v. Shaar Fund, Ltd.,*[91] in which it stated that manipulation "refers generally to practices, such as wash sales, matched orders, or rigged prices, that are intended to mislead investors by artificially affecting market activity."[92]

The Second Circuit's analysis in *Fezzani* went further:

> [M]anipulation "connotes intentional or willful conduct designed to deceive or defraud investors by controlling or artificially affecting the price of securities." The critical question then becomes what activity "artificially" affects a security's price in a deceptive manner. . . . [C]ase law in this circuit and elsewhere has required a showing that an alleged manipulator engaged in *market activity* aimed at deceiving investors as to how other market participants have valued a security.[93]

This language suggests the Second Circuit has moved away from the view of the Third Circuit.

The D.C. Circuit takes a strong view in favor of open market manipulations' illegality.[94] In *Markowski v. SEC,*[95] a case with facts somewhat analogous to what we have termed a market manipulation with an external interest, the D.C. Circuit interpreted § 10(b) to have proscribed manipulations involving trades made "solely because of the actor's purpose" when that purpose was improper, without necessitating any further unlawful act.[96]

This circuit split has not gone without notice. In 2016, the D.C. Circuit reiterated its position that trading alone could give rise to liability for manipulation.[97] In response, the accused manipulator petitioned the Supreme Court, seeking review.[98] The defendants' petition for a writ of certiorari to the Supreme Court noted—correctly—that the current split among the federal circuits creates significant confusion for market participants and disparities of outcome for those accused. The Court, however, denied the petition, so the confusion will continue for now.

## B. Assessing the Law on Open Market Manipulation

As developed in Sections II and III, both naked open market manipulation and open market manipulation with an external interest are strategies that can move market prices. Moreover, each can yield expected profits under certain circumstances, and each is socially undesirable. For each of these two kinds of manipulation, we have identified objectively observable factors that can serve as a condition for imposing legal sanctions on undesirable trades, while minimizing prosecution of socially desirable trades. This analysis also shows how rules against the two practices based on these objectively observable factors fit within the prohibitory scope allowed by the language of §§ 9 and 10(b).

Against this background and the preceding review of the case law, we can now evaluate what the courts have done to date in interpreting these provisions and what they should do in the future.[99] First, the reluctance of many courts to even recognize the existence of open market manipulation and its potential unlawfulness under § 10(b) is unjustifiable. In this connection, the Supreme Court should resolve the circuit split in favor of the Second and D.C. Circuits' stance. Second, even courts that do recognize the existence and potential unlawfulness of open market manipulation seem at a loss in formulating coherent, consistent rules that make policy sense. We suggest that they move toward the four-question approach we have proposed here. Specifically, at a concrete level, where there is a lack of documentary evidence that the sole purpose of a trade was to move price, courts should look for evidence of one of two phenomena beyond profitable buying and selling: 1) superficially unprofitable trading designed to generate information about the likelihood of an asymmetric price response (what we have referred to as a more general idea of exploratory trading); or 2) an external transaction that renders critically timed, facially unprofitable trading behavior profitable in expectation.

Our analysis leads us to an additional conclusion regarding the case law's best path toward optimal deterrence of manipulative trading. Because of the pre-2010 limitations on § 9(a)(2)'s reach (discussed earlier)—particularly, its applicability solely to exchange-listed securities—the common law jurisprudence of securities manipulation has overwhelmingly developed around Rule 10b-5. Though the ambit of § 9(a)(2) is now wide, path dependency seems to have resulted in § 10(b), rather than § 9(a)(2), continuing to be regulators' and private litigants' statute of choice. They may be making a mistake. Section 9(a)(2) can now be more actively deployed, and offers the conspicuous advantage of being free from the confused Rule 10b-5 case law suggesting that "deceit" is a necessary feature of manipulation. Our approach is well suited to act as a guide to the development of new § 9(a)(2) case law.

## C. Misstatement Manipulation

Unlike the two kinds of open market manipulation, there has long been a basis in court-made law for imposing sanctions on traders engaging in misstatement manipulation. Rule 10b-5(b) makes it unlawful for any person "to make any untrue statement of a material fact or to omit to state any material fact necessary in order to make the statements made, in light of the circumstances under which they were made, not misleading . . . in connection with the purchase or sale of a security." As far back as 1968, the Second Circuit ruled in *SEC v Texas Gulf Sulphur* that whenever an *issuer* makes a statement that is "reasonably calculated to influence the investing public," such statement satisfies Rule 10b-5's requirement that it be "in connection with the purchase or sale of a security," even if neither the issuer nor its managers buy or sell shares themselves.[100] This broad interpretation of the "in connection with" requirement rule has subsequently been further expanded to reach other persons besides the issuer and its officials and to include the statements of these other persons when they would predictably affect investors' judgments. Moreover, the courts have made clear that in government-based actions, there need not be a showing of reliance by the particular purchasers or sellers of shares. Indeed, one might reasonably argue that there is no reason to call "misstatement manipulation" manipulation at all: it is just fraud. Still, this evolution extends the reach of Rule 10b-5(b) far beyond that of common law fraud, which contemplates a one-on-one transaction with reliance on the misstatement by the counterparty. The application of Rule 10b-5(b) to misstatement manipulation goes to the distortive effect of the misstatement on overall market pricing.

Given this background, for our purposes, it matters little whether what we label misstatement manipulation is considered manipulation or simply a fraud outlawed by the explicit terms of Rule 10b-5(b). Courts, however, do struggle to distinguish between what they consider to be just fraud and what they consider to be a manipulation that involves a misstatement. They have generally held that manipulations involving misrepresentations require something more than mere misrepresentations. As the Second Circuit has put it, a manipulation claim under Rule 10b-5, even when it involves misrepresentations, requires in addition "manipulative acts."[101] These acts must "create a false impression of how market participants value a security."[102] "[A]llegations of misrepresentations or omissions alone cannot support a claim of market manipulation."[103]

This nebulous distinction between fraud and manipulation involving a misstatement matters for reasons that are not at the center of our concerns in this chapter. It nevertheless is not just semantics. Federal Rule of Civil Procedure Rule 9(b) adds a special obstacle to bringing any fraud suit by requiring the complaint to plead the fraud with specificity. On top of this, the Private Securities Litigation Reform Act (PSLRA), enacted by Congress in 1995, imposes significant additional pleading requirements on some securities claims, but these arguably do not stand in the way of private claims based on misstatement manipulation.[104] If they do not, the litigation advantages of manipulation claims over those in fraud may become highly consequential. The PSLRA responded to the perception that securities fraud class actions had become the centerpiece of significant abuse of the civil legal system, with private plaintiffs bringing "strike suits" that extracted costly settlements from public corporations to dispose of meritless claims.[105] To counteract these perceived abuses, the PSLRA created heightened pleading requirements that apply to all private damages actions under the Exchange Act requiring a showing of the defendant's state of mind.[106]

Some courts have questioned whether these heightened pleading requirements apply to the kind of intent involved in manipulation-based claims and have ruled that as a general matter manipulation claims are subject to lower pleading requirements than misrepresentation claims.[107] This makes sense in the case of what we describe as a misstatement manipulation because such a manipulation combines a misstatement with a purchase and sale. It makes no real sense in the case of the typical fraud-on-the-market Rule 10b-5 suit, which was the kind of action that primarily prompted the PSLRA. This is because there is no requirement in a fraud-on-the-market suit that the issuer or any other defendant have engaged in any transactions at all. Consider such a claim: a case in which the defendant made a misrepresentation that affected the securities market but did not himself engage in any transaction. If this claim were allowed to be characterized as a manipulation claim, plaintiffs would be able to do a simple end-run around the PSLRA's heightened pleading standards. Nothing in our analysis suggests that there is a good reason for allowing such an end run.[108]

## VI. CONCLUSION

Preventing the manipulation of securities has long preoccupied the popular and political imaginations. Yet, much of the scholarly literature has remained suspicious of manipulation as a coherent and useful concept. This chapter has synthesized various existing forms of manipulation, and attempted to identify who is harmed by each from the perspective of microstructure economics, and the economic welfare effects of these harms. It then turned to the legal landscape, which shares with the academic literature the fog surrounding manipulation. The federal courts disagree among themselves about some of manipulation law's most basic questions. We attempted to offer a resolution to those questions and provide practical advice for regulators by developing a more precise approach to the evidentiary burdens they should impose in optimally prosecuting manipulation, while avoiding the deterrence of desirable trades.

# Appendix

The complaint of the Securities and Exchange Commission against Joseph Taub and Elazar Shmalo[109] presents a striking example of an alleged naked open-market manipulation which, at least ex-post, turned out to be tremendously profitable. Over two years it is alleged that defendants engaged in 23,000 market manipulations netting over $26 million in trading profits. It appears that the defendants made these millions of dollars from OTC internalizers, exploiting the agreements they had with retail brokerage houses. The logic is the following: both marketable and nonmarketable orders placed at exchanges will generally have price impact and potentially significant price impact. On the other hand, orders sent to a retail brokerage account will be sent to OTC internalizers who guarantee execution at the inside spread. Transactions affected by the internalizers will be reported by the Trade Reporting Facility (TRF), which transactions are likely to have much lower price impact since they are assumed to be the result of either retail order flow or dark pool transactions, both of which are thought to be less likely to be motivated by private information. So, the strategy requires two brokerage accounts—one in which order flow can be directed to an exchange (the SEC calls this the Helper Account), and the other which uses OTC internalization (The SEC calls this the Winner Account). The Helper Account is used to move the price, the Winner Account to profit from the manipulation. Notice, that since there are two accounts, there will be, in effect, two manipulations to get both accounts back to a zero position.

An example, taken from actual numbers in the complaint, but modified a bit for clarity, will illustrate the strategy. The company is labeled Company C. On September 25, 2015, starting with orders on the exchange, and using the Helper Account, fifteen orders for one hundred shares each are sold at prices starting around 19.70, falling to 19.50. Then, ten buy market orders of 1,500 shares each are sent to the Winner Account. These orders are executed at or close to the offer which rises from 19.50 to 20.13. The Helper Account is now short while the Winner Account is long. So, buy orders executed on the exchange are sent from the Helper Account in a variety of sizes, but totaling 1,500 shares at prices

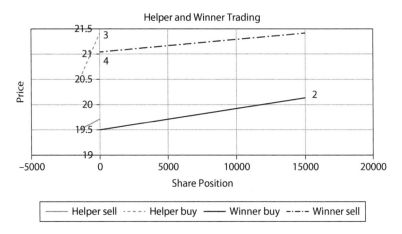

Figure 7.1 Helper and Winner trading

starting from 20.44 rising to 21.40. Finally, seven sell market orders of between 1,000 and 2,500 shares each are sent to the Winner account at prices falling from 21.40 to 21.04. The price response from orders in the Helper account is roughly .013 cents per share, while the price response in the Winner account is .004 cents per share per share.

Figure 7.1 presents a simplified graph of the trading activity. The light solid line on the lower left indicates the Helper sells that drive the price down. The line starts at a zero position and ends up at a short position. The dark gray line on the lower right represents the 15,000 shares bought in the winner account. The light gray dotted line on the upper left shows the buys in the Helper account bringing the position in the Helper account back to zero. Finally, the dark dash-dot line on the upper right shows the Winner position starting at 15,000 shares reduced to zero, with a final price of about $21.

Profit from trading in the Winner account is the area between the dark dash-dot and dark gray lines. The loss in the Helper account is the area between the light dotted and light gray lines. By inspection, the profit in the winner account is much larger than the loss in the Helper account.

Short Selling | **EIGHT**

No subject in securities regulation has generated more heat and less light than short selling. A *short sale* is the sale of a share that is borrowed from a third party rather than owned by the seller. At a later time, the short seller extinguishes her obligation to return the share to this third party by "covering"—purchasing an identical share in the market and then returning it to the third party. If the share price drops, the cost of covering will be less than the proceeds received earlier from the sale and the short seller will make money. Politicians and CEOs rail against short selling as a manipulative tool that artificially pushes share prices below their fundamental values.[1] In contrast, most finance theorists extol short selling's virtues as a practice that helps to quickly incorporate new information into share prices, and thus enhances price accuracy.[2] Short selling, in their view, also provides valuable liquidity to the market and aids investors in hedging against risk.[3] According to one study, short sales accounted for 31 percent of all sales of NASDAQ-listed stocks and 24 percent of all sales of New York Stock Exchange (NYSE) listed stocks.[4] They are thus an important phenomenon, certainly big enough to affect prices.

This chapter discusses the theory, law, and empirical literature concerning short selling. Section I discusses what theory suggests are the potential socially beneficial and socially harmful effects of short selling. The possibility of negative effects has been sufficiently compelling to legislators and regulators to result in varying kinds of regulation over the past seventy-five years, a brief history of which is presented in Section II. Section III surveys the existing empirical literature concerning the causes and effects of short selling and the consequences of attempts to regulate it.

## I. THEORY

What does theory suggest about the social consequences of short selling's effects on share prices, capital market efficiency, and corporate governance more generally?

## A. Socially Beneficial Price Effects

The free availability of short selling can improve share price accuracy in two ways. First, it can increase the incentives for sophisticated traders to gather and analyze new information relevant to predicting an issuer's future cash flows. Second, short selling can make prices better reflect already-existing information relevant to making such predictions when such information is disparately spread among the potential traders in a market or when prices are distorted by mistake traders.

### 1. Incentives to gather and analyze new information

The availability of short selling increases the expected return on the hard work of fundamental value informed trading: gathering bits of publicly available information or observable features of the world and analyzing that information in a sophisticated way that allows a superior assessment of an issuer's future cash flows than is implied by the issuer's current stock price. These increased incentives arise out of the fact that anyone can be a buyer of an issuer's shares, but, without short selling, only a current holder can be a seller.

The direction of a new, better prediction of an issuer's future cash flow is inherently unpredictable (otherwise it would not be new and better). Thus, when gathering and analyzing new information about an issuer reveals that its future cash flows are different than previously thought, there is a 50 percent chance that those cash flows look better than the market's current estimate. In this event, the person can buy shares of the issuer, whether he currently holds any shares or not, effectively utilizing the results of his hard work to earn an expected profit. He may also benefit from these results by transferring this information and analysis to someone else for a profit. Although the well-known imperfections in the market for information mean that substantial transaction costs are involved in obtaining revenues from such a transfer,[5] any transferee, whether or not she currently holds any shares of the issuer, can also buy shares and hence earn an expected profit based on the transferred information and analysis. This means that the market for such transfers is broader than if the usefulness of the information were restricted to only those transferees who already owned shares.

There is also a 50/50 chance that the hard work will instead turn out to reveal that the issuer's future cash flows look worse than previously thought. In this event, without short selling, the person who did the hard work can only sell shares of the issuer if he currently holds such shares, thereby limiting his sales to the number of shares, if any, that he holds. Thus, he will either be entirely unable, or limited in his ability, to directly use the results of his hard work to earn an expected profit. Moreover, it is harder to profit by transferring these results to someone else than when the prediction turns out to be better than previously thought. The transaction costs of making a transfer are enlarged by the fact that the person who did the hard work has to identify, from among all market participants, only those who currently hold shares of the issuer. Also, he must do so without making the results public to the world at large, thereby destroying their trading value. Thus, without short selling, the rewards for the individual's hard work if the results turn out to be negative are less than the rewards if the results turn out to be positive.

In contrast, if short selling is freely available, just as anyone can be a buyer, anyone can be a seller. If the results generated by the hard work turn out to be negative, the rewards for this work are no longer handicapped. If the results turn out to be positive, the rewards for this work are just as large as if short selling were prohibited. Because the availability of short selling increases the likelihood of profiting if one of the outcomes of hard work materializes (negative results), without decreasing the likelihood of profiting if the other outcome materializes (positive results), short selling increases the overall expected return on performing such work.

An increase in the expected return on such hard work will increase the amount that will be done, resulting in more accurate predictions of future cash flows, which will in turn result in more accurate share prices as such information becomes the basis of trades. As discussed in chapter 2, more accurate share prices enhance efficiency in the economy by improving corporate decision making related to the selection of new investment projects as well as to the operation of already-existing projects.

A possible illustration of the importance of short selling in providing incentives for gathering and analyzing information is the reported unhappiness of hedge funds during the summer and fall of 2008 when temporary restrictions were placed on the short selling of certain financial firms.[6] Although these complaints were probably viewed by many as reflecting an inappropriate desire to further profit from the misery in the financial sector,[7] the actual picture was more complicated. The efficient market hypothesis suggests that at any given moment in time, there is no more reason to believe that a financial institution's share price will continue to decrease rather than increase, and that this is true even in a crisis such as the one experienced in 2008.[8] Which direction these prices will go depends on new information as it becomes available, and new information is, by definition, unpredictable in its implications. Hedge funds and the individuals working for them had invested heavily in the capacity to make better predictions, as new information became available, concerning the future cash flows of such issuers than the predictions made by others in the market.[9] To the extent that the new regulations prevented them from engaging in short selling, they were more restricted in their ability to earn a return on these investments when their analysis of new information turned out to suggest lower future cash flows than what was suggested by previously available information.[10]

## 2. Better reflection of disparately spread information

Short selling can also improve price accuracy by helping prices better reflect the implications of information that market participants have already gathered and analyzed. Such information is likely to be disparately spread over the range of market participants, with some participants possessing some bits of such information and other participants possessing other bits.[11] Without short selling, an issuer's share price reflects more fully, or at least more precisely, the views of investors whose information sets yield an optimistic assessment of the issuer's future cash flows than it reflects the views of investors whose information sets yield pessimistic assessments.[12] This, again, is due to the fact that while all members of the investment community whose information results in an optimistic view can be buyers, for members whose information yields a pessimistic view, only those who happen to already hold an issuer's stock can be sellers.

The exact way in which the lack of short selling undermines price accuracy, however, depends on one's assumptions about investor behavior. An assumption that all investors are fully rational yields one conclusion. The contrasting assumption that a substantial percentage of investors are mistake traders, who irrationally follow fads, fashions, and trends, yields a different conclusion.

## A. RATIONAL-INVESTOR MODEL

If one assumes that all investors are fully rational, an absence of short selling, combined with the fact that the distribution of information among investors makes some investors more optimistic than others, will *not* bias share prices to be on average too high. Participants in the market will know about the unavailability of short selling and its implications in terms of the level of trading activity by investors with different views. Therefore, the market will consistently discount prices to compensate for what would otherwise be an upward bias.[13]

Even under this rational-investor model, however, share prices will be less accurate without short selling. Imagine that the information sets of those investors who have pessimistic views about certain issuers make such investors only mildly pessimistic about the issuers' prospects. In contrast, the information sets of those investors who have pessimistic views about the rest of the issuers in the market make such investors severely pessimistic about these other issuers' prospects. When there is no short selling, the discount imposed on all issuers is an average of the views of the mild and the severe pessimists. This is because the market cannot distinguish into which of the two groups any given issuer falls; rather, the market only knows that the pessimist investors' views concerning the issuer, whether as a group they are mild or severe pessimists, are underrepresented in trading.

If short selling were available, the views of pessimists would instead be fully represented in trading. The issuers whose investors are only mildly pessimistic would have their shares priced higher than the prices that would have resulted from the general discount imposed on all issuers in the absence of short selling. Similarly, the issuers whose investors are severely pessimistic would be priced lower than what would have resulted from this general discount. Thus, under the rational-investor model, the free availability of short selling would lead to prices that more fully and accurately reflect the stock of information in the world concerning an issuer's prospects. Prices would differentiate between an issuer where the negative fraction of investors possess mildly negative information and an issuer where the negative fraction of investors possess severely negative information.

## B. MISTAKE TRADER MODEL

Now, instead of full rationality, assume that many investors are mistake traders who are driven by fads or fashions. Recall from chapter 3 that mistake traders believe they have information not reflected in price that permits a more accurate appraisal of an issuer's future cash flows, but in fact they do not. When mistake trading is driven by fads or fashions, it tends to drive price away from being the best estimate of an issuer's future cash flows given all publicly available information.[14] With this assumption, different implications arise from the fact that without short selling, investors whose information sets give them a pessimistic assessment of an issuer's future cash flows are not as fully represented in trading as investors whose information sets give them an optimistic assessment. Unlike the rational-investor model, knowledge by some traders of this difference in trading representation will not necessarily lead to share prices being adequately discounted in the market. The mistake traders, who do not consider these trading representation differences in their decisions, are sufficiently numerous that their influence on prices is not, at least in the short run, totally counterbalanced by the anti-mistake traders—the "smart money" arbitrageurs who do consider this fact.[15] As a result, share prices may be biased upward for sustained periods of time. If a bubble begins to form with respect to an issuer, persons who trade on the basis of a rational evaluation of future cash flows will all be pessimists.[16] After these investors sell whatever shares they hold of the issuer, they no longer have any influence on its share price.

Short selling is not necessarily a complete cure to the problems caused by mistake traders, but if short selling were freely available, the imbalance in how much the optimists and the pessimists are represented in trading would cease, and bubbles would in turn be more likely to burst before growing too large.[17] Under the mistake trader model, freely available short selling thus enhances share price accuracy because bursting bubbles before they become large keeps prices closer, on average, to their fundamental values.

## B. Other Socially Beneficial Effects

The availability of short selling also greatly facilitates the ability of a professional liquidity supplier to provide liquidity. This is because, absent short selling, holding a huge inventory is the only alternative way for a liquidity supplier consistently to provide liquidity in front of heavy selling, and holding such an inventory is very expensive.[18] As a result of this concern, traditional dealers have usually been exempted from any short selling restrictions imposed on other traders in the market. As we saw in chapters 1 and 3, however, designated dealers have become far less important. HFTs have now, through the placement of limit orders, taken over the role of providing much of the liquidity in the market. The ability of HFTs and other nonmarketable limit order users to provide liquidity would be similarly hindered if they were unable to short-sell.[19]

Thus, unlike the early days of NASDAQ, the ability of all traders, not just deal-ers, to short-sell freely enhances the amount of liquidity in the market.[20]

## C. Socially Harmful Price Effects

The concerns that short selling results in social harms have tended not to be as precisely articulated as the claims regarding short selling's socially beneficial effects. This is most likely because negative concerns are more often expressed by politicians and corporate executives engaged in ordinary public discourse, rather than by financial economists in the more rigorous language of professional academia. Behind some of the seemingly exaggerated rhetoric of short selling's critics, however, a number of coherent stories can be told—some potentially more serious than others—about situations in which the availability of short selling might have socially harmful effects.

### 1. Naked open market manipulation: depressing price and repurchasing

One story of how the availability of short selling can have socially harmful effects involves the use of short selling to profit from naked open market manipulation, discussed in chapter 7. Under this scenario, the manipulator does not believe the stock to be overpriced. She nevertheless sells short a substantial block of its shares, perhaps in a series of transactions, expecting that these sales in the aggregate will push down the price of the shares. At a subsequent time, she will need to repurchase the same number of shares in order to cover. If, because of an asymmetric price response, she can repurchase these shares at prices that on average are less than what she sold them short for, she can profit.[21]

As we noted in chapter 7, naked open market manipulation can, under cer-tain (though limited) circumstances, generate positive expected profits. When it does, it will have the two socially harmful effects result discussed in chapter 7. First, on average, it moves share prices, at least temporarily, away from their fun-damental values because the decrease in price is unrelated to any change in infor-mation about the future cash flows of the issuer involved. Second, it decreases liquidity because it adds to the costs of being a professional liquidity supplier. Obviously, the less short selling is restricted, the more opportunities there will be to engage in naked open market manipulation involving a sale followed by a repurchase, and hence the larger the number of occasions leading to these socially undesirable effects. This observation is not a very persuasive reason for general limits on short selling, however. Rather, it just calls for an effort to deter all naked open market manipulation where there are objective indications that it is occurring: both short sales followed by purchases and purchases followed by ordinary sales of the shares that were purchased.

*2. Open market manipulation with an external interest: depressing price in order to profit on a contract with a third party*

As we also noted in chapter 7, a wide variety of contracts have terms that provide one of the parties with a payoff that depends on the market price of an issuer's shares at a particular point in time. For the other party to such a contract, the lower the issuer's price, the less it must pay out under the contract. The party that benefits under the contract from the lower price (the low-price beneficiary) has an incentive to push down the market price of the issuer's shares at the point in time specified in the contract for determining the payoff. Just in advance of this point in time, the low-price beneficiary, without any belief that the shares are priced above their fundamental value, pushes the price down by selling short a substantial block of stock. When she later covers, she may end up repurchasing at prices that are on average as great as, or even greater than, the prices at which she sold short. She nevertheless may, on a net basis, profit handsomely as a result of the gains she experienced from having reduced her payout under the contract.

As we saw in chapter 7, one harmful social consequence of open market manipulation with an external interest is that, like the use of short selling for naked open market manipulation, it moves share prices away from their fundamental values. The other harmful social consequence is that open market manipulation with an external interest makes the valuable practice of contracting based on share price more costly. Again, the less short selling is restricted, the more opportunities there will be to engage in open market manipulation by the party to a share-price-term-based contract who would benefit from a lower price, and hence the larger the number of occasions leading to these socially undesirable effects. Nevertheless, this observation is also not a very persuasive reason for general limits on short selling. Rather, it just calls for an effort to deter all open market manipulation with an external interest, whether by a short-selling party benefiting from a lower price or by a purchasing party benefiting from a higher price.

In sum, these problems are really just ways in which short selling sometimes facilitates some other kind of bad practice. Thus the focus, as in chapter 7, should be on deterring the bad practice, whether it arises on the side that would lead to the use of short selling or on the other side, involving long purchases.

*3. Diminishing the underlying value of the firm*

As we mentioned in chapter 7, though possible under the right conditions, it is normally difficult, on an expected basis, to buy back for a profit shares that have been sold short. This analysis, however, assumes that the underlying value of the firm is unchanged by the initial drop in price caused by the short seller's sell orders. This is a reasonable assumption for most firms: the operations of their underlying businesses, and hence the cash flows generated by their operations, are largely unaffected by short-term changes in the price of their shares.

However, the operations of some kinds of firms, especially at certain times, may be significantly affected by such short-term share price changes. A financial firm during a time of a financial crisis is the most obvious example. Such a firm's ability to perform its day-to-day underlying businesses—lending, trading, or underwriting—depends on its ability to maintain its capital base. An insurance firm can be in a similar position. As we saw in 2008–2009, the capital base of such a firm can erode rapidly in a financial crisis and the lost capital can only be replaced with new sales of equity. When there has been such an erosion in an issuer's capital base, if the price of its equity is temporarily depressed, the financial firm either has to forgo business or dilute equity. Thus, its future cash flows per share, and hence its fundamental value, can be reduced by a temporary drop in share price.[22]

Consider a trader during a crisis who thinks that the decline that has already occurred in the share price of a given financial firm is sufficient to reflect the new realities brought on by the crisis. This trader therefore does not believe that the firm's shares are overpriced. The trader nevertheless sells short a substantial block of these shares. The initial share price drop caused by her short sale may become a self-confirming hypothesis, in the sense that the share price drop may lead to a drop in the share's fundamental value because of the damage of the lower share price to the firm's underlying business. Moreover, because of this self-confirming aspect, short selling the issuer's shares could easily become contagious. Short sales in such a situation could be profitable on an expected basis because the price at which the short sellers cover would be lower on average than the price at the time of the short sale. This is because the price at the time of covering would reflect the decline in fundamental value caused by the contagious short-selling-induced share price drop.

Fear that this sort of phenomenon was underway at points during the summer and fall of 2008 appears to have underlain the thinking that led to the imposition of greater restrictions on short selling of shares in U.S. financial firms during this period.[23] Nevertheless, even a financial firm is not seriously vulnerable to this kind of problem most of the time. Absent a financial crisis that erodes its capital basis, it too can, without much damage, wait out a temporary dip in share price before selling new equity. Thus, this kind of social harm from short selling, if it occurs at all, is probably an exceptional event. It would at most call for only temporary restrictions on short selling that are limited to the shares of firms in the sector or sectors vulnerable to this contagious self-confirming hypothesis.

*4. A first cut on misstatement manipulation: short selling combined with the creation of false news*

Two potentially profitable strategies can be based on combining short selling with the spreading of false news. One is to short-sell first, then spread false negative news that depresses prices, and thereafter cover at the depressed price. The other is to first spread false positive news that increases share price, next short-sell at the inflated price, and finally cover after the market realizes the falsity of the news and the price inflation has dissipated. Both strategies involve misstatement manipulation, and, as discussed in chapter 7, would result in two socially negative effects: reductions in both price accuracy and liquidity. As also discussed in chapter 7, misstatement manipulation violates § 10(b) of the Exchange Act and Rule 10b-5.[24] Thus again, there is no call for a prohibition on short selling to prevent this practice. These two strategies constitute a subset of a more general bad practice—misstatement manipulation—and cannot be distinguished from the more general practice in terms of the social harms that they create. This more general practice is already subject to legal regulation.

*5. Short selling combined with the creation of false news: a more nuanced approach*

The fraudulent practice of spreading false news and trading to take advantage of the resulting distortion is, as just discussed, clearly socially harmful. The prohibitions applicable to misstatement manipulation more generally are probably sufficient in terms of rules. However, for issues such as detecting violations of these prohibitions and determining what is appropriate evidence for proving that the violations occurred, a relevant question is whether the availability of short selling significantly increases the level of this harmful more general practice. Arguably it will not, because there are alternative ways of profiting from spreading both negative and positive news without the use of short sales. The alternative strategy for profiting from spreading false negative news is to spread the news first, next purchase the shares at the resulting depressed price, and then resell the shares after the market realizes the falsity of the news and the depression in price dissipates.

The alternative strategy for profiting from spreading false positive news is to purchase the shares before spreading the news and then sell immediately after the news has been spread, at the resulting inflated price.

A more sophisticated approach to the question, though, reveals flaws in this reasoning. It suggests that the availability of short selling does increase the level of the fraudulent practice of spreading false news and trading to take advantage of the distortion in price. Understanding this more sophisticated approach starts with two observations. The first observation is that for some kinds of information (at least some of the time), convincingly spreading false negative information may be easier than convincingly spreading false positive information, and that for some other kinds of information the opposite may be the case. For example, positive false news is sometimes easier to spread because it is probably less likely to be immediately corrected by the company. During rising times, false positive news may also be more believable because people want to believe it and it is consistent with the overall mood of euphoria. In contrast, when avoiding specificity is desirable, false negative information, because of the power of innuendo, is probably easier to spread than false positive information.[25]

The second observation is that the legal and financial risks associated with the fraud of spreading false news and trading to take advantage of the resulting distortion in price may, under some circumstances, be affected by whether the initial trade is made in advance of spreading false information and the second transaction is made immediately after the false news has had its full impact on price, or whether the initial trade is made after the false information has been spread but is still distorting the price and the reverse trade is made after the market realizes the truth and the price distortion dissipates.[26] A variety of considerations affect which order is preferable with respect to each of these risks.[27]

These two observations suggest a variety of possible combinations of the relevant factors. For situations representing many of these combinations, the more advantageous way of undertaking the fraud involves the use of a short sale. In at least some of these situations, if short selling were not available, the fraud would no longer be attractive enough to be worthwhile. Thus, the availability of short selling would increase the prevalence of fraud involving the spreading of false news and its associated social harms.

## D. Short Selling on the Basis of Negative Inside Information and Its Effects

One other practice—trading on the basis of negative inside information—will also likely be more prevalent if short selling is available, because ownership of an issuer's shares will not be necessary to take advantage of any such information that a trader might come to possess. The trader can simply sell short and then cover when the price declines after the information becomes public. Again, however, use of short selling in this fashion is just a subset of the larger practices of either issuer insider trading or other-entity insider trading that are analyzed in detail in chapters 5 and 6. As we saw there, each of these more general practices increases price accuracy while decreasing liquidity, but on balance is undesirable. Again also, there would appear to be no call for a general prohibition on short selling, because each of these uses of short selling is a subset of a more general practice—issuer insider trading and other-entity insider trading—and neither can be distinguished from the more general practice in terms of the social harms that it creates. Exchange Act § 16(c) prohibits issuer officers and directors from selling their firm's shares short. A coherent rationale for a blanket prohibition on this claim of sales, but no blanket prohibition on purchases, would appear to be more closely related to avoid perverse managerial incentives than to prevent issuer insider informed trading.

## II. HISTORY OF REGULATION

Since the onset of the Great Depression, the perception that short selling can be socially harmful has led to a varying set of regulations over time.[28]

### A. The Depression and Establishment of a Regulatory Structure

In September 1931, the NYSE briefly banned short selling altogether.[29] Soon after the lapse of this ban, the NYSE began to prohibit short sales at a price below the price of the immediately preceding last sale and to regulate the lending of shares.[30] Although we believe, based on today's knowledge, that the range of conditions allowing for positive expected profits is fairly narrow, the legislative hearings and investigations leading up to the passage of the Securities Act and the Exchange Act led many persons to conclude that a substantial cause of the enormous drop in share prices beginning in the latter part of 1929 was the predatory practice of *raids*—a group of traders selling short a large amount of an issuer's securities with the hope that they can profit by covering through repurchases at the depressed price resulting from their sell orders.[31] As a result, when the Exchange Act was passed in 1934, it included § 10(a), which prohibits short sales in violation of any rule promulgated by the SEC in furtherance of the public interest or for the protection of investors.[32]

The SEC did not utilize its authority under § 10(a) immediately. Shortly after the market break of 1937, though, when officials believed concentrated short selling to have occurred, the SEC adopted Rule 10a-1, which imposed, subject to certain exceptions, the "uptick" test on short sales of exchange-listed securities. This test allowed short sales only if they were either (i) at a price above the price of the last reported sale, or (ii) at a price equal to the last reported sale when the last reported sale was above the price of the reported sale immediately preceding it.[33] Eventually, with a several-decade delay, more heavily traded NASDAQ securities were also subjected to similar regulations, but with a test based on the most recent best bids rather than reported sale prices.[34]

## B. Recent Developments

Notwithstanding these restrictions, the extent of short selling grew substantially,[35] as did theoretical and empirical understanding of its social effects, resulting in a number of changes in SEC policy in recent years.

### 1. The Rule 202T test suspension of regulations

In 2004, in the midst of a five-year period of strongly increasing stock prices,[36] the SEC adopted Rule 202T of Regulation SHO, which established procedures for the SEC to suspend its short-sale restrictions for a test set of issuers in order to perform a study comparing their pricing with issuers that continued to be subject to the restrictions.[37] The test period ultimately ran from May 2, 2005 through August 6, 2007. Essentially, one-third of the three thousand issuers composing the Russell 3000 Index were selected at random to be the test group for whom restrictions were suspended, with the remaining two-thirds serving as a control group.

### 2. Evaluation of the test results and elimination of restrictions

The SEC had the staff at its Office of Economic Analysis (OEA) analyze the data collected in connection with the test and made this data available to outside researchers as well. Upon conclusion of the test, the SEC issued a Release stating that "OEA found little empirical justification at that time for maintaining short sale price restrictions, especially for actively traded securities."[38] The Release went on to say that this analysis, combined with the studies of outside researchers, "generally . . . supported removal of short sale price test restrictions at that time."[39] Reflecting these findings, the SEC eliminated all restrictions on short selling effective July 3, 2007.[40]

### 3. The financial crisis reversal

The sharp drop and high volatility displayed by market prices in the summer and fall of 2008 led the SEC to reverse course. It issued two temporary emergency orders relating to the short selling of financial issuer stocks: the first, in July 2008, reinforced rules relating to the borrowing and delivery of shares,[41] and the second, in September 2008, prohibited, for a two-week period, all short selling of the shares of about 800 financial issuers.[42]

In February 2010, after continued trouble in the markets, the SEC adopted a rule imposing restrictions on short selling when a stock is subject to significant price erosion.[43] Under that "alternative uptick" rule, if a stock experiences a 10 percent price decline in a single day, then short selling is permitted only if the price of the security is above the current national best bid.[44] In the press release announcing the rule, the SEC chairman observed that "short selling can potentially have both a beneficial and a harmful impact on the market," but noted that "[i]t is important for the Commission and the markets to have in place a measure that creates certainty about how trading restrictions will operate during periods of stress and volatility."[45]

## III. EMPIRICAL RESEARCH

What does the empirical research to date tell us about the theories relating to the possible social benefits and harms caused by short selling and the effects of the various regulatory interventions discussed in this chapter?

Determining the effect of short-selling restrictions on the level of share prices of the issuers involved is important for sorting out the various theories discussed earlier concerning short selling's social effects, both positive and negative. One theory, relating to how short selling helps prices better reflect disparately spread information, suggests that restrictions on short selling bias prices upward to a level above their fundamental value. A second theory, also relating to how short selling helps prices better reflect disparately spread information, suggests that restrictions would make prices less accurate but would not consistently bias them one way or the other. A third theory, relating to how short selling can be used by traders to engage in naked open market manipulation, implies that restrictions would inhibit a practice that, at least temporarily, would otherwise bias prices downward.

The conclusions of empirical literature on the effect of short-selling restrictions on share price levels are mixed. A study by Charles Jones, concerning various restrictions imposed in the 1930s, concludes that the respective impositions of restrictions were associated with a positive share price reaction.[46] This result is consistent with the first theory (that restrictions, by diminishing the influence of investors holding negative information, bias prices above their fundamental level) and the third theory (that the lack of restrictions, by making purely manipulative bear raids easier, biases prices below their fundamental level). However, it is not consistent with the second theory: that restrictions do not consistently bias prices one way or the other, they just make them less accurate. The fact that the price reaction to each restriction occurred at the time that the rule became effective, rather than at the time the rule was announced, is also inconsistent with the rational-expectations assumption underlying the second theory.

A study of much more recent trading by Diether, Lee, and Werner comes to a different conclusion.[47] This study analyzed data concerning the daily level of shorting activity and price behavior of issuers that composed the approximately one thousand issuers in the SEC's Rule 202T test group, for which, during the test period of May 2005 through August 2007, all short sale restrictions were eliminated, and compared it with the same data for the approximately two thousand issuers in the control group, on which the existing restrictions continued to be imposed.[48] The authors found that the level of shorting activity for the test group increased relative to the control group, but that daily returns and volatility were essentially the same for each group.[49] The test group's relative increase in shorting activity suggests that the restrictions were having a real effect on behavior. The lack of a statistically significant difference between the two groups in terms of returns is consistent with the second theory's implication that restrictions on short selling, while reducing price accuracy, will not bias prices, but does not support the first and third theories.[50] The lack of a statistically significant difference with respect to volatility has ambiguous implications in terms of support for the second theory, because no consensus exists among financial economists concerning the relationship between volatility and share price accuracy.[51]

In contrast, Grullon, Michenaud, and Weston found evidence supportive of the first and third theories.[52] These authors compared the shorting activity and price behavior of the issuers in the SEC's Rule 202T test group with those of the issuers in the control group. Using a short event window around the date the SEC announced the list of the issuers in the test group, these authors found no price effects for issuers in the test group, similar to Diether, Lee, and Werner. However, using wider event windows around the date of announcement,

Gustavo, Grullon, and Weston found that prices of issuers in the pilot group decreased relative to those in the test group. These authors also found that this negative price response persisted in the long term for a sample of small firms in the pilot group.

## Appendix A

Our discussion in this chapter was concerned primarily with the extent to which short selling makes abuse easier. We ignored one abuse, commonly known as *naked short selling*, which is the act of selling without bothering to borrow the shares needed for delivery at the settlement date. This leads to *failures to deliver*, more succinctly known as *fails*. A discussion of this requires a description of the mechanics involved in a model short sale.

We start by supposing that a hedge fund wants to short 100 shares of Alphabet (GOOG) currently priced at $1,000 per share. It informs its broker of its desire to do so. The broker either makes arrangements to borrow the shares or has reasonable grounds to believe that the GOOG shares can be borrowed. The broker then sends the sell order to a trading venue, marking it as "short." At settlement, typically two business days after the trade, the hedge fund's broker delivers 100 shares to the broker or brokers of the buyer or buyers. The buyer's brokers deliver $100,000 to the hedge fund's broker, who sends this money on to the share lender along with the required 50 percent margin that the hedge fund must provide.[53] Thus, the share lender has control over a $150,000 account.

While the short position is maintained, the hedge fund broker sends any dividends to the share lender and the share lender sends money based on the "rebate rate" to the hedge fund. This rebate rate is the interest earned on the margin account less the "shorting fee" kept by the share lender. This fee, which varies stock by stock, is determined in the market for shorting that stock and may be so large as to make the rebate rate negative.[54] When the fee is large, the stock is said to "go on special." The hedge fund will have to add to the margin account if the stock goes up sufficiently. Although the initial margin is 50 percent, the maintenance margin is no less than 25 percent.[55] That is, if the stock price is P, the margin must be maintained at $1.25 \times P$. So, in our example, if the stock price rises above $1,200 (= 1,000 \times 1.5/1.25$), each dollar increase in the price leads to a $1.25-per-share addition to the margin account. In contrast, should the stock price fall below $1,000, the short seller can withdraw $1.50 per share for each dollar drop in the stock price.

The short position is "closed out" when the hedge fund purchases the shares in the market and delivers those shares to the lender. The share lender then returns the contents of the margin account to the hedge fund's broker.

This discussion concerning the opening of the short position shows that short selling does not free up capital for the investor. Quite the contrary: the investor does not receive the proceeds of the sale and must, on top of this, put up an additional 50 percent of the value of the sale. There is thus a nice symmetry between buying on margin and short selling. Both require capital in the amount of 50 percent of the transaction.[56]

We have already discussed a major impact of Reg. SHO, namely the replacement of the uptick rule with a circuit breaker rule. Most of the text of Reg. SHO, however, deals with preventing naked shorting and subsequent fails. A first observation is that the onus falls on the short seller's broker. This broker must have in place procedures to minimize the possibility of failing to borrow and hence failing to produce shares at settlement of the short-sale transaction. If a broker has a fail in a particular security, that broker is prohibited from accepting other short-sale orders from anyone. Thus, if a short seller is to do so naked, he or she must have the complicity of the broker.

The incentive for naked shorting is clear, particularly for hard-to-short securities, because the rebate rate is so much less than the interest earned on the cash that the short seller has put up as security. This becomes particularly salient in low-interest-rate environments in which the rebate rate becomes negative.

Some commentators have argued that fails are innocuous—indeed, actually beneficial—because the person buying from the short seller merely becomes the share lender and effectively a competitor in the share lending market.[57] Although these commentators admit that the buyer did not choose to be a lender, they do not consider this to be important. This position ignores the fact that this share lender is not protected by the overcapitalization of the margin account held by an actual share lender. Moreover, naked shorts create problems in terms of voting shares. It is true that the actual share lender, as a theoretical proposition, loses the opportunity to vote the shares lent out, just as the borrower does not have a vote. However, as a matter of practice, it turns out that share lenders frequently do vote their lent shares. This has led to instances of vote totals exceeding 100 percent.[58] For these and other reasons, most financial economists and legal experts view fails negatively and advise that they should be deterred by appropriate regulation.

Regulation of Broker-Dealers

**PART 4**

Finance is pervaded by intermediation, and trading markets are no exception. Among the most important intermediaries in trading markets are entities commonly referred to as *broker-dealers*. This term covers any individual or institution whose business involves any one or more of three broad securities-intermediating activities: (i) an agent executing orders on behalf of a customer (i.e., a *broker*); (ii) a principal transacting with other traders for the intermediary's own account (i.e., a *dealer*); and (iii) a trading venue that is not registered as a stock exchange. Broker-dealers occupy a panoply of roles within securities markets. In some cases, the *same* institution can potentially advise an individual on which stock to buy and then either arrange execution of the order on that person's behalf on a trading venue or act as counterparty on the other side of the order. Moreover, in the case where it arranges execution, the trading venue can be one owned by the broker dealer. The fact that the same regulated institution often serves the very different functions as *broker*, *dealer*, and *trading venue* has proved a subject of much confusion for commentators, students, and courts.[1] It is thus important to be clear that despite the same overarching regulatory status, the same financial institution will be regulated very differently based on whether and when it is serving in its brokerage, dealer, or venue function.

This chapter proceeds as follows. Section I defines broker-dealers as a general matter and touches on the overall web of legal directives governing them. Section II addresses the brokerage function, defining the main economic problem the law must address in connection with it (the agency problem), and the principal doctrine that the law has developed to address that problem (the duty of best execution). Section III addresses the relevant rules that address the dealer function. Section IV discusses the future of the law's regulatory regime for trading venues. Unlike most of the chapters in parts II through IV of this book, this chapter is almost entirely descriptive, offering an account of the basic law governing broker-dealers in their various functions.

## I. WHAT IS A BROKER-DEALER?

*Broker-dealer* is a regulatory term of art. The SEC requires that an individual or institution performing any one or more of three functions—a broker, a dealer, or a nonexchange trading venue—register under the Securities Exchange Act of 1934 (the Act) as a "broker-dealer" using Form BD.[2]

The Act defines a broker as "any person engaged in the business of effecting transactions in securities for the account of others."[3] A *dealer* is defined as "any person engaged in the business of buying and selling securities . . . for such person's own account through a broker or otherwise."[4] Both definitions are crafted so as to include those actors whose "business" is intermediating others' trading interests, as opposed to being simply an active trader of securities. Section 15(a) of the Act prohibits acting as either a broker or dealer in securities without first registering as such with the SEC.[5] The Act also authorizes the SEC to establish standards for the capabilities of broker-dealers and the natural persons associated with the broker-dealer, and empowers the SEC to deny or revoke a broker-dealer's registration.[6] Lastly, any operator of a trading venue that is not a national securities exchange is also required to register with the SEC on the same Form BD. In essence, any person that is in any business of helping to effect transactions in securities must register as a broker-dealer. The only exception is a trading venue that is registered with the SEC as an exchange.

Broker-dealers are regulated by an interacting web of federal statutory law, federal administrative rulemaking, self-regulatory rules, and state law. The most important piece of legislation governing broker-dealers is the Exchange Act, which first defined *broker* and *dealer*, and established a basic regulatory apparatus. Since then, the 1975 Amendments to the Exchange Act, Regulation ATS, and Regulation NMS have proved important supplements.

Changes in equity market structure have also placed new pressures on the self-regulatory organization model of stock exchange regulation. Self-regulation and applicable state law go back before the arrival of comprehensive federal securities regulation in the 1930s. For example, much earlier, the New York Stock Exchange had already developed an extensive system of self-regulation, which the Exchange Act was designed to supplement, rather than displace.[7] Federal securities law expanded the self-regulatory system. It recognized the status of stock exchanges as self-regulatory organizations (SROs) and empowered the SEC to regulate them.[8] It also authorized the formation of self-regulatory organizations for brokers and dealers, and imposed a requirement that every broker-dealer must join a self-regulatory organization.[9] Ultimately, a single such SRO was formed—the National Association of Securities Dealers (NASD)—which is now the Financial Industry Regulatory Authority (FINRA). FINRA is the SRO that regulates all broker-dealers today.[10] Each of the SROs—FINRA and each of the registered exchanges—promulgates its own rules, but these rules must be approved by the SEC.[11] The SEC can also "abrogate, add to, and delete" an SRO's rules.[12] Both the SRO and the SEC (but not private persons) can bring proceedings to enforce the SRO's rules.[13] FINRA and the registered exchanges have produced an extensive body of regulatory rules for broker-dealers. These rules often parallel or enlarge upon the duties imposed by federal law. In the following discussion, we include reference to SRO rules when relevant.

## II. BROKERAGE

Brokerage services involve assisting customers in effecting securities purchases and sales that they wish to make by representing them as agents to get these trades done. Brokers also advise customers as to what to purchase and sell, but this has been discussed extensively elsewhere[14] and will not be our concern here. Rather, we focus on the economics and regulation of a broker's role in providing trading services.

## A. The Economics of the Brokerage

The trading services provided by brokers serve three important purposes. One is the provision of trade execution services. This simply reflects an efficient division of labor. Most households lack the time, inclination, and resources to specialize in executing the trades necessary to buy and sell securities. Brokers provide these trade execution services to customers, which can include breaking a customer's total buy or sell request into a set of separate orders and deciding to which venue to send each order and when.

The second function of a broker is to vouch that its customer is good for the promise she is making when she enters into a trade on an exchange. Such a trade is simply an executory contract, whereby one party promises to provide a certain number of shares on a certain date and the other party promises to pay a specified amount of money for those shares. The parties' respective brokers vouch that their customers will in fact live up to their promises on the day of closing. This vouching arises from a complex set of rules that allows each party in an anonymous market to be willing to commit to participate in a transaction that, by the time of closing, might turn out to be disadvantageous to her. She will not be willing to make this commitment unless she is confident that the other party will perform if instead the transaction turns out to be disadvantageous to the other party. The vouching by the parties' respective brokers provides this confidence.

A third function is to serve as a gatekeeper that the law can use to regulate the behavior of traders. This is needed because a customer's order, by the time it arrives at a trading venue, is anonymous. Enforcement authorities who detect a possible trading violation can find out the broker that represented the order, however, and then have the broker identify the customer behind the order.

From the economic point of view, the first function—providing execution services—is the most interesting. This function sets the stage for a classic agency problem. An *agency problem* arises whenever a principal relies on an agent to act on its behalf and the quality of the agent's service is not completely observable.[15] In the brokerage context, the customer is the principal and the broker is the agent. Customers rely on their brokers to accomplish their trading objectives. Naturally, this raises the possibility that the incentives of the principal and agent may not be perfectly aligned, because the principal wants the agent to execute its transactions in the manner that best serves the principal's interests, while the agent may want to execute orders in the manner that involves the least effort or is otherwise most profitable for it.

The mere possibility of an agency problem does not necessarily mean that it is significant in practice. The question is whether the broker and the customer can agree on a mutually beneficial contract the terms of which credibly require the desired performance of the broker for the promised price. The key potential problem is the observability of the broker's performance by the customer. The severity of the observability-of-performance problem will depend on (i) the complexity of the customer's trading objectives; (ii) the sophistication of the customer; and (iii) the quality of the data available on quotes, transactions, and market structure within a given market. A retail customer typically lacks the ability and skill to monitor, or assess the quality of, his agent's performance, particularly with regard to a more complicated trade. Nor would it likely be cost-effective for him to do so even if he had the ability and skill. Even for a more sophisticated customer, however, it is difficult to resolve by contract the principal-agent problem he has with his broker, because of the noisy character of trading outcomes. There is only a limited correlation between even a highly skilled broker's efforts and trading success. This noise means that the broker's level of effort and skill—the quality of performance—cannot be perfectly observed. As a result, a contract cannot be written in which compensation purely tracks skill of performance, and that completely resolves the agency problem facing investors.[16] The law responds with a foundational tool for addressing agency problems: a *fiduciary duty*. In the brokerage context, this duty is limited to a concept called *the duty of best execution*, which we discuss in the next section.

Within the world of equity trading, it is worth noting that the duty of best execution is nested within the constellation of broader rules governing how orders within the national market system can be executed. Importantly, Rule 611 of Reg. NMS substantially resolves the principal-agent problem for small marketable orders. Rule 611 imposes a one-size-fits-all solution that works through the regulation of trading venues. As discussed in chapter 1, Rule 611 requires each trading venue to establish procedures designed to prevent "trade throughs" (executions that occur at prices inferior to the NBBO). In essence, if a broker sends a marketable order to a venue where the order would not execute at the NBB or NBO, that venue must send it on to a venue where it will not receive execution at a price inferior to the NBBO. For small retail marketable orders, the only dimension of execution that likely matters is price. Thus, Rule 611 makes a bad execution relatively unlikely for a retail investor, no matter how poorly his broker performs the execution services.

## B. The Duty of Best Execution

As noted in subsection II.A, brokers acting on their customer's behalf in providing trading services owe a duty of best execution. This duty exists under the common law principles of agency; under self-regulatory organization rules; and, according to some court opinions, under § 10(b) and Rule 10b-5 of federal law. At a descriptive level, perhaps the most transformational change in the brokerage industry over the past few decades has been the diminished significance of brokers' role in providing financial advice to clients, leaving the role of brokers in providing *trading services* as the more important one. As a result, the relative importance of the duty of best execution has only grown with time.[17]

In interpreting the duty of best execution, the case of *Newton v. Merrill Lynch*[18] provides a seminal analysis.[19] *Newton* was a putative class action by thousands of investors against a number of prominent broker-dealers that traded on NASDAQ, alleging violations of § 10(b) and Rule 10b-5 based on breaches of the duty of best execution. The litigation emerged out of the infamous NASDAQ "odd-eighths" scandal of the early 1990s. The "tick size" or minimum price increment at the time was an eighth of a dollar, and yet a series of financial economics working papers documented that NASDAQ market makers in a number of prominent stocks quoted almost exclusively in even eighths (e.g., $0.25, $0.50, $0.75, $1.00, etc.) and rarely, if ever, quoted in odd eighths. This suggested that a narrowing of the spread to $0.125 was being prevented by collusive behavior or a lack of competition among Nasdaq dealers.[20] At the same time, the dealers were trading among themselves on other venues, predominantly SelectNet and Instinet, at prices that were better than the NBBO on Nasdaq. The investors claimed that their brokers had failed in their duty of best execution by not providing them with executions that would have resulted from matching their orders against the superior quotes available on SelectNet and Instinet.[21]

Although the Third Circuit in *Newton* ultimately held in favor of the defendant brokerage firms, based on a view of SelectNet and Instinet as essentially still experiments with unclear implications, its dicta provided a clear definition of the duty of best execution as "requiring a broker-dealer to 'use reasonable efforts to maximize the economic benefit to the client in each transaction.' "[22] The court also provided an illuminating discussion of the multidimensional character of the duty of best execution, noting that "[o]ther terms in addition to price are also relevant to best execution."[23] In providing best execution for customers, a broker-dealer must also "take into account order size, trading characteristics of the security, speed of execution, clearing costs, and the cost and difficulty of executing an order in a particular market."[24]

Brokers satisfying customer orders are subject to this general duty of best execution, which grows out of the common law of agency. FINRA rules have further elaborated on the duty in terms that apply not only to brokers, but also sometimes to security firms interacting with customers in a principal transaction role, as described in the next section. Specifically, FINRA Rule 5310 describes the duty of best execution: In any transaction for or with a customer, a broker must use *reasonable diligence* to ascertain the best market for a security, and trade in that market so that the resultant price for the customer is "as favorable as possible under prevailing market conditions."[25] Reasonable diligence by a broker will include considering "the character of the market for the security (e.g., price, volatility, relative liquidity, and pressure on available communications)"; "the size and type of transaction"; "the number of markets checked"; the "accessibility of the quotation"; and "the terms and conditions of the order which result in the transaction."[26]

## III. DEALERS

When a securities firm acts as a dealer, it intermediates trade by purchasing shares from those interested in selling, and selling to those interested in buying. Activity fitting this description can be divided into two rather separate functions. One is the market-making role, in which the dealer is in essence providing liquidity to the market. The other is serving customers in a fashion very much resembling the way a securities firm serves customers as a broker. The difference in the latter role is that the firm itself acts as the counterparty to the customer in the transaction she wishes to undertake, rather than seeking to find a counterparty by sending the customer's order to a trading venue.

### A. Market Making

The economics of the market-making function are critical to the operation of trading markets, as has already been extensively considered in chapters 3 and 4. The regulation of liquidity suppliers is also an important topic, but one that departs in several ways from the style of regulation with which this book is usually concerned. Federal law effectively imposes no regulatory regime on the dealer function *per se* in terms of the trading of NMS stocks. As a result, there is little "law" governing how a market maker must supply liquidity in terms of NMS stocks. Individual exchanges still retain some institutional roles for liquidity suppliers that choose to occupy a formal market-making function on that venue. For instance, the New York Stock Exchange has its "Designated Market Makers" (DMMs)—the successors of NYSE's far more famous and historically significant specialists. As was the case with specialists, each stock has only one specific DMM. Each DMM takes on obligations to maintain a "fair and orderly" market, including obligations to quote (i.e., post limit orders) at the NBBO during at least a designated percentage of trading hours.[27] Other exchanges typically also have institutional roles for market makers.

## B. Acting as a Counterparty to Customers

The most likely opportunity for a securities firm to engage in the other kind of dealer function—being the counterparty to a customer in the transaction the customer wishes to undertake—is when the transaction involves an over-the-counter stock. There is federal law addressing the dealer function in the over-the-counter market for stocks, however. In particular, compensation of a broker-dealer when acting as a principal has been the subject of both federal court decisions and SRO rules. The primary object of this regulation is the protection of a retail investor dealing with a broker-dealer firm. To the retail customer placing an order for stock, the securities firm trading with her directly in a principal transaction looks very much the same as when such a firm acts as an agent playing the brokerage role. Indeed, she may be completely unaware of whether the firm is acting as a broker, by obtaining or disposing of the stock for her; or as a dealer, by buying the stock from, or selling it to, the customer. To the securities firm, however, the incentives are very different depending on which role it is taking.

### 1. General rules governing compensation in principal transactions

FINRA Rule 2121 governs the compensation that a broker may receive when satisfying a client order from the broker-dealer's own account. Whether the security is listed or unlisted, the broker must transact "at a price which is fair." This is determined by considering all relevant circumstances, including market conditions for that security at the time of the transaction, the cost involved, and the fact that the broker is entitled to a profit.[28]

The fairness of the price to the customer is generally measured in terms of the markup, in the case of a purchase, and the mark-down in the case of a sale. As noted, such principal transactions mainly occur in non-NMS stocks, which are available only in the OTC market and are typically relatively thinly traded.[29] Often, the broker-dealer to which the retail customer brings her order and that acts as a counterparty to this order is also a dealer making a market in the stock. Alternatively, when the broker-dealer is not a market maker in the stock, it may engage in a "riskless principal transaction" and purchase shares in the market and then resell them to the customer (or sell the shares short and purchase them from the customer). In either of these situations, the broker-dealer is entitled to some kind of compensation for performing the retail service that it is providing the customer. The markup and markdown represent, respectively, a portion of the price paid or received by the broker-dealer and constitutes compensation for its retail services. Two regulatory issues arise. One is how large the markup or markdown can be and still be considered fair. The other is how to calculate the markup or markdown: what the customer pays or receives must be compared to some other price, where the markup or markdown is the difference. The issue is what this other price should be. Both of these questions have been a constant source of controversy in disputes involving broker-dealer conduct in their dealings with retail customers.[30] For ease of discussion, we will consider these questions in terms of the markup for customer purchases; however, the same ideas apply in mirror-image fashion to markdowns for customer sales.

*2. The permissible size of the markup*

Consider first the permissible size of the markup. In 1943, the Board of Governors of the National Association of Securities Dealers (NASD) adopted a policy, still adhered to by FINRA, which suggests that markups or markdowns of more than 5 percent are presumptively excessive.[31] This policy has received explicit judicial support from the Second Circuit.[32] Supplementary commentary on Rule 2121 clarifies that under some circumstances a pattern of markups or markdowns of less than 5 percent can still be unfair or unreasonable. The commentary also states that determining the fairness of a markup or markdown must involve consideration of all relevant factors, including the type of security involved, its availability, price, the amount of money involved in the transaction, disclosure of the markup or markdown, the pattern of markups and markdowns, and the nature of the broker-dealer's business.[33]

In addition to FINRA rules, case law also suggests that excessive markups may violate Rule 10b-5.[34] For instance, in *Alstead, Dempsey & Co.,*[35] a broker-dealer dominated market-making in a stock and charged its customers markups of more than 10 percent and 20 percent when they purchased that stock. The SEC stated that "a dealer violates antifraud provisions when he charges retail customers prices that are not reasonably related to the prevailing market price at the time the customers make their purchases," and found that this had been the case with the defendant broker-dealer.[36] The SEC concluded that the broker-dealer had willfully violated § 17(a)(1)-(3) of the Securities Act and § 10(b) of the Exchange Act and Rule 10b-5 thereunder.[37]

There is some question, however, as to whether these SEC rulings and earlier court rulings with regard to Rule 10b-5 would hold up today. These earlier rulings seem to be based on the "shingle theory," which holds that the broker-dealer has made an implicit statement to the customer that its terms would involve a reasonable markup or markdown and that then imposing terms with an unreasonable markup or markdown makes that implicit statement an untrue statement of a material fact. By implying a misrepresentation, this theory appears to be a back-door way of using Rule 10b-5 to impose a federal duty on a broker-dealer in a principal transaction situation not to charge an unreasonable markup or markdown, even though the broker-dealer made no actual statement and there is no statutory or SEC rule explicitly prohibiting high markups or markdowns. The shingle theory may well run contrary to the Supreme Court's ruling in *Santa Fe Industries v. Green*. In *Santa Fe*, the Supreme Court flatly rejected the view that violations of fiduciary duties without any element of deception could violate § 10(b).[38] As the Court put it, "[t]he language of § 10(b) gives no indication that Congress meant to prohibit any conduct not involving manipulation or deception."[39]

### 3. Calculation of the markup

With regard to the calculation of the markup or markdown, the point from which it is calculated is generally said to be the "prevailing market price."[40] When the dealer is engaged in a riskless principal transaction—purchasing the security after the order has been received from the customer and then reselling it to the customer—the comparison price is simple: the dealer's own contemporaneous cost in acquiring the security.[41]

In other principal transactions, the prevailing market price has to be calculated somewhat differently. If the broker-dealer is a market maker in an actively traded stock, then the markup for a customer's buy order should be calculated on the basis of the prices of the broker-dealer in its market-maker role, and those of any other market makers in stock, in recently executed *sales* transactions (i.e., executed transactions at their offers).[42] The markup for a customer's buy order should *not* be based on the prices of the broker-dealer in its recently executed purchase transactions (i.e., executed transactions at its bid), even though that is the broker-dealer's actual out-of-pocket cost of acquiring the shares. This is because doing so would treat the market maker as if it had incurred no costs in maintaining the bid-ask spread. A broker-dealer that both makes a market in a stock and provides the service of handling orders for retail customers incurs separate costs with respect to each of these activities, and both are involved when it handles the order by acting as the counterparty. It needs to be compensated for playing each of these roles. Using the market makers' buying prices as the prevailing market price for customer purchase orders would compensate the broker-dealer only for this second role, not for the costs of market making.

An example can help clarify this point. Imagine a situation in which several market makers in a stock are all executing their buy orders at $20 and sell orders at $30, prices that are equal to current bid and ask quotes. A customer buys that stock from one of these broker-dealers that acts in a principal capacity. If the bid was used as the measure of the broker-dealer's contemporaneous cost, then the broker-dealer, even at a 5 percent markup, would only be paid $21 by the customer for this transaction. Although $20 is what the broker-dealer paid for the share, using this figure to calculate the markup fails to recognize that $30 is the price at which the broker-dealer in its market-making role is selling this stock, and that $30 likely represents the opportunity cost of selling the share to the customer. Also, if the broker-dealer instead acted as an actual broker and obtained the share from another market maker on behalf of the customer, $30 is the price that would have to be paid and a commission would then be added to this higher figure.

If the broker-dealer is selling from its inventory, but either has not sold shares recently as a market maker or is not a market maker at all, then the determination of the proper comparison price for the markup can be even more complex. If there are other market makers in the stock and they have sold shares recently, their sale prices can be used as the basis for calculating the markup. If this is not the case, then it looks more like the broker-dealer is simply distributing the stock to the public rather than providing in one transaction two services: liquidity supply and retail services. In that event, a plausible case can be made for using the broker-dealer's purchase price as the basis. Nevertheless, even this can become problematic if the stock was purchased some period back.

Lastly, there is a general rule against using quotes rather than transaction prices when calculating a broker-dealer's markup. This is because the broker-dealer can quote an offer well above what anyone would be willing to pay for the stock. More generally, quotations will not be a reliable indicator of price where there is little interdealer trading activity.[43] In such a market, quotations may merely represent starting points for negotiation, rather than a measure of the price of completed trades. Accordingly, for thinly traded or obscure securities, bids and asks may be just opening moves in a potential negotiation, making the spread appear wider than what typically ultimately turns out to be the difference in price between completed purchases and sales. Thus, quotations for such stocks may be poor indicators of the actual prices at which transactions occur. However, where a stock is actively traded and has competing market makers, and where the broker-dealers' market-making quotes have been demonstrated to frequently lead to executions, then quotes may serve as viable indicators of prices.[44]

## IV. NON-EXCHANGE TRADING VENUES

Currently, there are three principal types of equity trading venues: stock exchanges, alternative trading systems (ATSs), and non-ATS off-exchange trade, which is mostly internalization. A *stock exchange* is regulated by law as a self-regulatory organization (SRO). The exchange's SRO rules are subject to SEC scrutiny and approval, and the exchange enjoys absolute immunity from private suit when pursuing its regulatory functions. All other trading venues are regulated as *broker-dealers*. Recall from chapter 1 the wide variety of non-exchange trading venues. An ATS is simply an exchange-like trading venue—a facility in which buyers and sellers of stocks can post orders and transact—that does not take on any self-regulatory functions or operate as an SRO. ATSs can be either electronic communication networks (ECNs), now largely disappeared, or dark pools. ECNs are open to all traders and generally either make their quotations part of the public data feeds for quotes or act as "crossing networks," whereby the venue connects buyers and sellers each willing to execute at the midpoint between the best offer and best bid available in the larger market. Dark pools, which are discussed in more detail in chapter 10, can restrict who has access and do not make their quotes available. Lastly, there is non-ATS trade, which is largely internalization (discussed in more detail in chapter 12), whereby a retail broker-dealer sells its customers' order flow to another broker-dealer that acts as the counterparty to the flow of buy and sell orders sent to it. In significant part for historical reasons, the law freights this distinction between an exchange operating as an SRO, and a broker-dealer, which is instead required to be a member of an SRO, with considerable regulatory baggage.

It is worth pausing to recount the history of how it is that non-exchange trading venues came to be regulated as broker-dealers. Forty years ago, there were several stock exchanges, but trading volume was dominated by the New York Stock Exchange (NYSE).[45] The only major non-exchange trading venue was NASDAQ, a system in which multiple dealers would make readily available quotes in a given stock and where brokers, on behalf of their customers, could send orders to execute against these quotes. Though technically not an exchange, NASDAQ was operated by the National Association of Securities Dealers, which functioned as a self-regulatory organization and, much like an exchange, was closely supervised by the SEC. Thus, the backbone of the equity trading market consisted of marketplaces regulated as SROs and had not evolved dramatically since the adoption of the 1933 and 1934 Acts.

That landscape shifted with the entrance of a significant new market participant in 1969.[46] Institutional Networks Corporation, later known as Instinet, established an electronic facility in which institutional investors could trade directly with one another without a broker or specialist.[47] Instinet easily met the statutory definition of an exchange,[48] yet then-current regulation barred exchanges from allowing institutional traders to become members—a practice that was key to Instinet's business model.[49] Instinet's legal status thus fell into a kind of gray zone. The SEC considered creating a new regulatory category for Instinet and related new businesses.[50] In the meantime, however, Instinet had already applied to register as a broker-dealer and eventually did so. This allowed Instinet to be regulated and supervised by the SEC under a different guise—that of a broker-dealer—and the SEC permitted this patchwork solution to become the status quo.[51] Thus, in the 1960s, what would later be called alternative trading systems appeared.[52] The consequential character of this decision, however, was almost certainly not appreciated. Nonetheless, it set the stock market on a path to regulating all equity trading venues that are not exchanges as broker-dealers. Fast-forwarding to the present, as we have seen, there are now a wide range of equity trading venues that are regulated as broker-dealers and are responsible for perhaps 35–40 percent of total trading volume.[53]

As defined by the Exchange Act, an *exchange* is simply any rule-based marketplace for transacting securities.[54] Exchange Act § 5 prohibits engaging in transactions on any exchange that is not registered as a national securities exchange pursuant to § 6 of the Act unless the exchange is granted an exemption under § 5. Section 6(b) in effect requires a national securities exchange to be organized as a self-regulatory organization.[55] In other words, in the language of the statute, all rules-based marketplaces for securities are "exchanges," but in the parlance of general commentary in recent decades (which is followed in this book), only rules-based marketplaces that are SROs—i.e., the ones that are registered as national securities exchanges—are referred to as exchanges. The other rules-based marketplaces operate pursuant to an exemption based on their registration as broker-dealers and in that status must be regulated by an SRO.

Exchanges' statuses as SROs play an important role in current market structure, so it is worth discussing what that status involves and the benefits and burdens that it confers. Under the self-regulatory system, exchanges act as quasi-public institutions that are delegated regulatory functions by the SEC. The exchanges are charged with partly regulating their own markets, including establishing rules compliant with regulation, supervising the conduct of their members (i.e., the broker-dealers who are the persons entitled to trade directly on the exchange), and participating in the governance of the systems that interlink the various exchanges and other equity trading venues.[56] Important benefits also accompany SRO status, including dramatic limits on an exchange's potential civil liability to private individuals and institutions. A stock exchange is absolutely immune from liability to private plaintiffs when conducting regulatory activities.[57]

A dark pool, as discussed in chapter 1, is a nonexchange trading venue that promises to keep confidential the existence of the orders sent to it and to restrict the kinds of parties allowed to trade there. Properly operated, it can provide a venue where uninformed buyers and sellers that are seeking to trade substantial amounts of stock can minimize the movement of prices against them and transact at prices potentially superior to the NBO and NBB. Critics suggest, however, that dark pools often break their promises with respect to order secrecy and customer restrictions and in the process disadvantage traders who send orders to these venues.[1] A trader is also hurt if her broker, in sending her order to a given dark pool, fails to send her order to the trading venue where it will execute at the best price or in the most timely and reliable fashion. This chapter investigates how, ideally, a dark pool should operate, addresses certain criticisms of how they are actually operated in practice, and finally considers various potential reforms.

## I. DARK POOLS AND THE FATE OF CUSTOMER ORDERS

There are two major criticisms of practices in today's stock market that are associated with dark pools, each involving the fate of customer orders that end up in such venues.[2] The first practice involves large investment banks, which are both important providers of brokerage services and operators of most of the largest dark pools.[3] They are accused of routing their brokerage customers' orders to the banks' own dark pools even when the orders will receive inferior execution there.[4] As an example, consider an institutional investor that uses a large investment bank as its broker to handle a nonmarketable buy limit order.[5] The bank steers the institution's order to a dark pool that the bank operates. The bank's proprietary traders learn through an internal source of the existence of the institution's order. Unless cancelled, this order may sit in the dark pool until such time the bank's proprietary traders decide it is advantageous for them to send in an order to execute against the institution's limit order (which, in the zero-sum world of secondary trading, would mean the execution is disadvantageous for the institutional investor). Related to this first practice is the claim that it is common for a dark pool operator to misrepresent the nature of other parties trading in its pool in order to induce brokerage customers to agree to have their orders sent to this pool.

The second alleged practice involves large investment banks ignoring their brokerage customers' instructions to direct their orders to specific venues, and instead routing the orders to their own dark pools, where, again the orders receive an inferior execution.[6] Again, as an example, suppose that an institution using this investment bank as a broker fears its order will be sent to the bank's dark pool and suffer the fate described just above. The institution therefore specifies that its order be sent to an alternative venue. The bank ignores the direction and sends the order to its own dark pool anyway. Even if the trader detects that this has happened, which may be difficult to do, it may not switch brokers because it may feel tied to the large bank due to the free "soft money" research services the bank provides.[7] Market solutions to such a violation of the investment bank's duty of best execution may not work effectively under these circumstances.

Dark pool operators have been no strangers to legal actions involving allegations that they have engaged in these kinds of practices. The SEC has brought a number of successful proceedings against dark pool operators.[8] Former New York Attorney General Eric Schneiderman filed a civil suit against Barclays alleging that Barclays' dark pool, Barclays LX (then the second largest in the United States) misrepresented to users 1) the involvement of HFTs in LX; 2) the informational advantages given to HFTs; and 3) that Barclays, as a broker, treated all venues the same based on quality, when it actually disproportionately routed client orders to its own pool.[9]

We do not know whether any of these practices is in fact widespread. As discussed later in this chapter, however, they are clearly illegal, and their wealth-transfer and efficiency effects appear completely negative. We close this chapter by suggesting some policy reforms that would make enforcement more effective if, despite the illegality of these practices, evidence emerges that they are in fact widespread.

## A. Understanding the Function of Dark Pools

First, recall from chapter 1 that a dark pool, like an exchange, is typically an electronic limit order book. Unlike an exchange, however, it does not publicly reveal the limit orders that are posted on it.[10] Moreover, it has the ability to restrict who can post limit orders and submit marketable orders.[11] Dark pools, despite their nefarious-sounding moniker, can provide useful, legitimate services to their customers. They arose because of the more liberal regulatory environment established by the NMS Amendments to the Exchange Act and the information-technology revolution. A key force driving their rise—as with so many other institutions and practices within the new stock market—was a concern about mitigating adverse selection. A dark pool's most valuable characteristic, from this perspective, is to provide a venue where uninformed buyers and sellers that are seeking to trade substantial amounts of stock can minimize the movement of prices against them and transact at prices potentially much better than the NBO or NBB.[12] These advantages arise from the fact that quotes on a dark pool are not publicly displayed and exist because dark pool operators have the ability to exclude traders they believe to be informed.

An ideal dark pool could function in the following way. One party would post a midpoint limit order going in one direction which would be executed against by another party sending in either a midpoint limit order going in the opposite direction or just any other marketable order. Both parties are completely uninformed. In this situation, the midpoint is a substantially better price for the buyer relative to the NBO, and it is the same for the seller relative to the NBB.

The system begins to break down to the extent that either kind of party is in fact informed. Assume for purposes of illustration that the posted midpoint limit order is a buy order. Consider first the situation in which the party posting the midpoint buy limit order is informed, and accordingly she posts a large order. The uninformed parties sending sell orders to the dark pool will be disadvantaged because they will not be able to see the size of the posted sell limit order and hence draw an inference that an informed party might be on the other side. The system similarly begins to break down if instead it is the counterparty who is informed. The counterparty submits its order only because its information suggests that the midpoint is a price that would make a purchase or sale advantageous to it. Because trading is a zero-sum game, this is a disadvantageous transaction for the uninformed party that posted the standing midpoint sell limit order. Thus, the dark pool operator provides a service to the extent that it can effectively screen all parties sending in orders to assure that each side is relatively unlikely to be informed.[13]

The extent to which dark pools can in fact successfully filter out the informed is not clear. Theory, supported by empirical work, suggests, however, that the informed themselves do not find dark pools an ideal place to trade. A big advantage of sending an order to a dark pool is the price improvement provided by mid-point orders. However, an informed trader with good news is unlikely to be the only one with such news and so its buy order will likely be joined by other informed buy orders. If these orders are sent to dark pools, the result is limited execution.[14] This theory enjoys empirical support in work by Carole Comerton-Forde and Talis Putnins who show that there is less price discovery in dark pools.[15]

## B. Wealth-Transfer and Efficiency Considerations

To the extent that a dark pool does not function in accordance with the ideal described in subsection A, an order sent there may execute at less-desirable terms than if it were sent to another venue. An investment bank that operates a dark pool has intimate knowledge of the extent to which it in fact falls short of this ideal. If a brokerage unit of an investment bank sends a trader's order to the bank's own dark pool when the broker knows, or should know, that the order would receive superior execution elsewhere, the bank gains from the extra volume of trade in its dark pool and in other possible ways,[16] and the customer loses from the inferior terms of execution. The same result is likely to arise if the trader, having tried to determine where its order is most likely to get best execution, instructs its broker that the order be sent to a venue other than the bank's dark pool, but the instruction is ignored. The same result is also likely if the bank operating the dark pool misrepresents to customers the nature of the parties allowed to trade on the bank's dark pool, in order to create the impression that there exists less danger of informed counterparties there than is in fact the case. Such a misrepresentation is likely to attract non-marketable orders that could execute on better terms elsewhere. All of these results generalize if these failures are common practices: they make investment banks richer and traders poorer.

At the simplest level, the negative efficiency consequences arising from these failures of brokers or dark pool operators track the negative efficiency consequences of breaching contracts or engaging in misrepresentations more generally. As we saw in chapter 9, a broker has a duty of best execution in the way it routes a customer's order. This requires the broker to exercise "reasonable diligence to ascertain the best market" for a transaction to ensure that an order receives a price "as favorable as possible under prevailing market conditions."[17] In essence, the duty of best execution is a default term in the contract between the broker and its customer. Its violation leads to the same efficiency concerns that any other breach would: the fact that the parties voluntarily entered into the transaction no longer leads to the presumption that it can be expected to advance the interests of both and that it thus enhances efficiency. The same analysis applies to a broker disregarding customer instructions as to where to route an order, which is also clearly illegal.[18] When a misrepresentation induces a party to enter a contract—in this case agreeing to have an order sent to a dark pool that has different counterparties than represented—the same problem is again created: the transaction no longer carries the presumption of being efficiency enhancing. Finally, if an investment bank that is both a broker and an operator of a dark pool provides information concerning a customer order to its trading affiliates (or anyone else), it would be violating its agency law duties of confidentiality, provisions of Regulation ATS, and probably its own marketing material.[19] Again, one can view these duties as default provisions in a contract, the breach of which robs the transaction of the presumption that it enhances efficiency.

If we, however, look at the efficiency question from the more nuanced mode of inquiry that we have generally used in this book, the story becomes a bit more complicated. Suppose these practices are in fact widespread. In that case, they increase the effective costs of trading for those uninformed traders whose orders go to dark pools. They also discourage some traders from using dark pools who would use them, and who would enjoy lower costs of trading as a result, if these practices did not occur. The lower level of liquidity experienced by these two groups because of dark pools falling short of ideal will reduce the efficiency of both the allocation of resources over time and the allocation of risk in the economy.

In contrast, though, these practices may improve share price accuracy and hence enhance the real economic-efficiency effects flowing from that. This is true to the extent that fundamental value informed traders get advantages trading in dark pools because these practices lower their cost of trading. It is also true to the extent that uninformed investors are scared off from the dark pools because of these practices. When more uninformed investors instead trade on exchanges, the spreads are lower for informed investors. The uninformed investors trading on exchanges reduce the trading costs of informed investors, and this cost reduction encourages those in the business of generating and trading on fundamental value information. As explored in chapter 5, whether the positive efficiency effects from increased price accuracy are worth the negative efficiency effects from the increased costs of trade depends on the mix of informed trader types that enjoy the benefits of dark pool misconduct. Indeed, *even if* the positive efficiency effects from these alleged practices dominated the negative ones— which we have no reason to believe—we would not recommend abandoning the traditional rules of upright commercial practice that are breached by these practices. Other methods exist for achieving the same objective, such as prohibiting or limiting dark pools.[20]

## II. REGULATORY RESPONSES

In Section I we examined two problematic practices associated with an investment bank playing the dual roles of a broker for customers' orders and as an operator of a dark pool. The first potential problem concerns brokers directing customer orders to their own dark pools even when the customer receives inferior execution there. The second concerns brokers ignoring client instructions to direct an order to a specific venue and instead routing it to the broker's own dark pool.

A series of regulatory proposals that seek to rein in the growth of dark pool volume generally could affect these two practices, but with the added and potentially undesirable effects of affecting access to dark pool trading in general. These proposals include eliminating retail investors' access to dark pools and reserving them solely for institutional investors;[21] requiring that dark pools offer price improvement before an order can be routed to one;[22] and caps for the volume that can transact on dark venues.[23] All of these proposals seem insufficiently targeted, however, if the problems with dark pools are solely the potential conflicts of interest noted in this chapter, rather than more fundamental features.

More targeted and less intrusive would be a reform proposal focused on disclosure. This would be designed to assist customers in determining whether their orders are being routed to venues offering best execution and whether order-routing directions are being ignored. FINRA has recently taken steps in the direction of greater disclosure, requiring various new disclosures by different forms of off-exchange trade.[24] The most relevant proposal would require dark pools to provide FINRA with more extensive order-book information than they currently provide to the Order Audit Trail System (OATS).[25] OATS is an order-tracking system designed to assist FINRA's surveillance activities.[26] Brokers could be required to disclose what percentage of orders routed to their own venue were executed there, at what price, and what instructions, if any, were associated with those orders. Economist James Angel has called for such greater disclosure by brokers, suggesting that "brokerage firms themselves . . . disclose execution quality directly to their customers."[27]

More could also be done to strengthen the stock market's mandatory disclosure regime. Currently, brokers are not required to disclose to customers on their transaction confirmation slips the venue in which an order was executed.[28] The cost of requiring disclosure of the venue of execution should not be onerous, because records of where execution occurred must already be retained. Such disclosures would provide customers with the ability to check whether their requests were being followed.

Proposals based on disclosure, however, share at least two vulnerabilities. First, if brokers are submitting inaccurate disclosures, then the SEC or private litigants must feasibly be able to detect such conduct. Second, disclosure to customers will be effective only if customers actually examine and act on those disclosures, which is unlikely to be the case with retail (as opposed to institutional) clients. The SEC could mitigate these problems by conducting periodic audits to verify whether these disclosures and confirmations are accurate. Investor organizations, the financial media, or commercial services might well develop easily understood scoring systems to inform retail customers about how well different brokerage firms perform. If none of these private entities do (perhaps because of the public-goods nature of such scores), the SEC could develop a scoring system itself.

Beyond the problems with dark pools discussed in chapter 10, there are two other major controversies today involving broker-dealers' role in secondary market structure. Each concerns practices that critics claim result in customer orders not being sent to the trading venue where they will receive the best execution. Specifically, critics suggest that brokers often fail in this way, sending the order instead to the venue that pays the most to the broker. There are two such monetary inducements: maker-taker fees and payment for order flow.[1] This chapter and chapter 12 address these two different inducements. This chapter is focused on maker-taker fees and their mirror image, taker-maker fees. Chapter 12 is focused on payment for order flow.

## I. UNDERSTANDING MAKER-TAKER FEES

It is common for an exchange to make payments to brokers that prompt the brokers to steer certain kinds of orders in the exchange's direction and to charge brokers for other kinds of orders they send to the exchange. Under the maker-taker model, the exchange pays for nonmarketable limit orders it receives that ultimately transact and charges for each marketable order it receives that executes against a limit order posted on it. Under the taker-maker model, the venue does the opposite.

In a typical maker-taker structure, a venue charges in the range of $0.0025–$0.0030 per share for marketable orders and pays rebates for executed non-marketable orders in the range of $0.0020–$0.0025 per share.[2] In contrast, the taker-maker scheme will typically charge executed nonmarketable limit orders $0.0007–$0.0010 per share and rebate $0.0002–$0.0005 for marketable orders. The actual fees and rebates vary somewhat across exchanges and over time,[3] but under either scheme the venue typically nets in the neighborhood of $0.0005 per share for each executed transaction.

The maker-taker and taker-maker fee structures have been subject to vigorous criticism as essentially a system of bribes. Critics argue that they create incentives for brokers to direct customer orders to the venue that pays the highest rebate, rather than the one that delivers best execution for the customer. In a letter to the SEC, Senator Charles Schumer argued that they "create[d] a conflict of interest, as brokers may be incentivized to execute trades on a particular venue even if that venue is not offering the best price," creating "room for brokers to arguably put their own interests ahead of their clients by maximizing the rebates they receive from exchanges."[4] Senator Carl Levin, asking a TD Ameritrade executive about the fact that TD Ameritrade had directed virtually all nonmarketable orders to a single trading venue, which happened to offer the highest rebate for such orders, suggested that "[y]our subjective judgment as to which market provided best execution for tens of millions of customer orders a year allowed you to route all of the orders to the market that paid you the most. . . . I find that to be a frankly pretty incredible coincidence."[5] Shortly after those hearings, a class-action lawsuit was launched against TD Ameritrade, alleging that it violated its duty of best execution in this way.[6]

## A. Modeling the Fee Structures

To see how these fee structures work, we will start with a model that makes several simplifying assumptions. These assumptions are that the maker rebate and taker fee are the same and equal $r$; that there is a single, consolidated trading venue; that all traders submit their orders directly to the trading venue rather than doing so through a broker; and that these traders are rational actors who are well informed about the terms of trade available in the market. Under these assumptions, maker-taker fees and rebates are benign: they have no effect on how liquidity is supplied or on anyone's wealth position. This will not necessarily be the case, however, when we relax these various assumptions.

## 1. Liquidity suppliers

Let us look at things first from the liquidity suppliers' point of view. These suppliers, often HFTs, are in the competitive business of supplying liquidity through posting nonmarketable limit orders, as well as other traders who post such orders to transact at better prices than they would get from marketable orders. Consider first the HFTs. Let $s$ equal half of the spread HFTs need to cover their costs associated with making a market given the possibility of informed trading. Let $p$ be the consensus value of a security at the time a quote is made. Absent a liquidity maker rebate, the limit orders posted by the HFTs at the trading venue will, in accordance with the adverse selection model of liquidity provision set out in chapter 3, put the offer at $p + s$ and the bid at $p - s$. When there is rebate of $r$ ($r < s$), the offer will be $p + s - r$. This is because an HFT will receive $r$ every time a limit order it posted transacts, and so receiving $p + s - r$ is, from an economic point of view, the equivalent to receiving $p + s$ if there were no rebate (that is, the amount the HFT would need to receive to break even without a rebate). Under the same logic, the bid will be $p - s + r$, which is the economic equivalent for the HFT of paying the breakeven price of $p - s$ per share in a world without rebates.[7] Rational regular traders who submit nonmarketable limit orders will also set the limit that they specify, so, relative to the limit they would have set in the absence of a rebate, they adjust any buy order limit down by $r$ and any sell order limit up by $r$.

## 2. Liquidity takers

Now consider liquidity takers: traders who submit marketable orders. On the one hand, because of the adjustments to the available offers and bids described in subsection 1, posted by liquidity suppliers in reaction to receiving rebates, the offer price which traders submitting marketable orders pay for shares, and the bid price at which they sell them, are each improved by $r$ relative to what they would have paid or received in the no-rebate world, respectively. On the other hand, this narrowing of the spread is exactly offset by the fee $r$ that, as takers of liquidity, they must pay the venue for each share bought or sold.

### 3. The benign effect of the fees and rebates given the simplifying assumptions

This analysis shows that the combination of maker rebates and taker fees leads to precisely the same terms of trade from an economic point of view as would prevail in their absence. Thus, there is no reason to think, at least under the assumptions we have employed so far, that anyone would behave differently than in a world without rebates. This same analysis holds for taker rebates and maker fees, because, if they are equal, they simply correspond to a negative $r$ in the expressions from subsection 2.

## B. Relaxing the Assumptions of the Model

Now consider what happens when we relax various assumptions of the model.

### 1. Relaxing the assumptions about the trading venues

Relaxing the simplifying assumptions that we made about trading venues does not change the conclusions. We started with the assumption that the maker rebate and the taker fee are equal. In reality, they are not, because exchanges typically require a fee for the service of providing a place to trade. As we have seen, this fee is the difference between the two. The size of the venue's fee is irrelevant to the current discussion, and, with it taken out, the maker rebate and taker fee are by definition always going to be equal.

We also assumed a single, consolidated trading venue. The real world, with competing venues, should work the same way, however, at least as long as we continue to hold onto our assumptions about the nature of the traders in the market: i.e., that they can send their order wherever they desire, and that the order will execute where it is sent. That is, there is no order protection rule. This is because both liquidity suppliers and liquidity takers, when deciding whether to send an order to any given venue, can make the same calculations as in the preceding model concerning the venue's fee and rebate system—and again the bids and offers will adjust in a way that just offsets these fees and rebates.

### 2. Relaxing the assumptions about regular traders

The assumptions about traders may play a more critical role. To start, we assumed that regular traders send their orders directly to the market without broker intermediation. That means that in maker-taker venues, traders who submit nonmarketable limit orders that execute would receive the rebate directly and those who submit marketable orders would pay the fee directly (and the reverse in each case for taker-maker venues). In fact, few traders are allowed to send orders directly to trading venues; instead, they must use a broker. So, for a trader, the broker is the one who receives the rebate and pays the fee. Typically, nothing in the trader's contract with its broker provides that the rebates and fees be passed through directly to the trader,[8] nor is this required by regulation.

If we continue to assume competitive exchanges, a competitive market for brokerage services, and regular traders who are rational and sufficiently informed to be able to effectively monitor the quality of service their brokers are delivering, the effects of the maker-taker fee structure (and the taker-maker one) remain benign. As set out later, the maker rebates offered by a given venue will lead to commensurately lower brokerage fees for nonmarketable limit orders sent to this venue and the taker fees will lead to commensurately higher brokerage fees for marketable orders there. Hence, the rebates and fees are simply passed on indirectly through their effects on brokerage fees.

To see how introducing a broker into the picture affects things, consider first a trader who wishes her broker to submit on her behalf a *nonmarketable* buy limit order. This buy order will be competing with bids posted by HFTs. Recall that each HFT will increase its bid price commensurately to the size of the rebate, if any, at the venue where it is posting its offer. The trader's limit order, to have the same likelihood of timely execution as it would in a venue without a rebate, would have to have a commensurately higher limit price as well. If the trader's limit order ultimately does transact, the cost of buying a share to the trader is her limit price plus $bnm$, where $bnm$ is the broker's commission for nonmarketable orders posted on that venue. If $cnm$ is the cost to the broker for the act of servicing a nonmarketable order, but the broker receives $r$ as a rebate, then the broker's net cost is $cnm - r$. In a competitive brokerage market with informed, rational consumers of the service, the forces of competition would assure that $bnm = cnm - r$, whatever $r$ is at the venue. When $r$ is higher, the trader will need to submit a commensurately higher limit price to get the same likelihood of timely execution, and so would need a commensurately lower brokerage fee to come out even.

Now consider another trader, one who instead wishes his broker to submit on his behalf a *marketable* buy order. The price he will need to pay will be $p + s + bm$, where $bm$ is the broker's commission for marketable orders posted on this venue. If $cm$ is the cost to the broker for the act of servicing a marketable order and the broker must pay the venue a taker fee of $r$ as a rebate, then the broker's net cost is $cm + r$. In a competitive brokerage market with informed consumers of the service, the forces of competition would assure that $bm = cm + r$, whatever $r$ is. When $r$ is lower, $s$ will be commensurately higher, and so the brokerage fee will have to be lower for the trader to end up paying the same net price for a share.[9]

This story, though, has two flaws. These flaws raise, but do not prove, the possibility that rebates affect how participants in the market behave. First, at least for most retail trades, brokerage fees are fixed on a per-execution basis and do not depend on the venue in which a particular order transacts. Second, it is not easy for many traders to monitor the performance of their brokers. With brokerage commissions invariant, regardless of where an order is sent, a broker has an incentive to send a nonmarketable limit order to the venue with the highest maker rebate and marketable orders to the venue with the lowest taker fee. The quality of execution may be lower as a result, but this can be difficult for the trader to ascertain.

This problem is especially acute with a nonmarketable limit order because determining whether or not it received best execution is more difficult to figure out than with marketable orders. The quality of a limit order execution includes whether it executes or not, how long it takes to get executed, and how likely the market is to move in a disadvantageous direction following an execution.

A 2013 paper sheds some light on this question.[10] To take the extremes at the time of their data, Edge X had a nonmarketable rebate rate of $0.0030 per share and provided a partial or full fill rate (the percentage of such orders ultimately executed against) of 54 percent, an average fill speed of 111 seconds, and a good-fill ratio (measured as the proportion of time the midpoint of the market quotes 5 minutes after a transaction was above the transaction price at the bid or below the transaction price at the ask) of 49 percent. In contrast, Boston, with a rebate rate of −$0.0014 per share, had a fill rate of 74.5 percent, a fill speed of 33 seconds, and a good-fill ratio of 55 percent. Four retail brokerage houses each sent roughly half of their limit orders to Edge X and only Interactive Brokers spread its limit orders around.[11] Evidently, nonmarketable limit orders posted on high-rebate venues are not getting very good execution. Yet that is where many retail brokerages are sending nonmarketable limit orders when the customer does not specify a venue for execution.

## C. Wealth-Transfer Considerations

Even if traders are unable to monitor the quality of broker execution completely, especially with regard to nonmarketable limit orders, the level of competition among trading venues and among brokers probably assures that neither type of enterprise is making excess returns as a result of the maker-taker and taker-maker rebate and fee structures that abound. In terms of traders, there appears to be excess liquidity on the maker-taker venues, and this benefits large traders who place marketable orders there. Those who are harmed are the ordinary traders whose nonmarketable limit orders get inferior execution.

## D. Efficiency Considerations

Extra liquidity of the kind that appears to be generated by venue rebates and fees may be valuable to certain informed traders and hence may add to share price accuracy. The welfare effects of poor execution quality for traders placing nonmarketable limit orders are harder to trace without a better sense than we have of who they are and what they are trying to accomplish. They too may be informed traders, or they may be mistake traders (uninformed traders who think they are informed). In any event, as with dark pool misconduct, it is illegal for a broker to route an order to a venue in a way that violates its duty of best execution. Best execution is an implicit term in a broker's contract with its customers. Even if the failure of brokers to provide best execution results in greater price accuracy, due to the resulting extra liquidity, there are more appropriate ways to increase share price accuracy than allowing the breach of an understanding between broker and customer.

## II. REGULATORY RESPONSE

With regard to maker-taker and taker-maker fees, we saw that with different venues providing different rebates and charging different fees—something we observe in the real world—if brokerage commissions do not vary depending on the venue to which an order is sent (which again in the real world they do not[12]), the broker has an incentive to send nonmarketable limit orders to the venue with the highest rebate and marketable orders to the venue with the lowest fee. In each case, the venue to which the order is sent will probably not provide best execution, a proposition for which there is, as we have seen, some empirical evidence.[13] If customers were perfect monitors of their brokers, this incentive might not matter, but they are not perfect monitors, especially with respect to limit orders. This leads us to the conclusion that rebates should be passed directly through to customers and fees directly charged to them, each independent of whatever commission the broker chooses to charge. Such a reform would not guarantee best execution, but it would eliminate an incentive for poor execution. In an era of electronic recordkeeping, the cost of such a reform appears trivial, especially if the disclosure obligation can be satisfied by an estimate based on an algorithm providing an unbiased estimate of rebates or fees related to a customer's order. The important point of the proposed reform is to remove the broker's incentive to provide less than best execution and to provide customers with a payment that is at best a largely unbiased, if not fully accurate, reflection of the rebates that her orders generated. To paraphrase an old saying, "if it might be broke, fix it."[14]

Payment for Order Flow | **TWELVE**

This chapter addresses the pervasive phenomenon of payment for order flow. For a fee, a brokerage firm may sell to another firm (an order-execution facility) its order flow of buy and sell marketable orders from a certain kind of customer—typically a retail investor—who is considered generally uninformed. The other firm, as we have noted before, is called an *internalizer*. It promises that each purchased order that it executes will be at a price that is at least slightly improved over the best offer or bid available in the market at the time the order is placed by the customer.[1] For instance, shares might be purchased from sell-order customers at perhaps $0.0001 over the NBB and shares sold to buy-order customers at that amount below the NBO. Selling order flow in this fashion essentially outsources what a retail broker might otherwise do itself, internally, by transacting against incoming customer orders as principal, buying from the seller at a price slightly over the best bid in the market and selling to the buyer at a price slightly below the best offer in the market, and making the difference between the price paid and the price received as a profit. Internalizers typically only pay for marketable orders, but will often accept nonmarketable limit orders. The payments the broker selling customer order flow receives from the internalizer is referred to as *payment for order flow*.[2]

The extent of the practice was first noted in a 2010 SEC Concept Release on Equity Market Structure. It reports that an analysis of eight brokerage houses with a significant retail customer business revealed that nearly 100% of market orders were sent to internalizers.[3] Financial economist Robert Battalio and his coauthors show that nine out of the ten retail brokers studied send virtually all marketable orders to order-flow purchasers.[4]

Critics characterize payment for order flow as another kind of bribe. They argue that it creates an incentive for the broker to direct its customer orders to the venue that pays the highest rebate, rather than the one that most improves the prices sellers receive and buyers pay. For instance, one critic criticized the practice as potentially "creat[ing] . . . conflicts of interest" between brokers, who seek to maximize revenue from selling order flow, and customers, who might receive better execution elsewhere.[5] Indeed, in a letter to then-SEC Chair White, Senator Carl Levin stated that "[c]onflicts of interest erode public confidence in the markets" and that "payments [for order flow] create another incentive for brokers to maximize their own profits at the expense of best execution of customer orders," and called for their elimination.[6]

## I. UNDERSTANDING PAYMENT FOR ORDER FLOW

As usual, the best way to analyze the social consequences of the practice of payment for order flow is to consider its wealth distribution effects and its efficiency effects.

### A. Wealth Effects

If the internalizer and broker markets are each competitive, then the analysis of the wealth effects of payment for order flow is very simple: there are none. The internalizers pay the brokers the revenue that they are able to make above their costs (plus a market return on capital) from executing the buy and sell orders on the promised terms of slight price improvement. What the brokers receive reduces the costs of providing brokerage services, and in a competitive brokerage market these savings are passed on through lower commissions.

If, however, the internalization market is not competitive, then internalizers are the monopsonist equivalent of oligopolists and may have the market power to pay less for order flow than what they make above their costs (plus a market return on capital) from executing orders at a slight improvement over the

NBO and NBB. What brokers then pass on to customers in the form of lower brokerage fees may be insufficient, leaving traders worse off. Alternatively, the internalization market may be competitive, but the broker market may not be. In that case, the brokers may sell the order flow for an appropriate price but only pass a portion of those savings on to customers. If so, then just as with maker-taker fees, payment for order flow could create a genuine agency problem by aligning brokers' incentives with receiving payments for order flow, whereas better execution may be obtained on an exchange.[7] In this noncompetitive version of the market, customers receive inferior execution because their orders are not routed to exchanges and the customers receive only a portion of the savings obtained.

## B. Efficiency Effects

Liquidity suppliers on the exchange do not get the opportunity to interact with internalized order flow. The removal of uninformed order flow from the exchange alters its adverse-selection environment.[8] As we learned in chapter 4, the probability that liquidity providers face informed traders increases, which in turn increases the spread that informed traders need to pay. This, as we have seen, reduces the incentives of fundamental value information traders to engage in their information-generating activity and thus reduces share price accuracy. In contrast, it is possible that execution at terms slightly better than the NBO and NBB, when combined with lower brokerage fees resulting from the indirect passing-on of at least part of the payment for order flow, reduces the effective cost of trading for uninformed traders. If so, the practice of brokers selling order flow to internalizers improves the efficiency with which resources are allocated over time and the efficiency with which risk is allocated. Still, for these efficiency gains to be fully realized, internalizers must pay competitive rebates for order flow, and these must be fully passed on to traders one way or another.

## II. REGULATORY RESPONSE

What, if any, is the appropriate regulatory response to payment for order flow? If we are confident that the markets for internalization services and for brokerage services are both completely competitive, then no response would be needed. This is because payment for order flow would promise retail market order traders a low effective cost of trading, once brokerage commissions are counted as part of the calculation. If one or both of the markets is not fully competitive, however, the practice leads to these traders having higher effective costs of trading than could be achieved by some other arrangement.

In considering this problem, it is important to remember that we are looking at a situation in which brokers have the ability to segregate out retail order flow, which is uninformed, and match buyers and sellers without the adverse-selection concerns that generate much of the spread on exchanges. Thus, the cost of execution should be very low, presumably considerably lower than the spread that remains after the small price improvement provided by the internalizer. Indeed, it is even possible that if much of the reduced costs of execution do not make their way through to the customer in the form of reduced brokerage fees, these traders would be better off with all their trades being sent to the exchanges. This is because now the retail market orders execute at prices only slightly better than an NBB or NBO that is generated in a market deprived of the uninformed order flow that has be siphoned off by internalization. If the exchanges had this additional uninformed order flow, the NBB would be higher and the NBO lower, quite possibly by amounts greater than the sum of the small price improvement.

The key question, thus, is whether brokers pass on to customers the substantial payments they receive for order flow in the form of lower commissions, given that internalizers offer only nominal price improvement. We do not know the answer to this question, and it is possible that it happens. Still, if there is a problem, passing through the payments would solve it. Such a reform should also not be very costly in an age of electronic recordkeeping.[9] In essence, this again appears to be a situation in which the cure is sufficiently cheap that "if it might be broke, fix it."

# Conclusion

This book has aimed to provide a systematic legal and economic analysis of a wide range of important issues in the modern equity market. As a conclusion, we hope to point to three major open questions about the structure of financial markets that stand in need of much greater empirical and theoretical exploration. We will quickly discuss how market structure differs across asset classes; the question of the optimal degree of pooling of informed and uninformed traders; and how technological innovations at exchanges might affect the character of liquidity provision. For each, our emphases will be two-fold: first, to demonstrate the continuing power of the informational paradigm to cast light on these issues, but second, to also use them as an occasion for appreciating its limits.

The first open issue is to consider the similarities and differences between the equity market's structure and the many other markets important to finance—including debt (whether corporate, municipal, or government bonds), options, commodities, futures, and over-the-counter derivatives—and whether and how those differences should make for distinct regulatory treatment of those other markets. To our knowledge, the legal literature has only begun to see the importance of thinking about the differences—often subtle and surprising—of microstructure across asset classes.[1] Yet, as we hope to illustrate, it is an issue of potential first-order importance for regulators.

In keeping our focus on the adverse selection model of liquidity provision, a key axis for thinking about different financial markets is their distinctive *information structure*. By this, we mean the importance, if any, of the role played by private information and information asymmetries in that market. Consider, as a quick case study, a market with a very different informational structure than corporate equities, the corporate bond market.

The structure of trading corporate bonds today is markedly different from the structure of the equity market. In fact, the corporate bond market more closely resembles the equities market of 1990 or even 1980. Recall that today's equities market is dominated by electronic limit order books open to the provision of liquidity by any market participant. In contrast, the debt market resembles a pure dealer market, where every purchase order is filled by a sale from a dealer and every sell order is filled by a purchase from a dealer. There are no national corporate bond exchanges where marketable orders execute against nonmarketable limit orders and electronic trading platforms have made surprisingly limited inroads. In terms of law, the regulatory structure governing the market is minimal. Public offerings of corporate debt securities must generally be registered under the federal securities laws. Institutions that act as dealers in those securities must register with the SEC as broker-dealers, and transaction data is publicly disclosed.[2] In terms of secondary market structure, however, there is no mandated transparency for quotations in corporate bonds, no order-handling rules requiring dealers to post customer limit orders, and no trade-through rule proscribing transactions at prices inferior to superior quotations available elsewhere. In fact, as late as 2001 there was no consolidated data on transaction prices. Furthermore, as we have seen, a major preoccupation of federal securities law for equities is insider trading, discussed extensively in chapters 5 and 6. Rule 10b-5 may apply to bond transactions, but current SEC activity suggests that there are few, if any, insider trading prosecutions based on individuals' or institutions' trading of debt instruments.

Against the background of these regulatory differences between equity and debt markets, we note that spreads in the corporate bond markets are orders of magnitude higher than for NMS stocks. Does this fact call for any regulatory response? If so, what kind? Is is time for a Reg. NMS for corporate bonds or for more vigorous prosecution of insider trading? We suggest that the answers to these questions are helpfully informed by the informational perspective, and that they should be shaped by the answer to a more basic question: What role, if any, does private information play in the trading of corporate bonds?

On the one hand, if private information is pervasive, shaping the provision of liquidity in a manner similar to the equities market, then active insider trading prosecutions in the corporate bond market could play an important role in shaping market outcomes. Specifically, insofar as there is private information, then the cost of liquidity will reflect a component due to adverse selection and reducing adverse selection can reduce the cost of liquidity. If, on the other hand, the role of private information is minor, then there is little need for regulatory tools like the prohibition on insider trading. In that case, the large spreads that we observe may be the result of a substantial shortfall in the competitiveness of the bond dealer market, suggesting that a very different kind of regulatory intervention is called for, presumably focusing on market structure rules and quote and transaction transparency.

At the broadest level, leading economic theories of the role played by the trading of corporate bonds suggests that their "informational insensitivity" is a crucial feature.[3] The basic idea is that market participants often trade corporate bonds precisely because they value the fact that they—and their counterparty—are unconcerned with attempting to discern whether the actual value of the instrument differs from the current trading price. This is light-years from the world of equities and the pervasive concern with adverse selection that shapes that market. But is this true of all corporate bonds? Perhaps not.

The bonds of highly distressed issuers are unlikely to be informationally insensitive or to be providing the same financial service as the "safe" corporate bonds that Gary Gorton and others have emphasized. Indeed, the debt of distressed issuers is traded by hedge funds and other institutions that seem to invest considerable resources to become highly informed as to their cash-flow prospects. It seems like such debt securities might be usefully subjected to an insider trading regime under the misappropriation theory. The details we leave to future empirical research and theory, but the lesson seems worth emphasizing. Naturally, the nature of an asset—its cash flow profile, governance rights, contractual details—matters to a market. And both the bonds of a blue-chip issuer and the bonds of a company considering bankruptcy share fundamental similarities in terms of maturity dates, term structure, and fixed repayment of principal and interest. Yet, the informational structure of the secondary market for those two assets varies considerably, and these differences—the insignificance of information asymmetries in the market for high-quality debt, and their pervasive role in the market for distressed debt—can matter considerably to whether a given regulatory policy is unnecessary or important.

Before closing this discussion of corporate bond trading, it is worth investigating another, non-informational dimension on which debt and equity differs.

This will suggest that some market phenomena may not be explained by our informational paradigm and that other areas of investigation will no-doubt be needed. Specifically, it should be noted that the other costs of liquidity provision that we have discussed may play a role. While the typical listed firm has only one series of equity, it might have hundreds of series of bonds, each with its own maturity, coupon rate and contractual provisions. Managing an inventory of all the series of bonds in all listed issuers would be prohibitively costly, and require a huge amount of capital. As a result dealers carry a smaller inventory but even this is costly because many corporate bonds trade quite infrequently. They then rely on searching for the counterparty to a trade that a client wants in a particular bond. How costly is all of this? We do not know.

We turn now to a second open question. A basic fact of the equity market, familiar from earlier chapters, is that a liquidity provider on an exchange cannot tell whether its counterparty is informed or uninformed. Indeed, this fact generates the fundamental dynamic in which liquidity providers lose money to the informed by trading with them and charge the uninformed a higher price than they would otherwise need to pay. Using the terms informally, stock exchanges thus reflect a kind of "pooling equilibrium"—a state of affairs in which traders of different "types" in terms of adverse selection risk all transact together, from the mistaken to the uninformed to those with various degrees of private information. Indeed, the stock market is routinely characterized as anonymous. However, if anonymity is taken to mean that liquidity providers simply have no idea of the type of their counterparty, then this is frequently false.

In myriad ways, liquidity providers often are aware, probabilistically, of the type of their counterparty. The internalization of purchased order flow is a clear example. If, say, Citadel purchases the order flow from Bank of America's retail customers then it can safely assume that the vast majority of incoming marketable order flow is uninformed. The internalizer does not know the precise identity of the person on the other side of the trade, but that is not really the characteristic of interest. What liquidity providers are interested in is a counterparty's *type* for the purposes of adverse selection risk, and an internalizing broker-dealer certainly has a good idea about its counterparties' type when it purchases all of a retail brokerage's marketable order flow. Or consider NYSE's retail liquidity program.[4] The program empowers liquidity providers to quote non-displayed subpenny orders that will only interact with specifically designated orders from retail traders whose brokers vouch for their retail status. This offers liquidity providers a lower adverse selection risk and retail traders price improvement. Dark pools may also be run in a fashion that attempts to keep out informed traders.

We mention these three examples of the many possible to make clear that the current stock market also reflects a partial *separating equilibrium* in which the "type" of different traders is sometimes signaled, perhaps by the origin of their order flow (internalization), by disclosure by their broker (as with NYSE's retail liquidity program), perhaps by their trading style, etc.

As a result, the degree to which any secondary market reflects a pooling versus a separating equilibrium is to a significant extent a choice variable for regulators. It is thus a live and important policy question to ask: *What is the optimal degree of pooling of the informed and uninformed?* In principle, Congress could mandate that all equity trade occur on a single stock exchange. This would represent a significantly greater degree of pooling than the current multi-venue system reflects. Market forces themselves seem to be pushing in the opposite direction of greater separating.

This is a profound issue, which we raise largely to illustrate how major architectural questions remain for microstructure theory to address and the value of the adverse selection perspective in thinking about them. A few quick things can be said now, however. In general, the issue of pooling versus separating reflects a basic trade-off in the extent to which the uninformed will subsidize the informed by sharing in the adverse-selection component of the spread when there is pooling. Thus, more pooling should generally mean the informed find their information gathering and trading activities more profitable. More separating means that liquidity providers are able to offer the uninformed cheaper liquidity, reflecting the diminished or nonexistent adverse selection risk, while the informed find their activities less profitable due to costlier liquidity. One background question then is whether there is enough information production in a given market.

Here, too, in terms of finding the optimal degree of pooling, it will be important for regulators to appreciate that the degree of optimal pooling will likely differ across asset classes. Indeed, the degree of separation of the informed and uninformed not only varies in dizzying ways in equities across global jurisdictions, but it varies considerably across asset classes in any one jurisdiction. Even in those markets in which there are both the informed and uninformed, if the informational signals that a market generates are of less usefulness to the real economy than the equity market, then the degree of optimal pooling may be lower.

Lastly, looking to the future of financial markets one cannot help but observe how technology is transforming their market structure. Consider just a few of these technological innovations in equity market structure. One innovation that has frequently appeared in the headlines has been "speed bumps" at exchanges. This began with the exchange IEX, whose speed bump imposes a 350-microsecond delay on all incoming messages to the IEX order book and an equally timed delay on all information disseminated from the order book. After some vacillation, it seems that the Chicago Stock Exchange's quite different speed bump will become operational. This speed bump is different because it is asymmetric, imposing a 350-microsecond delay on most incoming orders, but not on the ability of certain designated market makers to alter their limit orders. Or consider IEX's discretionary peg order, which prevents non-displayed midpoint orders from executing during algorithmically defined periods of rapid change in quotations for a stock. IEX may seek to allow the discretionary peg functionality to apply to displayed orders.

To all of these innovations, the adverse selection view has much to say. For the speed bumps, it suggests the need for solving for a complex equilibrium in which some speed bumps make liquidity provision more difficult by slowing down receipt of transaction data, while other speed bumps enable market participants to readjust limit orders in the face of new information, while slowing everyone else down. The discretionary peg order, intriguingly, may effectively prevent limit orders from executing precisely when the adverse selection environment is greatest, making IEX a "safer" environment for the posting of limit orders. We note this not because we are confident about the accuracy of these speculations, but because we are confident in the distinctive explanatory power of the informational paradigm to cast light on new questions and markets. We have focused on the U.S. stock market—perhaps the world's best functioning market of any kind—as an avenue for studying how markets function—their dynamics, their mathematical properties, their social utility—in one of their purest and most elegant forms. Even there, much more remains to be understood. But we must leave all that to others, and to another day.

# Notes

## INTRODUCTION

1. World Bank, *Market Capitalization of Listed Domestic Companies*, https://data.world-bank.org/indicator/CM.MKT.LCAP.CD. In aggregate, large commercial banks hold slightly more than $15 trillion in assets. Federal Reserve, *Federal Reserve Statistical Release: Large Commercial Banks* (Sept. 30, 2017), https://www.federalreserve.gov/releases/lbr/current/. In total, all U.S. investment companies similarly hold less in assets. INVESTMENT COMPANY INSTITUTE, 2016 INVESTMENT COMPANY FACTBOOK (2016), https://www.ici.org/pdf/2016_factbook.pdf.

## 1. THE INSTITUTIONS AND REGULATION OF TRADING MARKETS

1. *See generally* George T. Simon & Kathryn M. Trkla, *The Regulation of Specialists and Implications for the Future*, 61 BUS. LAW. 217, 225–27 (2005) (explaining the history of NYSE and NASDAQ procedures).
2. *See* LAWRENCE E. HARRIS, TRADING AND EXCHANGES 89–111 (2002) (discussing the structure of the traditional NYSE and NASDAQ exchanges).

3. Laura Tuttle, Alternative Trading Systems: Description of ATS Trading in National Market System Stocks 5–6 (2013), http://www.sec.gov/market-structure/research/ats_data_paper_october_2013.pdf. *See also* https://otctranspar-ency.finra.org/Agreement.

4. *See infra* in this Part II.A. For a posted sell limit order, this stated limit price is an *offer*. For a posted buy limit order, this stated limit price is a *bid*.

5. As discussed in more detail in V.A.2 *infra*, marketable orders include both "market orders" and "marketable limit orders." A *market order* is created when the person submitting the order commits to trading at whatever is the best available price in the market. The computer will also match the limit orders posted on the venue with "marketable limit orders." A buy limit order is marketable when it has a limit price greater than or equal to the lowest offer in the market and a sell limit order is marketable when it has a limit price less than or equal to the highest bid.

6. *See* Jonathan A. Brogaard, Terrence Hendershott, & Ryan Riordan, *High Frequency Trading and Price Discoverv*, 27 Rev. Fin. Studies 2267 (2013) (finding based on a NASDAQ data set that HFTs supply liquidity for 51 percent of all trades and provide the market quotes 50 percent of the time). This is confirmed by Allen Carrion, *Very Fast Money: High-Frequency Trading on the NASDAQ*, 16 J. Fin. Mkts. 680 (2013); *see also generally* Albert J. Menkveld, *High Frequency Trading and the New Market Makers*, 16 J. Fin. Mkts. 712 (2013) (exploring the role of HFTs as market makers in today's market).

7. *See* Charles R. Korsmo, *High-Frequency Trading: A Regulatory Strategy*, 48 U. Rich. L. Rev. 523, 540 (2014) (defining attributes of HFTs).

8. Laura Tuttle, OTC Trading: Description of Non-ATS OTC Trading in National Market System Stocks 11 (2014), https://www.sec.gov/marketstructure/research/otc_trading_march_2014.pdf.

9. For a discussion of internalization, *see* Chapter 12.

10. Securities Acts Amendments of 1975, Pub. L. No. 94–29, 89 Stat. 97 (codified as amended in scattered sections of 15 U.S.C.) (amending the Securities Exchange Act of 1934, 15 U.S.C. §§ 78akk (1976 & Supp. IV 1980)).

11. Alexander P. Okuliar, *Financial Exchange Consolidation and Antitrust: Is There A Need for More Intervention?*, 28 Antitrust, Spring 2014, at 66, 67 (explaining changes implemented by the SEC to satisfy Congress's vision for Regulation NMS).

12. When the NMS amendments were adopted, Congress expected a proliferation of competing venues. It self-consciously rejected a proposal for an electronic limit order book in which all order flow was directed to a single trading venue, known as a central limit order book (CLOB). *See, e.g.,* S. Rep. No. 94-75, at 12 (1975), *as reprinted in* 1975 U.S.C.C.A.N. 179, 190 (rejecting the role for "the SEC . . . as an 'economic czar' for the development of a national market system" and noting that

"a fundamental premise of the bill is that . . . a national market system . . . will depend upon the vigor of competition within the securities industry").

13. *See* James J. Angel, Lawrence E. Harris, & Chester S. Spatt, *Equity Trading in the 21st Century: An Update* 11-12 (2013), http://www.q-group.org/wp-content /uploads/2014/01/Equity-Trading-in-the-21st-Century-An-Update-FINAL1.pdf (showing significant increases in the speed of execution, decreases in the bid-ask spread, decreases in commissions, and increases in the number of quotes per minute); *see also* James J. Angel, Lawrence E. Harris, & Chester S. Spatt, *Equity Trading in the 21st Century* 7–26 (Marshall Research Paper Series, Working Paper No. FBE 09–10, 2010), http://modernmarketsinitiative.org/wp-content/uploads/2013/10/Equity-Trading-in-the-21st-Century.pdf (discussing recent technology improvements in trading systems and their impacts).

14. *See generally, e.g.*, Jean-Edouard Colliard & Thierry Foucault, *Trading Fees and Efficiency in Limit Order Markets*, 25 REV. FIN. STUD. 3389 (2012); Thierry Foucault & Albert J. Menkveld, *Competition for Order Flow and Smart Order Routing Systems*, 63 J. FIN. 119 (2008); *see also* Regulation NMS, 70 Fed. Reg. 37,496, 37,530 (June 29, 2005) (to be codified at 17 C.F.R. pt. 200); Craig Pirrong, *The Thirty Years War*, 28 REGULATION, no. 2, Summer 2005, at 54, 56 (discussing Regulation NMS).

15. Cboe Global Markets, *U.S. Equities Market Volume Summary*, BATS GLOB. MKTS., http://www.bats.com/us/equities/market_share (operating by corporate parent: BATS, four exchanges; NYSE, four; NASDAQ, three). Two other exchanges are operated independently. *Id.*

16. *Id.*

17. Securities Exchange Act of 1934 § 3(a)(1) (1934); *see also* 15 U.S.C. § 78c(a)(1) (2012) (defining an *exchange* as "any organization, association, or group of persons . . . which constitutes, maintains, or provides a market place or facilities for bringing together purchasers and sellers of securities"); 17 C.F.R. § 240.3b-16(a)(2) (2005) (defining an *exchange* as involving "established, non-discretionary methods" for when orders interact).

18. Securities Exchange Act of 1934 § 3(a)(26) (1934); 15 U.S.C. § 78c(a)(26) (2012).

19. *See generally* Concept Release Concerning Self-Regulation, Exchange Act Release No. 50700, 84 SEC Docket 619 (Nov. 18, 2004).

20. A "self-regulatory organization 'when acting in its capacity as a SRO, is entitled to immunity from suit when it engages in conduct consistent with the quasi-governmental powers delegated to it pursuant to the Exchange Act and the regulations and rules promulgated thereunder.' " DL Capital Grp. v. Nasdaq Stock Mkt., 409 F.3d 93, 97 (2d Cir. 2005) (citations omitted) (*citing* D'Alessio v. N.Y. Stock Exch., Inc., 258 F.3d 93, 106 (2d Cir. 2001)). Self-regulatory organizations are discussed in more detail in Chapter 8.

21. *See* LAURA TUTTLE, Alternative Trading Systems: Description of ATS Trading in National Market System Stocks 5–6, 11 (Oct. 2013), https://www.sec.gov/divisions /riskfin/whitepapers/alternative-trading-systems-10-2013.pdf (providing an overview of ATSs and statistics on trade size distribution across venues).
22. Regulation of Exchanges and Alternative Trading Systems, 63 Fed. Reg. 70,844 (Dec. 22, 1998) (codified at 17 C.F.R. pts. 202, 240, 242, 249) (Regulation ATS Adopting Release); 17 C.F.R. § 242.300(a).
23. 15 U.S.C. §§ 78c(a)(4)–(5).
24. *See* Rhodri Preece, *Dark Pools, Internalization, and Equity Market Quality*, CHARTERED FIN. ANALYST INST. 15–19 (Oct. 2012), https://www.cfainstitute.org/en /advocacy/policy-positions/dark-pools-internalization-and-equity-market-quality (discussing internationalization and its use by broker-dealers).
25. *See also* Concept Release on Equity Market Structure, Exchange Act Release No. 34–61358, 75 Fed. Reg. 3594, 3599 (Jan. 21, 2010). Internalization is discussed in more detail in Chapter 12.
26. Strictly speaking, the NYSE and NASDAQ turnovers are not directly comparable because NYSE-listed shares traded on both NYSE and NASDAQ, whereas NASDAQ-listed shares were traded only on NASDAQ. In the early days (up until the issuance of Regulation NMS), this was not much of a problem, as the NYSE had such a large market share in the trading of its listed shares.
27. If there are at least 200 shares available at $95.29 at the venue to which Maria's broker sends the order, the order will execute on this venue. If not, NMS Rule 611 requires that the venue have procedures in place to send all, or the unsatisfied part, of the order on to another venue where shares are available at the NBO of $95.29. *See infra* II.C. A market sell order would work the same way if she instead wished to sell 200 shares, and, unless the NBB changed, would execute almost immediately at $95.28.
28. A *sell limit order* would be a sell order with the caveat that the person placing it would not accept less than a certain price.
29. A sell limit order in which the NBB at the time the order is sent is above—that is, at least as favorable as—the order's limit is referred to as a *marketable sell limit order*.
30. Quotes in fact can move quite quickly. In the ten minutes following when Maria first contacted her broker and noted the best offer of $95.29, the offer was at one point as low as $95.28 and as high as $95.33. If, by the time the order arrives, the NBO had moved above $95.31, Maria's limit order would not execute even though it was considered "marketable" when sent. Note, however, that the order, until its expiration or cancellation, remains a commitment to buy 200 shares at $95.31 or less.
31. Similarly, the best bid quote is $95.28 with a depth of 500 shares. This is the result of persons who had previously posted still-in-effect nonmarketable buy orders with

a limit of $95.28 that aggregate to 500 shares (that is, buy orders with a limit price below the NBO, which in our example is $98.29).

32. This priority rule holds for all but one of the U.S. exchanges. As of this writing, PSX, the Philadelphia Stock Exchange uses a complicated priority rule which involves size priority (largest standing order at a price trades first for part of the trade); the remainder of the arriving order is filled pro-rata among the standing limit orders.

33. This is the way a CLOB market would work. As already noted, though the matter is controversial, some commentators believe it would have been better if Congress had required that there be a single venue rather than pushing for the competitive, multi-venue system that has in fact developed. *See supra* note 12 and accompanying text.

34. Note that the lowest offer of $30.50 is above the highest bid of $30.48. If that were not the case, then the seller and buyer should transact given that the seller would be willing to accept less than the buyer is willing to pay. Thus, the lowest offer resting on a venue must exceed the highest bid.

35. *See* 17 C.F.R. § 242.601(b)(2) (2015).

36. *Id.*

37. *See* 17 C.F.R. § 242.602 (2015).

38. *See, e.g.*, Concept Release on Equity Market Structure, Exchange Act Release No. 61,358, 75 Fed. Reg. 3594, 3601 (Jan. 14, 2010) (to be codified at 17 C.F.R. pt. 242).

39. Federal regulation requires trading venues to establish procedures reasonably designed to prevent the purchase or sale of a stock at a price inferior to the lowest offer or highest bid, respectively, which is disseminated on the national reporting system for quotations. *See* Regulation NMS Rule 611(the "no trade through rule"),17 C.F.R. § 242.611 (2015) (establishing the rule); *id.* § 242.600(b) (defining relevant terms). Regulation NMS is the most important body of federal regulation governing trading in the stock market.

40. 17 C.F.R. § 242.611(a)(1).

41. Section 11A(c)(1)(B) provides, *inter alia*, that the SEC should "assure the prompt, accurate, reliable, and fair . . . distribution" of transaction information. Securities Acts Amendments of 1975, Pub. L. No. 94-29 (June 4, 1975), 89 Stat. 97, 115 (1975).

42. Regulation NMS, Exchange Act Release No. 51,808, 70 Fed. Reg. 37,496 (June 25, 2005).

43. 17 C.F.R. §§ 242.600(b)(21), 242.601, 242.603, 242.608 (2015) (establishing plan requirement and rules).

44. *See id.* § 242.602.

45. *See id.* §242.608.

46. *See id.* § 242.601.

47. *See* 17 C.F.R. §§ 242.601, 242.602.

48. *See* 17 C.F.R. § 242.600(b)(42).

49. Rule 604 codifies earlier regulation by the SEC known as the "Order Handling Rules." Order Execution Obligations, Rules 11Ac1-4 and 11Ac1-1, Exchange Act Release No. 37619A.

50. *See* 17 C.F.R. § 242.611(a)(1). This rule is subject to various exceptions. 17 C.F.R. § 242.611(a)–(b). More precisely, the rule aims to prevent the purchase (or sale) of a stock at a price higher than a protected offer (or lower than a protected bid); a *protected bid* or *offer* is a quotation that is the best bid or offer on a stock exchange. *See* 17 C.F.R. § 242.600(b)(57)(i)–(iii). The best bid and best offer mean the highest priced bid and the lowest priced offer. *See* 17 C.F.R. § 242.600(b)(7).

51. *See* 17 C.F.R. § 242.600(b)(78).

52. *See* Jonathan Macey & David Swensen, *Recovering the Promise of the Orderly and Fair Stock Exchange*, 42 J. Corp. L. 777, 782 (2017). *See also* Andre E. Owens & Cherie Weldon, *SEC Issues Regulation NMS Adopting Release, Starting the Clock on Sweeping Overhaul of the National Market System*, (2005) https://www.wilmerhale.com/pages/publicationsandnewsdetail.aspx?NewsPubId=91392.

53. 17 C.F.R. §§ 242.300-242.303.


## 2. THE SOCIAL FUNCTION OF STOCK MARKETS

1. This figure was calculated on the basis of data in Compustat.

2. In 2016, private (i.e., nongovernment) nonresidential investment in the United States was $2.32 trillion. FRED Economic Data, https://fred.stlouisfed.org/series/PNFIA.

3. In 2016, real GDP was $18.62 trillion. World Bank, *Gross Domestic Product* (2016), https://data.worldbank.org/indicator/NY.GDP.MKTP.CD.

4. Only 114 of the S&P 1500 Composite are controlled companies. IRRC Institute, Controlled Companies in the Standard & Poor's 1500: A Ten Year Performance and Risk Review (Oct. 2012), https://irrcinstitute.org/wp-content/uploads/2015/09/FINAL-Controlled-Company-ISS-Report1.pdf.

5. For the seminal articulation of this problem associated with the separation between ownership and control in the modern large corporation, *see* Adolf Berle, Jr. & Gardiner C. Means, The Modern Corporation and Private Property (1932); *see also* Michael C. Jensen & William H. Meckling, *Theory of the Firm: Managerial Behavior, Agency Costs and Ownership Structure*, 3 J. Fin. Econ. 305, 308–10 (1976).

6. For a more detailed discussion of the severe collective action problems associated with smaller holders, *see* Merritt B. Fox, *Required Disclosure and Corporate Governance*, 62 Law & Contemp. Prob. 113, 116–18 (1999).

7. Jay C. Hartzell & Laura T. Starks, *Institutional Investors and Executive Compensation* (September 2002), AFA 2003 Washington, DC Meetings 7 (in a sample including

all the firms in the S&P 500 Index, the S&P Midcap Index, and the S&P Smallcap Index, the average aggregate institutional holdings are 53.1 percent of shares outstanding and the average holdings of the top five institutional investors in a firm are 22 percent of the outstanding shares and 44 percent of the aggregate institutional holdings). *Accord* Anthony Saunders, Marcia Millon, Alan J. Marcus, & Hassan Tehranian, *The Impact of Institutional Ownership on Corporate Operating Performance*, NYU Stern Fin. Working Paper No. 03-033, 14 (November 7, 2003) (in a sample of the firms in the S&P 100, 59.3 percent of shares outstanding were held by institutions and the average holdings of the top five institutional investors in a firm were 20.1 percent of the outstanding shares).

8. William W. Bratton, *Hedge Funds and Governance Targets*, GEORGETOWN L.J. 95 (2007, rev. 2010), at 1375, http://papers.ssrn.com/sol3/papers.cfm?abstract _id=928689&high=%20william%20bratton (hedge funds have a high record of success in using the proxy system to achieve corporate change); Alon Brav et al., *Hedge Fund Activism, Corporate Governance, and Firm Performance*, 63 J. FIN. 1729 (2008), (activists are at least partially successful at achieving corporate outcomes two-thirds of the time, and there are statistically significant abnormal returns in the range of 5 percent to 7 percent around the time of the announcement that a hedge fund has become active with respect to a particular issuer).

9. *See* James Dow & Gary Gorton, *Stock Market Efficiency and Economic Efficiency: Is There a Connection?*, 52 J. FIN. 1087 (1997) (showing how, with properly designed incentives, more accurate secondary market stock prices can guide managers to make more efficient decisions); Qi Chen, Itay Goldstein & Wei Jiang, *Price Informativeness and Investment Sensitivity to Stock Prices*, 20 REV. FIN. STUDIES 619 (2006); Artyom Durnev, Randall Morck & Bernard Yeung, *Value Enhancing Capital Budgeting and Firm Specific Stock Return Variation*, 59 J. FIN. 65 (2003) (demonstrating the relationship between the informedness of share prices and the efficient choice of real investment projects by firm managers).

10. There is empirical evidence that a reduction in the riskiness of an issuer's stock will increase the proportion of stock-based compensation that a manager is willing to accept. Clifford G. Holderness, Randall S. Kroszner & Dennis P. Sheehan, *Were the Good Old Days That Good? Changes in Managerial Stock Ownership Since the Great Depression*, 54 J. FIN. 435 (1999).

11. The discussion in this paragraph in the text roughly follows the reasoning behind the so-called First Welfare Theorem (FWT) in welfare economics. The FWT states that, under certain circumstances, a market economy will achieve an equilibrium that is at a welfare optimum in the sense that no feasible reallocation of resources or goods can make any individual better off without hurting someone else. The FWT is sometimes referred to as the "invisible hand" theorem because it shows that

the market works as the invisible hand guiding allocations to this desirable end. It appears that the first statement of the FWT with a discrete time dynamic economy and uncertainty with a finite number of states was made by Gerard Debreu in his THEORY OF VALUE: AN AXIOMATIC ANALYSIS OF ECONOMIC EQUILIBRIUM 100–102(1959). The first part of the theorem requires that an equilibrium exist. This is guaranteed if certain technical conditions on production and preferences are met. The characteristics of this equilibrium are that, at the resulting prices, producers maximize firm value, consumers choose consumption plans that are feasible and most preferred, and markets clear. The conditions for the theorem are (1) there are no production or consumption externalities, (2) firms and consumers are price takers, (3) all economic actors have the same information, (4) there are no transactions costs, and (5) markets are complete in the sense that any risk can be hedged.

12. For a review of the discussion among commentators on this issue, see Richard M. Frankel, S. P. Kothari & Luo Zuo, *Why Shareholder Wealth Maximization Despite Other Objectives* (2018,) available at: https://papers.ssrn.com/sol3/papers .cfm?abstract_id=3165085.

13. A proposed new investment project might involve a new product or process never before undertaken by the firm, but it could also just involve expansion of something the firm was already doing or a replacement of existing productive assets that have worn out.

14. *See* RICHARD A. BREALEY ET AL., PRINCIPLES OF CORPORATE FINANCE 22, 105 (11th ed. 2013).

15. *Id.* at 215–17.

16. The converse proposition that a firm should avoid negative net present value projects is the rule that the firm, to maximize share value, should seek to identify, and then implement, as many positive net present value investment projects as possible. Investing in zero net present value projects has no effect on share value one way or the other.

17. One of us has argued elsewhere that to the extent the managers of a management-controlled firm can do so without risk of a hostile takeover, it is in management's best interests to maximize the firm's aggregate available cash flow (AACF)—that is, its aggregate future earnings, before deductions for depreciation and management compensation and perquisites, discounted to present value at a rate reflecting management's time preference and risk aversion. MERRITT B. FOX, FINANCE AND INDUSTRIAL PERFORMANCE: THEORY, PRACTICE AND POLICY 121-27 (1988).

 The greater the AACF, the greater the capacity of the firm over time to satisfy the interests of each of the top managers: compensation, luxury perquisites, respect, power, affection of those around them, and a sense of rectitude. Striving to make AACF as large as possible also implies, after deduction for management compensation and expenses, the largest possible growth in firm assets (subject, of course, to the constraint that each project invested in is not expected to actually lose money). The idea that managers gain utility simply from the size of the firm they run has a long history. *See, e.g.,* FRANK KNIGHT, RISK, UNCERTAINTY, AND PROFIT (1921); JOSEPH A. SCHUMPETER, THE THEORY OF ECONOMIC DEVELOPMENT (1934); R. GORDON, BUSINESS LEADERSHIP IN THE LARGE CORPORATION (1945). Moreover, the greater the rate of growth of the assets, the more opportunities for promotion, thereby improving the relations between top managers and those directly below them. OLIVER WILLIAMSON, MARKETS AND HIERARCHIES 120 (1975). The idea that managers of public corporations will under many circumstances have an interest in investing in negative net present value projects is also behind Jensen's so-called "free cash flow" hypothesis. Michael C. Jensen, *Agency Costs of Free Cash Flow, Corporate Finance and Takeovers*, 76 AM. ECON. REV. (May 1986), at 323.

18. *See* Frank H. Easterbrook, *Two Agency-Cost Explanations of Dividends*, 74 AM. ECON. REV. 650, 654 (1984); FOX, FINANCE AND INDUSTRIAL PERFORMANCE, *supra* note 17, at 132–40.

19. *See, e.g.,* GORDON DONALDSON, CORPORATE DEBT CAPACITY (1961); William J. Baumol et al., *Earnings Retention, New Capital and the Growth of the Firm*, 52 REV. ECON. & STAT. 345 (1970). For a critical review of these and several other studies, along with an estimate of the magnitude of the effects on the economy, see FOX, FINANCE AND INDUSTRIAL PERFORMANCE, *supra* note 17, at 233–37. *See also* Jensen, *supra* note 17; Reinier Kraakman, *Taking Discounts Seriously: The Implications of "Discounted" Share Prices as an Acquisition Motive*, 88 COLUM. L. REV. 891, 898 (1988). There are good reasons to believe that the forces that push managers toward share value maximizing behavior have, for a number of reasons including more accurate share prices, become stronger in the past several decades. *See* Jeffrey N. Gordon, *The Rise of Independent Directors in the United States, 1950-2005: Of Shareholder Value and Stock Market Prices*, 59 STAN. L. REV. 1466 (2007) (tracing the history of this change in focus to shareholder value); Bengt Holmstrom & Steven N. Kaplan, *Corporate Governance and Merger Activity in the United States: Making Sense of the 1980s and 1990s*, 15 J. ECON. PERSP. 121 (2001) (documenting a move toward a more market-oriented style of corporate governance in the United States); Merritt B. Fox, *Promoting Innovation: The Law of Publicly Traded Corporations*, 5 CAPITALISM AND SOCIETY 1, 39–41 (2010,Issue 3).

20. LARRY HARRIS, TRADING AND EXCHANGES, 206–214 (2003).

21. *See* Yakov Amihud & Haim Mendelson, *Asset Pricing and the Bid-Ask Spread*, 17 J. FIN. ECON. 223, 230 (1986); Yakov Amihud & Haim Mendelson, *Liquidity and Asset Prices: Financial Management Implications*, 17 FIN. MGMT. 5, 6 (1988).

22. *See* THIERRY FOUCAULT, MARCO PAGANO&AILSA RÖELL, MARKET LIQUIDITY: THEORY, EVIDENCE, AND POLICY 307 (2013) (discussing how illiquidity acts as a wedge between transaction prices and the fundamental value of assets).

23. HARRIS, *supra* note 20, at 214–15.

24. *See* HARRIS, *supra* note 20, at 206–14.

25. Thomas Philippon, *Has the US Finance Industry Become Less Efficient? On the Theory and Measurement of Financial Intermediation*, 105 AM. ECON. REV. 1408, 1411 (fig. 2) (2015).

26. *See* Grace Xing Hu, Jun Pan & Jiang Wang, *Early Peek Advantage* (Working Paper, Hong Kong University and MIT), 2013 (documenting the existence of traders who profit due to rapidly trading on the release of market-moving information).

27. Even without considering the resource costs, the negative social consequences from the effect of this practice on liquidity almost certainly dominate the benefits from the fleeting improvement in price accuracy. We suggest in chapters 4 and 6 that this is a reason not to alter market structure rules to prevent "electronic front running," which can be used by liquidity suppliers to protect themselves against announcement traders and in the process narrow spreads and improve liquidity.

28. There is, of course, an argument that a system of venues in which each competes to be the CLOB for any given company's stock could in fact be more effective at prompting innovation. Jonathan Macey & David Swensen, *Recovering the Promise of the Orderly and Fair Stock Exchange*, 42 J. CORP. L. 777, 790–91 (2017). *See generally* Paul G. Mahoney & Gabriel Rauterberg, *The Regulation of Trading Markets: A Survey of Evaluation* (Law and Economics Research Paper Series 2017–07, University of Virginia School of Law) 46–49 (2017).

29. John Hicks, *The Foundations of Welfare Economics*, 49 ECON. J. 696 (1939); Nicholas Kaldor, Welfare Propositions in Economics and Interpersonal Comparisons of Utility, 49 ECON. J. 549 (together introducing the Kaldor-Hicks conception of efficiency). The Kaldor-Hicks approach defines efficiency as the maximization of persons' willingness to pay for a change. When the individual(s) positively affected by a policy shift are willing to pay more for it than those adversely affected would be willing to pay to avoid it, then the policy change is Kaldor-Hicks efficient. The Kaldor-Hicks conception has been criticized vigorously and with considerable merit, but with all its limitations, it remains the standard welfare criterion in law-and-economics analyses of corporate and securities law. Cf. REINIER KRAAKMAN ET AL., THE ANATOMY OF CORPORATE LAW: A COMPARATIVE AND FUNCTIONAL APPROACH 23 n. 87 (3d ed. 2017). In large measure, this is simply because of the lack of a tractable alternative measure to get at improvements in overall welfare.

30. *See, e.g.*, MICHAEL LEWIS, FLASH BOYS: A WALL STREET REVOLT (2014). *See also* Frank H. Easterbrook & Daniel R. Fischel, *Optimal Damages in Securities Cases*, 52

U. Chi. L. Rev. 611, 641 (1985). *But see* Alicia J. Davis, *Are Investors' Gains and Losses from Securities Fraud Equal Over Time? Theory and Evidence*, (2015). 3rd Annual Conference on Empirical Legal Studies Papers; CLEA 2008 Meetings Paper; U of Michigan Law & Economics, Olin Working Paper No. 09-002. Available at SSRN: https://ssrn.com/abstract=1121198 or http://dx.doi.org/10.2139/ssrn.1121198.

31. Luigi Guiso, Paola Sapienza & Luigi Zingales, *Trusting the Stock Market*, 63 J. Fin. 557 (2008).
32. Merton H. Miller & Frances Modiglani, *Dividend Policy, Growth and the Valuation of Shares*, 34 J. Fin. 411 (1961).
33. Brealey et al., *supra* note 14, at 215–17.
34. *See* Daniel Fischel, *The Law and Economics of Dividend Policy*, 67 Va. L. Rev. 699, 701–02 (1981).
35. *See* Homer Kripke, The SEC and Corporate Disclosure: Regulation in Search of a Purpose 123 (1979).
36. Brealey et Al., *supra* note 14, at 465–67.

# 3. THE ECONOMICS OF TRADING MARKETS

1. The value of a stock is generally regarded as equal to the expected future cash flows to a holder of the issuer's shares (discounted to present value). *See* Richard Brealey, Stewart Myers & Franklin Allen, Principles of Corporate Finance 80–84 (11th ed. 2013).
2. This taxonomy bears a significant resemblance to Larry Harris's division of informed traders, whose value traders and news traders parallel our fundamental value and announcement traders. *See* Larry Harris, Trading and Exchanges 194 (2002). While we do not go as far as Harris to treat insider trading as a form of news or announcement trading, we share the general view that their contribution to the social good of informative prices is similarly low. *Id.* at 228.
3. *See* Grace Xing Hu, Jun Pan & Jiang Wang, *Early Peek Advantage* (Working Paper, Hong Kong University and MIT, 2013) (documenting the existence of traders who profit due to rapidly trading on the release of market-moving information).
4. *See* ch. 6.
5. *See* ch. 6.
6. Facilitating such consumption deferral is one of the social functions that a well-functioning securities market can provide. *See* ch. 2.
7. Facilitating adjustments for risk-related reasons is another social function that a well-functioning securities market can provide. *See* ch. 2.
8. Brealey, Myers & Allen, *supra* note 1, at 302–308, 689.

9. What we refer to as "mistake traders" are labeled in some of the relevant literature as "noise traders." *See, e.g.,* Andrei Shleifer & Lawrence Summers, *The Noise Trader Approach to Finance,* 4 J. ECON. PERSP. 19 (1990). The term *noise trader* is ambiguous, however, because other financial economists use the term instead as a label for uninformed traders who are willing to trade at any price. *See, e.g.,* Albert Kyle, *Continuous Auctions and Insider Trading,* 53 ECONOMETRICA 1315 (1985).

10. *See* MERRITT B. FOX, FINANCE AND INDUSTRIAL PERFORMANCE: THEORY, PRACTICE AND POLICY, 34–43, 55–57 (1988).

11. *See* HARRIS, *supra* note 2, at 158 (discussing analyses indicating that in most markets adverse selection accounts for the majority of the bid-ask spread).

12. Given the assumption in this part of the discussion that liquidity supply requires no capital and that there are no costs to doing business other than adverse selection— factors that will be added in later—the best that a liquidity supplier operating in a fully competitive market could hope to do is break even.

13. Because of adverse selection, it is possible for the market to break down completely so that there is no trade. The smaller the portion of trading attributable to uninformed traders, the bigger the spread must be to compensate for the losses from the informed traders. But the bigger the spread, the fewer the uninformed investors willing to tolerate the associated trading losses. These problems are explored in more detail in Appendix B of this chapter.

14. *See* HARRIS, *supra* note 2, at 320–21.

15. *Id.*

16. *See* Lawrence R. Glosten & Paul R. Milgrom, *Bid, Ask and Transaction Prices in a Specialist Market with Heterogeneously Informed Traders,* 14 J. FIN. ECON. 71, 93–94 (1985).

17. An analysis coming to the same results can be done without this assumption, but the added complications make the model much less elegant and less easily understood.

18. *See generally* Glosten & Milgrom, *supra* note 16 (providing model of trading behavior under information asymmetries in securities markets).

19. *See generally* Glosten & Milgrom, *supra* note 16 (providing model of trading behavior under information asymmetries in securities markets). Applying Bayes' Rule, the bid-ask spread generated by the information perspective leads to exactly the same calculation of the bid and ask as was generated by the accounting perspective. *Id.* at 93–94.

20. Earlier work has made this point with regard to the operations of a dealer market. Albert Kyle, *Continuous Auctions and Insider Trading,* 53 ECONOMETRICA 1315(1985).

21. More precisely, the price will be within half of the bid-ask spread from fully reflecting the information.

22. *See* Lawrence R. Glosten & Lawrence E. Harris, *Estimating the Components of the Bid-Ask Spread*, 21 J. FIN. ECON. 123 (1988); Kalok Chan, Y. Peter Chung & Herb Johnson, *The Intraday Behavior of Bid-Ask Spreads for NYSE Stocks and CBOE Options*, 30 J. FIN. & QUANT. ANAL. 329 (1995).

23. *See* BREALEY, MYERS & ALLEN, *supra* note 1, at 302–8, 689.

24. *See, e.g.*, Mark B. Garman, *Market Microstructure*, 3 J. FIN. ECON. 257, 265 (1976); Thomas S.Y. Ho & Hans R. Stoll, *Optimal Dealer Pricing Under Transactions and Return Uncertainty*, 9 J. FIN. ECON. 47 (1981); Hans R. Stoll, *The Supply of Dealer Services in Securities Markets*, 33 J. FIN. 1133 (1978); Yakov Amihud & Haim Mendelson, *Asset Pricing and the Bid-Ask Spread*, 17 J. FIN. ECON. 223, 223–24 (1986).

25. As discussed in the text of this chapter, price-sensitive fundamental traders are uninformed in the sense that they do not possess any nonpublic information suggesting that the price of a share is incorrect. Rather, each such trader has her own best estimate of the issuer's future cash flows based on her particular analysis of publicly available information, and this estimate forms a reservation price for buying or selling the share.

26. The direction of causation of course goes the other way as well, because the extent to which this opportunity cost enlarges bid-ask spread will have an effect on volume. To isolate the concerns being explored here, however, we will take V as exogenous, essentially a measure of the underlying demand to trade shares in a given stock.

27. Hans R. Stoll, *The Supply of Dealer Services in Securities Markets*, 33 J. FIN. 1133 (1978); Yakov Amihud & Haim Mendelson, *Dealership Market: Market-Making with Inventory*, 8 J. FIN. ECON. 31, 32 (1980); Thomas S.Y. Ho & Hans R. Stoll, *Optimal Dealer Pricing Under Transactions and Return Uncertainty*, 9 J. FIN. ECON. 47 (1981); Maureen O'Hara & George S. Oldfield, *The Microeconomics of Market Making*, 21 J. FIN. & QUANT. ANAL. 361 (1986).

28. Carole Camerton-Forde et al., *Time Variation in Liquidity: The Role of Market-Maker Inventories and Revenues*, 65 J. FIN. 295, 326 (2010).

29. Stewart Mayhew, *Competition, Market Structure, and Bid-Ask Spreads in Stock Option Markets*, 57 J. FIN. 931 (2002).

30. *Id.*

31. FINRA, *Statistics*, https://www.finra.org/newsroom/statistics.

32. This paragraph is informed by Christine Parlour & Uday Rajan, *Payment for Order Flow*, 68 J. FIN. ECON. 379 (2005).

33. William G. Christie & Paul H. Schultz, *Why Do NASDAQ Market Makers Avoid Odd-Eighth Quote?*, 49 J. FIN. 1813 (1994).

34. For an example of such punishment, which seemed to involve verbal abuse, *see* Scot J. Paltrow, *Nasdaq Studies May Prove Academic*, L.A. TIMES, Apr. 7, 1995, http://articles.latimes.com/1995-04-07/business/fi-52023_1_hard-evidence. Game theoretic formulations would say that retaliation might consist of a narrowing of the

spread for a period of time. It is not clear, however, if 1/8 of a dollar could be a narrow enough spread to be much of a punishment.

35. William G. Christie & Jeffrey H. Harris, *Why Did NASDAQ Market Makers Stop Avoiding Odd-Eighth Quotes?*, 49 J. FIN. 1841 (1994). It is remarkable to note that this paper is based on data through July 1994 and was published in December 1994. This may be a record in financial economics for speed from first draft to publication.

36. United States Department of Department of Justice, *Competitive Impact Statement* (1996).

37. See *Order Execution Obligations* (Rules 11Ac1-4 and 11Ac1-1), Exchange Act Release No. 37619A (Sept. 6, 1996), https://www.sec.gov/rules/final/37619a.txt. The order handling rules are now incorporated in NMS Rule 604.

38. Eric Budish, Peter Cramton & John Shim, *The High-Frequency Trading Arms Race: Frequent Batch Auctions as a Market Design Response*, 130 Q.J. ECON. 1547, 1548 (2015).

39. James J. Angel, *Tick Size, Share Prices, and Stock Splits*, 52 J. FIN. 655 (1997).

## 4. HIGH-FREQUENCY TRADING

1. *See* Jonathan A. Brogaard, Terrence Hendershott & Ryan Riordan, *High Frequency Trading and Price Discovery*, 27 REV. FIN. STUD. 2267 (2013) (finding based on NASDAQ dataset that HFTs supply liquidity for 51 percent of all trades and provide the market quotes 50 percent of the time). This is confirmed by Allen Carrion, *Very Fast Money: High-Frequency Trading on the NASDAQ*, 16 J. FIN. MKTS. 680 (2013); *see also generally* Albert J. Menkveld, *High Frequency Trading and the New Market Makers*, 16 J. FIN. MKTS. 712 (2013) (exploring the role of HFTs as market makers in today's market).

2. Matthew Baron, Jonathan Brogaard, Björn Hagströmer & Andrei Kirilenko, *Risk and Return in High-Frequency Trading*, J. FIN. & QUANTITATIVE ANAL. (2018), at https://papers.ssrn.com/sol3/papers.cfm?abstract_id=2433118.

3. Laura Tuttle, *OTC Trading: Description of Non-ATS OTC Trading in National Market System Stocks* (Division of Economic and Risk Analysis, 2014), https://www.sec.gov/marketstructure/research/otc_trading_march_2014.pdf. Most of the remaining trades involve a broker internally matching the buy and sell orders received from its own retail customers, which is discussed in ch. 12.

4. Sam Mamudi, *Charlie Munger: HFT Is Legalized Front-Running*, BARRON'S (May 3, 2013), http://blogs.barrons.com/stockstowatchtoday/2013/05/03/charlie-munger-hft-is-legalized-front-running/.

5. Linette Lopez, *New York's Attorney General Has Declared War on Cheating High-Frequency Traders*, BUS. INSIDER (Sept. 24, 2013), http://www.businessinsider.com/schneiderman-targets-hft-front-running-2013-9.

6. *See, e.g.*, MICHAEL LEWIS, FLASH BOYS: A WALL STREET REVOLT (2014), at 108, 126, 172. Since the publication of the book in the spring of 2014, a host of other commentators have chimed in with criticism equating electronic front-running with traditional illegal front-running. *See* Gene Marcial, *High-Frequency Trading Mainly Hurts the Traders and Short-Term Investors*, FORBES (Apr. 2, 2014), http://www.forbes.com /sites/genemarcial/2014/04/02/high-frequency-trading-mainly-hurts-the-traders- and-short-term-investors/ (stating "front-running on Wall Street, which is what high-frequency trading is all about and what it really intends to be, is old news," and arguing that only the speed with which HFTs front-run other investors is new); Ellen Brown, *Computerized Front Running: Another Goldman-Dominated Fraud*, HUFFINGTON POST (Apr. 26, 2010, updated May 25, 2011), http://www.huffington- post.com/ellen-brown/computerized-front-runnin_b_548148.html.

7. Amended Complaint, City of Providence, R.I. v. Bats Global Mkts, Inc., No. 14-cv- 2811 (S.D.N.Y. Sept. 2, 2014), at 26. The complaint was later dismissed.

8. Traditional front-running is prohibited under the common law, federal law, and industry self-regulatory standards. *See* Opper v. Hancock Secs. Corp., 250 F. Supp. 668 (S.D.N.Y. 1966), *aff'd*, 367 F.2d 157 (2d Cir. 1966) (holding front-running to be illegal under principles of agency and federal law). The SEC prosecutes such front-running as a violation of § 10(b) of the Securities Exchange Act and Rule 10b-(5). *See, e.g.*, SEC v. Bergin, No. 3:13-cv-01940 (N.D. Tex. May 23, 2013) (charging trader for front-running clients under § 10(b)); *see also* Concept Release on Equity Market Structure, Exchange Act Release No. 34–61358, 97 SEC Docket 2115, at 26 (2010) (discussing illegality of front-running). FINRA Rule 5270 prohibits trading in a security if an individual has "material, non-public market information concerning [a customer's] imminent block transaction in that security," until that block transaction has become public. *See* FINRA Rule 5270.

9. This example fleshes out the story by Michael Lewis of how anticipatory order cancellation could occur with Agilent stock in such a situation. LEWIS, FLASH BOYS, *supra* note 6, at 33–34. Lewis asserts that the HFT could profit at the expense of others by cancelling its quotes on another exchange, but he does not discuss exactly why it would be profitable for the HFT to do so. Nor does he analyze how the quotes initially available might be different if the practice of electronic front-running were eliminated. The discussion that follows fills in these gaps.

10. *See* ch. 3 for a discussion of the different types of private information. We will revisit this discussion later in this chapter with a more nuanced analysis that focuses on the fortunes of each of the four kinds of informed traders: fundamental value information traders, announcement traders, and the two kinds of inside information traders.

11. For reasons of expository simplicity, this statement assumes that the increase in spreads would not decrease the volume of trading. Therefore, it is assumed that the

increase in the absolute number of HFT trades with informed traders that would occur from the elimination of electronic front-running would be the same with the increase in spreads as without it. In fact, an increase in spreads makes trading more costly, suggesting that the volume would be lower with the increase in spreads than without it. As a consequence, as discussed *infra* concerning the ultimate incidence of the practice, its elimination would result in a reduction in the rents paid to the industry's specialized inputs. The simplification here, however, does not alter the basic logic of the analysis concerning the effects on informed and uninformed traders.

12. Regulation NMS precludes exchanges from restricting access to trading on their facilities. *See* Regulation National Market System Rule 610(a), 17 C.F.R. § 242.610(a) (2005) (prohibiting "national securities exchange[s] [from] . . . prevent[ing] or inhibit[ing] any person from obtaining efficient access" to trading against the buy and sell quotes posted on exchanges); Securities and Exchange Act § 6, 15 U.S.C. § 78f (1934) (providing that "the rules of [a registered] exchange [must] provide that any registered broker or dealer . . . may become a member of such exchange").

13. *See, e.g.*, LEWIS, FLASH BOYS, *supra* note 6, at 104; *see also* Providence Amended Complaint, *supra* note 7, at 93–95.

14. Jonathan B. Berk & Richard C. Green, *Mutual Fund Flows and Performance in Rational Markets*, 112 J. POL. ECON. 1269 (2004).

15. *See, e.g.*, LEWIS, FLASH BOYS, *supra* note 6, at 126, 176; *see also* Providence Amended Complaint, *supra* note 7, at 6, 26, 93–95.

16. However, the impact of eliminating any of these practices is uncertain because HFTs desire colocation for a number of reasons. *See* Charles M. Jones, *What Do We Know about High-Frequency Trading* (Columbia Business School Research Paper No. 33–36, 2013), at 10, 26 (discussing that HFTs seek colocation to minimize their latency in learning of quote changes and in altering their quotes and analyzing empirical evidence that the introduction of colocation improves liquidity).

17. The exchange business, however, has become much more competitive than in the past, making the exchanges' longer run ability to collect rents questionable. In the very long run, the revenues of firms in a competitive industry can be expected to just equal their costs, including an ordinary market return on capital. Thus, to the extent that the exchange business has in fact become competitive, eventually any revenues lost from colocation fees would have to be made up through higher charges to all investors who trade on the exchange.

18. Implicit in this analysis is that the improvements in the real economy from more accurate prices in terms of better capital allocation and better utilization of the economy's existing productive capacity are greater than the value of the additional real resources that are brought to the task of gathering and analyzing bits of publicly available information, topics discussed in chapter 2. There is ample empirical

evidence to suggest that accurate price signals do in fact have efficiency-enhancing effects on managerial decisions. *See* THIERRY FOUCAULT, MARCO PAGANO & AILSA RÖELL, MARKET LIQUIDITY: THEORY, EVIDENCE, AND POLICY 361–68 (2013) (collecting relevant empirical studies). Theory also suggests that accurate financial information will often be underproduced due to its status as a public good. *See, e.g.,* Philip Bond, Alex Edmans & Itay Goldstein, *The Real Effects of Financial Markets*, 4 ANN. REV. FIN. ECON. 339 (2012).

19. *See* Form 10-K of Virtu Financial, Inc., https://www.sec.gov/Archives/edgar/data /1592386/000155837017001698/virt-20161231x10k.htm.

20. *Id.* at 42.

21. *Id.* at 10.

22. *Virtu Financial Annual Report*, available at the Virtu Financial website, http:// ir.virtu.com/financials-and-filings/default.aspx.

23. *See* ch. 2.

24. The latter factor has been explored incisively in earlier work. *See, e.g.,* Michael J. Fishman & Kathleen M. Hagerty, *Insider Trading and the Efficiency of Stock Prices*, 23 RAND J. ECON. 106, 110 (1992); Zohar Goshen & Gideon Parchomovsky, *On Insider Trading, Markets, and "Negative" Property Rights in Information*, 87 VA. L. REV. 1229, 1238–43 (2001).

25. Sugato Chakravarty, Pankaj Jain, James Upson & Robert Wood, *Clean Sweep: Informed Trading Through Intermarket Sweep Orders*, 47 J. FIN. & QUANTITATIVE ANAL. 415 (2012).

26. In fact, as will be discussed later, exploitation of inter-venue latencies may owe more to the regulatory "one-second rule" than to technological delays.

27. LEWIS, FLASH BOYS, *supra* note 6, at 172.

28. *See, e.g.,* Nanex, *Latency on Demand?* (Aug. 23, 2010), http://www.nanex.net/Flash-Crash/FlashCrashAnalysis_LOD.html (discussing discrepancies between NYSE quotes in the public quotation system and its private feeds and the potentially manipulative gaming of those feeds by HFTs); Tyler Durden, *'Do It Yourself' Latency Arbitrage: How HFTs Can Manipulate the NBBO at Whim Courtesy of NYSE Empty Quote Gluts*, ZEROHEDGE (Aug. 23, 2010, 9:29 PM), http://www.zerohedge.com /article/do-it-yourself-latency-arbitrage-how-hfts-can-manipulate-nbbo-whim-courtesy-nyse-quote-stuff.

29. City of Providence Amended Complaint, *supra* note 7, at ¶ 6. The complaint was later dismissed, however.

30. In the example, if Lightning did not engage in slow market arbitrage, it is possible that it would be another HFT engaging in slow market arbitrage, not an ordinary trader, who would transact against the $161.13 offer. The ultimate question we are asking, however, is what would happen if no HFT engaged in the practice.

31. *See, e.g.*, Alex Paley, *Navigating the Dark Pool Landscape*, DEUTSCHE BANK 46 (2010), https://autobahn.db.com/microSite/docs/Navigating_Dark_Pool_Landscape .pdf. This point was also picked up in Flash Boys. *See* LEWIS, FLASH BOYS, supra note 6, at 113–18.

32. *See, e.g.*, Kit R. Roane, *How NYSE Plans to Use 'Flash Crash' to Reclaim Its Glory*, CNN MONEY (2010), http://money.cnn.com/2010/05/12/markets/NYSE_flash _crash.fortune/index.htm (reporting attempts by NYSE executives to connect HFTs with the flash crash); Bob Dannhauser, *Debating Michael Lewis' 'Flash Boys': High-Frequency Trading Not All Bad*, SEEKING ALPHA (Apr. 7, 2014, 11:42 AM), http://seekingalpha.com/article/2129253-debating-michael-lewis-flash-boys -high-frequency-trading-not-all-bad.

33. LEWIS, FLASH BOYS, *supra* note 6, at 112.

34. THE RECENT BEHAVIOUR OF FINANCIAL MARKET VOLATILITY 1 (Bank for International Settlements Papers No. 29, 2006), at 1.

35. *See* JAMES J. ANGEL, LAWRENCE E. HARRIS, & CHESTER S. SPATT, EQUITY TRADING IN THE 21ST CENTURY: AN UPDATE 11 12 (2013), http://www.q-group.org/wp -content/uploads/2014/01/Equity-Trading-in-the-21st-Century-An-Update -FINAL1.pdf, at 11–12; *see also* John Y. Campbell, Martin Lettau, Burton G. Malkiel & Yexiao Xu, *Have Individual Stocks Become More Volatile? An Empirical Exploration of Idiosyncratic Risk*, 56 J. FIN. 1 (2001) (finding significant spikes in both firm-specific and market volatility during periods of major economic crisis for the period 1962–1997); Edward G. Fox, Merritt B. Fox & Ronald J. Gilson, *Economic Crises and the Integration of Law and Finance: The Impact of Volatility Spikes*, 116 COLUM. L. REV. 325, 335–36 (2016) (finding the same with respect to firm-specific volatility for the period 1925–2010).

36. Angel et al., *supra* note 35, at 2.

37. *See, e.g.*, Joel Hasbrouck & Gideon Saar, *Low-Latency Trading*, 16 J. FIN. MKTS. 646 (2013) (finding that HFT activity reduces volatility); Jonathan Brogaard, Thibaut Moyaert & Ryan Riordan, *High-Frequency Trading and Market Stability* (Working Paper, May 2014). *But see* Sandrine Jacob Leal, Mauro Napoletano, Andrea Roventini & Giorgio Fagiolo, *Rock Around the Clock: An Agent-Based Model of Low- and High-Frequency Trading* (Working Paper, Jan. 2014).

38. Report of the Staffs of the CFTC and SEC to the Joint Advisory Committee on Emerging Regulatory Issues, FINDINGS REGARDING THE MARKET EVENTS OF MAY 6, 2010, http:// www.sec.gov/news/studies/2010/marketevents-report.pdf (hereinafter the "Flash Crash Report"); Alexandra Twin, *Glitches Send Dow on Wild Ride*, CNN MONEY (May 6, 2010, 7:36 PM), http://money.cnn.com/2010/05/06/markets/markets_newyork/.

39. *See* Tom Lauricella & Peter A. McKay, *Dow Takes a Harrowing 1,010.14-Point Trip*, WALL ST. J., May 7, 2010, at https://www.wsj.com/articles/SB100014240527487043 70704575227754131412596.

40. *Id.*

41. Tom Lauricella & Scott Patterson, *Legacy of the "Flash Crash": Enduring Worries of Repeat*, WALL ST. J., Aug. 6, 2010, http://www.wsj.com/articles/SB100014240 52748704545004575353443450790402. Many of the most outlandish transactions executed during the Flash Crash were later cancelled or "broken" by regulators. *See* Deborah L. Jacobs, *Why We Could Easily Have Another Flash Crash*, FORBES, Aug. 9, 2013, http://www.forbes.com/sites/deborahljacobs/2013/08/09 /why-we-could-easily-have-another-flash-crash/.

42. Lauricella & Patterson, *supra* note 41.

43. *See, e.g.*, Andrew Smith, *Fast Money: The Battle Against the High Frequency Traders*, THE GUARDIAN, June 7, 2014, http://www.theguardian.com/business/2014/jun/07 /inside-murky-world-high-frequency-trading; Michael Ono, *High Frequency Trading May Magnify Market Woes*, ABC NEWS, Aug. 11, 2011, http://abcnews.go.com /Business/high-frequency-trading-accelerating-market-woes/story?id=14280847 (suggesting that "computer-driven high frequency trading is partially responsible for accelerating stock gyrations").

44. Flash Crash Report at 6.

45. This chapter focuses on HFTs as liquidity providers, and there is ample evidence that they play this role. *See, e.g.*, Albert J. Menkveld, *High-Frequency Trading and the New-Market Makers*, 16 J. FIN. MKTS. 712 (2013).

46. *See* chapter 3, Appendix B, for a model in which these effects are so extreme that the market unravels completely and there are no transactions.

47. Flash Crash Report at 2–3.

48. David Easley, Marcos López de Prado & Maureen O'Hara, *The Microstructure of the 'Flash Crash': Flow Toxicity, Liquidity Crashes and the Probability of Informed Trading*, 37 J. PORTFOLIO MGMT. 118, 120–26 (2011) (suggesting that order flow was especially informed and hence toxic for market makers in the period preceding the Flash Crash).

49. Flash Crash Report at 29; *see* Jones, *supra* note .

50. Flash Crash Report at 45–57. Such a market failure is described in chapter 3, Appendix B.

51. It should be noted that a significant portion of retail marketable orders and index -based institutional orders execute off exchanges in venues where the trades can be identified as largely uninformed. *See* SEC Release No. 34-68937, File No. SR-NASDAQ-2012-129 (February 15, 2013), at 17; Rhodi Preece, *Dark Pools, Internalization, and Equity Market Quality* (CFA Institute Codes, Standards, and Position Papers 3, 2012), at 16 ("Internalization is also thought to account for almost 100% of all retail marketable order flow."). In a fully competitive market, the spreads associated with these trades should not include a significant adverse selection component. Thus, they should be unaffected by whether or not electronic

front-running occurs on the exchanges, where, in the absence of the practice, the spreads would be wider to reflect the greater risk that the HFTs are dealing with informed traders. In reality, however, the spreads are barely smaller in these off-exchange executions (i.e., there is only a small amount of "price improvement"). As analyzed in chapter 12, it is an open question as to whether the benefits of the lack of adverse selection are ultimately passed through to retail investors in the form of reduced brokerage commissions. The answer would determine whether, in the absence of electronic front running, the wider spread on exchanges in fact would affect the total cost of trading for the retail customer.

52. *See* Kevin S. Haeberle, *Stock-Market Law and the Accuracy of Public Companies' Stock Prices*, 2015 COLUM. BUS. L. REV. 121, 15154, 16265 (2015) (arguing that off-exchange trading venues, by attracting uninformed trade, lead to less uninformed trade on exchanges, thereby increasing the probability of adverse selection on exchanges and widening spreads).

53. Although nothing close to systematic empirical proof is yet available, van Kervel's work suggests the very significant prevalence of "electronic front-running" or order cancellation in a European venue, whereas Bartlett's and McCrary's work suggests that there is little, if any, evidence of slow market arbitrage. *See* Vincent van Kervel, Liquidity: What You See Is What You Get? (May 2012) (unpublished Ph.D. thesis, Tilburg University), 2–6, http://www.rsm.nl/fileadmin/home/Department_of_Finance__VG5_/LQ5/VanKervel.pdf; Robert P. Bartlett III & Justin McCrary, *How Rigged Are Stock Markets? Evidence from Microsecond Timestamps* (working paper, Aug. 5, 2016).

54. *See* Jones, *supra* note 16, at 42–51.

55. *Id.* at 45.

56. *Id.* at 46.

57. *Id.* at 47.

58. *Id.*

59. *See* Eric Budish, Peter Cramton & John Shim, *The High-Frequency Trading Arms Race: Frequent Batch Auctions as a Market Design Response*, 130 Q.J. ECON. 1547, 1548 (2015).

60. *See* Linette Lopez, *New York Attorney General Endorses a Radical Change to the Way the World Trades Stocks*, BUS. INSIDER (March 18, 2014), http://www.businessinsider.com/schneiderman-endorses-batch-auctions-2014-3.

61. *See* 17 C.F.R. § 242.603(a)(2). Section 11A(c)(1) of the Exchange Act authorizes the SEC to regulate market data.

62. *See* Regulation NMS, 70 Fed. Reg. 37,496, 37,567, & 37,569 (June 29, 2005) (adopting release), http://www.sec.gov/rules/final/34-51808fr.pdf.

63. *See* 17 C.F.R. §§ 242.601, 242.602 (rules requiring exchanges to report last sales [price and size of the most recent trades] and current best bids and offers); NetCoalition v. SEC, 615 F.3d 525, 529 (D.C. Cir. 2010) (discussing core data regime).

64. *See, e.g.,* Concept Release on Equity Market Structure, 75 Fed. Reg. 3594, 3601 (Jan. 21, 2010), http://www.sec.gov/rules/concept/2010/34-61358.pdf at 26 (discussing that the consolidation processing time of the SIP "means that [private] data feeds can reach end-users faster than the consolidated data feeds").

65. *See* In re New York Stock Exchange LLC, and NYSE Euronext, Securities Exchange Act Release No. 67857, 2012 WL 4044880 (2012), http://www.sec.gov/litigation/admin/2012/34-67857.pdf.

66. *See* Nanex, *HFT Front Running, All The Time* (Sept. 30, 2013), http://www.nanex.net/aqck2/4442.html; Nanex, *Direct vs. SIP Data Feed* (Apr. 2014), http://www.nanex.net/aqck2/4599.html.

67. SEC v. Texas Gulf Sulphur, 401 F.2d 833, 854 (2d Cir. 1968); In re Investors Management Co., 44 S.E.C. 633 (1971).

68. SEC Release Nos. 33-7881, 34-43154, IC-24599 (August 10, 2000).

69. Faberge, Inc., 45 S.E.C. 249, 255 (1973); *see also* Selective Disclosure & Insider Trading, SEC Release No. 7787 (Dec. 20, 1999).

70. Selective Disclosure and Insider Trading, SEC Release No. 33-7881, at § II.B (Aug. 15, 2000).

71. Regulation NMS Plan to Address Extraordinary Market Volatility, https://www.sec.gov/news/press/2011/2011-84-plan.pdf; *see also* SEC, Investor Bulletin: New Measures to Address Market Volatility (July 1, 2012), http://www.sec.gov/investor/alerts/circuitbreakersbulletin.htm.

72. *See* NYSE, Designated Market Makers (2014), https://www.nyse.com/publicdocs/nyse/listing/fact_sheet_dmm.pdf.

73. *See, e.g.,* Khaldoun Kashanah, Ionut Florescu & Steve Yang, *On the Impact and Future of HFT* (IRRC Institute White Paper, 2014).

74. *See* Jones, *supra* note 16, at 13–11, 38 ("While some observers suggested greater obligations for market-makers, experience in other rapid downdrafts, including the stock market crash of October 1987, when Nasdaq market-makers and others refused to answer their phones or provide market-making activity, indicates that market-makers will almost always choose to withdraw from the market in the face of such extreme volatility"); *see also* Ian Domowitz, *Take Heed The Lessons From The 1962 Flash Crash*, INFORMATIONWEEK (June 21, 2010), http://www.wallstreetandtech.com/exchanges/take-heed-the-lessons-from-the-1962-flash-crash/a/d-id/1263651?.

75. *See* Angel et al., *supra* note 35, at 33.

## 5. THE ECONOMICS OF INFORMED TRADING

1. *See, e.g.,* LAWRENCE E. HARRIS, TRADING AND EXCHANGES 243 (2002) (explaining the pervasive role of trading in the stock market based on nonpublic information);

Kenneth French & Richard Roll, *Stock Return Variances: The Arrival of New Information and the Reaction of Traders*, 17 J. FIN. 5, 9 (1986).

2. For just a sampling of seminal early work in this area, *see* HENRY MANNE, INSIDER TRADING AND THE STOCK MARKET 131–45 (1966) (arguing that insider trading is efficient because it promotes pricing accuracy and entrepreneurialism); Stephen M. Bainbridge, *Insider Trading Under the Restatement of the Law Governing Lawyers*, 19 J. CORP. L. 1, 21 (1993) (arguing that the prohibition on insider trading is best justified as a property-right protection for information); Victor Brudney, *Insiders, Outsiders, and Informational Advantages Under the Federal Securities Laws*, 93 HARV. L. REV. 322, 343, 347–48 (1979) (analyzing the proper scope of the disclose-or-abstain rule); Dennis W. Carlton & Daniel R. Fischel, *The Regulation of Insider Trading*, 35 STAN. L. REV. 857, 862 (1983) (arguing that permitting insider trading may be an efficient way to compensate corporate managers); Zohar Goshen & Gideon Parchomovsky, *On Insider Trading, Markets, and "Negative" Property Rights in Information*, 87 VA. L. REV. 1229, 1238–43 (2001) (arguing that widespread insider trading would drive market analysts out of business with deleterious consequences for the informational quality of securities prices); Roy A. Schotland, *Unsafe at Any Price: A Reply to Manne, Insider Trading and the Stock Market*, 53 VA. L. REV. 1425 (1967) (arguing that insider trading may be injurious because it deters savers from investing in publicly traded securities).

3. *See* HARRIS, *supra* note 1, at 194 (introducing a general idea of informed trading).

4. In the legal literature, Stanislav Dolgopolov's work comes closest to ours in viewing informed trading as a more general phenomenon for regulators to appreciate, although his focus remains on insider trading. *See* Stanislav Dolgopolov, *Insider Trading, Informed Trading, and Market Making: Liquidity of Securities Markets in the Zero-Sum Game*, 3 WM. & MARY BUS. L. REV. 1 (2012).

5. *See* Markus Baldauf & Joshua Mollner, *High-Frequency Trading and Market Performance* (Working Paper, Oct. 2015), https://ssrn.com/abstract=2674767 (noting this basic microstructure trade-off).

6. 15 U.S.C. § 78j(b).

7. 15 U.S.C. § 78p(b).

8. SEC Regulation FD, 17 C.F.R. § 243.100 (2000) (Reg. FD).

9. *See infra* Sections IV.A and IV.B of chapter 6.

10. *Compare* Chiarella v. United States, 445 U.S. 222, 245, 246–47 (1980) (Blackmun, J., dissenting) (arguing to uphold petitioner's Rule 10b-5 conviction "even if he had obtained the blessing of his employer's principals"), *with* United States v. O'Hagan, 521 U.S. 642, 680, 689–90 (1997) (Thomas, J., dissenting) (arguing to reverse conviction because "in either case—disclosed misuse or authorized use . . . '[o]utsiders' would still be trading based on nonpublic information that the average investor has no hope of obtaining").

11. Press Release, A.G. Schneiderman Secures Agreement by Thomson Reuters to Stop Offering Early Access to Market-Moving Information (July 8, 2013), http://www .ag.ny.gov/press-release/ag-schneiderman-secures-agreement-thomson-reuters-stop-offering-early-access-market.

12. Dirks v. Sec. Exch. Comm'n, 463 U.S. 646, 663 (1983).

13. See Dirks v. Sec. Exch. Comm'n, 463 U.S. 646, 673 (1983) (Blackmun, J., dissenting) ("The fact that the insider himself does not benefit from the breach does not eradicate the shareholder's injury").

14. Salman v. United States, 580 U.S. ___ (2016).

15. A number of commentators have called for a "parity of information" approach to regulating insider trading, whereby all trades in which one party is better informed would be illegal because of the unfairness imposed on the other party. See, e.g., Edward Greene & Olivia Schmid, Duty Free Insider Trading, 2013 COLUM. BUS. L. REV. 369 (2013); Joel Seligman, The Reformulation of Federal Securities Law Concerning Nonpublic Information, 73 GEO. L.J. 1083, 1090 (1985); Louis Loss, The Fiduciary Concept as Applied to Trading by Corporate "Insiders" in the United States, 3 MED. L. REV. 34 (1970); Schotland, supra note 2. Some have also suggested that this is the predominant approach in Europe. See 3 BROMBERG & LOWENFELS ON SECURITIES FRAUD § 6:131 (2d ed. 1997). Although the logic of this approach extends easily to trades based on private fundamental value information, these commentators if pressed would probably not view their comments as applying to trades based on fundamental value information. For a discussion of the actual European approach, see also ch. 6, Section II.

16. This example has the informed trader ultimately making public the information he generated in order to lock in his profit. This is not a necessary step for profiting from informed trading, however. The informed trader instead might wait to sell until the event predicted by the information occurs or the prospect of it occurring becomes obvious to the public based on other news.

17. As noted in ch. 3, pure adverse selection models of liquidity supply do not address how liquidity suppliers reverse the inventory effects of executing on the order imbalance caused by informed trade, nor do they address the price impact when informed traders lock in their profits by reverse transactions once their private information becomes public. These other parts of the story become important, however, when we bring into the analysis the facts that liquidity suppliers need capital in order to trade and that their behavior is influenced by the risks associated with the use of this capital. As discussed in more detail in ch. 3, a fuller story that includes these considerations still ends up with liquidity suppliers needing the width of the spread to include an amount necessary to cover all the gains enjoyed by informed traders.

18. Some of these inputs are ordinary in the sense that they could be equally usefully deployed elsewhere in the economy. Other inputs are specialized: specifically, the efforts of key persons who possess abilities and skills uniquely useful for generating new fundamental value information. All of these inputs will be drawn into this business up to the point where, at the margin, the expected trading profits from successfully generating and trading on fundamental value information equal the costs of paying for the inputs.

19. Like fundamental value informed trading, liquidity supply requires both ordinary and specialized inputs. Lower demand will mean that less of both of these kinds of resources will be pulled into the business. Again, suppliers of the ordinary inputs will earn the same ordinary market return whatever the level of liquidity supply activity, so their wealth positions are unaffected. Persons with abilities and skills uniquely useful for liquidity supply will be paid less in rents and so their wealth positions will be negatively affected.

20. A large portion of retail trading, which is generally uninformed, is internalized and hence may occur on terms at least a little better than the NBB and NBO. The terms of the internalizers are keyed to the NBB and NBO and thus, to the extent that the terms themselves are not changed by the expected amount of informed trading, a wider spread on the exchanges means that internalized trading is more expensive as well.

21. This idea that shares' trading prices are discounted based on anticipated costs of trade has been familiar for decades. For early examples from the insider trading context, *see* Frank H. Easterbrook, *Insider Trading, Secret Agents, Evidentiary Privileges, and the Production of Information*, 1981 SUP. CT. REV. 309, 325; Kenneth E. Scott, *Insider Trading: Rule 10b-5, Disclosure, and Corporate Privacy*, 9 J. LEGAL STUD. 801, 807–9 (1980).

22. Uninformed traders who trade more often than average end up undercompensated by the discount and those who trade less often than average end up overcompensated by the discount, but it is hard to see how this makes a compelling argument that fundamental value informed trading is unfair because of these effects.

23. Nonetheless, there is an active and notable debate as to whether the size of the financial intermediation industry is excessive and whether wages are being competitively set within it. *See generally* Thomas Philippon, *Has the US Finance Industry Become Less Efficient?*, 105 AM. ECON. REV. 1408 (2015) (assessing the efficiency dynamics of financial services over time); Thomas Philippon & Ariell Reshef, *Wages and Human Capital in the U.S. Financial Industry: 1909–2006*, Q. J. ECON. (2012).

24. An argument can be made that when a corporate insider has the opportunity to trade on inside information, she will have a greater incentive to create good new ideas for her firm to pursue, in this sense therefore having an incentive to create news. We do not find this argument very convincing, however. See Section III.B.2 *infra*.

25. For a model that gives an important role to the lead time with which a price change better predicts a subsequent cash flow, *see* Kenneth D. West, *Dividend Innovations and Stock Price Volatility*, 56 ECONOMETRICA 37 (1988).

26. For an elaboration of this concept of informed prices, *see* Merritt B. Fox, Artyom Durnev, Randall Morck & Bernard Yeung, *Law, Share Price Accuracy and Economic Performance: The New Evidence*, 102 MICH. L. REV. 331, 344–48 (2003).

27. *See* Schotland, *supra* note 2, at 1443 (citing studies); Joseph E. Stiglitz, *Tapping the Brakes: Are Less Active Markets Safer and Better for the Economy?* (Paper presented at the Federal Reserve Bank of Atlanta, Apr. 15, 2014), 4, 8.

28. It also reduces the resources going into the business of liquidity supply and price-sensitive fundamental trading and thus to the level of the socially valuable services they perform. There is no obvious reason to believe that these services would not be operating at their socially optimal levels absent the informed trading.

29. The wider spread is paid as well by the other three kinds of informed traders. However, because we conclude that these three other types of trading are socially undesirable, the imposition of this wider spread on these traders is a positive, not a negative, feature of allowing fundamental value informed trading.

30. *See, e.g.*, Kenneth R. French & Richard Roll, *Stock Return Variances: The Arrival of New Information and the Reaction of Traders*, 17 J. FIN. 5, 9 (1986) (private information, as opposed to information from public announcements, plays an important role in informing prices); Joel S. Hasbrouck, *The Summary Informativeness of Stock Trades: An Econometric Analysis*, 4 REV. FIN. STUD. 571 (1991) (showing that in a sample of 177 NYSE equities, and using a vector autoregression (VAR) technique, 41 percent of the variance in spread midpoint changes is explained by transactions).

31. *See* THIERRY FOUCAULT, MARCO PAGANO & AILSA RÖELL, MARKET LIQUIDITY: THEORY, EVIDENCE, AND POLICY 361–68 (2013) (collecting relevant empirical studies); *see, e.g.*, Philip Bond, Alex Edmans & Itay Goldstein, *The Real Effects of Financial Markets*, 4 ANN. REV. FIN. ECON. 339 (2012); Artyom Durnev et al., *Does More Firm Specific Stock Price Variation Mean More or Less Informed Pricing?*, 41 J. ACCT. RES. 797 (2003); Artyom Durnev et al., *Value Enhancing Capital Budgeting and Firm-Specific Stock Return Variation*, 59 J. FIN. 65 (2004); Jeffrey Wurgler, *Financial Markets and the Allocation of Capital*, 58 J. FIN. ECON. 187 (2000). See also chapter 8, n. 5, *infra*.

32. *See generally* Grace Xing Hu, Jun Pan & Jiang Wang, *Early Peek Advantage?* (Working Paper), http://papers.ssrn.com/sol3/papers.cfm?abstract_id=2361311 (studying rapid trading and stock price adjustment in response to the release of market-moving information).

33. *See id.* (documenting prices fully adjusting to information in less than 20 milliseconds).

34. *See* Friese v. Super. Ct., 36 Cal. Rptr. 3d 558, 566 (Cal. Ct. App. 2005) (classifying insider trading as "a manifestation of undue greed among the already well-to-do, worthy of legislative intervention if for no other reason than to send a message of censure on behalf of the American people"). For scholars focused on understanding insider trading through a fairness lens, *see generally* John A. C. Hetherington, *Insider Trading and the Logic of the Law*, 1967 Wis. L. REV. 720; Homer Kripke, *Manne's Insider Trading Thesis and Other Failures of Conservative Economics*, 4 CATO J. 945 (1985); Schotland, *supra* note 2; Seligman, *supra* note 15; Green & Schmid, *supra* note 15; Loss, *supra* note 15.

35. MANNE, *supra* note 2, at 94–95.

36. MANNE, *supra* note 2, at 94; Henry Manne, *In Defense of Insider Trading*, HARV. BUS. REV., Nov.Dec. 1966, at 114. *See also* Carlton & Fischel, *supra* note 2, and accompanying text. Other critics of the prohibition of insider trading have provided a public choice analysis of insider trading regulation as essentially "purchased" by market professionals from regulators. *See* David D. Haddock & Jonathan R. Macey, *Regulation on Demand: A Private Interest Model, with an Application to Insider Trading Regulation*, 30 J.L. & ECON. 311 (1987).

37. *See* HARRIS, TRADING AND EXCHANGES, *supra* note 1, at 82.

38. See note 17 *supra* and the discussion in ch. 3 as to why, however liquidity suppliers reverse the inventory effects of executing on the order imbalance caused by informed trade, they will on average lose an amount equivalent to the gains enjoyed by informed traders and, to stay in business, the spread must reflect this prospect.

39. *Compare* LUCIAN BEBCHUK & JESSE FRIED, PAY WITHOUT PERFORMANCE: THE UNFULFILLED PROMISE OF EXECUTIVE COMPENSATION (2004) (arguing that executive compensation is excessive because managers control boards and compensation contracts are not negotiated at arm's length) *with* Frank H. Easterbrook, *Managers' Discretion and Investors' Welfare: Theories and Evidence*, 9 DEL. J. CORP. L. 540 (1984) (arguing that executive contracting reflects the result of an efficient contracting process). Even assuming, as we do, that, in the long run, the market's pressures set managerial wages at competitive levels, the adjustment could be quite slow.

40. Utpal Bhattacharya & Hazem Daouk, *The World Price of Insider Trading*, 57 J. FIN. 75, 104 (2002) (the 38 countries included a majority of developed countries).

41. *Id.* at 78.

42. In the example, Y purchased at the offer for an average price of $61.55, which implies that the average sale at the bid by uninformed sellers would have been at $61.45.

43. In contrast, the price-sensitive fundamental trader has a reasonable claim that but for the insider's purchase, he would not have sold and would instead be holding

shares that could be sold for about $18.50 more, because his sale was prompted by the rise in EDF's share price resulting from Y's purchases. However, as noted earlier, in a world where a certain level of issuer insider trading occurs, the bids that draw such investors in when liquidity suppliers rebalance their portfolios to cover their short positions include a premium to cover for this possibility.

44. *See* Michael J. Fishman & Kathleen M. Hagerty, *Insider Trading and the Efficiency of Stock Prices*, 23 RAND J. ECON. 106, 110 (1992); Joseph E. Stiglitz, *Tapping the Brakes: Are Less Active Market Safer and Better for the Economy?* (Paper presented at the Federal Reserve Bank of Atlanta, Apr. 15, 2014), 4, 8. This is the fundamental argument of the seminal piece, Zohar Goshen & Gideon Parchomovsky, *On Insider Trading, Markets, and "Negative" Property Rights in Information*, 87 VA. L. REV. 1229, 1238–43 (2001).

45. For a political economy explanation of SEC insider trading enforcement prompted by fundamental value informed traders and liquidity suppliers seeking to protect profits, *see* Haddock & Macey, *supra* note 36.

46. Laura Nyantung Beny, *Insider Trading Laws and Stock Markets Around the World: An Empirical Contribution to the Theoretical Law and Economics Debate*, 32 J. CORP. L. 237, 275–77 (2007) (finding that, cross-nationally, more rigorous insider trading laws are associated with more accurate stock prices and greater liquidity).

47. *See, e.g.*, Easterbrook, *supra* note 21, at 332.

48. For empirical evidence that various indirect methods of insider trading can negatively affect the quality of issuer disclosure, *see* Jesse M. Fried, *Insider Trading Via the Corporation*, 162 U. PA. L. REV. 801, 831 (2014) (disclosures in advance of issuer share repurchases where managers own issuer stock); Robert M. Daines, Grant R. McQueen & Robert J. Schonlau, *Right on Schedule: CEO Option Grants and Opportunism* (January 27, 2016), http://papers.ssrn.com/sol3/papers.cfm?abstract_id=2363148 (disclosures in advance of upcoming scheduled option grants based on the current share price).

49. *See* Ronald Gilson & Reinier Kraakman, *The Mechanisms of Market Efficiency*, 70 VA. L. REV. 549, 568–69 (1984); Eugene F. Fama, *Random Walks in Stock Market Prices*, 21 FIN. ANALYSTS J. (Sept.-Oct. 1965), at 55 (describing how information is incorporated into price). Capital constraints limit the amount of trading that issuer insider informed traders can trade, and noise hampers the ability of others trying to decode what the insiders know based on observed price changes. Sanford J. Grossman & Joseph E. Stiglitz, *On the Impossibility of Informationally Efficient Markets*, 70 AM. ECON. REV. 393 (1980).

50. Carlton & Fischel, *supra* note 2, at 879 (insider trading may accelerate the speed of disclosure).

51. Of course, we cannot rule out that there may be instances in which insider trading's improvement in price accuracy can make a meaningful contribution to the efficiency

of the real economy, particularly when a firm is contemplating a real investment project that can only be funded by a public offering of equity. An example is illustrated in Appendix A of this chapter. As elaborated there, however, we still think that on average the practice is socially disadvantageous and for this reason should be illegal.

52. MANNE, *supra* note 2, at 110–20.

53. This proposition assumes that the manager waits until she sees the ultimate results of the decision but before the results are publicly known. The ability to inside-trade provides the manager with an option that is exercised only if the results are positive. All else equal, the riskier an option is, the more valuable it is. *See* Lucian Arye Bebchuk & Chaim Fershtman, *Insider Trading and the Managerial Choice Among Risky Projects*, 29 J. FIN. & QUANTITATIVE ANALYSIS 1, 12–13 (1994) (insider trading leads to riskier projects). That insider trading could lead to riskier choice of projects is a familiar insight of the insider trading literature. *See, e.g.,* Thomas Ulen, *The Coasian Firm in Law and Economics*, 18 J. CORP. L. 301, 324–25 (1993); Joel Seligman, *The Reformulation of Federal Securities Law Concerning Nonpublic Information*, 73 GEO. L.J. 1083 (1985).

54. *See, e.g.*, Easterbrook, *supra* note 21, at 332.

55. *Cf.* Bruce Chapman, *Corporate Liability and the Problem of Overcompliance*, 69 S. CAL. L. REV. 1679 (1996) (firms are generally superior risk-bearers relative to managers).

56. *See* Rafael Gely & Leonard Bierman, *The Law and Economics of Employee Information Exchange in the Knowledge Economy*, 12 GEO. MASON L. REV. 651, 674 (2004) ("employees have a fairly limited ability to diversify their human capital portfolio" relative to investors' ability to diversify their wealth).

57. *See* Robert J. Haft, *The Effect of Insider Trading Rules on the Internal Efficiency of the Large Corporation*, 80 MICH. L. REV. 1051 (1982) (exploring the potentially adverse effects of permitting insider trading on decision making within large businesses).

58. The negative effects of insider trading on liquidity, and to a lesser extent price accuracy, have already been noted by a vast and rich legal literature, often arguing in favor of existing legal bans. For just a sampling of classic papers, *see* Bainbridge, *supra* note 2, at 11–12; Mark Loewenstein & William K. S. Wang, *The Corporation as Insider Trader*, 30 DEL. J. CORP. L. 45, 74–77 (2005); William K. S. Wang, *Stock Market Insider Trading: Victims, Violators, and Remedies—Including an Analogy to Fraud in the Sale of a Used Car with a Generic Defect*, 45 VILL. L. REV. 27, 38 (2000); H. Nejat Seyhun, *Insiders' Profits, Costs of Trading, and Market Efficiency*, 16 J. FIN. ECON. 189, 190–92 (1986); Jonathan R. Macey & Maureen O'Hara, *From Markets to Venues: Securities Regulation in an Evolving World*, 58 STAN. L. REV. 563, 589 (2005). Others have come to more ambivalent conclusions based on the finance literature. *See* Donald C. Langevoort, *Rereading "Cady, Roberts": The Ideology and Practice of Insider Trading Regulation*, 99 COLUM. L. REV. 1319, 1324 (1999).

59. *See* Carlton & Fischel, *supra* note 2, at 866–68.

60. Laura Nyantung Beny & Anita Anand, *Private Regulation of Insider Trading in the Shadow of Lax Public Enforcement: Evidence from Canadian Firms*, 3 HARV. BUS. L. REV. 215 (2013) (showing that many firms adopt precisely such policies).

61. *See* David D. Haddock & Jonathan R. Macey, *A Coasian Model of Insider Trading*, 80 Nw. U.L. REV. 1449, 1467–68 (1987).

62. *See* JONATHAN R. MACEY, INSIDER TRADING: ECONOMICS, POLITICS, AND POLICY 6 (1991) (monitoring insiders' trading activities likely to display considerable economies of scale); *see also* Jonathan R. Macey, *From Fairness to Contract: The New Direction of the Rules Against Insider Trading*, 13 HOFSTRA L. REV. 9, 59 (1984) (contract law remedies available to firms damaged by insider trading are insufficient to achieve an optimal level of enforcement).

63. *See generally* H. Nejat Seyhun, *The Effectiveness of the Insider-Trading Sanctions*, 35 J.L. & ECON. 149, 157, 172–75 (1992).

64. An unapproved trade by an institution's insider does improve price accuracy in the sense that the information generated by the institution is reflected sooner in price. Like issuer insider trading, however, the non-issuer insider is most likely to trade only shortly before the outside institution itself would have transacted or made an announcement. Again, such a brief improvement in price accuracy will not enhance the efficiency of the real economy in any meaningful way.

65. These terms include, unless the institution affirmatively reverses them, obligations that arise because of the status of the recipient (e.g., the obligation of an agent of the institution, such as its lawyer or investment bank, not to use for its own purposes confidential information received from the institution). *See* RESTATEMENT (THIRD) OF TORTS § 8.05 (AM. L. INST. 2009).

66. The unapproved trade does improve price accuracy in the sense of getting the information that is generated by the institution reflected sooner in price. Like trading by an issuer insider, however, the nonissuer insider is most likely to trade only shortly before the outside institution itself would have transacted itself or made an announcement. Again, such a brief improvement in price accuracy will not enhance the efficiency of the real economy in any meaningful way.


# 6. THE REGULATION OF INFORMED TRADING

1. 15 U.S.C. § 78j(b) (2012); 17 C.F.R. § 240.10b-5 (2015).

2. 15 U.S.C. § 78j(b) (2012).

3. 17 C.F.R. § 240.10b-5 (2015).

4. 40 S.E.C. 907 (1961).

5. *Id.* at 908.

6. *Id.* at 909.

7. *Id.* at 912.

8. *Id.*

9. 401 F.2d 833 (2d Cir. 1968).

10. *Id.* at 848 (emphasis added). The statement was dicta because the actual defendants were officers or high-level employees of the company.

11. 445 U.S. 222, 235 (1980). For a fascinating discussion of the history around *Texas Gulf Sulphur, see* Donald C. Langevoort, *From* Texas Gulf Sulphur *to* Chiarella: *A Tale of Two Duties*, 71 SMU L. Rev. __ (2018).

12. *Id.* at 230. Powell's discussion of the reach of Rule 10b-5 assumed that the non-disclosed information was material, thus suggesting that a trade on the basis of immaterial information would be legal even by an insider. Insiders are always in possession of immaterial nonpublic information. If Congress had wished to pro-hibit all informed trading by corporate insiders, whether or not material, there would have been a simple way of doing so: ban all purchases or sales of an issuer's stock by corporate insiders for as long as the insiders maintain that status. This path was not taken.

13. *Id.* at 232–33.

14. *Id.* at 240.

15. *Id.* at 243–44.

16. *Id.* at 237–38.

17. *Id.* at 251.

18. United States v. O'Hagan, 521 U.S. 642 (1997).

19. 521 U.S. 650.

20. *Id.* at 652 (emphasis added). Justice Ginsburg, in an effort to better connect this breach with the language of § 10(b) and its reference to a "deceptive device," argued that "misappropriators . . . deal in deception" because "[a] fiduciary who '[pretends] loy-alty to the principal while secretly converting the principal's information for personal gain' . . . 'dupes' or defrauds the principal." *Id.* at 653–54.

21. *Chiarella*, 445 U.S. at 228.

22. 445 U.S. at 230, n.12.

23. 463 U.S. 646, 660 (1983) (citation omitted).

24. *Id.* at 662. For an extensive discussion of the genesis of the personal benefit test, *see* Adam C. Pritchard, Dirks *and the Genesis of Personal Benefit*, 68 SMU L. REV. 857 (2015).

25. *Dirks*, 463 U.S. at 664.

26. *Id.* at 658–59. An online Symposium at the Stanford Law Review included several notable discussions of the personal benefit test, *see* Jill E. Fisch, *Family Ties: Salman*

*and the Scope of Insider Trading*, 69 Stan. L. Rev. Online 46, 48-50 (2016); Donald C. Langevoort, *Informational Cronyism*, 69 Stan. L. Rev. Online 37, 38-40 (2016); Jonathan R. Macey, *The Genius of the Personal Benefit Test*, 69 Stan. L. Rev. Online 64, 69 (2016); Donna M. Nagy, Salman v. United States: *Insider Trading's Tipping Point?*, 69 Stan. L. Rev. Online 28, 29-31 (2016); A.C. Pritchard, *The SEC, Administrative Usurpation, and Insider Trading*, 69 Stan. L. Rev. Online 55, 55 (2016). *See also* Michael D. Guttentag, *Selective Disclosure and Insider Trading*, 69 Fla. L. Rev. 519, 524 (2017); John P. Anderson, *Poetic Expansions of Insider Trading Liability*, 43 J. Corp. L. 367 (2018). Guttentag argues that the kind of information-sharing that motivated Powell to create the personal benefit test has been subsequently prohibited by Reg. FD, undercutting the rationale for the test. Our emphasis on the value of the selective disclosure of *immaterial* information by issuer representatives—which is not prohibited by Reg. FD—leads us to a different view.

27. *Dirks*, 463 U.S. at 662.

28. *See, e.g.*, SEC v. Musella, 678 F. Supp. 1060, 1062–64 (S.D.N.Y. 1988) (defendants "should have known that fiduciary duties were being breached with respect to confidential, non-public information"); *In re* Motel 6 Sec. Litig., 161 F. Supp. 2d 227, 242 (S.D.N.Y. 2001) ("a defendant's subjective belief that information received 'was obtained in breach of a fiduciary duty . . . may . . . be shown by circumstantial evidence'").

29. In each of these two cases, if someone who himself is prohibited from trading instead, or in addition, tips someone else, he would violate Rule 10b-5 as a tipper.

30. Salman v. United States, 580 U.S. __ (2016).

31. 773 F.3d 438 (2d Cir. 2014).

32. *Cert. granted*, No. 15-628 (U.S. Jan. 19, 2016) (granting petition for a writ of certiorari as to Question 1 presented by Petition for Writ of Certiorari in Salman v. United States, http://www.scotusblog.com/wp-content/uploads/2016/01/Salman -v-US-petition-for-writ-of-certiorari.pdf).

33. Slip op. at 10. The language from *Newman* quoted in the grant of certiorari would appear to eliminate the gift branch of the test. A gift by definition cannot involve an exchange, but the quoted language seems to require one. Yet, it is not clear that eliminating the gift branch of the test was the intention of the Second Circuit. The very next sentence after the quoted language says "in other words . . . this requires 'a relationship between the insider and the recipient that suggests a quid pro quo from the latter, *or* an intention to benefit the [latter].'" *Newman*, 773 F.3d at 452 (quoting United States v. Jau, 734 F.3d 147, 153 (2d Cir. 2013) (emphasis added)). Moreover, a holding eliminating the gift branch of the benefit rule was not necessary to support the Second Circuit's decision to reverse the conviction of the defendants in the case, because the Second Circuit also concluded that "no reasonable jury could have

found that [the defendants] knew, or deliberately avoided knowing, that the information originated with corporate insiders." 773 F.3d at 455.

34. Slip op. at 10 ("*Dirks* specifies that when a tipper gives inside information to 'a trading relative or friend,' the jury can infer that the tipper meant to provide the equivalent of a cash gift"). Although there was additional evidence that in fact the tipper intended to help his direct-tippee brother, it does not appear there was evidence that Salman knew anything other than that the two brothers had a close relationship (and that the tipper, in violation of the employer's confidentiality requirement, was the source of the information on which Salman was trading).

35. *See, e.g.*, SEC v. Yun, 327 F.3d 1263, 1274–75 (11th Cir. 2003); SEC v. Gansman, 657 F.3d 85, 92 (2d Cir. 2011); 18 INSIDER TRADING REGULATION, ENFORCEMENT AND PREVENTION § 6:13 (Donald C. Langevoort 2015).

36. *See, e.g.*, United States v. Falcone, 257 F.3d 226, 234 (2d Cir. 2001) ("the government was simply required to prove a breach by Salvage, the tipper, of a duty owed to the owner of the misappropriated information, and defendant's knowledge that the tipper had breached the duty").

37. *See* SEC v. Sargent, 229 F.3d 68, 76–77 (1st Cir. 2000) (reviewing case law but declining to decide the issue). The issue arose, but was not decided by the Supreme Court, in *Salman*. The case appears to involve only information coming from investment banks the clients of which were not the issuers of the shares that were traded. Thus, the alleged Rule 10b-5 violation would have to be grounded on the misappropriation theory (although the government maintained it was grounded on the classical theory as well). *Salman*, slip op. at 8, n.2. The Court said "we do not need to resolve the question [of whether the personal benefit test applies to the misappropriation theory]." The Court also said that the parties "do not dispute" that it does and so "we will proceed on the assumption that it does." *Id.*

38. SEC v. Musella, 748 F. Supp. 1028, 1038 n.4 (S.D.N.Y. 1989), *aff'd*, 898 F.2d 138 (2d Cir. 1990) ("The misappropriation theory of liability does not require a showing of a benefit to the tipper"). Also, in United States v. Chestman, 903 F.2d 75 (2d Cir. 1990), the Second Circuit focused on whether a marital relationship by itself created a duty of confidentiality which is breached when the recipient of the information uses it to tip, and made no mention that the recipient also needed a personal benefit in return for the tip. In a later opinion, it affirmatively suggested that *Chestman* supported the notion that the personal benefit was not required for a misappropriation case. United States v. Libera, 989 F.2d 596, 600 (2d Cir. 1993). More recently, however, in United States v Newman, 773 F.3d 438 (2d Cir. 2014), the court stated that "[t]he elements of tipping liability are the same, regardless of whether the tipper's duty arises under the 'classical' or the 'misappropriation'

theory." *Id.* at 446. There is no real analysis of the issue, however, and the statement is dicta because the case is clearly based on the classical theory: it involves information coming from within the issuer whose shares were being traded and there was no allegation that the tippee owed any duty of confidentiality to the tipper.

39.  United States v. Parigian, 824 F.3d 5, 15 (1st Cir. 2016).

40.  SEC v. Yun, 327 F.3d 1263, 1274–75 (11th Cir. 2003). The court expressed the concern that any insider tipping case could be reframed as a misappropriation case, instead of a *Dirks*-type classical insider trading case, thereby rendering the *Dirks* personal benefit requirement a dead letter. *Id.* at 1279. Another way in which the courts could deal with this problem, however, would be to rule that the misappropriation theory, which was developed to deal with a different situation not involving the breach of duties to the persons on the other side of a trade, is simply not applicable to the issuer insider tipper.

41.  For a detailed discussion of these points and of the history of the case law to date, *see* Merritt B. Fox & George Tepe, *Personal Benefit Has No Place in Misappropriation Tipping Cases*, 71 SMU L. Rev 767 (2018).

42.  82 F.3d 1194 (1st Cir. 1996).

43.  82 F.3d at 1203. *Cf.* Freeman v. Decio, 584 F.2d 186, 194 (7th Cir. 1978) ("If the corporation were to attempt to exploit such non-public information [usually involved in insider trading] by dealing in its own securities, it would open itself up to potential liability under federal and state securities laws, just as do the insiders when they engage in insider trading"); Arlia *ex rel.* Massey Energy Co. v. Blankenship, 234 F. Supp. 2d 606, 610 (S.D. W. Va. 2002) ("insider trading does not rob the corporation of an opportunity, because securities laws prohibited the company itself from trading on its own nonpublic information").

44.  *See, e.g.*, Hyman v. N.Y. Stock Exch., 46 A.D.3d 335, 337, 848 N.Y.S.2d 51, 53 (2007) ("it is well settled that a corporation does not owe fiduciary duties to its members or shareholders"); Powers v. Ryan, No. CIV. A.00-10295-00, 2001 WL 92230, at *3 (D. Mass. Jan. 9, 2001) ("The case law is less settled on whether a corporation owes a fiduciary duty to a shareholder"); *see also* W. WANG & M. STEINBERG, INSIDER TRADING § 5.2.3 (3d ed. 2010) (§ 5.2.3(c)(1) discusses this issue in depth). In terms of *ex post* fairness, it should be noted that unlike trades by insiders, the resulting losses suffered by the shareholders (or shareholders to be) transacting with the corporation are exactly counterbalanced by the gains enjoyed by the shareholders who did not transact. *See also* Donald C. Langevoort & Gaurang Mitu Gulati, *The Muddled Duty to Disclose Under Rule 10b-5*, 57 VAND. L. REV. 1639, 1644–64 (2004) (discussing the distinctive features of issuer insider trading and *Shaw*).

45.  *Chiarella*, 445 U.S. at 240 (Burger, J., dissenting) (citation omitted).

46. In contrast, we also concluded that trades based on one or more bits of nonpublic immaterial information from within an issuer were not socially undesirable, and existing interpretations of Rule 10b-5 in fact do not find them illegal.

47. *Chiarella*, 445 U.S. at 230, n.12.

48. Dirks v. SEC, 463 U.S. 646, 663 (1983) (directing courts to look to "whether the insider receives a direct or indirect personal benefit from the disclosure, such as a pecuniary gain or a reputational benefit that will translate into future earnings").

49. The same reasoning is also behind our conclusion that trades by insiders themselves based on nonpublic immaterial information are on average socially desirable.

50. An authorized selective disclosure of material information raises very different issues. As noted earlier, the prevailing view of the lower courts is that trading by an issuer when in possession of such information would violate Rule 10b-5. By logical extension, it would presumably also be the view of these courts that the issuer would violate Rule 10b-5 if its agent made an authorized tip of such information, as would a trade by its direct tippee or any indirect tippees if the trader were aware that the tip was authorized.

51. Moreover, the issuer has an interest in preventing such accidents because the resulting effect on liquidity will lower its share price. Admittedly, there is the possibility that the firm, while not formally authorizing the disclosure, would wink at its agent trading the occasional material tip in return for either continued analyst coverage where there otherwise would not be any, or for more favorable coverage. Whether tips in return for analyst coverage are socially undesirable requires its own complex analysis, as does calculating the likelihood of tips in return for favorable coverage, a topic we consider later in this chapter in the discussion concerning Regulation FD.

52. Under *O'Hagan*, the only exception would be in the surreal situation in which the insider, just in advance of breaching her duty of confidentiality to her employer, informs the employer of her intention to do so. 521 U.S. at 653–54. This is because the Court requires deceit for a trade to violate Rule 10b-5, but includes, within the reach of what it understands as deceit, the situation in which an insider breaches her duty of confidentiality without affirmatively telling her employer that she is doing so.

53. 521 U.S. at 655, 657 (a misappropriator's trades harm members of the investing public).

54. Justice Thomas, in dissent, points to this incoherence to conclude that such trading should not violate Rule 10b-5 whether or not the trader has permission. O'Hagan, 521 U.S. 680, 689–90 (Thomas, J., dissenting) (whether a trade is based on "disclosed misuse or authorized use [of information]—the hypothesized 'inhibiting impact on market participation,' would be identical to that from behavior violating the misappropriation theory") (citation omitted).

55. We recognize that respected commentators have taken a different view. *See, e.g.,* 18 D. LANGEVOORT, INSIDER TRADING: REGULATION, ENFORCEMENT AND PREVENTION § 6.13, at 6-43-44 (2009); *see also* WANG & STEINBERG, *supra* note 44, at § 5.4.4 (collecting sources). Langevoort suggests that "a desire to assure a relatively free flow of information in the marketplace . . . applies just as well to situations where information comes from a source other than the issuer," but we are inclined to see engagement between firm representatives and the analyst community (and perhaps other market participants, like major shareholders) as having a distinctly greater role in the equity market than engagement between non-issuer representatives and other participants. For a more extensive analysis concluding that the personal benefit test should not be inserted in misappropriation cases, *see* Fox & Tepe, *supra* note 41.

56. There should also be evidence that the tippee knows, or has good reason to believe, that the information came from an insider source.

57. *See* ch. 5, Section IV.A.1.b.

58. Slip op. at 10.

59. If the indirect tippee cannot reliably determine that the information is reliable and from an insider source, a Rule 10b-5 violation is unlikely in any event. Materiality is a necessary element for a Rule 10b-5 insider trading violation, and the materiality of a rumor depends in part on "it[s] reliability in light of its nature and source and the circumstances under which it was received." Investors Management Co., 44 S.E.C. 633, 670 (1971).

60. Ronald J. Colombo also advances a presumption of personal benefit. While there is much to be said for his proposal, a major difference between his approach and ours is that his presumption is only rebuttable by a "showing of good-faith, whistle-blowing conduct." *See* Ronald Colombo, *Tipping the Scales Against Insider Trading: Adopting a Presumption of Personal Benefit to Clarify* Dirks, 45 Hofstra L. Rev. 117, 118 (2016). Because we believe Powell's policy concern for analyst communications is a worthy one, we view our approach as an improvement on both policy and doctrinal grounds. Both Colombo and Pritchard have also noted that if a personal benefit is read as generously as possible—as some prosecutors have urged—it almost amounts to a presumption of personal benefit. Unrelatedly, note the distinction between the third and fourth reasons. Neither involves the insider tipper enjoying a personal benefit. In the fourth, however, the selective disclosure of confidential material information has been authorized by the issuer. Disclosures for the third reason typically occur within the context of analyst interviews. So, in contrast to disclosures for the fourth reason, the selective disclosure of the particular information at issue was not authorized even though the conversation within which the disclosure occurred was. The non-personal-benefit reason that the insider tipper disclosed information she is supposed to keep confidential would most often be that

she mistakenly believes either that the information is immaterial or that it is already public. The *Dirks* case itself provides a very unusual example of an unauthorized tip where there is no personal benefit: to publicly reveal a fraud within the corporation. If this, or some other unusual but meritorious motivation, were the reason, the source should be able to provide evidence to this effect and thus, appropriately, would not be found to violate Rule 10b-5.

61. In trades motivated by one of the first two reasons, the facts, if known, would establish the personal benefit required by *Dirks* and so there would be a Rule 10b-5 violation. In the trade motivated by the fourth reason, there would be no personal benefit, but the tipper would nevertheless be participating in the issuer's Rule 10b-5 violation.

62. When the analyst herself does not trade, but makes a private recommendation based on a professional relationship with the actual trader, it is socially undesirable to punish the recipient's trade, because doing so would chill analyst interviews. This relationship means, however, that the analyst would likely provide the actual trader with the evidence needed under the alternative approach to protect her from punishment.

63. Despite the policy desirability of punishing the indirect tippee's trade, if he can provide evidence that the initial disclosure was motivated by the third reason, he would not be found under the proposed alternative approach to have violated Rule 10b-5. This is because it would then be possible for the indirect tippee to establish that the insider source did not commit a Rule 10b-5 type breach. Thus, there would be no breach in which the indirect tippee could be a participant after the fact.

64. 445 U.S. at 230, n.12 (citations omitted).

65. *See, e.g.*, Francis v. Franklin, 105 S. Ct. 1965 (1985) (reversing conviction based on jury instruction imposing presumption); Sandstrom v. Montana, 442 U.S. 510 (1979). Still, the combination of civil remedies available to the government and private damages suits is sufficiently threatening to create a significant deterrent. *See* § 21(d)(2) of the Exchange Act, 15 U.S.C. § 78u(d)(2) (authorizing various forms of SEC penalties and remedies). Pritchard, *supra* note 25, at 61–62, highlights a variety of related concerns about the aggressive enforcement of insider trading law by the SEC and DOJ based on a vague, catch-all statutory provision.

66. An even more ambitious revision would be to make the alternative approach applicable only to the insider source and his initial outside recipient and to deny the affirmative defense to any indirect tippee. This would bring the reach of Rule 10b-5's prohibitions closer to the ideal set out in ch. 5, but would begin to be in tension with the doctrinal roots found in *Chiarella*.

67. The Martin Act prohibits "any fraud, concealment, suppression [or] false pretense" in connection with the purchase or sale of a security. It has been interpreted as banning "all deceitful practices contrary to the plain rules of common honesty"

including "all acts . . . which do by their tendency . . . deceive or mislead the public." People v. Federated Radio, 244 N.Y. 33, 38–39 (1926). For an insightful and broadly parallel analysis of this issue, see Kevin S. Haeberle & M. Todd Henderson, *Informal-Dissemination Law: The Regulation of How Market-Moving Information is Revealed*, 101 CORNELL L. REV, 1373 (2016).

68. Thomson Reuters in turn had purchased distribution rights to these results from the developers of the survey. *See generally* Grace Xing Hu, Jun Pan & Jiang Wang, *Early Peek Advantage?* (Working Paper, Oct. 8, 2016), http://papers.ssrn.com/sol3 /papers.cfm?abstract_id=2361311.

69. Press Release, A.G. Schneiderman Secures Agreement by Thomson Reuters to Stop Offering Early Access to Market-Moving Information (July 8, 2013), http://www.ag.ny .gov/press-release/ag-schneiderman-secures-agreement-thomson-reuters-stop -offering-early-access-market.

70. *See, e.g.*, Press Release, A.G. Schneiderman Announces Agreement with BlackRock to End Its Analyst Survey Program Worldwide (Jan. 9, 2014), http://www.ag.ny.gov /press-release/ag-schneiderman-announces-agreement-blackrock-end-its-analyst -survey-program-worldwide (analyst survey was considered the world's largest).

71. Broad as the Martin Act's actual language and court interpretations of this language are, it is hard to argue that a non-issuer institution violates the Act simply by staying silent at the time that it provides information to select traders and then, after these traders have had a chance to trade, announcing the information publicly. Still, one cannot rule out the possibility that the Attorney General could have persuaded a court to find a violation if he had been able to show that the investing public clearly assumed that no trader was receiving the information in advance of its public announcement. This possibility was not tested, however. The Attorney General was ultimately able to obtain the agreement of Thompson Reuters and Bloomberg not to engage in the practice in the future simply by issuing them a subpoena—a procedure that did not require him to provide a coherent explanation, subject to court review, of how the available evidence suggested the real possibility of a violation. This is because the Martin Act gives the Attorney General the power to issue such a subpoena on his or her own initiative. N.Y. Gen. Bus. Law art. 23-A, § 352. Thus, to get the subpoena, the AG is not required to get a court order by showing probable cause or to convene a court-supervised grand jury, unlike in an ordinary criminal proceeding. Nor is the AG required to file a complaint that is subject to court review pursuant to a defendant's motion to dismiss, unlike in a civil action.

72. *See* Council Directive 2003/6, 2003 O.J. (L 96) 16 (EC)7 [hereinafter Market Abuse Directive].

73. Insider Trading Prohibition Act (proposed), H.R. 1625, 114th Congress, https:// www.congress.gov/bill/114th-congress/house-bill/1625 [hereinafter H.R. 1625].

74. Market Abuse Directive art. 2(1).

75. Market Abuse Directive art. 1(1).
76. Market Abuse Directive § 31. For expository convenience, the text and notes from hereon are written as though the Directive has direct effect on persons engaging in, or associated with, informed trading. In fact, an EU directive simply directs member states to adopt legislation that has these effects.
77. Market Abuse Directive art. 1(1).
78. Market Abuse Directive art. 2(1).
79. The definition of *inside information* includes only information "likely to have a significant effect on [price]." *Id.*
80. Market Abuse Directive art. 3(1)(a).
81. The analyst would be prohibited from trading by the Directive's art. 2(1)(c) and from advising others to do so by its art. 3(b).
82. Market Abuse Directive art. 4.
83. Such a trade would very likely be a Rule 10b-5 violation in circuits that do not impose the personal benefit rule in cases where the information is not from within the issuer—the position that we believe is doctrinally correct.
84. This would not include the planned purchase or sale itself, which would be prompted by the analysis, not by the information that it was planned.
85. *See* John C. Coffee, Jr., *How to Get Away with Insider Trading*, N.Y. Times, May 23, 2016, http://www.nytimes.com/2016/05/23/opinion/how-to-get-away-with-insider-trading.html?_r=0.
86. Insider Trading Prohibition Act (proposed), H.R. 1625, 114th Congress, https://www.congress.gov/bill/114th-congress/house-bill/1625 [hereinafter H.R. 1625].
87. H.R. 1625, § 16A(a).
88. H.R. 1625, § 16A(b)(2).
89. H.R. 1625, § 16A(c)(1)(C).
90. H.R. 1625, § 16A(c)(2).
91. H.R. 1625, § 16A(a).
92. H.R. 1625, § 16A(c)(2).
93. H.R. 1625, § 16A(c)(C).
94. H.R. 1625, § 16A(b).
95. *See, e.g.*, Securities Exchange Act of 1934, 15 U.S.C. § 12(a) (prohibiting the trading of a security on a national securities exchange that is not registered on such an exchange pursuant to the provisions of § 12); 15 U.S.C. § 12(g) (requiring issuers of stocks with more than specific numbers of holders of record and amount of assets to register pursuant to § 12); 15 U.S.C. § 13 (requiring any security registered on an exchange to provide mandated periodic disclosure); 15 U.S.C. § 15(d) (requiring registration in connection with a public offering).
96. Eugene F. Fama, *Efficient Capital Markets: A Review of Theory and Empirical Work*, 25 J. Fin. 383 (1970).

97. This result could be effected not only by government regulation, but instead by stock exchange rules. Currently the New York Stock Exchange provides that when a disclosure by a NYSE-listed issuer is to be made during trading hours, the NYSE should be notified and it will consider whether trading should be temporarily halted. NYSE, *NYSE Listed Company Manual* § 202.06(B), http://nysemanual.nyse.com /LCM/Sections/. NASDAQ has a similar rule for NASDAQ listed firms. NASDAQ Rule IM-5250-1.

98. Though important, the details of this discussion are beyond the scope of this chapter. *See* Merritt B. Fox, Finance and Industrial Performance: Theory, Practice and Policy, 34–43 (1988); John C. Coffee, Jr., *Market Failure and the Economic Case for a Mandatory Disclosure System*, 70 Va. L. Rev. 717, 728–29 (1984); Sanford J. Grossman & Joseph E. Stiglitz, *On the Impossibility of Informationally Efficient Markets*, 70 Am. Econ. Rev. 393, 405 (1980).

99. SEC Reg. FD, 17 C.F.R. §§ 243.100–243.103.

100. Selective Disclosure and Insider Trading, Exchange Act Release No. 43,154, 65 Fed. Reg. 51716, 51716 (Aug. 24, 2000).

101. *Id.*

102. *See, e.g.,* Anup Agrawal, Sahiba Chadha & Mark A. Chen, *Who Is Afraid of Reg FD? The Behavior and Performance of Sell-Side Analysts Following the SEC's Fair Disclosure Rules*, 79 J. Bus. 2811, 2822 (2006) (finding that analyst forecasts became less accurate following Reg. FD); Zhihong Chen, Dan S. Dhaliwal & Hong Xie, *Regulation Fair Disclosure and the Cost of Equity Capital*, 15 Rev. Accounting Stud. 106, 139 (2010) (finding that the cost of capital decreased following Reg. FD).

103. *See* Merritt B. Fox, *Regulation FD and Foreign Issuers: Globalization's Strains and Opportunities*, 41 Va. J. Int'l L. 653, 673–78 (2001).

104. *Id.* at 674–75.

105. *Id.* at 677–78.

106. Armando Gomes, Gary Gorton & Leonardo Madureira, *SEC Regulation Fair Disclosure, Information, and the Cost of Capital*, 13 J. Corp. Fin. 300 (2007) (cost of capital actually increases for small firms); Zhihong Chen, Dan S. Dhaliwal & Hong Xie, *Regulation Fair Disclosure and the Cost of Equity Capital*, 15 Rev. Accounting Stud. 106 (2010) (the cost of capital for large and medium-sized firms decreases). The two studies use different methodologies, however.

107. This discussion is drawn from the excellent survey by Adam S. Koch, Craig E. Lefanowicz & John R. Robinson, *Regulation FD: A Review and Synthesis of the Academic Literature*, 27 Accounting Horizons 619 (2013)

108. *See* Council Directive 2003/6, 2003 O.J. (L 96) 16 (EC)7 (31).

109. *Id.* Article 6 states, "Member States shall ensure that issuers of financial instruments inform the public as soon as possible of inside information which directly concerns the said issuers."

110. Securities Exchange Act of 1934, ch. 404, § 16(b), 48 Stat. 881, 896 (codified at 15 U.S.C. § 78p(b)) (1988).

111. *See* Merritt B. Fox, *Insider Trading Deterrence Versus Managerial Incentives: A Unified Theory of Section 16(b)*, 92 MICH. L. REV. 2088, 2107–38 (1994).

112. A derivative suit under state corporation law can provide a remedy similar to that under §16(b). The theory is that a corporate officer or director who trades on inside information breaches her fiduciary duty to the corporation, to which she therefore should return her profits. *See, e.g.*, Diamond v. Oreamuno, 248 N.E.2d 910, 912 (N.Y. 1969).

113. NYSE, *NYSE Listed Company Manual*, http://nysemanual.nyse.com/LCM/Sections/.

114. *Id.*

115. *See* MICHAEL LEWIS, FLASH BOYS: A WALL STREET REVOLT (2014).


# 7. MANIPULATION

1. *See infra* Section V.A (discussing splits among the federal circuit courts of appeal).

2. The literature on manipulation features a chorus of commentators arguing about the definition and usefulness of the concept of manipulation. *See, e.g.*, Daniel R. Fischel & David Ross, *Should the Law Prohibit "Manipulation" in Financial Markets?*, 105 HARV. L. REV. 503 (1991) (famously arguing that the effort to legally prohibit manipulation should be abandoned); Craig Pirrong, *Squeezes, Corpses, and the Anti-Manipulation Provisions of the Commodity Exchange Act*, 17 REGULATION, no. 4, 1994, at 54 ("[T]o define just what manipulation means . . . is a more difficult task than one might think, because the term 'manipulation' is used very imprecisely and indiscriminately").

3. *See, e.g.*, Fischel & Ross, *supra* note 2, at 503 ("The drafters of the Securities Act of 1933 and the Securities Exchange Act of 1934 . . . were convinced that there was a direct link between excessive speculation, the stock market crash of 1929, and the Great Depression of the 1930s"); William A. Roach, Jr., *Hedge Fund Regulation: "What Side of the Hedges Are You on?"*, 40 U. MEM. L. REV. 165, 178 (2009) ("The shocking results of the [congressional] investigation uncovered high levels of market manipulation and led Congress to pass the first federal securities laws, the Securities Act of 1933"). However, there is significant debate as to whether significant manipulation had in fact been occurring in the years preceding the Great Depression. *See* Guolin Jiang, Paul G. Mahoney & Jianping Mei, *Market Manipulation: A Comprehensive Study of Stock Pools*, 77 J. FIN. ECON. 147, 168–69 (2005); PAUL G. Mahoney, Wasting a Crisis: Why Securities Regulation Fails (2015).

4. *See* 15 U.S.C. § 78i(a)(2); 15 U.S.C. § 78j(b).

5. Be aware that the SEC has only recently begun reporting administrative proceedings when they are stand-alone administrative proceedings.

6. *See* 15 U.S.C. § 78i(a)(2).

7. *See* 15 U.S.C. § 78j(b).

8. *Id.*

9. *See, e.g.*, Robert C. Lower, *Disruptions of the Futures Market: A Comment on Dealing with Market Manipulation*, 8 YALE J. REG. 391, 392 (1991) ("Manipulation is difficult to define. . . . [D]rawing a line between healthy economic behavior and that which is offensive has proved to be too subjective and imprecise to produce an effective regulatory tool."); Fischel & Ross, *supra* note 3, at 506–07 ("no satisfactory definition of [manipulation] exists. . . . the concept of manipulation should be abandoned."). Even the Supreme Court has at times appeared to collapse any distinction between a "manipulative" device and a "deceptive" one by requiring that any violation of § 10(b) involve a misrepresentation. Schreiber v. Burlington N., 472 U.S. 1, 8 n.6 (1985) ("Congress used the phrase 'manipulative or deceptive' in § 10(b) and we have interpreted 'manipulative' in that context to require misrepresentation."); Santa Fe Indus. v. Green, 430 U.S. 462, 476–77 (1977). *See also* Steve Thel, *Regulation of Manipulation Under Section 10(b)*, 1988 COLUM. BUS. L. REV. 359.

10. *See, e.g.*, Hazen, *The Law of Securities Regulation*, 2 LAW SEC. REG. § 12.1 (6th ed. 2010) ("The purpose of the various statutes and rules prohibiting market manipulation is to prevent activities that rig the market and to thereby facilitate operation of the 'natural law' of supply and demand. . . . [M]anipulation consists of any intentional interference with supply and demand."). Another formulation defines *manipulation* "as *exercising unsupported price pressure* because this creates societal costs." Matthijs Nelemans, *Redefining Trade-Based Market Manipulation*, 42 VAL. U. L. REV. 1169 (2008) (emphasis added). In these formulations, the normative criticism of the relevant conduct is doing all the work in identifying exactly what kind of behavior is supposed to be prohibited, yet no guidance is provided as to what in fact violates the norm. Alternatively, the definition can be too narrow. For example, the requirement proposed by two well-known microstructure economists is that a strategy is manipulative only if it reduces both price accuracy and liquidity. Albert Kyle & S. Viswanathan, *How to Define Illegal Price Manipulation*, 98 AM. ECON. REV. 274, 274 (2008). This leaves out of the prohibition strategies that increase one and reduce the other, but where the negative social impact of the market characteristic that is reduced is greater than the positive impact from the one that is increased. Attempts to define manipulation in related regulatory areas such as commodities regulation show some of the same problems. *See, e.g., In re* Henner, 30 Agric. Dec. 1151 (U.S.D.A. 1971) ("'Manipulation' is a vague term used in a wide and inclusive manner, possessing varying shades of meaning, and almost always conveying the

idea of blame-worthiness deserving of censure"); 2 Timothy J. Snider, Regulation of the Commodities Futures and Options Markets 12.01, at 12–5 (2d
ed. 1995) (calling the law of manipulation "a murky miasma of questionable analysis
and unclear effect"). *See also* Edward T. McDermott, *Defining Manipulation in Commodity Futures Trading: The Futures "Squeeze,"* 74 Nw. U. L. Rev. 202, 205 (1979)
(calling manipulation law "an embarrassment—confusing, contradictory, complex,
and unsophisticated"); Jonathan R. Macey & Maureen O'Hara, *From Markets to
Venues: Securities Regulation in an Evolving World*, 58 Stan. L. Rev. 563, 565 (2005)
(discussing manipulation's negative effects on liquidity).

11.  Dean Starkman & Jim Puzzanghera, 5 *Global Banks to Pay $5.7 Billion in Fines Over
Currency Manipulation*, L.A. Times, May 20, 2015, http://www.latimes.com/business
/la-fi-banks-criminal-fines-20150521-story.html; *see also* Suzi Ring, Liam Vaughan
& Jesse Hamilton, *CitiGroup, JPMorgan to Pay Most in $4.3 Billion in FX in Rigging
Cases*, Bloomberg News (Nov. 12, 2014), http://www.bloomberg.com/news/2014
-11-12/banks-to-pay-3-3-billion-in-fx-manipulation-probe; *see also* Gina Chon &
Tom Braithwaite, *JPMorgan Settles Forex Manipulation Lawsuit*, Fin. Times, Jan.
5, 2015, http://www.ft.com/intl/cms/s/0/7c545192-9511-11e4-b32c-00144feabdc0
.html?siteedition=intl.

12.  A practice or regulation can lead to a social harm if it reduces economic efficiency
in a particular way or systematically leads to unfair results. It can lead to a social
gain if it improves economic efficiency or ameliorates some unfairness. *See* ch. 2.
Thus, the desirability of a regulation that seeks to prohibit a given practice depends
on whether, considering on a net basis all the social harms and benefits involved in
a comparison between a world with and without the regulation, the world with the
regulation is superior to the world without it.

13.  *See, e.g.*, Tālis J. Putniņš, *Market Manipulation: A Survey*, 26 J. Econ. Survs. 952
(2012).

14.  Precisely how the correction occurs, however, will still matter to how a manipulation affects the wealth of various market participants and how dramatically it harms
liquidity. *See infra* Section II.A.1.b (showing that if the correction occurs due to
informed trading, then liquidity providers will lose significantly again, whereas if it
corrects due to a public disclosure, they will not).

15.  The purchase referred to in the text may consist of just one buy transaction or a
series of buy transactions in a relatively short period of time.

16.  The concept also covers a sale of a certain number of shares, and their repurchase
under circumstances where the difference in the price reaction to the sale versus
the repurchase results in the average repurchase price being less than the average
sale price.

17.  *See* Lawrence E. Harris, Trading and Exchanges 158 (2003).

18. The concept also covers the mirror set of transactions, where the initial transaction is a sale, and the trader has an external interest allowing him to enjoy a greater gain from a lower share price.

19. They include seeking to profit through one of the several kinds of informed trading, mistake trading, anti-mistake trading, professional liquidity supplying, saving by making an uninformed share purchase to enable later consumption by making an uninformed share sale, seeking to obtain a more favorable or suitable risk/expected return ratio through the purchase or sale of shares, reacting to a price change that hits the purchase or sale reservation price set as the result of fundamental analysis of publicly available information, and seeking to profit by observing trends in bids, offers, and executed transactions to try to detect informed trading by others and then trading in the same direction.

20. Harris, *supra* note 17, at 266.

21. Fischel & Ross, *supra* note 2.

22. *See* note.

23. It should be noted that at least some cases involved multiple defendants.

24. Carole Comerton-Forde & Tālis J. Putniņš, *Stock Price Manipulation: Prevalence and Determinants*, 18 Rev. Fin. 23 (2014).

25. Mark M. Carhart, Ron Kaniel, David K. Musto & Adam V. Reed, *Leaning for the Tape: Evidence of Gaming Behavior in Equity Mutual Funds*, 57 J. Fin. 661 (2002).

26. Pierre Hillion & Theo Vermaelen, *Death Spiral Convertibles*, 71 J. Fin. Econ. 381 (2004).

27. This is a very simplified description. More detail is available in Lawrence R. Glosten, *Sedona: The End of a PIPE Dream*, available at Columbia CaseWorks; *also see* Hillion & Vermaelen, *supra* note 26, at 4.

28. Some simple calculations will show this result. Suppose the face value of a future price convertible bond is $250,000 and the current stock price is $10. Immediate conversion would thus yield 25,000 shares for a total value of $250,000. Now suppose that the holder of the bond shorts 50,000 shares and as a result expects the stock price to be driven down to $5. On average, the short seller expects to collect $7.50 per share for proceeds of $7.50 × 50,000 = $375,000. At conversion, the bond holder will receive 250,000/5 = 50,000 shares. These shares are used to close out the short position with no further cash flows. Thus, there is a 50-percent profit associated with the downward manipulation.

29. *See* SEC v. Badian, Civil Action No. 06 CV 2621 (LTS), Litigation Release No. 19,639, 87 SEC Docket 2175 (Apr. 4, 2006).

30. *See* SEC v. Badian, Civil Action No. 06 CV 2621 (LTS), Litigation Release No. 22,593, 105 SEC Docket 1917 (Jan. 15, 2013).

31. *See* Adam Clark-Joseph, *Exploratory Trading* (Working Paper, Jan. 13, 2013), http://www.nanex.net/aqck2/4136/exploratorytrading.pdf.

32. Again, the concept also covers a sale of a certain number of shares, and their repurchase under circumstances where the difference in the price reaction to the sale versus the repurchase results in the average repurchase price being less than the average sale price. Throughout this chapter, for simplicity, we will assume that the first transaction or set of transactions are purchases.

33. In its definition of *manipulate*, the *Merriam-Webster Dictionary* includes "to change by artful or unfair means so as to serve one's purpose." *See* http://www.merriam-webster.com/dictionary/manipulate.

34. *See* LARRY HARRIS, TRADING AND ELECTRONIC MARKETS: WHAT INVESTMENT PROFESSIONALS NEED TO KNOW (2015) (discussing that "[t]rading is a zero-sum game when gains and losses are measured relative to the market index").

35. This $2,000 loss assumes, as does the pure adverse selection model of informed trading discussed in ch. 3, that during Mani's buying period, the liquidity suppliers do not turn around and rebalance their portfolios and acquire shares to cover their short position. As explored in ch. 3, § IV, a more complicated story recognizes that liquidity suppliers likely would seek to rebalance their portfolios relatively quickly. Using the example again, one could imagine that after each hour's 5,000-share order imbalance resulting from their sales to Mani, liquidity suppliers would have a somewhat higher offer and bid than what would be called for by the pure adverse selection considerations. The object would be to find some price-sensitive fundamental value investors who would respond by sending in more sell orders and fewer buy orders than would otherwise have been the case. Recall that these investors are different from any of the informed market participants described in ch. 3. Each of these investors has its own reservation price for buying and for selling ABC shares that is a product of its own best estimate of ABC's future cash flows based on its particular analysis of publicly available information, how long or short it already is in ABC shares, and a discount to reflect the chance that what appears to be an attractive purchase or sale price might be the result of informed trading or manipulation. Because the liquidity suppliers are, as a result of needing to attract these price-sensitive sellers, buying at a higher bid, but not selling at a higher offer, this strategy too is costly to liquidity suppliers. The prospect that manipulation will lead to such costs being incurred will lead liquidity suppliers to widen their spreads in order to break even, just like the $2,000 lost in the example in the text.

36. For a more detailed discussion of the interaction between informed traders and liquidity suppliers, see *supra* ch. 3, Section III.

37. It is also possible that the price does not adjust to an accurate level. If this occurs, then the liquidity suppliers do not suffer this second set of losses during the adjustment period.

38. *See* Lydia Saad, *U.S. Stock Ownership Stays at Record Low*, GALLUP ECON. (May 8, 2013), http://www.gallup.com/poll/162353/stock-ownership-stays-record-low .aspx. Michael Lewis attributes this drop, which has occurred in the face of a sharply rising market over the past five years, to a sense that the market is unfair. MICHAEL LEWIS, FLASH BOYS: A WALL STREET REVOLT 200–1 (2014); *see also* Editorial, *The Hidden Cost of Trading Stocks*, N.Y. TIMES, June 22, 2014, http://www.nytimes .com/2014/06/23/opinion/best-execution-and-rebates-for-brokers.html.

39. Fischel & Ross, *supra* note 2, at 506.

40. *Id.* at 517–18.

41. *Id.* at 517.

42. *Id.* at 518.

43. *Id.*

44. Since their work was published, other commentators have recognized flaws in Fischel's and Ross's argument, often in different respects. *See* Steve Thel, *$850,000 in Six Minutes—The Mechanics of Securities Manipulation*, 79 CORNELL L. REV. 219, 240–47 (1994) (discussing how a manipulator may profit by trading so as to alter others' expectations); HARRIS, *supra* note , at 259, 265–68 (developing the possibility of asymmetric price response); Franklin Allen & Douglas Gale, *Stock Price Manipulation*, 5 REV. FIN. STUD. 503 (1992). *See also* Robert A. Jarrow, *Market Manipulation, Bubbles, Corners, and Short Squeezes*, 27 J. FIN. & QUANTITATIVE ANAL. 311 (1992); Franklin Allen & Gary Gorton, *Stock Price Manipulation, Market Microstructure and Asymmetric Information*, 36 EUR. ECON. REV. 624 (1992).

45. *See* Adam D. Clark-Joseph, *supra* note 31 (documenting the existence of a kind of price-decoding high-frequency trader in the futures market).

46. This situation can be distinguished from a test of the market which reveals that the book has substantial depth followed by a series of purchases and later sales, a strategy that is commonly used when the later purchases and sales are for some purpose other than to profit from an expected asymmetric price reaction.

47. Again, the concept also covers the mirror set of transactions in which the initial transaction is a sale and the trader has an external interest so that she enjoys a greater gain from a lower share price.

48. 938 F.2d 364 (2d Cir. 1991). It was Steve Thel who first noted how this case illustrates the weaknesses of Fischel's and Ross's arguments. *See* Thel, *supra* note 44.

49. *Mulheren*, 938 F.2d at 365–67.

50. Andrew Verstein, *Benchmark Manipulation*, 56 B.C. L. REV. 215, 220, 242–43 (2015); Gabriel Rauterberg & Andrew Verstein, *Index Theory: The Law, Promise and Failure of Financial Indices*, 30 YALE J. ON REG. 1 (2013) (describing the extensive use of market benchmarks in contracts).

51. *See* Thel, *supra* note 44, at 251–55—another seminal article on manipulation—for an extensive and illuminating discussion of the *Mulheren* case. Thel uses the case to respond to the Fischel and Ross argument that naked open-market manipulation cannot be profitable. Because the *Mulheren* case involves an open-market manipulation with an external interest, it does not really show that naked open-market manipulation can be profitable. Thus, Thel did not fully rebut the Fischel and Ross argument that a naked one cannot be profitable. The case does show, however, that one with an external interest can be very profitable.

52. Again, the mirror set of actions—making a falsely positive statement about an issuer that pushes its share price up, selling (or short selling) the shares, and then repurchasing (or closing the short position) after the truth comes out—would also be misstatement manipulation.

53. A more nuanced analysis would include price-sensitive fundamental value informed traders—traders who sell in response to the price increase resulting from the misstatement manipulator's purchases because, given the publicly available information including the false statement, they think that the stock has become overpriced. This does not change the basic conclusions, however.

54. SEC v. Competitive Techs., Inc., No. CIV.A.3:04CV1331 (JCH), 2005 WL 1719725, at *6 (D. Conn. July 21, 2005) ("In order '[t]o make out a violation of subsection 9(a)(1) . . . a plaintiff must prove the existence of (1) a wash sale or matched orders in a security, (2) done with scienter and (3) for the purpose of creating a false or misleading appearance of active trading in that security' ") (citations omitted); *see also id.* ("Section 9(a) claims must allege that defendants acted with the purpose of creating a false appearance of active trading (in the case of 9(a)(1) claims) and the purpose of inducing others to trade in the stock (in the case of 9(a)(2) claims)").

55. *See* 15 U.S.C. § 78i(a)(1) (prohibiting "effect[ing] any transaction in such security which involves no change in the beneficial ownership thereof, or (B) [ . . . ] enter[ing] an order or orders for the purchase of such security with the knowledge that an order or orders of substantially the same size, at substantially the same time, and at substantially the same price, for the sale of any such security, has been or will be entered by or for the same or different parties" where this is done for "the purpose of creating a false or misleading appearance of active trading in any security other than a government security, or a false or misleading appearance with respect to the market for any such security").

56. A wash or matched sale intended to create the appearance of a rising price would consist of the submission of a buy limit order constituting a higher bid than the current NBB followed by the submission of a marketable sell order that transacts against this higher bid. For this to work, the second submission must arrive faster than any sell order of an outside actor seeking to take advantage of the new, more

favorable bid. The more active the market is for the stock of the particular issuer, the less likely it is that the second submission will beat out the sell order of an outside actor—a necessary condition for the wash or matched sale to succeed. The same observation, using mirror submissions, applies to a wash or matched sale intended to create the appearance of a falling market.

57. *See* 15 U.S.C. § 78i(a)(2); *see generally* Cohen v. Stevanovich, 722 F. Supp. 2d 416, 424 (S.D.N.Y. 2010); Sharette v. Credit Suisse Int'l, 127 F. Supp. 3d 60, 78 (S.D.N.Y. 2015); AnchorBank, FSB v. Hofer, 649 F.3d 610, 616–17 (7th Cir. 2011); Chemetron Corp. v. Business Funds, Inc., 682 F.2d 1149, 1164 (5th Cir.1982), *vacated on other grounds*, 460 U.S. 1007 (1983); SEC v. Malenfant, 784 F. Supp. 141, 144 (S.D.N.Y. 1992).

58. *See, e.g.*, Nanopierce Techs., Inc. v. Southridge Capital Mgmt, No. 02 Civ. 0767, 2002 U.S. Dist. LEXIS 24049, at *6 (S.D.N.Y. Oct. 10, 2002); Markowski v. SEC, 274 F.3d 525, 528 (D.C. Cir. 2001).

59. *See* Sharette v. Credit Suisse Int'l, 127 F. Supp. 3d 60, 78 (S.D.N.Y. 2015); Anchor-Bank, FSB v. Hofer, 649 F.3d 610, 616–17 (7th Cir. 2011); SEC v. Malenfant, 784 F. Supp. 141, 144 (S.D.N.Y. 1992). A private suit under § 9(a)(2) would also require proof that the relevant transactions were relied on by the plaintiff, and affected the price of plaintiff's transaction. *Chemetron*, 682 F.2d at 1164.

60. Sullivan & Long, Inc. v. Scattered Corp., 47 F.3d 857, 864 (7th Cir. 1995) (citing Santa Fe Indus. v. Green, 430 U.S. 462, 476 (1977)).

61. 25 SEC 227 (Jan. 29, 1947).

62. *Id.* at *3.

63. *Id. See also In re* Charles C. Wright et al., 3 SEC 190 (Feb. 28, 1938) ("The very existence of an option when coupled with buying on the market by those having an interest in its exercise is an indication of a purpose to raise the market price, to increase market activity and thus to distribute profitably the stock covered by the option.").

64. 362 F. Supp. 964 (S.D.N.Y. 1973). Interestingly, the finding that § 9(a)(2) was violated in this case seems to be dicta, as it was conducted to show that by analogy § 10(b) must also have been violated. *Id.*

65. The broker-dealers undertaking the trading at the behest of the underwriter claimed that they believed the offering was oversold. *Id.* at 978. Although the court was highly skeptical of the claim, *id.*, the fact that the defendants could even make the claim suggests that it was not widely understood in the market that the offering was not fully sold. This explains how stock could continue to be offered in a primary market at $10 while there were bids in the secondary market in the neighborhood of $20.

66. *Id.* at 977.

67. *Id.* at 978 ("The apparent and actual trading was achieved with advancing pink sheet quotes, inducement of other brokers to enter quotes, and actual purchases. The price rise was effected by Nagler-Weissman's dominion and control of the market in the stock and total price leadership in both the sheets and actual purchase, as further evidenced by the virtual collapse of the market in the stock following the manipulation.").

68. *Id.*

69. 419 F.2d 787 (2d Cir. 1969).

70. *Id.* at 795. ("In furtherance of its interest in defeating the Crane tender offer and consummating its own merger with Air Brake, Standard took affirmative steps to conceal from the public its own secret sales off the market at the same time it was dominating trading in Air Brake shares at a price level calculated to deter Air Brake shareholders from tendering to Crane.").

71. *Id.*

72. *Id.*

73. An additional reason for the predominance of § 10(b) cases is that some courts have also interpreted § 9(a)'s scienter requirement as more exacting than that of Rule 10b-5, under which knowledge of the falsity of a material statement is sufficient. As one court put it, "the 'intent to induce' requirement . . . is distinct from the scienter requirement of Rule 10b-5(b). While one may intend to do a fraudulent act thereby fulfilling Rule 10b-5(b)'s scienter requirement, the intent that that act induce a purchase or sale is a distinct and more specific requirement. Thus the 'intent to induce' requirement creates a higher burden of proof for the plaintiff . . . than that borne under Rule 10b-5(b)." Chemetron Corp. v. Bus. Funds, Inc., 682 F.2d 1149, 1162 (5th Cir. 1982), *cert. granted, judgment vacated*, 460 U.S. 1007, 103 S. Ct. 1245, 75 L. Ed. 2d 476 (1983); *see also* Panfil v. ACC Corp., 768 F. Supp. 54, 59 (W.D.N.Y.), *aff'd*, 952 F.2d 394 (2d Cir. 1991); Salvani v. ADVFN PLC, 50 F. Supp. 3d 459, 477 (S.D.N.Y. 2014), *aff'd sub nom.* Salvani v. InvestorsHub.com, 628 F. App'x 784 (2d Cir. 2015). Although these cases address § 9(a)(4), its "intent to induce" language is identical to that of § 9(a)(2), so their logic might seem logically to extend to that section as well. *But see* SEC v. Competitive Techs., Inc., No. CIV.A.3:04CV1331(JCH), 2005 WL 1719725, at *7 n.7 (D. Conn. July 21, 2005) ("The standard for scienter in securities fraud cases has generally been stated in relation to section 10(b) manipulation claims rather than section 9(b) manipulation claims; however[,] courts have consistently applied the same standard to both sets of claims."). *See also* Fezzani v. Bear, Stearns, & Co., 2004 WL 744594, *14, Fed. Sec. L. Rep. (CCH) 92,773 (S.D.N.Y. 2004), SEC v. Schiffer, 1998 WL 226101, *3, Fed. Sec. L. Rep. (CCH) 90,213 (S.D.N.Y. 1998); SEC v. Malenfant, 784 F. Supp. 141, 145 (S.D.N.Y. 1992).

74. *See In re* NASDAQ Stock Mkt. LLC for Registration as a Nat'l Sec. Exchange; Findings, Opinions, and Order of the Common, SEC Rel. No. 34-53128 (Jan. 13, 2006), 71 Fed. Reg. 3550 (Jan. 23, 2006).

75. *See* 15 U.S.C. § 78j(b).
76. 17 C.F.R. § 240.10b-5 (1976) ("It shall be unlawful for any person . . . (a) To employ any device, scheme, or artifice to defraud, (b) To make any untrue statement of a material fact or [omission] . . . , or (c) To engage in any act, practice, or course of business which operates or would operate as a fraud or deceit upon any person, in connection with the purchase or sale of any security.").
77. Blue Chip Stamps v. Manor Drug Stores, 421 U.S. 723, 767 (1975) (Blackmun, J., dissenting) (*citing* Remarks of Milton Freeman, *Conference on Codification of the Federal Securities Laws*, 22 Bus. Law. 793, 922 (1967)).
78. *See, e.g.*, Ernst & Ernst v. Hochfelder, 425 U.S. 185, 198 (1976) ("the word 'manipulative' . . . is and was virtually a term of art when used in connection with securities markets. It connotes intentional or willful conduct designed to deceive or defraud investors by controlling or artificially affecting the price of securities.") (citations omitted); Santa Fe Indus. v. Green, 430 U.S. 462, 476 (1977) (manipulation "refers generally to practices, such as wash sales, matched orders, or rigged prices, that are intended to mislead investors by artificially affecting market activity.") (citations omitted); Schreiber v. Burlington N., Inc., 472 U.S. 1, 8 n.6 (1985) ("Congress used the phrase 'manipulative or deceptive' in § 10(b) and we have interpreted 'manipulative' in that context to require misrepresentation.") (citations omitted).
79. Chiarella v. United States, 445 U.S. 222, 234–35 (1980).
80. Louisiana Pac. Corp. v. Merrill Lynch & Co., 571 F. App'x 8, 10 (2d Cir. 2014), *citing* ATSI Comms., Inc. v. Shaar Fund, Ltd., 493 F.3d 87, 101 (2d Cir. 2007). In the case of a government action for manipulation under Rule 10b-5, there would presumably be no need for a showing of two of these elements—damages and reliance—just as there is no need for showing these elements in a government action for a materially false or misleading statement under Rule 10b-5(b). SEC v. Kelly, 765 F. Supp. 2d 301, 319 (S.D.N.Y. 2011) ("[U]nlike a private plaintiff, the SEC need not allege or prove reliance, causation, or damages in an action under Section 10(b) or Rule 10b-5.").
81. 272 F.3d 189 (3d Cir. 2001).
82. *Id.* at 205.
83. *Id.*
84. The Seventh Circuit appears to have joined the Third Circuit as part of this first group. In Foss v. Bear, Stearns & Co., the Seventh Circuit, in reply to a plaintiff who wanted to "call the [alleged] conduct 'manipulation' rather than 'fraud,' " stated that "this is a distinction without a difference" because in "securities law, manipulation is a *kind* of fraud; deceit remains essential." 394 F.3d 540, 542 (7th Cir. 2005). It should be noted, however, that this is dicta because the case had facts significantly different from the kinds of open-market manipulation being explored here.

85. 938 F.2d 364 (2d Cir. 1991).

86. *Id.* at 368.

87. *Id.* at 371.

88. Nanopierce Techs., Inc. v. Southridge Cap. Mgmt, No. 02 Civ. 0767, 2002 U.S. Dist. LEXIS 24049, at *6 (S.D.N.Y. Oct. 10, 2002). Other district courts in the Second Circuit went even further. *See* Sharette v. Credit Suisse Int'l, 127 F. Supp. 3d 60, 82 (S.D.N.Y. 2015) ("other courts in this district have found that open-market transactions that are not, in and of themselves, manipulative or illegal, may constitute manipulative activity within the meaning of Section 10(b) when coupled with manipulative intent."); *see also* SEC v. Masri, 523 F. Supp. 2d 361, 372 (S.D.N.Y. 2007) ("The Court concludes . . . that if an investor conducts an open-market transaction with the intent of artificially affecting the price of the security, and not for any legitimate economic reason, it can constitute market manipulation."); ATSI Comms., Inc. v. Shaar Fund, Ltd., 493 F.3d 87, 102 (2d Cir. 2007).

89. *See* Fezzani v. Bear, Stearns & Co., 777 F.3d 566, 571 (2d Cir. 2015). The case involves a broker-dealer that was accused of prompting its customers to purchase certain stocks and then later maintaining the price of these stocks by buying shares in the secondary market, presumably to increase its clients' appetites for its next round of recommendations. The case involves a defendant, who, rather than being the broker-dealer itself, was someone accused of allowing the broker-dealer to "park" these shares in his account (i.e., allowing the broker-dealer to sell him the shares it had purchased but with an understanding that he would be protected against any drop in price). The language quoted in the text is dictum because the court dismissed the complaint against the defendant. According to the court, the plaintiff failed "to allege acts by [the defendant] that amounted to more than knowingly participating in, or facilitating" the broker-dealer's fraud. *Id.* at 625. To be liable in a private damages action, the court concluded, the defendant himself would have had to make the false communication. *Id.*

90. *Id.* at 571–72 (citations omitted).

91. 493 F.3d 87 (2d Cir. 2007).

92. *Id.* at 99–100. The court went on to say that "[a] market manipulation claim . . . cannot be based solely upon misrepresentations or omissions. There must be some market activity, such as 'wash sales, matched orders, or rigged prices.' " *Id.* at 101 (citation omitted). It said as well: "[I]n some cases scienter is the only factor that distinguishes legitimate trading from improper manipulation." *Id.* at 102. The Second Circuit upheld the district court's grant of the defendant's motion to dismiss the complaint for different reasons, however. The type of security involved was a note convertible into common stock at a ratio determined by the share price at the time of conversion, very much like the security in *GFL* (and *SEC v. Badian* discussed at notes 29 and 30

*supra* and accompanying text). Unlike the plaintiff in *GFL*, however, the plaintiff in *ATSI* did not effectively plead facts showing that the defendant actually shorted the shares right before conversion.

93. 493 F.3d at 100–01 (citations omitted, emphasis added). *See also* Gurary v. Winehouse, 190 F.3d 37, 45 (2d Cir. 1999); Mobil Corp. v. Marathon Oil Co., 669 F.2d 366, 374 (6th Cir.1981); *cf.* Pagel, Inc. v. SEC, 803 F.2d 942, 946 (8th Cir.1986) ; Crane Co. v. Westinghouse Air Brake Co., 419 F.2d 787, 796 (2d Cir.1969).

94. The SEC also joins the Second and D.C. Circuits in recognizing trades done with a manipulative intent, without any further unlawful act, as potentially unlawful manipulation. In an administrative proceeding against Terrance Yoshikawa, the SEC embraced an expansive, if vague, interpretation of § 10(b), which would encompass pure market manipulation. *In re* Application of Terrance Yoshikawa for Review of Disciplinary Action Taken by NASD, Release No. 53731 (Apr. 26, 2006). The SEC took the position that manipulation is "'intentional interference with the free forces of supply and demand,'" *id.* at 4, whereas the specific allegations against Yoshi-kawa were that he had "engaged in a manipulative scheme by artificially moving the NBBO in the specified securities and thereby fraudulently affected the nature of the market for these securities." *Id.* at 6. In this case, the defendant had repeatedly placed a small limit order in one direction that reset the NBO or NBB and then placed a much larger order in the opposite direction that he had good reason to believe would be executed in a venue that used the NBO and NBB as reference prices even when the order it received was larger than the amount available in the market at the NBO or NBB. So, the practice involved was closely analogous to an open-market transaction with an external interest.

95. 274 F.3d 525, 528 (D.C. Cir. 2001).

96. *Id.* at 529. The case involved a broker-dealer that acted as an underwriter for an IPO of the shares of a small issuer, Mountaintop. The broker-dealer sold a large portion of the offering to its own retail customers. Then, for seven months, the broker-dealer "(1) maintained high bid prices for Mountaintop securities, and (2) absorbed all unwanted securities into inventory," *id.* at 527, until this unsustainable effort forced the broker-dealer to close. At this point, Mountaintop's share price dropped by 75 percent in one day. The D.C. Circuit noted that "[t]he activity in Mountaintop fur-thered an *external interest*. At least in the short term, the [broker-dealer] supported Mountaintop's price not to profit from later sales of Mountaintop, but to maintain customer interest in Global generally and to sustain confidence in its other securities." *Id.* at 529 (emphasis added).

97. *See, e.g.,* Koch v. SEC, 793 F.3d 147, 155 (D.C. Cir. 2015), *cert. denied*, 136 S. Ct. 1492, 194 L. Ed. 2d 586 (2016).

98. Koch v. SEC, U.S. No. 15-781 (Mar. 28, 2016).

99. In making these observations, we are not weighing in on the difficult question of what kind of higher showing, if any, should be required for violations of the rule to be considered criminal as opposed to some kind of SEC-enforced or private civil sanction.

100. SEC v Texas Gulf Sulphur, 401 F.2d 833, 859–61 (2d Cir. 1968).

101. ATSI Comms., Inc. v. Shaar Fund, Ltd., 493 F.3d 87 (2d Cir. 2007).

102. *Id.*

103. Sharette v. Credit Suisse Int'l, 127 F. Supp. 3d 60, 77 (S.D.N.Y. 2015).

104. *See* Damian Moos, *Pleading Around the Private Securities Litigation Reform Act: Reevaluating the Pleading Requirements for Market Manipulation Claims*, 78 S. CAL. L. REV. 763, 764 (2005).

105. *See* S. Rep. No. 104-98, at 4 (1995), *reprinted in* 1995 U.S.C.C.A.N. 679, 683; Richard M. Phillips & Gilbert C. Miller, *The Private Securities Litigation Reform Act of 1995: Rebalancing Litigation Risks and Rewards for Class Action Plaintiffs, Defendants and Lawyers*, 51 BUS. LAW. 1009 (1996).

106. The PSLRA requires that in any action "the complaint . . . state with particularity facts giving rise to a strong inference that the defendant acted with the required state of mind with respect to each alleged act or omission." 15 U.S.C. § 78u-4(b)(2). In a famous misstatement case, the Supreme Court ruled that this means the plaintiff must allege facts which give rise to "an inference of scienter [that] must be more than merely plausible or reasonable—it must be cogent and at least as compelling as any opposing inference of nonfraudulent intent." Tellabs Inc. v. Makor Issues & Rights Ltd., 551 U.S. 308, 314 (2007).

107. ATSI Comms., Inc. v. Shaar Fund, Ltd., 493 F.3d 87, 102 (2d Cir. 2007) (holding that a "plaintiff need not plead manipulation with the same degree of specificity as a plain misrepresentation claim"). As another court put it, "[W]here the principal allegations of wrongdoing involve market manipulation rather than false statements, the Complaint sets forth a sufficient level of detail by alleging the nature, purpose, and effect of the fraudulent conduct and the roles of the defendants." *In re* Blech Sec. Litig., 928 F. Supp. 1279, 1290–91 (S.D.N.Y. 1996). *See also* Baxter v. A.R. Baron, No. 94 Civ. 3913, 1996 WL 586338, at *8 (S.D.N.Y. Oct. 11, 1996) ("The degree of particularity required for pleading a market manipulation scheme is not as demanding as it is when Rule 9(b) is applied in other instances of fraud because the facts relating to a manipulation scheme are often known only by the defendants."); *In re* Initial Pub. Offering Sec. Litig., 241 F. Supp. 2d 281, 386 (S.D.N.Y. 2003).

108. Courts seem to have shown a careful awareness of this possibility. As a result, manipulation claims centered on misrepresentations are generally viewed as subject to the PSLRA's heightened requirements. For instance, in Lentell v. Merrill Lynch & Co., 396 F.3d 161 (2d Cir. 2005), the Second Circuit held that although the plaintiffs sought to cast their claims in terms of market manipulation under Rule

10b-5, "where the sole basis for such claims is alleged misrepresentations or omissions, plaintiffs . . . remain subject to the heightened pleading requirements of the PSLRA." *Id.* at 17-78; *see also* Schnell v. Conseco, Inc., 43 F. Supp. 2d 438, 447–48 (S.D.N.Y. 1999).

109. Case 2:16-cv-09130 in the United States District Court, District of New Jersey.

## 8. SHORT SELLING

This chapter borrows heavily from sections of Merritt Fox, Lawrence Glosten, & Paul Tetlock, *Short Selling and the News: A Preliminary Report on an Empirical Study*, 54 N.Y.L.S. Rev. 645 (2010).

1. *See, e.g.,* Ken Sweet, *Morgan's Mack: Short Sellers Destroying Our Firm*, FOXBusiness (Sept. 17, 2008), http://www.foxbusiness.com/story/markets/morgansmack -short-sellers-destroying-firm/ (Morgan Stanley CEO John Mack believed current short sellers are "irresponsible," and are "driving [Morgan Stanley] stock down"); Posting of Shepherd Smith Edwards & Kantas, *U.S. Representative Barney Frank Calls on SEC to Widen Investigation of Improper Trading Rumors Surrounding Bear Stearns's Stock*, Stockbroker Fraud Blog (Apr. 21, 2008), http://www.stockbroker-fraudblog.com/2008/04/us_representative_barney_frank.html (Rep. Barney Frank is concerned that short-selling in certain banks is being orchestrated to bring stock prices down).

2. *See infra* Section I.A.

3. *See infra* Section I.B.

4. Karl B. Diether, Kuan-Hui Lee & Ingrid M. Werner, *Short-Sale Strategies and Return Predictability*, 22 Rev. Fin. Stud. 575, 579 (2009).

5. The dilemma faced by the producer of such information is that he wants to maximize his rents and have the information used only as widely as the producer of any valuable input would want it used—that is, to the point where marginal revenue equals marginal cost. The revelation of the information to another undermines his monopoly position because, absent an agreement between the producer and the transferee, anyone who receives it can then "produce" additional units of it at very low marginal cost. Agreements between the original producer and another to limit the use and further transfer of the information are difficult to draft and enforce and thus entail significant transaction costs. Transfers are further burdened by the fact that it is hard for the potential transferee to evaluate information without learning it, at which point there is no need to pay for it. Kenneth J. Arrow, *Economic Welfare and the Allocation of Resources for Invention, in* The Rate and Direction of Inventive Activity 609, 616 (Richard R. Nelson, ed., 1962).

6. *See, e.g.,* The Brief: Institute for Law and Economics, *William Ackman Says a Ban on Short Selling Is Shortsighted,* PENN LAW J. ONLINE (Spring 2009), https://www.law.upenn.edu/alumni/alumnijournal/Spring2009/the_brief/page10.html (Ackman believed that the September 2008 ban on short selling is misguided and "strait-jacket[s]" hedge fund managers); James Mackintosh et al., *Ban on Shorting Banks Failed Badly, Say Experts,* FINANCIALTIMES.COM (Mar. 11, 2009), http://www.ft.com/cms/s/0/34c7e12a-0ddd-11de-8ea3-0000779fd2ac.html?nclick_check=1 (hedge funds and academics believe that the short selling restrictions did not work and short-selling funds are being "demonized"). For a discussion of these restrictions, see *infra* Section II.B.3.

7. *See, e.g.,* Sara Hansard, *Hedge Funds Alone in Fight Against Short-Selling Curb,* INVESTMENT NEWS (Aug.11, 2008), http://www.investmentnews.com/article/20080811/REG/827522981.

8. Financial economists describe a market displaying *"semi-strong"* efficiency as one where "prices will adjust immediately to public information," after which security returns are unpredictable. RICHARD A. BREALEY, STEWART C. MYERS & FRANKLIN ALLEN, PRINCIPLES OF CORPORATE FINANCE 359 (9th ed. 2008). In such a market, no ordinary investor, on an expected basis, can beat the market by collecting and acting on public information, because it is already reflected in price. *Id.*

9. *See, e.g.,* James Chanos, President, Kynikos Associates, *Prepared Statement for the U.S. Securities and Exchange Commission Roundtable on Hedge Funds,* Panel Discussion: "Hedge Fund Strategies and Market Participation" (May 15, 2003), http://www.sec.gov/spotlight/hedgefunds/hedge-chanos.htm; *An 'Abomination'? Critics Attack SEC's Short-Selling Ban,* L.A. TIMES, Money & Company Blog (Sept. 19, 2008, 1:07 PM), http://latimesblogs.latimes.com/money_co/2008/09/some-reaction-t.html (negative reactions of both hedge funds and academics to the ban on short selling); Posting of John Hempton, *In Defence of Naked Short Selling—Or Why the Crackdown on a Phoney Problem is Costing Taxpayers at Least a Billion Dollars,* Bronte Capital Blog (June 16, 2009), http://brontecapital.blogspot.com/2009/06/in-defence-of-naked-short-selling-or.html (arguing that the ban on short selling makes the market less efficient and costs taxpayers money). A less benign explanation of the hedge fund unhappiness at the short-sale restrictions is that during a financial crisis, short-selling the shares of financial firms might be profitable because the decline in share price resulting from the short-sale trade could damage the underlying business of the firm and hence lead to a decline in fundamental value that would be reflected in price longer term. *See infra* Section I.C.3.

10. Another illustration of the importance of short selling for incentives is the existence of hedge funds that specialize in looking for hints that an issuer's accounting is incorrect and is exaggerating earnings. Such funds would be unlikely to exist if short

selling were not available, because their whole business model is to look for bad news and to try to profit by selling when they find it. For example, Kynikos Associates described itself as a "private investment management company . . . [which] specializes in short selling . . . [and] profits in finding fundamentally overvalued securities." Chanos, *supra* note 9.

11. In this informal model which treats information as bits, one can imagine that the bits that are relevant to a given trader predicting an issuer's future cash flows would include not only the bits relating to the issuer itself and the input and output markets in which the issuer operates, but also the bits that inform the trader's particular approach to doing analysis. Thus, two persons might have the same set of the first type of bits, but come to different predictions concerning the issuer's future cash flows, because of differences in their sets of the second type of bits. This is a way that one person could be an "optimist," who thinks that the stock is priced below its fundamental value, and another a "pessimist," who thinks it is priced above.

12. For models working out this proposition, *see, e.g.*, Edward M. Miller, *Risk, Uncertainty, and the Divergence of Opinion*, 32 J. FIN. 1151 (1977).

13. Douglas W. Diamond & Robert E. Verrecchia, *Constraints on Short-Selling and Asset Price Adjustment to Private Information*, 18 J. FIN. ECON. 277, 278 (1987).

14. *See, e.g.*, Andrei Shleifer & Lawrence H. Summers, *The Noise Trader Approach to Finance*, J. ECON. PERSP., Spring 1990, at 19, 19–20.

15. *See* J. Bradford De Long et al., *Noise Trader Risk in Financial Markets*, 98 J. POL. ECON. 703 (1990).

16. *See* Jose A. Schienkman & Wei Xiong, *Overconfidence and Speculative Bubbles*, 111 J. POL. ECON. 1183, 1185–86 (2003).

17. *See* Christopher L. Culp & J.B. Heaton, *Naked Shorting*, Regulation (Apr. 26, 2007), http://papers.ssrn.com/sol3/papers.cfm?abstract_id=982898; Miller, *supra* note 12, at 1160–61; Eli Ofek & Matthew Richardson, *DotCom Mania: The Rise and Fall of Internet Stock Prices*, 58 J. FIN. 1113, 1113 (2003).

18. *See generally* Thomas E. Copeland & Dan Galai, *Information Effects and the Bid-Ask Spread*, 38 J. FIN. 1457 (1983); Lawrence R. Glosten & Paul Milgrom, *Bid, Ask and Transaction Prices in a Specialist Market with Heterogeneously Informed Traders*, 14 J. FIN. ECON. 71 (1985); Sanford J. Grossman & Merton H. Miller, *Liquidity and Market Structure*, 43 J. FIN. 617 (1988); Hans R. Stoll, *The Supply of Dealer Services in Securities Markets*, 33 J. FIN. 1133 (1978).

19. The wording of the short sale ban in 2008 exempted "registered market makers." Because HFTs that are in the business of supplying liquidity are typically registered market makers on most exchanges, they were likely not affected and would not be affected were the same exemptions applied today.

20. This negative influence has been demonstrated in the case of financial firms. *See* Ekkehart Boehmer, Charles M. Jones & Xiaoyan Zhang, *Shackling Short Sellers: The 2008 Shorting Ban*, 26 Rev. Fin. Stud. 1363 (2013).

21. This is the alleged tactic employed by participants in the "bear raids" of the early 1930s that so much disturbed the drafters of the Securities Exchange Act of 1934. 7 Louis Loss & Joel Seligman, Securities Regulation 3200 n.213 (3d ed. 2003).

22. This is typically less severe with a manufacturing or nonfinancial services firm, which, if it suffers a temporary decline in share price unrelated to its fundamentals can, without great damage to its future cash flows per share, either temporarily defer real investments or raise funds for the real investment in ways other than equity sales.

23. *See infra* Section II.B.3. On September 18, 2008, the SEC instituted a temporary emergency ban on the shorting of 799 financial services companies because of "[concern] about recent sudden declines in the prices of a wide range of securities . . . [which] can give rise to questions about the underlying financial condition of an issuer, which in turn can create a crisis of confidence without a fundamental underlying basis." Emergency Order Taking Temporary Action to Respond to Market Developments, Exchange Act Release No. 34,58592, 73 Fed. Reg. 55,169 (Sept. 18, 2008). The following day, the SEC reiterated its beliefs that "unbridled short selling is contributing to the recent, sudden price declines in the securities of financial institutions unrelated to true price valuation," and that "financial institutions are particularly vulnerable to this crisis of confidence and panic selling." It further stated that in addition to the new shorting ban and the previous emergency orders increasing short sale reporting and easing restrictions on issuer repurchase, it "may consider additional steps as necessary to protect the integrity and quality of the securities markets and strengthen investor confidence." Press Release, SEC Halts Short Selling of Financial Stocks to Protect Investors and Markets, SEC Release 2008-211 (Sept. 19, 2008), http://www.sec.gov/news/press/2008/2008-211.htm.

24. Deliberately spreading false news and trading to take advantage of the resulting distortion in price violates the Rule 10b-5 prohibition against the making of "any untrue statement of a material fact . . . in connection with the purchase or sale of a security." 17 C.F.R. § 240.10b-5 (2009). During the run-up to the financial crisis, the SEC reaffirmed its commitment to "vigorously investigate and prosecute those who manipulate markets with this witch's brew of damaging rumors and short sales." Michael J. de la Merced, *S.E.C. Accuses Trader of Spreading Rumors*, N.Y. Times, Apr. 25, 2008, at C6. This led to charges such as those filed in the Southern District of New York against trader Paul S. Berliner for shorting in connection with rumor-mongering. Complaint, SEC v. Paul S. Berliner, No. 08-CV-3859 (S.D.N.Y. Apr. 24, 2008), http://www.sec.gov/litigation/complaints/2008/comp20537.pdf (case settled in Administration Proceeding File No. 3-13035).

25. At the start of the financial crisis in the summer of 2008, the SEC, for example, appeared more concerned about the ease with which false negative rumors were spread than false positive ones. It justified the emergency imposition of new rules relating to the borrowing and delivery requirements on short sales of financial institution shares, in part, on concern that negative false rumors concerning them had fueled share price decline below the level that would have resulted from the normal price discovery process. Emergency Order Taking Temporary Action to Respond to Market Developments, Exchange Act Release No. 58,166, 73 Fed. Reg. 42,379, paras. 1–2 (July 15, 2008).

26. The legal risk associated with a trader engaging in this fraudulent practice is the risk of detection and hence of a legally imposed sanction. The financial risk is the variability in the possible return from engaging in this fraudulent practice and the effect of this variability on the overall level of riskiness of the trader's portfolio. Engaging in the practice un-diversifies the trader's portfolio, which in turn makes the riskiness of the trader's portfolio sensitive to the variability in the return from engaging in the fraudulent practice even though this variability represents potentially diversifiable idiosyncratic risk.

27. As for legal risk, on the one hand, engaging in the initial trade after, rather than before, spreading false news may be harder to detect because significant news tends to increase the overall volume of trading. Paul C. Tetlock, *Giving Content to Investor Sentiment: The Role of Media in the Stock Market*, 62 J. FIN. 1139 (2007). On the other hand, when the false news to be spread is positive, detection of the fraud may be more difficult if the initial trade is before the spreading of the news, because it avoids the necessity of engaging in a short sale to profit. Short sales are more conspicuous because they represent a smaller percentage of trades. As for financial risk, when the initial trade occurs first and the spreading of the false news occurs thereafter, the primary source of the variability in the possible return from engaging in the fraud stems from the inability of the trader, at the time she engages in the initial transaction, to predict precisely the extent, if any, to which the false news will affect price. The second source of variability is all the other factors that will push the issuer's price around during the period between the first transaction and the second transaction. The importance of this source of risk is limited by the fact that the time between the first and second fraudulent transactions is likely to be short, probably no more than a day or two. This is because the trader will presumably spread the false news as soon as the initial transaction is completed. For a stock trading in a market that is efficient with respect to public announcements of the issuer, even news that is publicly disseminated by a non-issuer source (for example, a news service or an analyst), and that has as its ultimate source a publicly unnamed person (the trader spreading the false news), is likely to have its full impact on price very quickly. Once the false news has

had its full impact on price, the trader will want to engage in the second transaction immediately in order to eliminate any further risk and lock in her profits. When the spreading of the false news occurs first and the initial trade occurs thereafter, the relative importance of these two sources of financial risk is reversed. The primary source of this variability in the possible return stems from all the other factors that will push the issuer's price around during the period between the fraudulent first transaction and the second transaction. This is because there may well be an extended period of time before the market fully realizes the falsity of the news and the impact of this news on price dissipates. Because the trader cannot make her full return from engaging in the practice until the impact on price completely dissipates, the trader remains undiversified for a considerable period of time and cannot lock in her profits. The other source of variability—the inability of the trader, at the time she engages in the initial transaction, to ascertain precisely the extent to which the false news has affected prices—is now the less important source of risk. Compared to the scenario in which the initial transaction precedes the spreading of the false news, the trader in this latter scenario has the advantage of being able to observe the price change before she commits by engaging in the first transaction. Because other factors may affect price at the same time as the false news is being spread, it may not be possible to ascertain perfectly the impact of the false news on price. Still, for assessing this impact, being able to observe the price change is a big advantage over not being able to observe it.

28. More detailed histories of U.S. short-selling regulation can be found at Charles M. Jones, *Shorting Restrictions: Revisiting the 1930s* (October 2008), https://www0.gsb .columbia.edu/mygsb/faculty/research/pubfiles/3233/JonesShortingRestrictions4a. pdf; Amendments to Regulation SHO, SEC Release No. 34-59748, 17 C.F.R. pt. 242, at 11–17 (Apr. 10, 2009).

29. Amendments to Regulation SHO, *supra* note 28, at 1.

30. *See id.*; *see also* U.S. Securities & Exchange Commission, REPORT OF THE SPECIAL STUDY OF THE SECURITIES MARKETS OF THE SECURITIES AND EXCHANGE COMMISSION, *reprinted in* H.R. Doc. No. 88-95 pt. 2, at 251 (1963) (sixteen exchanges adopted this rule in 1935).

31. *See* LOSS & SELIGMAN, *supra* note 21, at 3200 n.213.

32. Securities Exchange Act of 1934 § 10(a), 15 U.S.C. § 78j (2006).

33. Jones, *supra* note 28, at 20; *see also* Exchange Act Release No. 1548, 1938 WL 32911 (Jan. 24, 1938).

34. Originally adopted in 1994, NASD Rule 3550 (renumbered as Rule 5100 by SR-NASD-2005-087, effective Aug. 1, 2006) regulated short selling to allow short sales only when the current best bid is equal to or greater than the last best bid. Like the tick test, the bid test was developed in an attempt to stabilize the market by precluding shorts when prices are declining. The bid test allows more sales than the tick test, however, because "only the bid (rather than the actual price) must be rising

for a short sale to be allowed." White & Case LLP, *Nasdaq Securities Can Use Flexible Short Sale Rules* (Financial Services Advisory Update, Aug. 2006), at 2, http://www .whitecase.com/publications/detail.aspx?publication=993.

35. Holger Daske, Scott A. Richardson & Irem Tuna, *Do Short Sale Transactions Precede Bad News Events?* (May 2005), http://papers.ssrn.com/sol3/papers.cfm? abstract_id=722242.

36. Four of the five years in the period 2003–2007 showed substantial growth in the Dow Jones Index, and the decline in the year without growth (2005) was a modest 0.61 percent. The average annual growth during this five-year period was 10.12 percent. 1Stock1.com, *Dow Jones Industrial Average Yearly Returns*, http://www.1stock1 .com/1stock1_139.htm (last visited May 18, 2018).

37. Regulation SHO, 17 C.F.R. § 242.202T (2004).

38. Amendments to Regulation SHO, *supra* note 28, at 13.

39. *Id.* at 15.

40. Regulation SHO and Rule 10a-1, Exchange Act Release No. 34–55970, 72 Fed. Reg. 36,348 (July 3, 2007) (to be codified at 17 C.F.R. pts. 240, 242).

41. Emergency Order Taking Temporary Action to Respond to Market Developments, Exchange Act Release No. 34-58166, 73 Fed. Reg. 42,349 (July 15, 2008).

42. Emergency Order Taking Temporary Action to Respond to Market Developments, Exchange Act Release No. 34-58592, 73 Fed. Reg. 55,169 (Sept. 18, 2008).

43. Amendments to Regulation SHO, SEC Release No. 34-61595, 17 C.F.R. pt. 242. (Feb. 24, 2010).

44. *See* Press Release, SEC Halts Short Selling of Financial Stocks to Protect Investors and Markets, SEC Release 2008-211 (Feb. 24, 2010), https://www.sec.gov/news /press/2010/2010-26.htm.

45. *Id.*

46. Jones, *supra* note 28.

47. Karl B. Diether, Kuan-Hui Lee & Ingrid M. Werner, *It's SHO Time! Short-Sale Price Tests and Market Quality*, 64 J. Fin. 37 (2009).

48. *Id.*

49. Diether, Lee & Werner, *supra* note 47, at 38–40.

50. Beber and Pagano empirically examine the effects of short sale regulatory interventions adopted by regulators around the world in 2008–2009. *See* Alessandro Beber & Marco Pagano, *Short-Selling Bans Around the World: Evidence from the 2007–2009 Crisis*, 68 J. Fin. 343 (2013). They find, among other things, that bans on short selling did not result in better stock price performance, except possibly for U.S. financial stocks. *See id.* at 375–80.

51. *Compare* Kenneth D. West, *Dividend Innovations and Stock Price Volatility*, 56 Econometrica 37 (1988) (the lower the volatility as measured by the variance

(SSE) of the portion of an issuer's daily share price change not explained by the day's return on the market as a whole, the more accurate the issuer's share price), *with* Randall Morck et al., *The Information Content of Stock Markets: Why Do Emerging Markets Have Synchronous Stock Price Movements?*, 58 J. FIN. ECON. 215 (2000) (the higher the SSE relative to the variance of the issuer's total daily share price change, the more accurate the issuer's share price.). For a more detailed discussion of this point, see Merritt B. Fox et al., *Law, Share Price Accuracy, and Economic Performance: The New Evidence*, 102 MICH. L. REV. 331, 350–57 (2003).

52. Gustavo Grullon, Sébastien Michenaud & James P. Weston, *The Real Effects of Short-Selling Constraints*, 28 Rev. Fin. Stud. 1737 (2015).

53. This 50 percent is the statutory minimum. A broker can require a larger margin.

54. Recently, the rebate rate for Microsoft was 0 percent, whereas the rebate rate for Herbalife was –3 percent. That is, a shorter of Herbalife shares had to pay 3 percent per year to the share lender. This was at a time when the Fed overnight rate was 0.25 percent.

55. A recent survey of a few brokerage houses indicates that 30 percent is more representative.

56. The 50 percent requirement for buying on margin and short selling is a part of Regulation T.

57. Christopher L. Culp & J. B Heaton, *The Economics of Naked Short Selling*, REGULATION 31, 46–51 (2008).

58. This issue is discussed in Marcel Kahan & Edward Rock, *The Hanging Chads of Corporate Voting*, GEO. L.J. 96, 1227–81 (2008).

## 9. BROKER-DEALERS

1. *See* Newton v. Merrill Lynch, Pierce, Fenner & Smith, Inc., 259 F.3d 154, 162 (3d Cir. 2001).

2. 15 U.S.C. § 78o(b) (§ 15(b) of the Act).

3. Securities Exchange Act of 1934, § 3(4)(A), 15 U.S.C. § 78c.

4. *Id.*

5. Securities Exchange Act of 1934, § 15(a). The statute also identifies a range of exemptions from registration.

6. Securities Exchange Act of 1934, § 15(b)(1) (powers over registration); § 15(b)(7) (standard setting powers). The ability to operate as a broker-dealer thus depends on approval by the SEC, while the 1934 Act also requires a broker-dealer to (i) become a member of a self-regulatory organization (§ 15(b)(8) and Rule 15b9-1); (ii) become a member of the Securities Investor Protection Corporation; and (iii) comply with

a number of other state and federal statutory requirements. *See* § 3(a)(18) and Rule 15b7-1. There is a long-standing and vigorous debate about the merits of self-regulation in the securities markets. *See, e.g.,* Adam C. Pritchard, *Self-Regulation and Securities Markets,* REGULATION, Spring 2003, at 32 (arguing for the virtues of a self-regulatory approach); William A. Birdthistle & M. Todd Henderson, *Becoming a Fifth Branch,* 99 CORNELL L. REV. 1 (2013); Daniel M. Gallagher (SEC Commissioner), *Market 2012: Time for a Fresh Look at Equity Market Structure and Self-Regulation* (speech to SIFMA's 15th Annual Market Structure Conference, Oct. 4, 2012); Sam Scott Miller, *Self-Regulation of the Securities Markets: A Critical Examination,* 42 WASH. & LEE L. REV. 853 (1985).

7. *See, e.g.,* Securities Exchange Act of 1934, § 19(b).

8. Securities Exchange Act of 1934, § 6.

9. Securities Exchange Act of 1934, § 15A. The National Association of Securities Dealers (NASD) acted as this group for decades, until it merged with the NYSE's regulatory group and formed FINRA.

10. JOHN COFFEE & HILLARY SALE, SECURITIES REGULATION: CASES & MATERIALS 628 (12th ed., 2012). Exchanges, though SROs themselves, have also come to rely extensively on FINRA.

11. Securities Exchange Act of 1934, § 19(b).

12. Securities Exchange Act of 1934, § 19(c).

13. COFFEE & SALE, *supra* note 10, at 629); Brady v. Calyon Sec. (USA), 406 F. Supp. 2d 307, 312 (S.D.N.Y. 2005) ("While defendants may be subject to the rules and by-laws of NYSE and NASD, the rules of NYSE and NASD do not confer a private right of action."); SSH Co., Ltd. v. Shearson Lehman Bros., Inc., 678 F. Supp. 1055, 1058 (S.D.N.Y. 1987) ("[T]he [NYSE and NASD] rules contain no express provisions for civil liability and the courts in this circuit have refused to imply a private right of action to enforce these rules.").

14. *See, e.g.,* ARTHUR LABY & TAMAR FRANKEL, THE REGULATION OF MONEY MANAGERS: MUTUAL FUNDS AND ADVISERS (3d ed., 2015); Arthur Laby, *Fiduciary Obligations of Broker-Dealers and Investment Advisers,* 55 VILL. L. REV. 701 (2010) (symposium); Arthur Laby, *Reforming the Regulation of Broker-Dealers and Investment Advisers,* 65 BUS. LAW. 395 (2010).

15. *See* Michael C. Jensen & William H. Meckling, *Theory of the Firm: Managerial Behavior, Agency Costs and Ownership Structure,* 3 J. FIN. ECON. 305 (1976).

16. The lack of observability will matter whether it applies to the principal, to a subsequent court, or, as will usually be the case, to both.

17. Jonathan B. Berk & Jules H. van Binsbergen, *The Economics of Intermediaries, in* SECURITIES MARKET ISSUES FOR THE 21ST CENTURY, at 309 (Merritt B. Fox, Lawrence R. Glosten, Edward F. Greene & Menesh S. Patel eds. 2018),

https://www.law.columbia.edu/sites/default/files/microsites/capital-markets
/securities_market_issues_for_the_21st_century.pdf.

18. Newton v. Merrill Lynch, Pierce, Fenner & Smith, Inc., 259 F.3d 154, 162 (3d Cir. 2001). Subsequent cases interpreting best execution claims in the securities context rely heavily upon *Newton*. *See, e.g.*, Koch v. SEC, 793 F.3d 147, 155 (D.C. Cir. 2015), *cert. denied*, 136 S. Ct. 1492, 194 L. Ed. 2d 586 (2016); Gurfein v. Ameritrade, Inc., 312 F. App'x 410, 412 (2d Cir. 2009); Kurz v. Fidelity Mgmt. & Res. Co., 556 F.3d 639, 640 (7th Cir. 2009).

19. Newton v. Merrill Lynch, Pierce, Fenner & Smith, Inc., 259 F.3d 154, 162 (3d Cir. 2001), *as amended* (Oct. 16, 2001) (Newton II) ("They allege that defendants violated their duty of best execution by automatically executing each investor's trade at prices listed on the NBBO without consulting alternative sources that may have provided better value.").

20. William G. Christie & Paul H. Schultz, *Why Do NASDAQ Market Makers Avoid Odd-Eighth Quotes?*, 49 J. FIN. 1813 (1994); William G. Christie et al., *Why Did NASDAQ Market Makers Stop Avoiding Odd-Eighth Quotes?*, 49 J. FIN. 1841, 1858 (1994).

21. Newton v. Merrill Lynch, Pierce, Fenner & Smith, Inc., 135 F.3d 266, 271 (3d Cir. 1998).

22. Newton II, *supra*, note 19, at 173 (citation omitted). The theory of why a violation of this duty of best execution represents a Rule 10b-5 violation is that accepting a customer's order constitutes a representation that the broker will comply with its duty of best execution. The court stated that "[a] broker-dealer who 'accepts . . . an order while intending to breach that duty makes a misrepresentation that is material to the purchase or sale [of a security].' If the order was executed in a manner inconsistent with this duty, it was also performed with scienter." *Id.* at 173–74 (citations omitted).

23. Newton v. Merrill Lynch, Pierce, Fenner & Smith, Inc., 135 F.3d 266, 271 (3d Cir. 1998).

24. *Id.* For a more recent opinion fundamentally applying the analysis of *Newton*, *see* Gurfein v. Ameritrade, Inc., No. 04 CIV. 9526(LLS), 2007 WL 2049771, at *3 (S.D.N.Y. July 17, 2007), *aff'd*, 312 F. App'x 410 (2d Cir. 2009). In *Gurfein*, the plaintiff alleged that the major online brokerage Ameritrade, Inc. had breached its contractual duties to her and its duty of best execution by routing her order to the American Stock Exchange (AMEX), which provided inferior execution. Her support for this claim was a recent SEC report merely finding that AMEX provided execution inferior to options in other companies' stock during other time periods. The court found that there were no particular allegations of "an alternative exchange that was reasonably available to Ameritrade under the circumstances and that would have offered materially better overall execution." *Id.* ("even if such an alternative market did exist, numerous factors are relevant to execution, including

(in addition to speed) price, clearing costs, convenience, and others. . . . The mere allegation that the AMEX fell short of a hypothetical ideal market on one particular dimension (speed) is not enough to suggest that Ameritrade breached its duty of best execution, considered as a whole and in light of the numerous dimensions on which an investigator might measure quality of execution.").

25. FINRA Rule 5310, "Best Execution and Interpositioning" (emphasis added). Note that Rule 5310, by its terms, covers securities firms not only when they are acting as brokers, but also when they deal with customers in a dealer fashion if an order is routed to the dealer "for the purpose of order handling and execution." Rule 5310, Comment .04.

26. FINRA Rule 5310(a)(1)(A)-(E).

27. NYSE, *Designated Market Makers* (2018), https://www.nyse.com/publicdocs/nyse/listing/fact_sheet_dmm.pdf.

28. FINRA Rule 2121, "Fair Prices and Commissions."

29. NMS stocks are traded through the system of linked, multiple venues established by Reg. NMS, and are electronic limit order books. Non-NMS stocks, in contrast, are traded almost exclusively in electronic dealer markets.

30. *See, e.g.*, Lehl v. SEC, 90 F.3d 1483 (10th Cir. 1996) (sanctioning broker for excessive markups); Alstead, Dempsey & Co., Exchange Act Release No. 20,825, 30 S.E.C. Docket 208, 1984 WL 50800, at *2 (Apr. 5, 1984) (sanctioning broker-dealer for excessive markups). That seminal case also analyzes other relevant issues related to the markups discussed here.

31. FINRA Rule 2121.01.

32. *See* First Indep. Group, Inc. v. SEC, 37 F.3d 30, 32 (2d Cir. 1994) ("When a securities firm acts as a dealer, it is entitled to charge a reasonable markup on the wholesale price it pays for the securities. In general, markups in excess of 5 percent of the prevailing market price are not justified."), *citing* NASD Rules § 4, "Interpretation of the Board of Governors-NASD Markup Policy."

33. NASD Rule 2121.01(a)(5), (b).

34. *See* Ettinger v. Merrill Lynch, 835 F.3d 1031 (3d Cir. 1987) (suggesting that excessive markups on bonds can be litigated under Rule 10b-5 and holding that "a broker-dealer's compliance with the disclosure requirements of Rule 10b-10 does not, as a matter of law, shield it from possible liability under Rule 10b-5"); Alstead, Dempsey & Co., Exchange Act Release No. 20,825, 30 S.E.C. Docket 208, 1984 WL 50800, at *2 (Apr. 5, 1984); Orkin v. SEC, 31 F.3d 1056 (11th Cir. 1994).

35. Exchange Act Release No. 20,825, 30 S.E.C. Docket 208, 1984 WL 50800, at *2 (Apr. 5, 1984).

36. Given that there was no active market in the stock beyond the defendant's market-making, the prevailing market price was determined by assessing the "contemporaneous prices that registrant was willing to pay other dealers" for the stock.

37. *See* 15 U.S.C. 77q(a)(1)-(3); 15 U.S.C § 78j(b); 17 C.F.R. § 240.10b-5.
38. *See* Santa Fe Indus. v. Green, 430 U.S. 462, 473–74 (1977) ("the claim of fraud and fiduciary breach in this complaint states a cause of action under any part of Rule 10b-5 only if the conduct alleged can be fairly viewed as 'manipulative or deceptive' within the meaning of the statute") (citations omitted).
39. *See* Santa Fe Indus. v. Green, 430 U.S. 462, 473 (1977); *id.* at 472 (relying "on the use of the term 'fraud' in Rule 10b-5 to bring within the ambit of the Rule all breaches of fiduciary duty in connection with a securities transaction . . . would . . . 'add a gloss to the operative language of the statute quite different from its commonly accepted meaning.' ") (citations omitted).
40. FINRA Rule 2121.01(a)(3). These conclusions have also received explicit judicial approval. *See* First Indep. Group v. SEC, 37 F.3d 30, 32 (2d Cir. 1994); Alstead, Dempsey & Co., Exchange Act Release No. 20,825, 30 S.E.C. Docket 208, 1984 WL 50800, at *2 (Apr. 5, 1984).
41. FINRA Rule 2121.02(b)(1). *See, e.g.,* First Indep. Group v. SEC, 37 F.3d 30, 32 (2d Cir. 1994); Alstead, Dempsey & Co., Exchange Act Release No. 20,825, 30 S.E.C. Docket 208, 1984 WL 50800, at *2 (Apr. 5, 1984).
42. FINRA Rule 2121.02(b)(1).
43. *Id.*
44. *See generally* Alstead, Dempsey & Co., Exchange Act Release No. 20,825, 30 S.E.C. Docket 208, 1984 WL 50800, at *2 (Apr. 5, 1984).
45. Gary Shorter & Rena S. Miller, *Dark Pools in Equity Trading: Policy Concerns and Recent Developments*, CONG. RES. SERV. 1 (Sept. 16, 2014), https://fas.org/sgp/crs/misc/R43739.pdf ("Traditionally, the exclusive locales for stock trades were exchanges such as the New York Stock Exchange . . . , the American Stock Exchange . . . , and NASDAQ.").
46. JERRY W. MARKHAM, A FINANCIAL HISTORY OF THE UNITED STATES 146 (2015).
47. George T. Simon & Kathryn M. Trkla, *The Regulation of Specialists and Implications for the Future*, 61 BUS. LAW. 217, 336 (2005).
48. *See infra* notes 79 and accompanying text.
49. Simon & Trkla, *supra* note 47, at 336.
50. Automated Trading Information Systems, 34 Fed. Reg. 12,952, 12,953 (proposed Aug. 9, 1969) (to be codified at 17 C.F.R. pt. 240).
51. Eventually, the SEC issued a no-action letter authorizing Instinet to operate pursuant to compliance within the context of broker-dealer regulation. *See* Instinet Corp., SEC No-Action Letter, 1986 SEC No-Act. LEXIS 1 (Sept. 8, 1986).
52. Luis A. Aguilar (SEC Commissioner), *Shedding Light on Dark Pools* (Nov. 18, 2015), https://www.sec.gov/news/statement/shedding-light-on-dark-pools.html#_ednref1.

53. *Id.*

54. Securities Exchange Act of 1934, § 3(a)(1) (1934); *see also* 15 U.S.C. § 78c(a)(1) (2012) (defining an *exchange* as "any organization, association, or group of persons . . . which constitutes, maintains, or provides a market place or facilities for bringing together purchasers and sellers of securities"); 17 C.F.R. § 240.3b-16(a)(2) (2005) (defining an *exchange* as involving "established, non-discretionary methods" for when orders interact).

55. Securities Exchange Act of 1934, § 3(a)(26) (1934); 15 U.S.C. § 78c(a)(26) (2012).

56. *See generally* Concept Release Concerning Self-Regulation, Exchange Act Release No. 50700, 84 SEC Docket 619 (Nov. 18, 2004) (discussing "the foundations of the self-regulatory system and new considerations that the Commission and the industry are facing").

57. A "self-regulatory organization 'when acting in its capacity as a SRO, is entitled to immunity from suit when it engages in conduct consistent with the quasi-governmental powers delegated to it pursuant to the Exchange Act and the regulations and rules promulgated thereunder.' " DL Capital Group, LLC v. Nasdaq Stock Mkt., 409 F.3d 93, 97 (2d Cir. 2005) (citations omitted) (citing D'Alessio v. N.Y. Stock Exch., 258 F.3d 93, 106 (2d Cir. 2001)); *In re* NYSE Specialists Sec. Litig., 503 F.3d 89, 96 (2d Cir. 2007); Weissman v. Nat'l Ass'n of Secs. Dealers, 500 F.3d 1293, 1296 (11th Cir. 2007) ("SROs are protected by absolute immunity when they perform their statutorily delegated adjudicatory, regulatory, and prosecutorial functions"); Sparta Surgical Corp. v. Nat'l Ass'n of Secs. Dealers, 159 F.3d 1209, 1214 (9th Cir. 1998); Austin Mun. Secs., Inc. v. Nat'l Ass'n of Secs. Dealers, 757 F.2d 676, 692 (5th Cir. 1985) ("[T]he NASD . . . requires absolute immunity from civil liability for actions connected with the disciplining of its members") (citations omitted); *In re* Series 7 Broker Qualification Exam Scoring Litig., 510 F. Supp. 2d 35, 42 (D.D.C. 2007). This feature of SROs has also been a fulcrum of scholarly controversy. *See generally* Rohit A. Nafday, *From Sense to Nonsense and Back Again: SRO Immunity, Doctrinal Bait-and-Switch, and a Call for Coherence*, 77 U. CHI. L. REV. 847 (2010) (arguing that SRO immunity is unwarranted); William A. Birdthistle & M. Todd Henderson, *Becoming a Fifth Branch*, 99 CORNELL L. REV. 1 (2013) (describing SROs as the fifth branch of government).

# 10. DARK POOLS

1. Sam Mamudi, *UBS Hit With Record Dark Pool Fine for Breaking U.S. Rules*, BLOOMBERG (Jan. 15, 2015, 12:25 PM), http://www.bloomberg.com/news/2015 -01-15/sec-fines-ubs-dark-pool-more-than-14-million-for-breaking-rules

(imposing on UBS the largest fine ever given a dark pool operator); Sam Mamudi, *Dark Pools Opening Up Amid Increased Scrutiny*, BLOOMBERG BUS. WEEK (May 21, 2014, 12:01 AM), http://www.bloomberg.com/news/2014-05-21/dark-pools-opening-up-amid-increased-scrutiny (reporting on industry unease with dark pools). These practices, and the criticisms of them, are discussed in more detail in Section V.E.

2. *See, e.g.*, Nathaniel Popper, *As Market Heats Up, Trading Slips into Shadows*, N.Y. TIMES, Mar. 31, 2013, at B1; A.M., *Shining a Light on Dark Pools*, THE ECONOMIST: SCHUMPETER (Aug. 18, 2011, 4:08 PM), http://www.economist.com/blogs/schumpeter/2011/08/exchange-share-trading; David Zeiler, *How High-Frequency Traders Use Dark Pools to Cheat Investors*, MONEY MORNING (Apr. 22, 2014), http://moneymorning.com/2014/04/22/how-high-frequency-traders-use-dark-pools-to-cheat-investors (discussing how HFTs may be abusing dark pool access).

3. An underlying premise of these criticisms is that the largest investment banks are also among the most prominent brokers and dark-pool operators. For instance, Michael Lewis often discusses dark pools as being operated by Wall Street banks, which is accurate: six of the ten largest dark pools are run by major investment banks. *See* MICHAEL LEWIS, FLASH BOYS: A WALL STREET REVOLT at 182–87, 264–65 (2014); *see also* RHODRI PREECE, & CFA INSTITUTE, DARK POOLS, INTERNALIZATION, AND EQUITY MARKET QUALITY 14–15 (2012). All of the ten largest brokers on NYSE are also global investment banks. *See NYSE Broker Volume*, NYSE MARKET DATA, http://perma.cc/YC2V-XUAG.

4. Michael Lewis, for example, claims that dark-pool operators sell access to their trading venues to HFTs—without disclosing this practice to other users—and that these HFTs then exploit other traders. Lewis, *supra* note 3, at 123. Inferior execution could also occur on a dark pool if the counterparties trading there were informed traders or were given information about the existence of the customer limit orders posted there.

5. Marketable orders sent to a dark pool enjoy the same protection provided by Rule 611 that orders sent to an exchange have. If a better price is available on an exchange, the dark pool must route the order there.

6. *See, e.g.*, Lewis, *supra* note 3, at 182–87, 264–65.

7. "Soft money" research consists of ancillary services provided to an institutional investor by a broker free of direct charge (that is, "hard money") in return for that investor directing order flow to that broker. Soft-money arrangements can be desirable from an institutional investor's perspective because they pass the cost of the soft-money research on to their clients in the form of higher brokerage fees, rather than as part of the direct cost of the institutional investor's own services to clients. *See* OFFICE OF COMPLIANCE, INSPECTIONS & EXAMINATIONS, U.S. SECURITIES &

EXCHANGE COMMISSION, INSPECTION REPORT ON THE SOFT DOLLAR PRACTICES OF BROKER-DEALERS, INVESTMENT ADVISERS AND MUTUAL FUNDS 6 (1998), http://www.sec.gov/news/studies/softdolr.htm.

8. *See, e.g.*, Liquidnet Inc., Exchange Act Release No. 72,339, 2014 WL 2547522 (June 6, 2014); Pipeline Trading Sys., Exchange Act Release No. 65,609, 2011 WL 5039038 (Oct. 24, 2011).

9. Complaint at 2–4, Schneiderman v. Barclays Capital, Inc., No. 451391/2014 (N.Y. Sup. Ct. 2014).

10. *See* 17 C.F.R. § 242.602(b)(1) (2015) (defining scope of reporting requirements); *id.* § 242.600(b)(65) (defining *broker-dealer*); *id.* § 242.600(b)(73)(ii)(A) (defining *subject security*).

11. *See* Regulation of Exchanges and Alternative Trading System Rule 301(b)(5), 17 C.F.R. § 242.301(b)(5) (2015); Concept Release on Equity Market Structure, Exchange Act Release No. 61,358, 75 Fed. Reg. 3594, 3614 (proposed Jan. 14, 2010) (to be codified at 17 C.F.R. pt. 242) ("As [trading systems] that are exempt from exchange registration, [off-exchange platforms] are not required to provide fair access [to all traders] unless they reach a 5 percent trading volume threshold in a stock, which none currently do[es]" and that "[a]s a result, access to . . . [these platforms] . . . is determined primarily by private negotiation.").

12. *See, e.g.*, PREECE & CFA INSTITUTE, *supra* note 3, at 12–13.

13. The operator provides a similar service to the extent that it keeps out HFTs that engage in midpoint order exploitation.

14. This point is made in Haoxiang Zhu, *Do dark pools harm price discovery?*, 27 REV. FIN. STUDIES 747 (2014).

15. Carole Comerton-Forde & Talis Putnins, *Dark Trade and Price Discovery*, 118 J. FIN. ECON. 70 (2015).

16. A broker can make money off transactions occurring on its dark pool for several additional reasons. If it is executing marketable orders on its dark pool, then a broker will receive its commission without having to subtract the taker fee charged marketable orders on most exchanges. If the broker is internalizing orders on its own dark pool and transacting against them as principal, then it can make half the spread on each trade. Even more nefarious inducements are suggested by the criticisms, such as exploitation of orders by a broker's HFT affiliate that has improperly been given details about orders.

17. FINRA Rules, FIN. INDUS. REGULATORY AUTH., at Rule at Rule 5310(a)(1). Reasonable diligence requires a broker to consider "the character of the market for the security (e.g., price, volatility, relative liquidity, and pressure on available communications)"; "the size and type of transaction"; "the number of markets checked"; the "accessibility of the quotation"; and "the terms and conditions of the order which

result in the transaction, as communicated to the member and persons associated with the member." FINRA Rule 5310(a)(1)(A)–(E).

18. Ignoring a principal's instructions would violate the agent's duties noted earlier, as well as an agent's specific duty of obedience to the principal. *See, e.g.*, Gagnon v. Coombs, 654 N.E.2d 54, 61 (Mass. App. Ct. 1995) (discussing agent's duty of obedience). Though many retail brokers do not provide customers any choice as to execution venue, some do, and brokers for institutional customers would be expected to provide options in this respect. *See, e.g., SmartRouting*, INTERACTIVE BROKERS, https://www.interactivebrokers.com/en/index.php?f=1685 (providing comparison of security prices offered by Interactive Brokers versus industry average).

19. *See* RESTATEMENT (THIRD) OF AGENCY § 8.05(2) (2006) (outlining agent's duty of confidentiality). Rule 301(b)(10) of Regulation ATS requires an ATS (essentially, a non-exchange stock market venue, such as a dark pool) to protect users' confidential information. 17 C.F.R. § 242.301(b)(10) (2014).

20. *See* Kevin S. Haeberle, *Stock-Market Law and the Accuracy of Public Companies' Stock Prices*, 2015 COLUM. BUS. L. REV. 121) (manuscript at 25–27, 44–45), https://papers.ssrn.com/sol3/papers.cfm?abstract_id=2410422 (arguing that off-exchange trading venues increase the probability of adverse selection on exchanges).

21. *See* Philip Stafford, *HK Plans Retail Investor Dark Pool Ban*, FIN. TIMES (Feb. 27, 2014, 11:53 PM), http://www.ft.com/intl/cms/s/0/32ab7298-9fba-11e3-94f3-00144feab7de.html#axzz3I1IB1vhn [http://perma.cc/D4AX-CS3W].

22. *See* Nicole Bullock, *Financial Regulators Probe Dark Pools*, FIN. TIMES (Sept. 16, 2014, 12:07 AM), http://www.ft.com/intl/cms/s/0/50428000-220d-11e4-9d4a-00144feabdc0.html#axzz3FU6kj2LE [http://perma.cc/EM92-86BS].

23. *See* Philip Stafford & Alex Baker, *Europe Deal Will Cap 'Dark Pools' Trading*, FIN. TIMES (Nov. 21, 2013, 5:26 PM), http://www.ft.com/intl/cms/s/0/ac3ce0f8-52ce-11e3-8586-00144feabdc0.html#axzz3CAa8BKBz [http://perma.cc/K4LB-DXXS].

24. FINRA, Equity Trading Initiatives: OTC Equity Trading Volume (Apr. 2, 2016), http://www.finra.org/sites/default/files/Regulatory-Notice-15-48.pdf; FINRA, FINRA Announces Implementation Date for Publication of ATS Block-Size Trade Data (Oct. 3, 2016), http://www.finra.org/sites/default/files/notice_doc_file_ref/Regulatory-Notice-16-14.pdf.

25. FINRA, *Update: FINRA Board of Governors Meeting*, Sept. 9, 2014, http://www.finra.org/industry/update-finra-board-governors-meeting-091914 ("The Board authorized the publication of a Regulatory Notice requesting comment on a proposal to require alternative trading systems (ATSs) to provide FINRA with order book information that is not currently reported by the ATS to the Order Audit Trail System (OATS), with such information to be reported to FINRA using existing OATS interfaces.").

26. *See generally* FINRA, *Order Audit Trail System (OATS) OATS Basics*, http://www
.finra.org/sites/default/files/AppSupportDoc/p016184.pptx [http://perma.cc/TB65
-TYPP].

27. *The Role of Regulation in Shaping Equity Market Structure and Electronic Trading: Hearing Before the S. Comm. on Banking, Hous. & Urban Affairs, 113th Cong.
(2014)*, at 55 (statement of James J. Angel, Associate Professor, Georgetown University McDonough School of Business). Several other commentators have also
called for greater disclosure by dark pools. *See, e.g., id.* at 33 (statement of David
Lauer, President and Managing Partner, KOR Group LLC, urging that the SEC
update Rules 605 and 606 to increase ATS reporting); *id.* at 23 (statement of Tom
Wittman, Executive Vice President and Global Head of Equities, NASDAQ OMX,
recommending that brokerage firms should disclose execution quality directly to
customers).

28. Brokers do have limited disclosure requirements under Regulation NMS. Rule 605
requires trading venues to provide monthly reports with various measures of execution quality, and Rule 606 requires broker-dealers that route customer orders to
provide quarterly reports that identify at an aggregate level the venues where client
orders are executed. *See* 17 C.F.R. §§ 242.605–242.606 (2015).

## 11. MAKER-TAKER FEES

1. *See, e.g.,* William Alden, *At Senate Hearing, Brokerage Firms Called Out for Conflicts*, N.Y. TIMES: DEALBOOK (June 17, 2014, 9:30 AM), http://dealbook.nytimes
.com/2014/06/17/trader-who-called-markets-rigged-tempers-his-critique (discussing scrutiny of payment for order flow at recent congressional hearings); Editorial,
*The Hidden Cost of Trading Stocks*, N.Y. TIMES (June 22, 2014), http://www.nytimes
.com/2014/06/23/opinion/best-execution-and-rebates-for-brokers.html?_r=0
(criticizing the practice of maker-taker fees).

2. *See generally* Larry Harris, Maker-Taker Pricing Effects on Market Quotations 2
(Nov. 14, 2013) (unpublished manuscript), http://www.securitiesmosaic.com
/gateway/sec/speech/hujibusiness_Maker-taker.pdf (discussing typical maker-taker
pricing scheme).

3. The actual fees and rebates imposed must be publicly available and must be the same
across all stocks traded on the exchange. The fees and rebates for any exchange are
available on the exchange's website. *See generally* Securities Exchange Act of 1934,
§ 19(b)(3)(A)(ii)(4), 15 U.S.C. § 78s(b)(3)(A)(ii) (2012); 17 C.F.R. § 240.19b-4(f)
(2) (2013).

4. Letter from Sen. Charles Schumer to Mary Schapiro, Chairman, SEC (May 10, 2012), http://www.schumer.senate.gov/Newsroom/record_print.cfm?id=336748. Flash Boys added its own criticism, declaring that "[t]he maker-taker system of fees and kickbacks used by all of the exchanges was simply a method for paying the big Wall Street banks to screw the investors whose interests they were meant to guard." MICHAEL LEWIS, FLASH BOYS: A WALL STREET REVOLT (2014), at 168–69.

5. *See* Alden, *supra* note 1. A *New York Times* editorial suggested that maker-taker fees are "corrupting" brokers, who "under the guise of making subjective judgments about best execution, . . . were routinely sending orders to venues that paid the highest rebates," and concluded by calling for greater regulation or elimination of maker-taker fees. *See* Editorial, *supra* note 1 (using TD Ameritrade data from the fourth quarter of 2012).

6. *See, e.g.*, Complaint at 20, Klein v. TD Ameritrade Holding Corp., No. 14-cv-5738, 2014 WL 5018542 (D.N.J. Sept. 15, 2014).

7. For expository simplicity, the analysis assumes that the tick size (the minimum difference allowed by the market between one price and the prices above and below) is infinitesimal, whereas, pursuant to NMS Rule 612, for most stocks it is in fact a penny; however, including this complication in the analysis leaves the conclusion largely unchanged.

8. *Conflicts of Interest, Investor Loss of Confidence, and High Speed Trading in U.S. Stock Markets: Hearing Before the Permanent Subcomm. on Investigations of the S. Comm. on Homeland Sec. & Governmental Affairs*, 113th Cong. 2 (2014) (statement of Sen. Carl Levin) [hereinafter *High Speed Trading Hearings*], at 8 (statement of Robert Battalio, Professor of Finance, University of Notre Dame). Interactive Brokers offers such a contract, but it also offers a fixed-price-for-execution contract. *See Commissions: Stocks, ETFs and Warrants—Overview*, INTERACTIVE BROKERS, https://www.interactivebrokers.com/en/?f=commission (last visited May 20, 2018).

9. A mirror image of these stories applies to nonmarketable and marketable sell orders.

10. Robert Battalio, Shane Corwin & Robert Jennings, *Can Brokers Have It All? On the Relation Between Make-Take Fees & Limit Order Execution Quality*. 71 J. FIN. 2193 (2016).

11. *Id.*

12. Interactive Brokers offers a commission schedule in which exchange fees and rebates are passed in whole or in part to the customer. It also offers a per share commission which passes through exchange fees, but not rebates.

13. That this is the case is not obvious a priori. Consider the maker/taker exchange EDGEX and the taker/maker exchange EDGEA. EDGEX has a 6% market share whereas EDGEA has a 1.3% market share (early July, 2018, Source Cboe Global Markets). A broker might plausibly believe that a nonmarketable order sent to the more active exchange would receive a better fill rate.

14. A memo from the SEC's Division of Trading and Markets notes that such a plan may be very difficult for investment advisors, in particular, to administer. With trading done centrally, it is not obvious how rebates and fees should be allocated to different accounts, particularly since fees and rebates are tiered so that the final amount is only determined at the end of the month. The memo is available at: https://www.sec.gov/spotlight/emsac/memo-maker-taker-fees-on -equities-exchanges.pdf. As we point out in the text, however, as long as the scheme makes a reasonably unbiased estimate of how much is owed to or from each trader, the incentive problem is eliminated.

## 12. PAYMENT FOR ORDER FLOW

1. By shares traded, the three largest internalizers are Citadel Securities, Goldman Sachs and Virtu Americas, accounting for about a half billion shares of Tier 1 NMS stock trading per day (Tier 1 stocks are those in the S&P500, the Russell 1000 and other selected indices). These data are available at the FINRA website that provides share volumes for ATSs and OTC (non-ATS) or internalizers here: https://otctransparency.finra.org/ .

2. Allen Ferrell, *A Proposal for Solving the "Payment for Order Flow" Problem*, 74 S. Cal. L. Rev. 1027, 1028 (2001).

3. Available at: https://www.sec.gov/rules/concept/2010/34-61358.pdf.

4. Robert Battalio, Shane a. Corwin & Robert Jennings, *Can Brokers Have It All? On the Relation Between Make-Take Fees and Limit Order Execution Quality*, 71 J. Fin. 2193 (2016).

5. *Conflicts of Interest, Investor Loss of Confidence, and High Speed Trading in U.S. Stock Markets: Hearing Before the Permanent Subcomm. on Investigations of the S. Comm. on Homeland Sec. & Governmental Affairs*, 113th Cong. 2 (2014) (statement of Sen. Carl Levin) [hereinafter *High Speed Trading Hearings*], at 33 (statement of Joseph P. Ratterman, CEO, BATS Global Markets); *id.* at 2 (opening statement of Sen. Carl Levin) ("'[P]ayment for order flow' can add up to untold millions, and almost every retail broker keeps these payments rather than passing them on to clients").

6. Letter from Sen. Carl Levin to Hon. Mary Jo White, Chairman, SEC (July 9, 2014), http://www.hsgac.senate.gov/download/levin-letter-to-sec-chairman-mary-jo -white-re-equity- market-structure-july-15_2014 [http://perma.cc/WBK5-G56C].

7. Since the internalizers use the NBBO for their trades, for an order to get consistently better execution on an exchange, it must be that either the internalizer strategically times order executions to its benefit, legally ignores quote improvements or there is nondisplayed liquidity on the exchanges. We tend to doubt the first two, but find the third to be plausible.

8. *See* Kevin S. Haeberle, *Stock-Market Law and the Accuracy of Public Companies' Stock Prices*, 2015 Colum. Bus. L. Rev. 121 (2015), at 44–45.
9. If it is difficult to track the payment for every specific order, any perverse incentives caused by the practice could be corrected just as effectively by passing on to customers an amount equal to an unbiased estimate of the payment.

## CONCLUSION

1. For some notable papers making efforts in this direction, see, e.g., Dan Awrey, *The Mechanisms of Derivatives Market Efficiency*, 91 NYU L. Rev. 1104 (2016); Andrew Verstein, *Insider Trading in Commodities Markets*, 102 Va. L. Rev. 453 (2016); Yesha Yadav, *Insider Trading in Derivatives Markets*, 103 Geo. L. J. 381 (2015).
2. SEC, Division of Market Regulation, Debt Market Review, *U.S. House of Representatives Subcommittee on Finance and Hazardous Materials Hearing on Improving Price Competition for Mutual Funds and Bonds* (September 29, 1998).
3. *See, e.g.*, Gary Gorton et al., *The Safe-Asset Share*, 102 am. Econ. Rev. 101 (2012); Gary Gorton & George Pennacchi, *Financial Intermediaries and Liquidity Creation*, 45 J. Fin. 49, 65–66 (1990); *see also* Bengt Holmström, *Understanding the Role of Debt in the Financial System* 7 (Bank for International Settlements, Working Paper No. 479, 2015).
4. NYSE, *NYSE Liquidity Programs*, https://www.nyse.com/markets/liquidity-programs.

# Name Index

Florescu, Ionut, 319n73

Foucault, Thierry, 301n14, 308n22, 315n18, 323n31

Fox, Edward G., 316n35

Fox, Merritt B., 304n6, 306n17, 307n19, 310n10, 316n35, 323n26, 331n41, 333n55, 337n98, 338n111, 351, 358n51, 359n17

Frank, Barney, 351n1

Frankel, Richard M., 306n12

Frankel, Tamar, 359n14

French, Kenneth, 320n1, 323n30

Fried, Jesse, 324n39, 325n48

Galai, Dan, 353n18

Gale, Douglas, 343n44

Gallagher, Daniel M., 359n6

Garman, Mark B., 311n24

Gely, Rafael, 326n56

Gilson, Ronald J., 316n35, 325n49

Ginsburg (Justice), 165, 328n20

Glosten, Lawrence R., 310n16, 310n18, 310n19, 311nn22, 341n27, 351, 353n18, 359n17

Goldstein, Itay, 305n9, 315n18, 323n31

Gomes, Armando, 337n106

Gordon, Jeffrey N., 307n19

Gordon, R., 307n17

Gorton, Gary, 295, 305n9, 337n106, 343n44, 370n3

Goshen, Zohar, 315n24, 320n2, 325n44

Green, Richard C., 314n14, 324n34

Greene, Edward, 321n15, 359n17

Grossman, Sanford J., 325n49, 337n98, 353n18

Grullon, Gustavo, 255, 256, 358n52

Guiso, Luigi, 309n31

Gulati, Gaurang Mitu, 331n44

Guttentag, Michael D., 329n26

Haddock, David D., 324n36, 327n61

Haeberle, Kevin S., 318n52, 366nn20–21, 370n8

Haft, Robert J., 326n57

Hagerty, Kathleen M., 315n24, 325n44

Hagströmer, Björn, 312n2

Hamilton, Jesse, 340n11

Hansard, Sara, 352n7

Harris, Jeffrey H., 312n35

Harris, Larry, 206, 299n2, 301n13, 307n20, 308n23, 308n24, 309n2, 310n11, 311n22, 316n35, 319n1, 320n3, 324n37, 340n17, 342n34, 343n44, 367n2

Hartzell, Jay C., 304n7

Hasbrouck, Joel, 316n37, 323n30

Hazen, 339n10

Heaton, J. B., 353n17, 358n57

Hempton, John, 352n9

Hendershott, Terrence, 84, 300n6, 312n1

Henderson, M. Todd, 359n6, 363n57

Hetherington, John A. C., 324n34

Hicks, John, 308n29

Hillion, Pierre, 207, 341n27

Ho, Thomas S.Y., 311n24

Holderness, Clifford G., 305n10

Holmstrom, Bengt, 307n19, 370n3

Hu, Grace Xing, 308n26, 309n3, 309n5, 323n32, 335n68

Icahn, Carl, 223–24

Jacobs, Deborah L., 317n41

Jain, Pankaj, 315n25

Jarrow, Robert A., 343n44

Jennings, Robert, 368n10

Jensen, Michael C., 304n5, 307n17, 359n15

# Subject Index

www.ingramcontent.com/pod-product-compliance
Ingram Content Group UK Ltd.
Pitfield, Milton Keynes, MK11 3LW, UK
UKHW041650020225
454515UK00003B/148/J